Real Estate Appraisal

From Value to Worth

Sarah Sayce
Professor and Head, School of Surveying, Kingston University

Judy Smith
Senior Lecturer, School of Surveying, Kingston University

Richard Cooper
Chartered Surveyor

Piers Venmore-Rowland
Visiting Professor, School of Surveying, Kingston University

Blackwell
Publishing

© 2006 by Blackwell Publishing Ltd

Editorial offices:
Blackwell Publishing Ltd, 9600 Garsington Road, Oxford OX4 2DQ, UK
  Tel: +44 (0)1865 776868
Blackwell Publishing Inc., 350 Main Street, Malden, MA 02148-5020, USA
  Tel: +1 781 388 8250
Blackwell Publishing Asia Pty Ltd, 550 Swanston Street, Carlton, Victoria 3053, Australia
  Tel: +61 (0)3 8359 1011

First published 2006 by Blackwell Publishing Ltd

ISBN-10: 1-4051-0001-X
ISBN-13: 978-1-4051-0001-4

Library of Congress Cataloging-in-Publication Data
Real estate appraisal: from value to worth/Sarah Sayce . . . [et al.]. – 1st ed.
    p. cm.
Includes bibliographical references and index.
ISBN-13: 978-1-4051-0001-4 (alk. paper)
ISBN-10: 1-4051-0001-X (alk. paper)
1. Real property–Valuation. I. Sayce, Sarah

HD1387.R365 2006
333.33′2–dc22
2005016453

A catalogue record for this title is available from the British Library

Set in 10/12.5pt Times
by Graphicraft Limited, Hong Kong
Printed and bound in India
by Replika Press Pvt Ltd, Kundli

The publisher's policy is to use permanent paper from mills that operate a sustainable forestry policy, and which has been manufactured from pulp processed using acid-free and elementary chlorine-free practices. Furthermore, the publisher ensures that the text paper and cover board used have met acceptable environmental accreditation standards.

For further information on Blackwell Publishing, visit our website:
www.blackwellpublishing.com

To all our families

David, Charlotte and Edd
Geoff, Rebecca, Mark and Rosie
Lorna, Nina, Robyn and Sasha

Contents

Preface

The education of the real estate professional is changing. It has become far more integrated with the world of business and this means that the texts to support both practitioners and students need to change too.

Real estate was once a discipline bedded in an isolationist approach in which property was viewed as a discrete study area, but the realisation now is that professionals must view the assets on which they give strategic and operational advice in a more holistic context. This has two main implications for the role of real estate appraisal.

- The pricing mechanism on which real estate professionals advise must take into account the theories and practices used in other investment markets. However, even this is not enough: investors are in competition with owner-occupiers and therefore an understanding of how assets are appraised by owner-occupiers is vital to the process.
- The owner of real estate assets may be either an investor or an owner-occupier. Both have increased needs to ensure efficient and effective management of the asset, and this determines the need for performance management techniques that allow comparison and objective evaluation to be undertaken. However, in addition, investors and owner-occupiers alike must now take cognisance of the wider sustainability issues of social and environmental responsibility; to date, the study of this in relation to real estate is in its infancy.

This book seeks to address these issues by introducing and examining some of the latest techniques employed in the marketplace. Fundamental to this are the development of both an understanding of market appraisal *and* worth, and an appreciation of the emerging role of sustainability as a driver for real estate decision-making.

The catalyst for this book has been the authors' experiences gained from both their interaction with those who have attended courses delivered by them and their work in practice. The courses range from degree and masters programmes for those seeking to gain admission to the Royal Institution of Chartered Surveyors (RICS), to Assessment of Professional Competence (APC) courses, to CPD lectures for practitioners. Whilst theory is very important to these students, and increasingly so, what precipitates learning is practical application. Over the years our students, at all levels, have constantly challenged us to provide a *context* for the theories we present them with and a steer as to what the markets are really doing!

Whilst no book can fully address these desires, we have endeavoured to bridge what we perceive to be the gap between theory and practice and, we hope, to address the needs not just of our students, and those of other real estate courses in the UK and beyond, but also of the practitioners who are now facing changes in their established ways of working. Our intention has been to present the material in an approachable way that is accessible to those who come to the subject fresh as graduate students and to those in the latter stages of their undergraduate programmes. We hope that we have succeeded in our ambition.

In order to keep the book 'fresh', we have introduced a web link to examples. Details of this can be found in Appendix B.

Acknowledgements

Writing any book brings many challenges; this one was no exception. Take four people, all with heavy work schedules, and sometimes very different ideas, and you have a recipe that – without goodwill and long-suffering publishers – could prove difficult to bring to a result. Indeed, there were times when we all seriously wondered whether our collective endeavour would hit the printer's press.

Though not without some delay, we did deliver and we hope our readers find that the effort has produced what we intended: a book with a slightly different slant, and one that tackles some of the newer concepts of property appraisal and worth in ways that relate directly to practice but are within the grasp of students.

We wish to thank all those people who, by their help and encouragement and their preparedness to talk through ideas with us, have helped to stimulate our thought processes and inform our ideas. So thanks to all our colleagues and partners, both in practice and at Kingston University, who have helped us in so many ways – often without knowing it! Thanks also go to the students for their constant questioning and challenging of ideas.

There are two other special groups of people who deserve our particular acknowledgement: first of all, Madeleine Metcalfe and her team at Blackwell Publishing for being so understanding and patient with us; secondly, our friends and families who have been perhaps less patient – but with good reason! May they be rewarded with a little more of our time over the ensuing months.

Sarah Sayce, Judy Smith, Richard Cooper and Piers Venmore-Rowland

About the authors

Professor Sarah Sayce is Head of the School of Surveying at Kingston University, in which capacity she is responsible for a suite of undergraduate and postgraduate programmes and for the research programmes. She is a Chartered Surveyor and after some years in practice she moved into teaching and research. She has published widely on many aspects of commercial property from portfolio management to leisure property and sustainability.

Judy Smith is a Senior Lecturer in the School of Surveying at Kingston University, where she is Field Leader for the MSc in Real Estate. She lectures on both undergraduate and postgraduate courses specialising in property investment, valuations and IT applications. She is a Chartered Surveyor and joint author of *Property Construction and Economics*, and is currently involved in researching a sustainable model of worth.

Richard Cooper is a Chartered Surveyor with experience in investment property analysis and appraisal for UK and Continental European property fund managers. He currently works for a UK-based manager of pooled property funds.

Piers Venmore-Rowland is a property appraisal and IT consultant and trainer. Having worked both as a stockbroker and as a Chartered Surveyor, he developed extensive property and financial knowledge. After some years in practice Piers become an academic and was Head of Department at City University before deciding to set up his own business. He is Visiting Professor at Kingston University.

1 Introducing concepts of value and worth

Aims of the chapter

- To provide a context for the book.
- To distinguish it from others in the field.
- To introduce the concepts of value, worth and price in the context of the main players within the real estate field.
- To provide an historical context for the themes of the book.

1.1 Real estate: an introduction to the economic concepts

Within this book the concepts of worth, price and value are explored in terms of their changing application to real estate markets. Underpinning all of these concepts is the theory of market economics. Whilst this book is not a text on land economics, it is important to introduce the principles upon which the relevant market practices have developed.

Under neoclassical economic theory, the three factors that contribute to economic wealth are normally taken to be:

- people
- money
- land.

Each factor is a resource that is deemed to be scarce and hence has value both to the individual and to society, and the study of economics is concerned with the allocation of the use of that resource. Within the UK there is a mixed economy, in that resource allocation decisions are taken partly by government on the basis of need, and partly by private individuals and corporate bodies on the basis of economic demand. Where real estate allocation decisions are based on need (for example, the provision of public goods and services such as hospitals and schools), these decisions are, as a broad-brush rule, taken on the basis of least *cost* and *value for money*. Where the allocation decisions are based on demand (for example, the provision of shops, offices for corporate use and private leisure facilities), this is on the basis of economic demand, as expressed through the supply and demand pricing model.

Under this paradigm, price is the product of the interaction of supply and demand. Given any level of demand and any given supply, price will adjust to produce an equilibrium point at which the amount in supply matches the quantum of demand. If the demand for a good falls and supply remains constant, price will also fall until it triggers people for whom price was previously a barrier to enter the market. Conversely, if demand rises then price will rise too. However, over time – which is sometimes referred to as the fourth dimension of economics – there will be an adjustment in supply and/or demand in response to price change.

The assumptions on which the pricing model is deemed to work are that:

- there are a multiplicity of separate economic actors, so that no one individual can influence the operation of the market;
- there is homogeneity of product;
- all participants are both rational and perfectly informed;
- there are no barriers to entering and exiting the market; and
- the market can make immediate marginal adjustments to accommodate change.

This is of course a very simplified explanation, and it does not relate easily to the real estate market. Whilst the normal market relationship is for supply and demand to be in equilibrium, in certain circumstances the property market may suffer disequilibrium where turnover effectively ceases and no clearing price exists. Disequilibrium was observed in the property crash of 1973.

Real estate lies within both the public and the private realm, and any decisions regarding its use allocation (and hence pricing) are affected by government intervention in the form of taxation and land use controls. Real estate is also a unique commodity in that its supply is fixed in overall terms, though not in relation to its specific use. It is also unique in that each unit of land or building is individual, in terms of location if nothing else, and it is therefore said to be a heterogeneous product.

Real estate is also unusual in that the motivation for ownership may be for utility purposes (for example, the requirement for a factory as a production unit or a shop as an outlet for manufactured goods) or for investment (that is, as a means of receiving a prospective income and capital return on a capital outlay). A further complexity of real estate as a subject for economic analysis is the nature of the land conversion process, whereby land is a developable commodity to which value can often be added by the carrying out of a scheme of building works, or a change in the effective use of the land or/and the buildings upon it. This development process is constrained both by the nature and extent of demand and by possible and actual physical, legal, financial, political and planning restrictions.

In the light of the above, it is not surprising that the land markets have given rise to a complex set of models and theories as they seek to deal with the effects of legislation and the lack of perfect knowledge that interfere with the 'pure' operation of the market mechanism (for a fuller explanation see, for example, Ball *et al.*, 1998; Eccles *et al.*, 1999; Warren, 2000; Harvey and Jowsey, 2003).

In summary, the economics of land and real estate markets is particularly complex due to:

- *The relatively fixed nature of land*: whilst fixed in physical terms, the availability of land for use will alter depending on land use planning regulations; it is therefore capable of change over time.
- *A lack of transparency and published data*: one of the key features of the property markets is their lack of transparency. Unlike equities markets, there is no free and easily accessible source of information on transaction prices. Whilst this situation is changing rapidly with the development of web-based services and the opening of the Land Registry to enquirers, data may not be free. Within institutional property markets,

greater transparency has been afforded by the setting up of the Investment Property Databank (IPD) which for the past 20 years has monitored the movement of yields and rents in respect of values of many institutional owner assets, but it is neither complete nor capable of disaggregation at the local or individual asset level, except to the contributing property owner, although it is freely available at aggregated level.

- *The nature of legal interests*: unlike other assets, property can be held in many ways and, strictly speaking within the UK, it is not held outright as all title is vested in the Crown. In legal terms, the owner holds an 'interest' in land. This can be freehold (full legal rights to deal with the asset as the owner wishes subject only to planning and other statutory restrictions); leasehold (the owner has an interest in the asset for a fixed term only and on terms that are set by a legal relationship between the freeholder and the lessee); or – following the passing of the Leasehold Reform and Commonhold Act 2002 – commonhold, whereby a joint ownership may be achieved. Currently there is little analysis of the likely effects of commonhold, given its recent introduction in 2004.
- *Heterogeneity*: the nature of the commercial property markets is that each property will be different; not only is the location unique, but properties also tend to differ in size, shape, specification and amenities. This leads to difficulty in comparing one with another and hence in achieving consistency within any pricing model.
- *The motivation of ownership*: as stated above, real estate may be owned as a resource within which to carry out economic or social activity or as an investment. Fundamentally, it is the ability to provide utility that drives the economic worth of the asset. The demand for land is a *derived* demand; it relates to the surplus that can be achieved through its usage. If there is no possibility of real utility being achieved then there will be no occupational demand and hence no value.

  To the investor, however, it is not the utility of the asset that matters directly but the security of income flow that can be achieved through rent. Investors are also concerned not just with cash flow security but with capital security and the prospects for both the cash flow and capital growth. Against this they will balance the risks of default and the attractiveness and likely returns available through investment in other asset classes, such as equities and bonds.

In summary, the role of property within the economy is observed to be important as a *resource* to the business and social community. However, it also has a second role within the economy as a home for *investment* funds, for both domestic and overseas investors. Where an individual or company, institution or government has spare capital not required for immediate consumption, it can either be held as a cash investment or invested in a capital asset. In the main capital markets the options open to investors range from government stock, to equities, to property, to derivatives relating to these markets.

Historically, many property text books have focused on property valuations and appraisals from the perspective of institutional investors. In the late 1970s average institutional property weightings were over 20% of investment assets. By 2000 this figure had fallen to below 5%, but it recovered by 2004 to just under 8%.

However, the proportion of the property market owned by institutions is only a small part of the whole commercial property market. In Chapter 9 it is shown that UK corporates and the UK Government own an estimated £486 billion of property assets. In Chapter 10 the gross property assets of public and private property companies are estimated at £210 billion. In contrast, institutional property holdings are estimated at around £100 billion.

Institutional property investment has an important role to play in the workings of the commercial property market, but in practice the corporate, government and property company ownership is some seven times greater. The latter plays a major role in the workings of the property market and thus deserves detailed consideration. In consequence, any major rise or fall in demand for investment property or property that is capable of being valued using the investment method will have an affect on the wider economy.

1.2   Aims of the book

There are many books that provide a comprehensive cover of the subject of real estate economics and others that deal specifically with the pricing of property. Many of these cover in-depth issues within the field of investment valuation (see, for example, Baum and Crosby, 1995b); others concentrate overall on valuation as a technical discipline from the viewpoint of the consultant valuer (Davies *et al.*, 2000; Rees and Hayward, 2000). The aim of this book is not to revisit that which is already very adequately covered elsewhere, although inevitably there is a significant amount of overlap. Instead it discusses aspects of practice and theory that link the world of investment valuation with that of the owner-occupier.

It is the authors' contention that for too long the debate that has informed practice has concentrated on the needs of the institutional investment owner of real estate, almost to the exclusion of those of the occupier. Yet without an occupier ready and willing to take a lease, now or in the future, a property investment has little real worth.

This focus of approach on the institutional landlord has been understandable, and in part is a result of the dramatic growth of funds under investment from the mid 1970s to the early 1980s. However, property as a home for investment funds has a relatively short history, dating back only 30 to 40 years in the UK and a far shorter time in most other EU countries (see, for example, Dubben and Sayce, 1991; Ross Goobey, 1992; Fraser, 1993; Scott, 1996). Institutional investment in property grew in an environment where planning restrictions on the supply of new, developed property encouraged occupiers to take long lease terms (normally 25 years) with periodic upward only rent reviews and full tenant liability for the physical asset (McIntosh and Sykes, 1985).

These so-called institutional leases were influential in that they enabled the income stream from property to be viewed in much the same way as other financial assets in the capital markets. This stimulated a body of research-based books including those by MacLeary and Nanthakumaran (1988); Brown (1991); Baum and Crosby (1995a) and Brown and Matysiak (2000). All these aimed at exploring ways of applying equity-market-based financial appraisal techniques to property investment analysis. The fundamental economic paradigm on which all these works have been based is that of neoclassicism; hence the works have striven to pursue rational quantitative approaches to the pricing conundrum.

In recent years, however, changes have been discernable and the spotlight has moved across to occupiers and owner-occupiers. This book concentrates on the following themes in particular:

- The growth in the influence of the corporate occupier as related to a breakdown of institutional leasing patterns, and the growth in finance leases rather than operational leases.
- The growth of new models of finance that influence property decision-making.
- The increasing recognition of the simplistic nature of maximising the 'single bottom line' – that is, the economic return – and the rise of the sustainability agenda.

Our aim in this book is to begin to address these issues in relation to the financial appraisal of property for both investors and corporate occupiers, and to relate this at all times to the practice implications.

1.3   New influences on the real estate market

1.3.1   The role of property and its growth as a managed asset

Land, in its improved or unimproved state, is fundamental to most human activity. It also has enormous implications for commercial activity as the resource base within which most commerce takes place. Some years ago the London Business School calculated that commercial property alone was worth half the value of the companies traded on the stock market and over double the value of Government stock (Currie and Scott, 1991). But in presenting these findings, the authors were explicit as to the difficulties they had in developing a methodology for capitalising the value of the UK's corporate estate, as they had been unable to find any publicly available statistics. Even an examination of company accounts did not give a full and clear picture, as is explained later in this book.

Setting aside the issue of how property capital values in the balance sheet are calculated, the implication of the Currie and Scott report was that property requires strategic management to ensure that its use aligns to business objectives (Edwards and Ellison, 2003). However, a succession of research reports, from Avis *et al.* (1989) to Bootle and Kalyan (2002), have concluded that many businesses are underutilising and undermanaging their property assets.

The reasons for this observed underuse and undermanagement are many and complex. In part they relate to historical factors, and in part to the way assets are held on the balance sheet. However, they also relate to the failure, until recently, of many owners to measure the economic performance of their assets, in terms of either their return on capital employed or their added value to the business. This scenario is changing rapidly, and through this book a number of the issues of performance measurement that are fundamental to providing corporate owners with a deeper understanding of the performance of their real estate are explored.

As owners take a more analytical approach to their asset management, so it will be expected that the type and specification of the properties they require to occupy will also alter. Already there is evidence that occupiers are seeking to intensify their use of office properties by changing the space requirements and moving to new ways of working such as 'hot desking' and 'hotelling'. More radically, some activities, previously located in the UK are being outsourced to other countries (for example, call centres to India). These changes will affect the future aggregate levels of demand for property and, in addition, affect the location, specification and longevity of property. This will in turn influence the attractiveness of property as an asset and its price in the marketplace.

Another change explored in the book is that taking place in the structure of leases. For many years long leases were the norm; this is now breaking down, with companies demanding either freeholds or very long leases for their core occupational needs, and short flexible leases for their ancillary activities. Nowhere has this trend been more prevalent than in the office market, with average lease lengths a third of those prevailing in the early 1990s. The reasons for the shortening of lease patterns are complex but relate in part to changes in the accounting regulations in relation to the treatment of leaseholds on the balance sheet; in part they are a reflection of the needs of occupiers to be more dynamic in response to the changing business environment.

The shortening of lease patterns has had two discernible effects. First, it has begun to address the lack of separation between the property occupational and investment markets that has been a hallmark of both practice and the literature. Second, and of more consequence for this book, it has required the development of appraisal techniques that can accommodate more flexible and less predictable income flows and that can be applied to unravel comparable rental evidence of transactions where, for example, rent review patterns, rent-free periods or capital inducements are different. This has led to the growth of applications of discounted cash flow techniques, as explored in subsequent chapters.

1.3.2   The new financial paradigms

Investors in real estate are making a choice to allocate a proportion of their funds to property in preference to other asset classes. In doing so they will apply a series of financial analysis techniques to assist in their decision-making. It is therefore important that property appraisers and analysts have a grasp of these models in order that they can advise appropriately. However, appraisers in the real estate industry can be criticised for having in the past been slow to embrace new theories and methodologies.

One of the key debates within the real estate appraisal field in recent years has been the issue of whether properties should be appraised by comparison with other transactions (valuation) or by reference to their prospective cash flows using discounted cash flow (DCF) techniques. Proponents of DCF argue for its greater ability to compare property performance and deal with non-standard cash flows – key requirements in a market that is moving towards more flexible cash flows. In this book the DCF approach is both explained and promoted as a methodology that should be used alongside traditional valuation techniques.

Another issue related to appraisal techniques concerns the relationship between real estate and the financial markets. Whilst much of the research work from the competing equities and bonds markets in the finance literature is ground-breaking and potentially interesting, analysts recognise that real estate has fundamentally different characteristics from equities and bonds; this poses questions as to how far the theories from these markets are valid for and can be applied to the real estate market.

Within the real estate field, as will be detailed in later chapters, appraisal techniques that deal with assets in a portfolio context relate in the main to the conventional finance theories developed between the 1960s and 1980s. Under these theories, there has been an assumption that investment decision-making is driven by rational economic behaviour and that investors have sought always to maximise returns and minimise risk. Modern portfolio theory, developed by Markowitz (1959) and subsequently extended by others such as Sharpe, Lintner and Mossen, adopted the rational assumption. Furthermore, these authors worked on the basis that markets are 'efficient', that is, that prices fully reflect all relevant financial data (see, for example, Fama and Miller, 1972). Since the mid 1980s, and some twenty years after these theories began to be applied in the financial field, property analysts have sought to use them for real estate.

In the meantime, just as these 'modern' finance theories have begun to gain ground within the real estate field, new theories have emerged which relax the assumptions of rationality and efficiency. New finance models accept the reality of inefficient markets and adopt a range of techniques from econometrics to arbitrage (Chen *et al.*, 1986) and behavioural models (Tversky and Kahneman, 1981) to explain investor behaviour. These new developments are explored in order to illustrate how far they can be used within the property asset allocation process.

1.3.3   The rise of the sustainability agenda

The above sets out the conventional economic view as related to property. Whilst this still provides the framework within which the markets operate, it is coming under increasing challenge from what is called the 'fourth factor'. Lovins *et al.* (1998) and Hawken *et al.* (1999) argue that the industrial and service economies, which our current economic theories seek to analyse and which at present form the basis of economic decision-making, are flawed. This is, they argue, because they fail to integrate the basic resources of air, water and ecological balance within the economic value sets; instead they treat them as free goods, with the consequence that the natural capital essential to supporting our economic activity is being depleted at a fast and unsustainable rate.

Hawken *et al.* (1999) contend that industrial (and post-industrial) societies will need to adjust their decision and resource allocation models to include natural capital within the economic equation. In this they concur with the 'factor four' principle (Lovins *et al.*, 1998) that economic survival rests on resource productivity growing fourfold to enable economic life to be sustained into the future.

The notion of balancing the desire for economic development with society's ambition for sustainability in both social and environmental terms has gained very rapid ground since the so-called Brundtland definition of sustainability was published in 1987 (WCED, 1987). This definition, namely that sustainable development meets the needs of today without compromising the ability of future generations to meet their own needs, has been the subject of much debate. However, the concept has been increasingly enshrined within supranational and national legislation and policy. Within the UK, the first sustainable development strategy was produced by government in 1994, following the Rio Earth Summit's call in 1992 for all countries to produce such a strategy.

The Rio Summit laid out eight principles of sustainability, which can be summarised as follows:

- The fundamental right of all human beings to an environment that is adequate for their heath and well-being.
- The conservation and proper use of the environment (including the built environment) in a way that benefits both current and future generations.

- The promotion of bio-diversity to ensure ecosystem maintenance.
- The monitoring of environmental standards and the publication of data related thereto.
- The prior assessment of the environmental impacts of significant developments.
- That all individuals are informed of planned activities and given rights to justice.
- That conservation is integral to the planning and implementation of development activities.
- That states should co-operate towards mutual implementation.

Underlying these principles are three themes:

- The promotion of *environmental well-being*, so that environmental degradation is min-imised and natural resources are used to the greatest benefit. This implies *inter alia*:
  o conservation of non-renewable energy resources;
  o reduction of greenhouse gas emissions;
  o promotion of use of renewable energy sources; and
  o management of resources, including waste management.
- The *protection* of, and *proper respect* for, *people* so that the common human condition is improved, as measured by indices such as the United Nations Human Development Index. This implies progress towards:
  o improvements in working conditions;
  o adequate care of the less advantaged;
  o social legislation to ensure good governance at all levels; and
  o appropriate educational and employment opportunities in terms of education and work.
- The creation of an *economic context* in which social and environmental goals can be achieved. Whilst Hawken *et al.* (1999) are optimistic about the prospects for this, others are less so.

The implications of the rise of the sustainability agenda may seem on first view to be divorced from the issue of real estate pricing. This may have been the case some years ago, but now both environmental concerns and social well-being are beginning to influence the operation of the property markets and the pricing of property assets.

First, there is a rapidly emerging raft of social and environmental legislation that affects real estate directly (see, for example, the Planning and Compulsory Purchase Act 2004; the 2005 England and Wales Building Regulations and the Disability Discrimination Act 1995). The advent of more energy controls and the proposed introduction of energy labels for buildings are other examples of ways in which occupiers will be affected by the growth of concern for sustainability. In addition, social responsibility policies are now to be found within many corporate organisations (see, for example, Henry, 1999). Collectively, these factors will affect the levels of property pricing in the marketplace in the future, if they do not do so already (St Lawrence, 2003).

The impact of the sustainability agenda will also have an effect on the attitudes of investors in property and hence the prices that they are willing to pay. In the wider invest-ment field, the establishment of the Dow Jones Sustainability Index in the US and of the FTSE4Good in the UK have demonstrated high comparative performances by companies with a strong commitment to corporate social responsibility. In turn this has attracted investment funds to such companies. A further driver is to be found in the requirement, since 2000, for pension funds to have social responsibility policies. This has led to many of the major funds and other institutional investors seeking ways to implement such policies in their investment practice, including their property investment practice (Sayce and Ellison, 2003). A survey by Parnell and Sayce (1999) found little evidence of pricing being directly affected at that time, but respondents were very strong in their opinion that in the future these matters would be significant.

In summary, whilst the established supply and demand model of pricing continues, the rise of worldwide concerns about sustainability matters is likely to act as an increasing constraint on models and to influence the behaviour of all players in the economy, including property occupiers and investors.

1.4   Structure of the book

This book is structured to take readers through the key decision points within the property investment process, whether that investment is for rental and capital return or forms part of the corporate asset base. Before doing so, this chapter introduces the main techniques that are conventionally used by valuers and appraisers in determining the market *value* of a property asset. These techniques are not developed in any detail here, as this material is covered in many other books (for example, Isaac and Steley, 2000; Johnson *et al.*, 2000) and aspects of the methods are developed in later chapters. The focus in the book is on exploring the new market practices that are evolving in response to the shifting investment and corporate agenda, and these relate to *worth*. Whilst accepting that a dictionary may regard the words 'value' and 'worth' as synonymous, to the property appraiser they are not. Accordingly, this chapter introduces the notion of worth to provide a context for the subsequent analyses.

Chapter 2 deals with the property purchase decision in some detail by exploring the factors that influence this decision, both for investors and for corporate occupiers. The purchase process that is required of the consultant valuer is then explained.

Investors will wish to place their decision within the context of the entire investment spectrum of opportunities to ensure that they are purchasing an appropriate asset at an acceptable price; hence Chapter 3 considers the appraisal of property within the context of the multi-asset portfolio and Chapters 4, 5 and 6 explore the calculation of market value. Whilst the approaches adopted in these three chapters do not introduce any concepts that are radically different from those espoused by the established literature, they are considered from a professional practitioner's perspective, and some of the newer constraints in relation to the emerging corporate social responsibility agenda are introduced.

Price will be a major consideration for the purchaser of any property. However, more important than the market price is what an asset is *worth* to a prospective purchaser and, following purchase, an analysis of this continued value to the organisation is required. These aspects are developed in Chapter 7 where the calculation of worth to the individual is considered.

To the property owner, risk is also a major concern. There are two aspects to this: risk as it relates to the pricing of an individual asset, and risk in relation to the interaction of that asset with others in the portfolio. The ways in which each can be analysed and built into pricing models are detailed and discussed in Chapters 8 and 12, respectively.

The point that property values are ultimately dependent upon occupational demand has already been made. We have indicated that we are concerned with property investors and occupational ownership. Chapter 9 analyses some of the influences on occupational demand and considers in detail the buy or lease decision, whilst Chapter 10 explores some of the property funding and financing decision issues.

Once a property sits within either an occupational or an investment portfolio, its contribution to economic return should be measured and its future likely contribution to the portfolio estimated. Accordingly, Chapter 11 and Chapter 13 consider the measurement of return and forecasting, respectively.

One of our objectives in writing this book has been to minimise the number of mathematical equations used; however, no study of property pricing can avoid these altogether, and some mathematical examples have been included. Appendix A contains details of the formulae that have been used within the book and, to further assist readers, Appendix B contains details of a web site from which further detailed and updated examples that illustrate the techniques and principles put forward in the book can be downloaded for use.

1.5   Worth v. price v. value: definitions

This book is concerned with the concepts of worth and value and their relationship to price within the real estate markets. The differences between them and their relevance in practice are developed further in Chapter 7. In this chapter, the background and underlying distinctions are introduced.

The concepts of worth and value and their relationship to price are fundamental issues within the operation and regulation of real estate markets. If a dictionary is consulted, the words *worth*, *price* and *value* are normally found to be described as synonymous or to have definitions that are at least in part interchangeable. Additionally, in other countries there may be little or no distinction made between these words (for a discussion of this see Adair *et al.*, 1996). There may be significant differences in practice: for example, in the UK valuations are undertaken by a valuer and an appraisal is undertaken by an appraiser/ property investment surveyor advising the purchaser or employed by the purchaser, whilst in the US an appraiser undertakes both valuations and investment appraisals. However, in the UK in recent years, the distinction in meaning between worth, price and value has become an important matter in defining the activity of the real estate professional.

Until the 1990s, most professionals operating in real estate would have used the words price, worth and value interchangeably. A debate was then triggered, primarily by the rapidly changing market conditions of the late 1980s and early 1990s. During this period valuations prepared primarily for bank lending purposes came under the scrutiny of the courts as a succession of valuers were called to account for their valuations which (with the benefit of hindsight) had proved to be over optimistic. The professional response was to examine, amongst other things, the regulations under which valuers operated, and to clarify the terminology used by them. The Royal Institution of Chartered Surveyors (RICS) set up the Mallinson Committee, headed by Michael Mallinson, the then chief surveyor to Prudential Property Investment Managers.

From the publication in 1994 of the Mallinson Report (Mallinson, 1994) to the publication in 2003 of the overhauled RICS *Appraisal and Valuation Standards* (RICS, 2003) there was a lively debate. In the early 1990s the emphasis on valuation accuracy in the UK was intense (Drivers Jonas, 1991; Lizieri and Venmore-Rowland, 1991, 1993; Matysiak and Venmore-Rowland, 1995; Matysiak and Wang, 1995; McAllister, 1995 and Brown and Matysiak, 2000) and debate focused on the need for the consultant valuer/appraiser to be in tune with the needs of the client, an issue raised by Mallinson. However, following Mallinson the focus of debate shifted from accuracy – though this remains an issue – to semantics. Mallinson was of the view that a number of different bases of valuation were required and that a distinction should be drawn between value in exchange (market value) and value in use (worth). In response to this, RICS produced two guides: one to commercial valuations (RICS, 1996) and the other on worth (RICS, 1997). Since that time the understanding of a differential between the terms has developed.

Whilst in the UK some consensus has begun to emerge, the question of the definition of worth, price and value presents continuing problems in an international context (see, for example, McParland *et al.*, 2000). It is important to attempt to define the concepts before progressing to appropriate valuation methodologies.

The word *value* can be used to describe different but related concepts in terms of real estate. It may be viewed as a general, all-encompassing term that incorporates the three main types of value: price, market value and worth. The term *valuation* has specific professional definitions and for the UK is defined within the RICS *Appraisal and Valuation Standards* (RICS, 2003). Elsewhere, it is defined by both the European standards (TEGoVA, 2003) and the International Valuation Standards (IVSC, 2003). Although the wording differs in each case, the essence is that a valuation is an estimation of the most likely selling price on the open market, on the basis of both a willing seller and a willing buyer. However, in practice, the valuation figure may not be the same as the price actually achieved. This may be due to imperfections within the property market or the presence of a special purchaser to whom the property may have a value over and above its worth to other potential buyers; or it may reflect a timing discrepancy, since valuations assume that the property marketing has already been undertaken and the transaction is due for completion as at the valuation date. In reality, the length of time it takes for the marketing of a property investment and agreement of a price can be several months, during which time market movement may occur that places the agreed price out of line with the then prevailing market values. Another problem that can lead to differences between the valuation and the price achieved may relate to the lack of current comparable evidence on yields and rents upon which to base the valuation. Price is derived from the interaction of supply and demand, but the supply of land for specific uses is relatively fixed and is slow to adjust to changes in demand, leading to price anomalies.

In the context of value, price and worth, Hoesli and MacGregor (2000) distinguish between four different concepts:

- *Price* is the actual observable money exchanged when a property investment is bought or sold. In most other markets price is given, but in the property market every property interest is different and requires an individual estimate of value to guide the buyer and seller in their negotiations to agree a price. Price can be fixed by negotiation, through tender bids or at auction.

- *Value* is therefore an estimation of the likely selling price. In other markets, where homogenous goods are sold, the price is not estimated but is determined from market trading and is usually used to describe an assessment of worth.
- *Individual worth* is the true value to an individual investor using all the market information and available analytical tools and can be considered as the value in use.
- *Market worth* is the price a property investment would trade at in a competitive and efficient market using all market information and available analytical tools. A valid model of calculation of market worth should reflect the underlying conditions of the market at the time. This should therefore be distinguished from market *value*, which accepts a less than perfect knowledge of market information.

In practice in the UK property investment market, value and worth can currently be distinguished as follows:

- *Value* is obtained through the gathering and application of comparable evidence. The comparable evidence is gathered from transactions involving properties similar in terms of effective rents (for more on this, please refer to Chapter 4), and yields. The valuation methods use rents and rental levels as at the valuation date, and yields in which risk and growth are implied (i.e. traditional valuation methods are used).
- *Worth* is frequently calculated using discounted cash flow methods and is considered in terms of whether or not a required or hurdle rate of return is achieved.

The debate on definitions is not confined to the UK; nor is there yet a settled position. The role of the International Valuation Standards Committee in devising and promoting internationally recognised and accepted definitions and processes has become of increasing importance, with a significant majority of countries with established property markets now involved in the process of developing international definitions and standards. As time goes by there will doubtless come a point at which full professional understanding is reached, but we have not arrived at it yet!

1.6   Conventional approaches to establishing value

In the UK, valuation practice has traditionally used five different methods. A summary of these is set out below. Four are commonly used for assets that are normally traded in the marketplace; the fifth relates to assets that are seldom if ever traded except as part of the sale of a company.

Before detailing the methods used, it must be stressed that the choice of method will depend upon the *purpose* for which the valuation is being prepared. The most common purpose is for market transaction; however, valuations are also commonly required for loan security or for inclusion in company accounts. (Valuations are needed for other purposes as well, notably in relation to taxation, but these are not addressed in this book.)

For more details on the five methods of valuation, please refer to Scarrett (1991) and Davies *et al.* (2000), and for their application to specific property types see Rees and Hayward (2000).

1.6.1   The comparative method

The comparative method is used where there are comparable transactions involving properties with characteristics similar to those of the property in question. For example, in the case of vacant possession residential property, the prices of similar three-bedroom houses can be compared and used to determine the value of the three-bedroom property in question. The skill of the valuer is to make adjustments to reflect the differences between the comparable properties and the property being valued.

This method is also used for the valuation of agricultural land, such that the value per hectare is derived from similar farm land that has been sold. Where zoning for new development is uniform, this method can be used as a valuation method for development land, on a square metre or hectare basis.

In commercial property transactions in the UK, this method is increasingly used as an informative figure that can provide the valuer with background information relative to the property, such that the property being valued and the comparables being used are looked at in terms of the capital value per square metre of the gross or net usable floor area. However, the comparative method is unlikely to be used as a standalone valuation method in the UK.

1.6.2   The investment method

The investment method is used to value income-producing vacant possession property with the potential to produce a rental income and owner-occupied commercial property that could be let to produce a rental income. In the UK the investment method is seen as the main method of valuing commercial property.

This method considers in today's terms the net income streams that a property will produce currently and in the future. Using the present value of £1 methodology, each of these annual income streams is discounted to arrive at today's value. As the current and prospective net income streams are determined as at the valuation date, the present value multipliers can be aggregated to produce years purchase multipliers (for example, years purchase in perpetuity, years purchase single rate or years purchase deferred for a set period). Further information on these valuation formulae is set out in Appendix A.

In the investment method there are five key inputs

- The passing rent.
- The estimated open market rental value as at the valuation date. This is determined from comparable evidence of recent lettings and relates to the effective open market rental value and not the headline open market rental value. Please refer to Chapter 4 for more details on this.
- The valuation yield(s) are determined from comparable evidence of recent market transactions, from which the years purchase multiplier is derived and applied to the net rents.
- The purchaser's costs of undertaking the purchase transaction. Net valuation yields are calculated on the basis that the return to the investor includes the costs of the transaction.

- The length of the void period and the associated costs before the vacant accommodation becomes income-producing. These figures relating to voids are in many instances implied into the valuation yield: the valuation yield is adjusted in line with comparable evidence to reflect the impact of current or prospective voids. In practice, if the void or potential void is material then it is likely to be included explicitly in the valuation.

It is worth noting that the underlying methodology used in the investment method of valuation utilises the concept of the time value of money, namely that £1 today is worth more than £1 receivable in the future. The figure is a product of when the money is received and the discount rate used. This discounting methodology is the same as that used in the discounted cash flow appraisal method (see section 1.7.1). However, in the investment method of valuation it is the *current* levels of rents that are used, and future growth, risk and property-specific characteristics are implied within the valuation yield (the multiplier). In contrast, the discounted cash flow appraisal method uses a target or required rate of return as the discount rate, but makes explicit assumptions as to what the future net rental cash flows will be.

1.6.3   The residual method

The residual method is used to value development sites and existing properties that have the potential to be redeveloped. Additionally, where the land cost is known this method can be used to determine the developer's profit.

The method involves many variables, and the value derived for the site can be very sensitive to relatively small changes in these variables. The traditional assumption is that the development and site purchase are financed using 100% borrowed money.

A straightforward way of considering how the residual method of valuation works is to look at the time line of events in a development scheme (Fig. 1.1). The building costs and fees are rolled forward, together with the interest charges. To these are added the letting and sale costs and the developer's profit, to give the total development cost as at the date the property is expected to become substantially let. At this date a deemed sale is assumed. The valuation of the completed and let property is carried out, usually using today's rental levels and net yields for comparable new properties. This figure is known as the gross development value, and from it is deducted the total development cost. The difference is the value of the land as at the deemed sale date in the future. This future land value includes the interest cost of holding the land, and these interest costs are stripped out using the present value of £1 formula to produce the current value of the site/land.

When undertaking residual valuations, practical considerations come to the fore. These include the ability to gain the necessary planning consents and any likely conditions attached thereto, the site conditions, the availability of building contract labour, the cost of

Fig. 1.1   The timeline of events in a development scheme.

borrowings and the time likely to be required to complete the development. The simplicity of the residual method of valuation is both its strength and its weakness. To overcome its simplicity and a number of the assumptions used, a detailed discounted cash flow appraisal can be undertaken as well.

1.6.4   The profits method

The profits or accounts method is used where the occupier of commercial property uses the accommodation as an integral part of their business, such that the value is linked to the profitability of the business, and the level of profit expected determines the ability of the trader to pay for premises.

The method, which is normally regarded as specialist, is used primarily for the valuation of trading premises and is normally, though not always, restricted to types of properties that change hands most frequently on a freehold basis. Examples of properties where the profits method is used include hotels, public houses, petrol filling-stations and some leisure properties. Yet where sufficient transactions and comparable evidence exist for similar properties because of an increasing number of lettings, there is less reliance on this method. This is explored further in Chapter 4.

1.6.5   The cost approach

The cost approach to valuation is used when a property is occupied by an owner, but there is a real lack of comparable evidence of transactions for similar properties. In such cases a cost basis of valuation is used; however, the resultant figure will be finalised by the client, with the valuer reporting the figure 'subject to the ongoing profitability' of the business.

The underlying assumption for this method is that the property forms part of the assets used in an ongoing business and as such, in an accountancy context, can be treated similarly to plant and machinery. The method is used within both the private and public sectors so its use is not restricted to profit-orientated property (see, for example, Sayce and Connellan, 2000). In the case of public sector properties, the assumption is made as to the continuance of the service.

Because the method is only used in cases where there is a lack of market transaction evidence, it follows that it is not used for the purposes of open market sale; indeed, its use within the UK is restricted to book or company accounting and statutory purposes (for example, taxation and compensation for compulsory acquisition). The same is not true in some other countries, such as the US, where it is used as a check against market value (Gelbtuch *et al.*, 1997), and some European countries, particularly those that are emergent economies (Adair *et al.*, 1996).

The cost approach to valuation assumes that the value to the owner relates to the cost of reproducing the asset by rebuilding. The valuation comprises two elements: the land and the buildings. First the land is valued with due regard to comparables. At the time of writing (2005), the land will be valued in its existing use (see, for example, RICS, 2003; IVSC, 2003). However, changes to international accounting regulations mean that this assumption is set to change, and new guidance issued by IVSC in 2004 to ensure compliance with accounting standards introduces the concept of market value for the land element (IVSC, 2004)

The building element is then valued to determine the depreciated replacement cost of the building. The calculation of the depreciated replacement cost (DRC) requires the estimating of the current replacement cost of the building, normally assuming a modern substitute building then depreciating this in relation to the future potential life of the actual building. There is much debate as to how such depreciation should be conducted (see, for example, Britton *et al.*, 1991; RICS, 2003), but most valuers adopt a straight line approach. The value of the property is the sum of the land value and the depreciated replacement cost.

Examples where this method is used include power stations, chemical plants, jetties and other specialised properties. It is worth remembering that the cost approach to valuation is akin to an accounting method of assessing the asset's value to the *business* rather than its value to a third party or its open market value. For this reason, a valuation of this kind should not normally be used as a basis for secured lending; neither does it give any indication as to the likely realisable price in the marketplace.

Please see Spreadsheet 1 for worked examples of each of the five valuation methods.

1.7   Additional approaches to appraisal

In addition to the five conventional methods of valuation, other methods are discernible in the market place both in the UK and elsewhere. These are now introduced.

1.7.1   The discounted cash flow appraisal method

Absent from the above five methods of valuation is the discounted cash flow (DCF) appraisal method of valuation. In many countries, including the US, Australia and New Zealand and across Continental Europe, this DCF method of appraisal is used as a valuation method in its own right – effectively a sixth valuation method. Until recently in the UK, however, discounted cash flow (DCF) was considered to be an analytical tool and not a valuation method.

In the bond and equities markets, discounted cash flow is an established valuation methodology. In contrast, in the UK real estate investment market DCF is generally seen as an investment appraisal tool. However, in a growing number of countries that have established and sophisticated property investment markets (for example, the US and Australia) the use of DCF methodologies has been extended such that they are recognised as a valid valuation method. Increasingly this is also the case in the UK, for a number of reasons which are set out below.

The techniques used in DCF appraisals are detailed in Chapter 3, but to present a context for the explanation of why they are being adopted, the basic terminology is explained here.

In essence a DCF requires the valuer or appraiser to arrive at an estimate of the *actual* anticipated cash flows over a specified time horizon, normally between 10 and 15 years. These cash flows will be the rent currently passing together with any uplifted rent anticipated during the period as a result of reviews and market movement. Accepting both that cash flows in the future will be prone to risk and that there is a time value to money (see Chapter 3 for an explanation of interest rate theory), each cash flow in the future is discounted at a chosen rate of interest (known as the hurdle rate, the target rate or the investor's required return). Cash flows beyond the specified time horizon are then capitalised using a single capitalisation rate and discounted at the hurdle rate. The resultant figure is the estimated gross present value (GPV) of the asset. This represents the figure at which an investor with the specified required rate of return should be prepared to purchase the investment. Where the purchase price and costs are included the figure becomes the net present value (NPV), and this is usually the figure that is sought.

Clearly, altering the required rate of return will alter the resultant figure; an increase in the rate required will lower the NPV, and vice versa. For many investors it is useful to know, for any proposed price, what rate of interest (or discount rate) would result in the investment being just worthwhile. It is possible, using simple spreadsheet methodology, to calculate this rate, which is know as the *internal rate of return* (IRR).

Having described the nature of a DCF, it must be asked why this it set to become accepted as a legitimate sixth method of valuation. As has already been explained, within the UK there has been a tradition of long leases but this is not paralleled in most other countries. More commonly, leases are short, with structural repairing obligations being a landlord's responsibility; there are no upward only rent reviews and in their place is indexation in line with, for example, a cost of living index (Adair *et al.*, 1996). This results in major differences in the assessment of market value.

- The tendency is to use a simple investment approach or *initial yield valuation*, in which the passing rent is capitalised and any reversionary potential is simply incorporated into the capitalisation yield.
- Alongside the initial yield valuation method, DCF appraisal is used as a complementary valuation methodology.

In the UK, many factors are driving practitioners to consider the adoption of such an approach. These drivers, described in more detail in subsequent chapters, include:

- Changes to lease terms, including shortening of the term and the prospect of possible political intervention relating to lease terms.
- Changes to accounting standards which require the inclusion of property at 'fair value'.
- Changes to stamp duty on leases, which is a powerful driver towards shorter occupational leases.

As leases change in response to these market drivers, so too must valuation techniques. Before consideration is given to the application of DCF analysis techniques as a method of determining whether or not a property is fairly valued, DCF methodology will be examined briefly to demonstrate how it can be used as an explicit valuation technique.

In the US, DCF is used as a valuation method, such that IRRs for different properties (in particular shopping centres) can be quoted as comparables. In the UK, the use of DCF as a valuation tool operates in a slightly different manner. Unlike normal DCF analysis, which lumps together all the cash flows to produce a net cash flow which is then analysed, UK DCF valuation methodology often splits the anticipated cash flows into four main tranches:

- *Bond tranche number 1*: this relates to the rental income passing for the term of the lease, and excludes any potential uplifts. It is valued as if it were a government bond, with the discount rate reflecting the creditworthiness of each tenant.
- *Bond tranche number 2*: this relates to the difference between the rent passing and the current market rental value of the property. This income stream is deemed to be more risky than tranche number 1. It is valued as if it were a bond, with the discount rate reflecting the creditworthiness of each tenant, plus a margin to reflect the uncertainty of the increase actually being achieved at the next rent review.
- *Equity tranche number 1*: this relates to the expected increases in the rents receivable over and above the current passing rents and the estimated market rental value. These potential income streams are discounted at a relatively high discount rate to reflect their riskiness.
- *Equity tranche number 2*: this relates to the 'exit value' of the property at the end of the DCF analysis period. Again, an equity-type discount rate is used to reflect the risks of obsolescence, depreciation and poor market performance.

For buildings let on long leases to high-quality tenants, this explicit DCF valuation method can produce values higher than the traditional open market valuation methods, due to the current positive yield gap between bonds and property yields. In contrast, where the occupational leases are short the values can come in significantly lower. It is not surprising that this methodology is used internally by a number of life insurance companies who view commercial property as a substitute for bonds and a method of providing for their annuity contracts. However, the variance in end results from those achieved through conventional methods has resulted in considerable resistance amongst some members of the valuer community. Nonetheless, the move towards its adoption is gaining momentum and the RICS standards (RICS, 2003) now contain specific reference to DCF methodology for calculating investment worth.

Whilst DCF is gaining acceptance as a method to be used as complementary to established techniques, it is worth noting that in the US valuation practice dictates that a series of valuations should be undertaken by the appraiser: namely, that each of the six methods of valuation should be undertaken (subject to applicability), and the valuer should produce a valuation in the context of prevailing local market conditions and the figures produced under the various methods. In practice the investment method (also known in the US as the direct capitalisation method), in conjunction with the discounted cash flow appraisal method, are the main methods relied upon for commercial property investments.

Discounted cash flow as an appraisal method is considered in more detail in Chapter 3 and subsequent chapters.

1.7.2 Statutory valuations

There is a strong case for including a seventh valuation method, as it is used by German open end funds who are major players in the European property investment market. Where they exist as a genuine valuation method, statutory valuations should be added to the list.

In the UK such methods do not exist in the property investment market. They relate only to cases of taxation and compensation. However, in Germany, financial institutions (which include German open end funds) in particular are required by law to value property investments under the terms set out in statutes. In this context, the WertV. (Wertermittlungsverordnung) provides a detailed code of valuation concepts, which are used by practising valuers. The details of such valuation methods are outside the scope of this book, and for further information readers are referred to Adair *et al.* (1996). However, when such valuation methods are used it is important to compare the valuation figure with the market value. The statutory valuation method can frequently produce a significantly higher figure, and this should be acknowledged.

1.8   An introduction to the drivers for DCF

Until recently, there was a clear distinction between the use of traditional valuations and DCF appraisal techniques. This distinction has become blurred, such that DCF appraisal techniques are used as both a valuation and an appraisal technique, and this blurring is being accelerated by the shortening in occupational leases taken by tenants.

The forces for change in the UK property market that will impact on and shorten lease length are as follows:

- Changes to stamp duty in the 2004 Finance Act make the amount of tax charged a function of the lease length: the longer the lease, the greater the tax burden payable by the lessee. This has prompted a demand for shorter leases.
- Changes to the UK and International Accounting Standards coming through in 2005 will change the way in which occupational leases are shown in company accounts. Currently, occupational leases are not shown in the balance sheet, but under the new rules they will be shown as both an asset and a liability. This will raise the gearing levels of retail and hotel companies significantly.
- There is government pressure for shorter, flexible leases. In 2002 the Labour Government told the property industry that, unless it saw landlords offering more flexible lease terms to tenants, it would bring forward legislation. In particular, upward only rent reviews are seen as being too onerous for tenants, given the cyclical nature of property markets.

In other countries where short leases are common, tenants usually have the ability to quit at either three- or five-yearly intervals. In short leases, the lease terms tend to be different from those seen in the traditional 15 to 25 year UK lease, as shown in Table 1.1.

Table 1.1   Typical lease terms.

UK leases	EU and US leases
Full repairing • Tenant responsible for structural repairs	Internal repairing • Landlord responsible for structural repairs
Upward only rent reviews	In EU a link to indexation common
Break clauses not very frequent • Security of income linked to tenant quality	Break options frequent • Void risk potential at breaks
Rental cash flows relatively predictable	Rental cash flows relatively unpredictable

Table 1.2   Valuation methodologies.

UK	EU and US
Investment method as outlined above	Initial yield method predominantly used • Void risk and income changes incorporated implicitly into the yield • UK-based investment method seldom used
DCF rarely used as a valuation methodology but commonly used as a tool of analysis of worth	DCF often used alongside the initial yield method as a second view on the value

The style of lease contract influences the valuation methodology used. Where there are short leases, the tendency is for valuers to use different valuation methodologies from those used in the UK, where there is the benefit of long leases (Table 1.2). Thus in the EU and US, DCF is used alongside the initial yield method as a valuation method. It therefore seems reasonable to conclude that, as UK leases get shorter, UK lease terms will start to change and will move into line with those seen in countries where short leases are common.

A shift in the UK to shorter leases is thus likely to have a knock-on effect in terms of the valuation methods used. If the UK follows the US and EU experience, there will be a move to the use of initial yield-based valuations and a growth in the use of DCF techniques by valuers.

There is another driver for change in the way that property is valued. This is the increasing use by the investor of combined equity (the investor's own money) and debt finance (typically money borrowed from a bank). This move is in part to strive for increased returns, and also to enlarge the pot of money available to increase the portfolio size and reduce the exposure to specific risks. These issues are considered in more detail in Chapters 9 and 12, respectively.

The incorporation of debt into the property transaction renders traditional valuations only partially useful. Whilst valuations are required by the lender in order to satisfy a number of their lending ratios – for example, initial and exit loan to value ratios – traditional valuations do not help in defining the prospective net cash flow profile of the investment, which is required by the bank to determine their debt service cover and interest cover ratios. Furthermore, traditional valuations do not provide figures relating to prospective geared (equity) returns.

Thus a move to shorter leases and a growing use of debt finance is prompting a growing use of DCF methodologies alongside traditional valuations. This widening of valuation methodologies will require the UK valuation profession to become accustomed to using DCF techniques. From the authors' experience, DCF is a methodology of which many UK property professionals have little practical experience. In Chapter 3 there is an introduction to property appraisal and investment analysis techniques, which discusses how DCFs can be structured and the key inputs and outputs.

1.9 Summary

This chapter has sought to introduce the main themes that run through the book. Real estate is a key element within the economy; it therefore requires to be appropriately managed and this in turn requires reliable and accurate appraisals to be carried out. In particular, as the established economic paradigms are increasingly challenged by the rise of the sustainability agenda, so there will be a need for a response among property professionals. There is also a need both to better understand the role of property as an operational asset and investment medium and to relate its appraisal more closely to the methodologies used in other markets.

The role of the adviser has traditionally been that of advising on market value or likely price in the marketplace. In subsequent chapters we argue that this role now requires the acquisition of new skills within the field of appraisal.

Currently, property pricing is achieved using one or more of five valuation methods. These have been in place for many years and are generally well understood. However, where properties are being held as investments, the traditional methodology is increasingly under challenge by the sixth method in the adviser's armoury, namely discounted cash flow (DCF). The increasing use of DCF as an appraisal method in addition to valuation methods provides a key theme for this book. DCF is used within the investment and occupier market, and is widely used in risk and portfolio analysis.

The issue of risk is also critical to appraisal and we devote two chapters to its consideration. However, any consideration of property appraisal should not be done without due consideration of the operational needs that underpin demand, and a chapter is devoted to occupier considerations. These are addressed in other chapters too.

In presenting this book we have sought to balance the theories that underpin practice with the applications, and readers are advised to consult the web link provided in Appendix B to gain new and updated information on applications.

References

Adair, A., Downie, M.L., McGreal, S. and Vos, G. (1996) *European Valuation Practice: Theory and Techniques*. London: E&FN Spon.

Avis, M., Gibson, V. and Watts, J. (1989) *Managing Operational Property Assets*. Reading: University of Reading.

Ball, M., Lizieri, C. and MacGregor, B. (1998) *The Economics of Commercial Property Markets*. London: Routledge.

Baum, A. and Crosby, N. (1995a) *Property Investment Appraisal*, 2nd edn. London: Routledge.

Baum, A. and Crosby, N. (1995b) Over-rented properties: bond or equity? A case study of market value, investment worth and actual price. *Journal of Property Investment & Finance*, 13 (2): 31–40.

Bootle, R. and Kalyan, S. (2002) *Property in Business – A Waste of Space*. London: RICS.

Britton, W., Connellan, O. and Crofts, M. (1991) *The Cost Approach to Valuation*. London: RICS.

Brown, G. (1991) *Property Investment and the Capital Markets*. London: Chapman Hall.

Brown, G. and Matysiak, G. (2000) *Real Estate Investment: A Capital Markets Approach*. London: FT Prentice Hall.

Chen, N.-F., Roll, R. and Ross, S. (1986) Economic forces and the stock market. *Journal of Business*, 59 (3): 383–403.

Currie, D. and Scott, A. (1991) *The Place of Commercial Property in the UK Economy*. London: London Business School.

Davies, K., Johnson, T. and Shapiro, E. (2000) *Modern Methods of Valuation*. London: Estates Gazette Ltd.

Disability Discrimination Act 1995. www.legislation.hmso.gov.uk

Drivers Jonas (1991) *The Variance in Valuations*. London: Drivers Jonas.

Dubben, N. and Sayce, S. (1991) *Property Portfolio Management*. Routledge: London.

Eccles, E., Sayce, S. and Smith, J. (1999) *Property and Construction Economics*. London: International Thomson.

Edwards, V. and Ellison, L. (2003) *Corporate Property Management: Aligning Real Estate with Business Strategy*. Oxford: Blackwell Science.

Fama, E. and Miller, M.H. (1972) *The Theory of Finance*. New York: Holt, Rhinehart, and Winston.

Fraser, W.D. (1993) *Principles of Property Investment and Pricing*, 2nd edn. Basingstoke: Macmillan.

Gelbtuch, H., Mackmin, D. and Milgrim, M. (1997) *Real Estate Valuation in Global Markets*. Illinois: The Appraisal Institute.

Harvey, E. and Jowsey, J. (2003) *Urban Land Economics*. Basingstoke: Palgrave Macmillan.

Hawken, P., Lovins, A. and Lovins, L. (1999) *Natural Capitalism: Creating the Next Industrial Revolution*. Boston: Little, Brown and Co.

Henry, E. (1999) The value of environmental performance to financial stakeholders. *UNEP Industry and Environment*, Jan–Mar: 11.

Hoesli, M. and MacGregor, B. (2000) *Property Investment: Principles and Practice of Portfolio Management*. Harlow: Longman.

Isaac, D. and Steley, T. (2000) *Property Valuation Techniques*. Basingstoke: Palgrave Macmillan.

International Valuations Standards Committee (2003) *International Valuation Standards 2003*. London: IVSC.

International Valuations Standards Committee (2004) *International Valuation Standards 2004*. London: IVSC.

Johnson, T.A., Davie, K. and Shapiro, E. (2000) *Modern Methods of Valuation of Land, Houses and Buildings*, 9th edn. London: Estates Gazette.

Lizieri, C. and Venmore-Rowland, P. (1991) Valuation accuracy: a contribution to the debate. *Journal of Property Research*, 8: 115–122.

Lizieri, C. and Venmore-Rowland, P. (1993) Valuations, prices and the market: a rejoinder. *Journal of Property Research*, 10: 77.

Lovins, L., Von Weizsäcker, E. and Lovins, A. (1998) *Factor Four: Doubling Wealth, Halving Resource Use*. London: Earthscan.

MacLeary, A. and Nanthakumaran, N. (eds) (1988) *Property Investment Theory*. London: E&FN Spon.

Mallinson, M. (1994) *Commercial Property Valuations: The Report of the Mallinson Committee*. London: RICS.

Markowitz, H. (1959) *Portfolio Selection: Efficient Diversification of Investments*. New York: John Wiley & Sons.

Matysiak, G. and Venmore-Rowland, P. (1995) *Appraising Commercial Property Performance Rankings*. Paper to the RICS Cutting Edge Conference, Aberdeen University, September 1995.

Matysiak, G. and Wang, P. (1995) Commercial property market prices and valuations: analyzing the correspondence. *Journal of Property Research*, 12: 181.

McAllister, P. (1995) Valuation accuracy: a contribution to the debate. *Journal of Property Research*, 12: 203.

McIntosh, A.P.J. and Sykes, S.C. (1985) *A Guide to Institutional Property Investment*. London: Macmillan.

McParland, C., McGreal, S. and Adair, A. (2000) Concepts of price, value and worth in the United Kingdom – towards a European perspective. *Journal of Property Invesmentment & Finance*, 18 (1): 84–102.

Parnell, P. and Sayce, S. (1999) *Investment Attitudes towards Green Buildings*. London: Drivers Jonas/Kingston University.

Planning and Compulsory Purchase Act (2004) www.legislation.hmso.gov.uk

Rees, W. and Hayward, W.H. (eds) (2000) *Valuations: Principles into Practice*. London: Estates Gazette Ltd.

Ross Goobey, A. (1992) *Bricks and Mortals: Dream of the 80s and Nightmare of the 90s – Inside Story of the Property World*, London: Random House Business Books.

Royal Institution of Chartered Surveyors (1996) *Commercial Property Valuations: An Information Paper*. London: RICS.

Royal Institution of Chartered Surveyors (1997) *The Calculation of Worth: An Information Paper*. London: RICS.

Royal Institution of Chartered Surveyors (2003) *Appraisal and Valuation Standards*. London: RICS.

Sayce, S. and Connellan, O. (2000) *The Valuation of Non-Profit Oriented Leisure Property*. London: RICS Research Foundation.

Sayce, S. and Ellison, L. (2003) Integrating sustainability into the appraisal of property worth: identifying appropriate indicators of sustainability. *American Real Estate and Urban Economics Association Conference*, RICS Foundation Sustainable Development Session, Skye, Scotland, 21–23 August 2003.

Scarrett, D. (1991) *Property Valuation: The Five Methods*, London: E&FN Spon.

Scott, P. (1996) *The Property Masters*. London: E&FN Spon.

St Lawrence, S. (2003) *Review of the UK Corporate Real Estate Market with regard to availability of environmentally and socially responsible office buildings*. Paper for Cambridge Programme for Industry Sustainability Learning Network, 2003.

TEGoVA (2003) *European Valuation Standards* (the 'Blue Book'). London: TEGoVA.

Tversky, A. and Kahneman, D. (1981) The framing of decisions and the psychology of choice. *Journal of Science*, 211 (4481): 453–458.

Warren, M. (2000) *Economic Analysis for Property*. London: Architectural Press.

World Commission on Environment and Development (1987) Our Common Future. Oxford: Oxford University Press.

2 Introduction to the purchase decision

Aims of the chapter

- To introduce readers to the property purchase decision.
- To explore the criteria that drive the decision-making process.
- To examine the process that is required from the viewpoint of the consultant valuer or property investment analyst.
- To explain the regulatory framework within which the process of assessing value and worth is undertaken.

2.1   Introduction

The transaction process within which properties are bought and sold in the UK and other mature property markets is normally one of a free and relatively open market. This means the process assumes that neither the vendor nor the purchaser is under an obligation or compulsion to proceed with the deal. In reality, this may not always be the case. The pressures bearing on *both* parties may be extreme, particularly at times of economic, political or social change when the purchaser and/or vendor may have significant financial or non-financial reasons to proceed or abort a purchase/sale.

Accordingly, in order to understand what determines price in the market place it is desirable to examine the criteria that may drive the parties to the transaction. It is important to recognise that the criteria affecting transactions may not be restricted to property considerations.

In mature property markets, the assumption underlying the transaction process is of a well-defined system of property rights, in which the 'owner' can be defined as one who has a bundle of legal rights over a piece of land and/or the buildings on it. Further, it is assumed that the owner has the legal wherewithal to dispose of those rights without legal hindrance. This may be a simplification, as there can be restrictions on legal titles that affect the transference of property ownership rights.

In addition, there are a number of instances where price is determined other than through the normal operation of the supply/demand equation: for example, where property is acquired under compulsory purchase powers or in pursuance of any form of statutory obligation, or where price is determined on a notional transfer such as death. These non-open market transactions are outside the scope of this book, which concentrates on open market transactions and the process with which the consultant adviser/property investment analyst will be concerned.

When considering the framework within which the purchase decision is made, the seller and buyer will require a valuation of the property in question. This will normally be carried out by a valuer using one of the methods outlined in Chapter 1. In the case of the vendor, the valuation will almost certainly be conducted using the comparative, investment or profits approach, depending on whether the building is let or owner-occupied and its use. In the case of bare land or land with development potential, a residual approach will be adopted. It is unlikely that a discounted cashflow (DCF) would be undertaken within current UK practice.

However, prospective purchasers are concerned not just with the prevailing market view of the value; their concern will be to ensure that the property represents a fair value for their own purposes. In short, they will wish to establish its *worth* in addition to its market value. Where the purchase is for investment purposes, a range of financial measures will be undertaken in order to establish this; where it is for owner-occupation, the emphasis will be on business as well as property, considerations. The rest of this chapter considers the criteria that surround the transaction process.

2.2   Criteria for purchase: the investment purchaser

When considering the criteria for investment purchase it is important to view this from the perspective of the investor purchaser. Investment requirements may differ significantly from investor to investor. It is therefore important to distinguish between the different types of investor and their requirements.

There are four major categories of investor:

(1) Those seeking to match their liability profile with suitable assets. For example:
   o pension funds, which have long-term, inflation-linked liabilities;
   o life insurance companies, which have long-term fixed-interest (bond returns) linked liabilities.
(2) Those seeking a specified or a required rate of return over the holding period. For example:
   o public and private property companies seeking to maximise shareholder returns for a given level of risk;
   o investment banks and opportunity funds, which have high target rates of return and in consequence tend to have short-term holding periods.
(3) Those seeking to match or beat the returns on a competing investment class. For example:
   o open-ended funds and property unit trusts – these investors often view the returns on cash or short-dated bonds as the competing investment classes, and the aim is to find property investments with secure and stable returns.
(4) Those who view property as a business asset. For example:
   o the majority of corporate enterprises, which have a requirement for property to produce returns to the business that exceed the business's weighted average cost of capital – for these, flexibility is a key element in their property investment strategy.

Each of the above will have an investment framework that will influence the investment strategy. A number of investors (such as pension funds and life insurance companies) have statutory controls on their investments and asset allocation. In addition, there may be internal controls imposed (for example, no more than 50% of the property investment portfolio in offices) or peer group constraints (for example, the desire to broadly match the sector weightings of competing investors).

In the light of the above, consideration can be given to the investment characteristics of the desired property investment. This is developed in more detail in Chapter 3, where property is considered in the context of the multi-asset investment spectrum.

In straightforward terms, investments can be considered in relation to their ability to:

- provide security of income;
- provide security of capital;
- be readily and easily traded, with low transfer costs;
- provide a hedge against expected and unexpected inflation;
- provide diversification and performance benefits when included in an investment portfolio;
- be suitable for debt financing.

The first five points are useful when considering properties relative to each other and relative to equities and bonds. The sixth is a feature that property has over those of bonds and equities. The ability to 'gear up' a transaction will vary from property to property, and undoubtedly will have some bearing on the desirability of a property. This is considered further in Chapter 10.

The characteristics can be widened such that investors consider them in relation to their own investment criteria. The criteria that are normally adopted are considered below.

2.2.1   Risk/return requirements

Return may be taken in the form of either income in order to discharge current liabilities or capital growth for future liabilities. The latter, as we have seen, is very important. Some investments offer both income and capital growth, whilst others offer only one of these. The ability to achieve return is normally an investor's number one concern!

Although all investment involves some degree of risk, most investors are naturally 'risk averse' and will in general require much higher returns from any project that they regard as risky. The definition of risk and how it is built into the appraisal process is considered in Chapters 8 and 12.

2.2.2   Portfolio diversification issues

As most investors are risk averse, they will seek to 'spread their risk' by buying not just one investment but many, so that if one fails the loss does not have too devastating an impact on their total returns. Accordingly, investors normally acquire a range of investments of different types so that exposure to any one type of risk is not too high. Sometimes this can mean that lower-return investments have to be included within the portfolio – so overall return can be the result of gaining portfolio balance. Much work has been done to try to find mathematical ways round this conundrum, and investment houses have produced complex models that seek to shape the ideal portfolio so that risk can be reduced without sacrificing too much return.

Portfolios with small numbers of properties tend to exhibit higher levels of volatility of returns than diversified portfolios. It follows from what has been said above that the size of lot is important. An investor with say £100 million to spend will not normally wish to put it in just one investment. A minimum number of investments held may normally be regarded as 20+, so in this example an investor seeking to reduce the diversifiable risk in their property portfolio should be looking for opportunities each of which is no more than about £5 million to buy. Alternatively, the investor may consider bringing on board a level of gearing to increase the amount available for investment. These issues are addressed in Chapters 10 and 12.

2.2.3 Prospective performance

Although return does include growth, some investments by their very nature offer the prospect for growth whilst others do not. In particular, government stock does not offer high growth, whereas investing in a new company might. High growth prospects are often associated with higher risk. When property is the investment medium, growth will occur where development potential in the future is identifiable or where the property is let on a lease at a historic (low) rent.

2.2.4 Issues raised through the due diligence process

Due diligence, which is described in section 2.6, is the process of investigation that must be undertaken prior to a purchase. In recent years the number of factors included within this process has increased and there is evidence that new criteria are beginning to affect investment purchase decisions. These include consideration of some of the issues that are of particular concern to occupiers and hence may affect continued lettability. Some current concerns, which are considered in more detail later in this chapter and in subsequent chapters, include:

- *Contamination*: the discovery of contamination can have serious financial consequences. Environmental audits should be undertaken before a transaction price is agreed and warranties obtained from the current owner. Former use of the building, site or adjacent land may suggest potential contamination. If the real estate is being held as an investment, liability for clean-up may have to be accounted for irrespective of the identity of the actual polluter. Whilst this is as yet unlikely, 2004 saw the first successful prosecution under these provisions.

   The current land use planning requirements are driving developments towards re-use of land, with government policy indicating a minimum of 60% of all development being on so-called 'brownfield' sites. This means that, increasingly, modern prime commercial stock will be subject to environmental risk. Contamination is not the only environmental risk to which commercial property is prone (see, for example, Sayce *et al.*, 2004), but it is the one that has the highest profile.

- *Sustainability*: a small but growing number of corporates have placed sustainability, and in particular corporate social responsibility, high on their agendas. Where this is the case, the ambition will be to purchase stock that will meet sustainability criteria (Sayce and Ellison, 2003) and hence is likely to show superior performance over time as the regulatory framework on sustainability inevitably tightens.

- *Obsolescence and depreciation*: the ability of a property to remain competitive is important, particularly in a low-inflationary environment where property's declining attractiveness and hence returns are not disguised by the effects of inflation. For a long period between the 1950s and the 1980s the level of inflation within the UK economy resulted in an upward trend in values that led to over valuations if the real effects of obsolescence and depreciation were taken into account. The view that valuers were being unrealistic in their appraisals due to obsolescence was first expressed in 1982 by Bowie who sparked off interest in the area. Subsequent work by Salway (1985) and Baum (1991) revealed that commercial buildings do suffer from obsolescence at greatly differing rates, but despite further work on the subject it is acknowledged that insufficient is yet known as to the causes of obsolescence and why some buildings and categories of buildings, notably offices, are more susceptible than others.

- *Legal due diligence*: the small print in the legal documentation can reduce the value of a property – for example, a restrictive user clause in a lease may reduce the rent on review by in excess of 15% (indeed, a legal case has resulted in a loss of more than 30%). A restrictive covenant prohibiting development of back land can adversely affect the development potential, as can rights of way and rights of light. It is therefore imperative that appropriate searches are conducted.

2.3   Criteria for purchase: occupational property

2.3.1   Distinction between investment and occupational property markets

The factors that drive the occupational property market differ from those affecting the investment markets although it must be remembered that ultimately the investment market is dependent upon the ability to attract a tenant! Accordingly, it is unrealistic to regard the two markets as not interlinked. As argued above, the result of a strong occupational property demand, combined with the convention of leases of 20 years or more had, until recently, lured investors into regarding property too much as an asset that could be viewed in terms of income stream alone without due regard to the fundamental changes affecting the corporate tenants on which the rental security and growth is predicated. In Chapter 4 we explore in detail the drivers of rental value and in Chapter 8 we look at the considerations that impact on the occupier in terms of the decision to rent or purchase, but these elements are introduced below.

2.3.2   Occupational demand criteria

The first decision that any potential occupier will have to make will be whether to purchase or to rent, and the success of the investment market depends on the fact that many corporate occupiers will choose to rent rather than commit to purchase. The decision to buy or to rent will be affected by:

- The nature of the business and the requirement, or otherwise, for significant investment in specialist equipment.

- The image of the business and whether it requires to promote its own corporate 'stamp' on premises.
- The availability or otherwise of appropriate premises.
- The financial implications, including the effect of taxation.
- Company policy.

These elements are developed further in Chapter 8.

Whichever decision is made, it has been argued by Apgar (Rubin, 1997:6) that, at the level of building choice, occupiers will base their property requirements on the 'three Ls' of location, layout, and leasing; all of these will affect their cost levels.

- The demand and supply relationship affects *location* as the occupier will require the most cost-efficient and appropriate location for their type of business.
- *Layout* refers to the amount of space and how it is arranged. The quantity of space used will be affected by working practices and space efficiency initiatives such as hot desk-ing for offices. How the space is laid out, the quality and its specification and condition will affect productivity. How it is used and its relative cost will determine revenue from the business, and some strategic property managers may be required to link demand for space to profitability.
- *Leasing* costs is the third factor, although Apgar stresses that in a competitive economy leasing costs should correlate with changes in the occupier's revenue. However, the occupier will want to achieve the most favourable lease or purchase terms through effective negotiation for the property that most suits the business needs.

Whilst the 'three Ls' are indeed important, other factors are beginning to affect the corporate agenda such that to these 'three Ls' can arguably be added two others: the requirement for *loose fit* premises that can rapidly adapt to changing occupier needs, and the increasing push for premises that are *low energy* – or at least can meet increasingly stringent environmental legislation (see, for example, Sayce and Ellison, 2003; Sayce *et al.*, 2004).

In summary, the needs of the business will determine both the type and amount of occupational demand for property. However, the policy of the company and external factors such as fiscal provisions have an influence on the tenure decision.

In terms of the strength of tenant demand, a relationship exists between the business cycle and that of the occupational property market, as noted by several commentators (see IPD/University of Aberdeen, 1994; Ball *et al.*, 1998; IPD, 1999). However, it is not just a question of a simple demand and supply interaction based on constant types of needs. Increasingly, companies are seeking to re-examine their business need for property and this is resulting in changing occupier requirements. This theme is developed further in Chapter 8.

2.4   The purchase transaction process

The property purchase transaction process contains a number of steps. The time taken to progress from one step to the next is very much dependent upon the state of the property market at the time of the transaction. In the mid 1970s and early 1990s, when the property market was suffering from deep recession, very little activity took place and the speed of transaction effectively stalled. In normal markets the purchase transaction takes around six months from the date when the client decides to market the property to completion. This is subject to the proviso that the price at which the property is marketed is realistic and not excessively high, thereby putting off potential purchasers. When the property market

Table 2.1   The main steps in the property purchase transaction.

Activity	Parties involved
Receive details of potential acquisition/disposal	Investment surveyor
Conflict of interest check	Investment surveyor
Identify a purchaser	Investment surveyor
Introduce product, including address and investment rationale and basic figures	Investment surveyor and client's surveyor
Confirm with client instruction and fee, as buying agent	Investment surveyor and client's surveyor
Conduct property analysis – unexpired lease terms, covenants, location, property specifics, etc.	Investment surveyor and valuer
Collate information on the local and general property markets – investment and rental markets, etc.	Investment surveyor and valuer
Explain rationale for purchase aligned to purchaser's requirements	Investment surveyor and client's surveyor
Undertake valuation and, if required, undertake a cash flow analysis	Valuer and investment surveyor
Identify any planning/tax or other issues	Investment surveyor, client's surveyor, planning consultant, tax accountant and other specialist advisers
Formulate view on purchase price and year end value, and advise client	Valuer, investment surveyor and client's surveyor
Formulate a bid strategy	Investment surveyor and client's surveyor
Arrange finance if required	Client's surveyor and finance director with financial adviser
Negotiate with vendor's agent	Investment surveyor
Agree heads of terms with conditions and timescale	Investment surveyor and solicitor
Ensure property is removed from the market to allow exclusivity of negotiation	Investment surveyor
Pre-acquisition due diligence – instruct solicitors	Client's surveyor and solicitor
Instruct building surveyors, measure buildings, undertake environmental surveys, etc.; reports to client	Building surveyor, technician environmental consultant and client's surveyor
Obtain board or trustee approval, as necessary	Client's surveyor and board
Write purchase report/recommendation	Investment surveyor
Re-assess transaction following due diligence; renegotiate, if necessary	Solicitor, investment surveyor, valuer and client's surveyor
Exchange contracts and pay deposit; arrange insurance cover	Solicitor, client's finance director and insurance broker
Completion	Client's solicitor, lender's solicitor and client's finance director
Send out fees invoice	Investment surveyor
Receive feedback from client	Investment surveyor and client's surveyor

is 'hot', the time taken to effect a sale is reduced. Table 2.1 contains a summary of the main steps of a commercial property purchase transaction.

As can be seen, from Table 2.1 a number of surveyors become involved in the purchase process. A pivotal role is played by the agent's investment surveyor/investment team, who hold centre stage and oversee the whole property purchase process. The valuer has an important role to play in ensuring that the investment is bought at a realistic price.

There is a growing trend amongst some of the larger property investors, both property companies and institutions, to seek off-market deals. An off-market deal is one where the vendor and purchaser deal directly with each other, and the role of agents is removed. In this case the client's surveyor takes on the roll of the investment surveyor, and in some instances the role of the valuer as well!

The purchase process will be broadly similar for an investor purchaser and an owner-occupier purchaser; however, there are a number of differences. The aim of the property investor is to obtain acceptable returns from their property holdings and to maximise such returns wherever possible, subject to various constraints (such as risk). In considering the investment purchase decision, the investor should have due regard to both the value of the property and its worth. The seller will also undertake a valuation and an assessment of the property's worth.

The valuation by the buyer and seller will reflect the open market comparables available and will be based on completed transactions. It will reflect a market view of the best price likely to be achieved on the sale of the property. In addition, an assessment of worth should be undertaken separately by each of the parties. This will reflect their views of the future performance potential of the property in the context of their respective investment positions. The assessment of worth for the two parties will not necessarily produce the same figures and these figures will not necessarily be the same as the valuation figure, but in many instances they will influence the investment strategy of the parties.

In contrast, a prospective owner-occupier will view the property purchase in the context of their business. It will not be the prospective rental income flows that are considered but the way in which the property will benefit the business, in terms of, for example, its efficiency, profitability, employment retention, property cost benchmarks and sustainability issues. These aspects are far wider than a property valuation and a DCF appraisal, and are considered in more detail in Chapter 8.

2.5   The regulatory framework

The process by which valuers and appraisers are regulated and carry out their work is a matter of both national and international concern. In most countries there is some form of control, but the level and nature of this control will vary. (For a country by country examination see, for example, Gelbtuch et al., 1997.) Regulation of valuers effectively takes two forms:

- control of the education process through some kind of formal examination or state certification or licence (as occurs in many European countries); and/or
- regulation or legal control over the manner in which valuations are carried out (such as in Germany, as noted above).

Within the UK, state control of valuers is minimal. There is some control over the brokerage process through the Estate Agents Act 1979 and the Property Misdescriptions Act 1991: the former gives general regulatory powers over the estate agency process, whereas the 1991 Act was designed to prevent estate agents and property development companies from making misleading statements about property. In reality, neither Act provides strong control over the process, nor do they control property valuations at all. The only legislative controls over these are enshrined in Acts related to compulsory purchase and taxation.

If the state does not intervene, regulation of the valuation process depends on professional regulation. Within the UK, the RICS (Royal Institution of Chartered Surveyors) is the leading professional body. Since 2000 the RICS has had a global ambition and now has approximately 20 000 members – one sixth of the total membership – working in countries other than the UK. The RICS has exercised regulation over its members in terms of property valuation for some 30 years, initially in a non-enforceable manner, but since 1992 compliance to their standards has been mandatory.

From a historical perspective, it was the 1973 property crash combined with concerns over professional accounting practices that led to the adoption by the RICS of formal guidance notes on valuation practice to establish valuation consistency. The first 'Red Book' of guidance notes on asset valuation standards was published in 1974 (RICS 1974). This made the UK unique in Europe in having valuation standards that were highly developed and mandatory. These guidelines form the basis of today's standards.

The original standards were restricted to third-party valuations (those on which an unconnected third party would rely, such as valuations for company accounting purposes). This changed during the mid 1990s when it was recognised by the property profession that there was a need for coherent standards for the reporting of valuations for private and public purposes to avoid the potential for ambiguity and corrupt practices. In this context the RICS commissioned reports from both Michael Mallinson (Mallinson, 1994) and the Economist Intelligence Unit (Economist Intelligence Unit, 1997). Subsequently additional, more stringent measures on control of valuation practices have been introduced in line with the recommendations of a further commissioned report headed by Sir Bryan Carsberg (Carsberg, 2003).

2.5.1   The RICS *Appraisal and Valuation Standards*

The current RICS *Appraisal and Valuation Standards* (RICS, 2003) (colloquially known as the Red Book) can be viewed as a quality control framework, setting out the structure and due diligence required for a valuation. A summary of the main provisions is set out here.

In addition to RICS standards, compliance with which is mandatory for members, both the International Valuations Standards Committee (IVSC) and The European Group of Valuers' Association (TEGoVA) publish standards. Early versions were very much based upon the RICS Red Book guidance but increasingly the IVSC, which was constituted in 1981 as a non-government organisation and which now has a wide-ranging membership, is important as a standard setter. However, unlike the standards produced by RICS, those issued by IVSC and TEGoVA are not mandatory. The standards apply to the preparation and execution of appraisals, valuations, revaluations, valuation reviews and calculations of worth in respect of property in all countries for all purposes. Thus their remit encompasses both valuations and calculations of worth.

There are a number of exclusions that lie outside the scope of the manual. For example, advice during the course of litigation, valuations prepared for arbitration and dispute resolution or for negotiations, internal valuations and certain agency advice are excluded. Where the valuation is not one of the exclusions, any proposed departure from the standards must be agreed in writing in advance and with good reason; otherwise the valuer may face disciplinary measures.

The Red Book includes mandatory practice statements (PSs) to which all qualified RICS members must adhere, wherever they practise. In general these are worded to be consistent with the IVS and, in that they are mandatory, they give validity to international *guidance*. In addition to the universal practice statements, the standards also include guidance notes and a series of UK practice statements (UK PSs) and UK guidance. These latter sections acknowledge the reality that, although worldwide *principles* are now being established, local variations in practice and context still exist. There is an expectation that in due time other country-specific standards and guidance will be developed by national associations.

A brief commentary on some of the most important aspects contained in the statements is given below but, given that the standards are updated on an almost monthly basis, readers are advised to ensure that they check updates via www.rics.org.

Fundamental to the framework of valuation regulation is the definition of market value. Over the years the definition has changed, and at times there has been conflict between UK and international interpretations. This is now resolved, and there is no single internationally accepted definition of market value (IVSC, 2002; TEGoVA, 2003). Market value is 'the estimated amount for which a property should exchange on the date of valuation between a willing seller and willing buyer in an arm's-length transaction after proper marketing wherein the parties had acted knowledgeably, prudently and without compulsion'. This has been accepted by the RICS (2003) to apply to all valuations carried out under the terms of the Red Book.

PS 1 Qualifications and conflicts of interest

This statement sets out that every valuation must be carried out by or supervised by an appropriately qualified member who accepts responsibility for the valuation. Additionally, such a person must have appropriate skill and knowledge, including local knowledge, to enable them to undertake the valuation competently.

One of the key requirements for professionals is adherence to standards of ethical practice; this practice statement makes it clear that adherence to the RICS 'core values' code, which includes integrity, independence and objectivity, underlies all valuation work. One of the issues for the profession is the interpretation of these core values, given the widely varying business practices that prevail in different countries (see, for example, Plimmer and Sayce, 2003).

PS 2 Agreement of terms of engagement

Under this statement the valuer is required to confirm instructions in writing before issuing the valuation, and the client is to be made aware of any limitations in the valuation service. This confirmation must include the purpose of the valuation, and whether the basis is appropriate. It should also point out and agree with the client any 'special assumptions' that are to be made in conducting the valuation. The statement also includes provisions dealing with cases of limited inspection and/or revaluations without inspection.

PS 3 Valuation bases and applications

Only limited discretion in the approach to be adopted to the valuation is available to the valuer and, to avoid any potential misunderstandings, the purpose for which a valuation is undertaken must be stated in the valuation report. The RICS now recognises only two main bases of valuation. These are the market value approach (as set out above but including a variation to allow for market rent) and the depreciated replacement cost (DRC) basis, which is effectively as detailed in section 1.6.5 under the cost approach method. From 2005, the DRC basis is redefined as a method of valuation, not a basis. For a limited period a further basis, existing use value, continues to be recognised in some circumstances (see Chapter 8).

PS 4 Inspection and material considerations

This statement requires that the valuer carry out inspections and investigations 'to the extent necessary to produce a valuation which is professionally adequate for its purpose'. In order to do this, the statement sets out the normal requirements which include not just physical measurement and noting of uses but in addition an analysis of the characteristics of the location. The valuer must also be alert to environmental and contamination issues and the presence or otherwise of deleterious materials. If these are suspected, the valuer must bring the fact to the attention of the client in order that an informed decision may be taken as to whether or not further investigations are carried out. In such cases it is not sufficient to make an assumption that no hazard of contamination exists.

The statement places the valuer under a further duty to take 'reasonable steps' to verify legal and other information supplied and to clarify with the client any assumptions that are made.

PS 5 Valuation reports and references

One of the concerns that RICS has is to ensure that valuation reports are carried out to a consistent standard. This statement requires that valuation reports include the following:

- identification of the client;
- the purpose of the valuation;
- the subject of the valuation;
- the interest to be valued;
- the type of property and how it is used, or classified by the client;
- the date of valuation;
- the basis or bases of the valuation;
- the status of the member and disclosure of any previous involvements;

- where appropriate, the currency that has been adopted;
- any assumptions, special assumptions, reservations, special instructions or departures;
- the extent of the member's investigations;
- the nature and source of information to be relied on by the member;
- any consent to, or restrictions on, publication;
- any limits or exclusion of liability to parties other than the client;
- confirmation that the valuation accords with the standards;
- the opinion of value in words and figures; and
- signature and date of the valuation report.

PS 6 European Union valuation applications

This short statement relates to valuations carried out under European rules, as they apply to insurance company accounts and secured lending. The latter is important as it introduces the concept of mortgage lending value (MLV), which is used in some EU member states for secured lending purposes. The MLV is fundamentally different from MV. It is 'the value of the property as determined by a valuer making a prudent assessment of the future marketability of the property by taking into account long-term sustainable aspects of the property, the normal and local market conditions, the current use and alternative appropriate uses of the property'. There is no mention of current price within MLV and it is far more dependent on subjective valuer opinion. Accordingly, the statement makes it clear that MLV should be used only in conjunction with a market valuation and only if the valuer has the appropriate expertise.

National standards

In addition to the general statements, there are a series of national (UK) standards which deal with valuations for particular purposes. These are:

UKPS1: Valuations for financial statements
UKPS2: Valuations for financial statements: specific applications
UKPS3: Valuations for loan facilities
UKPS4: Residential property valuations
UKPS5: Regulated purpose valuations

Of these, the most important is UKPS1 relating to valuations for financial statements. This allows for a specific basis of valuation known as existing use value (EUV) to be adopted for owner-occupied assets. This basis excludes any possibility of development value, on the basis that development is inconsistent with the concept of a continuing business. However, the basis is incompatible with the International Accounting Standards (IASs) and, as these are to be adopted by the UK, it is likely that EUV will have to be phased out.

From the above it can be seen that the standards do not state the precise method that the valuer should use when calculating the figures; instead, they seek to lay out principles to which the valuer must adhere. Their importance cannot be overestimated. In the absence of government intervention they provide the basis on which clients may have confidence in their professional property advisers.

2.6   Due diligence and legal issues

Due diligence is an important part of the property purchase/sale transaction, as has been indicated above. Before purchasing a property, purchasers will wish to satisfy themselves as to exactly what they are purchasing. Whilst some of the process will be about verifying physical factors, much of the due diligence process relates to the legal documentation relating of the property, an activity carried out by the client's solicitors.

When a property is placed on to the market, the agent's selling particulars are required under the terms of the Estate Agency Act 1979 to be truthful and to bring out all factors that have a bearing on the price. It is argued that before any purchaser enters a legal agreement the following items should be investigated:

- Legal checks including:
  - proof of title;
  - scope of ownership – for example, restrictive covenants, rights of light and rights of way;
  - head and occupation leases;
  - identification of key terms, and disadvantageous covenants;
  - mortgage documentation.
- Structural and physical investigations including:
  - deleterious materials;
  - state of repair;
  - construction type;
  - services and their condition, and maintenance contracts.
- Planning considerations including:
  - planning consents;
  - relevant local authority and government policy documents;
  - any outstanding enforcement notices;
  - details of any listing orders.
- Environmental and sustainability issues including:
  - contamination;
  - noise pollution;
  - local environment;
  - potential legal implications (for example, energy usage).

Research by Reading University (Crosby and McAllister, 2004) has identified that around 30% of property transactions are renegotiated whilst in solicitors' hands as a result of due diligence enquiries. It is therefore imperative from a seller's perspective that the property is marketed in the light of the full information; otherwise the hoped-for price may not be achieved.

2.7   Summary

The purchase decision is driven by many factors. These factors will vary according to the profile and views of the investor.

Operating within the current UK property markets are four main categories of purchaser: institutional investors, property companies, pooled funds/private investors and corporate occupiers. In the past most of the literature has concentrated on developing a deep understanding of the institutional investor. Comparatively little attention has been paid to the needs of the corporate occupier, yet they have an important role to play both as owners and as tenants.

For the investor, the purchase decision is driven primarily by the requirement to obtain a financial return, balanced against consideration of risk. These issues are considered in detail in later chapters. However, for the corporate occupier the agenda is very different. It is one of meeting operational needs, balanced against corporate strategic objectives. Increasingly, though, there are overlaps as occupiers take a more financially driven approach to their property assets.

The role of the adviser has traditionally been in advising on market value. In providing this advice, the appraiser must undertake a process of due diligence in relation to the purchase. Not only will failure so to do possibly result in a claim for negligence, but it will lead to abortive negotiations. The valuer is also normally obliged to operate within the framework set down by professional body regulations, as is the third-party appraiser/consultant adviser who undertakes the calculations of worth. These requirements are set out within international and national standards and, for RICS members, are mandatory.

References

Ball, M., Lizieri, C. and MacGregor, B. (1998) *The Economics of the Commercial Property Market.* London: Routledge.

Baum, A. (1991) *Property Investment Depreciation and Obsolescence.* London: Thomson Learning.

Bowie, N. (1982) Learning to take account of depreciation. *Estates Times*, 13 June.

Carsberg, B. (2003) *Property Valuation: The Carsberg Report.* London: RICS.

Crosby, N. and McAllister, P. (2004) *Liquidity in Commercial Property Markets: Deconstructing the Transaction Process.* Working Paper 2. London: Investment Property Forum.

Economist Intelligence Unit (1997) *Global Direct Investment and the Importance of Real Estate.* Report. London: RICS.

Gelbtuch, H., Mackmin, D. and Milgrim, M. (eds) (1997) *Real Estate Valuation in Global Markets.* Chicago: Appraisal Institute.

International Valuation Standards Committee (2002) *International Valuation Standards 2002.* London: IVSC.

Investment Property Databank (1999) *The UK Property Cycle: A History from 1921–1997.* London: RICS.

Investment Property Databank/University of Aberdeen (1994) *Understanding the Property Cycle: Economic Cycles and Property Cycles.* London: RICS.

Mallinson, M. (1994) *Commercial Property Valuations: Report of the Mallinson Committee.* London: RICS.

Plimmer, F. and Sayce, S. (2003) Ethics and professional standards for surveyors – towards a global standard. *FIG Working Week* 2003, Paris, April.

Royal Institution of Chartered Surveyors (1974) *Guidance Notes on the Valuation of Assets RICS Appraisal and Valuation Standards.* London: RICS.

Royal Institution of Chartered Surveyors (2003) *RICS Appraisal and Valuation Standards 2003*. London: RICS.

Rubin, V. (1997) *The Business Occupier's Handbook*. London: E&FN Spon.

Salway, F. (1985) *Depreciation of Commercial Property*. CALUS, University of Reading.

Sayce, S. and Ellison, L. (2003) Towards sustainability indicators for commercial property occupiers and investors. *Eighth Annual International Sustainable Research Conference*, Nottingham, 24–25 March 2003.

Sayce, S., Walker, A. and McIntosh, A. (2004) *Building Sustainability in the Balance: Promoting Stakeholder Dialogue*. London: Estates Gazette.

TEGoVA (The European Group of Valuers' Association) (2003) *European Valuation Standards*. London: Estates Gazette.

Further reading

Adair, A., Downie, M.L., McGreal, S. and Vos, G. (1996) *European Valuation Practice*. London: E&FN Spon.

Adams, A., Booth, P., and Venmore-Rowland, P. (1993a) *An actuarial approach to property valuations*. Paper to the RICS Cutting Edge Conference (1993).

Adams, A., Booth, P., and Venmore-Rowland, P. (1993b) Theoretical volatility measures for freehold property investments. *Journal of Property Research*, 10 (3): 153–166.

Brown, G. and Matysiak, G. (2000) *Real Estate Investment: A Capital Markets Approach*. London: FT Prentice Hall.

Britton, W., Connellan, O. and Crofts, M. (1991) *The Cost Approach to Valuation*. London: RICS.

Drivers Jonas and Investment Property Databank (1991) *Valuation Accuracy Report*.

International Valuation Standards Committee (2003) *International Valuation Standards 2003*. London: IVSC.

International Valuation Standards Committee (2004) *International Valuation Guidance Note 8: The Cost Approach for Financial Reporting*. London: IVSC.

Isaac, D. (2001) *Property Valuation Principles*. Basingstoke: Palgrave Macmillan.

Lizieri, C. and Venmore-Rowland, P. (1992) Valuation Accuracy: A contribution to the Debate. *Journal of Property Research*, Volume 9.

Lizieri, C. and Venmore-Rowland, P. (1993) Valuations, Prices and the Market: A Rejoinder. *Journal of Property Research*, 10.

Matysiak, G. and Venmore-Rowland, P. (1995) *Appraising Commercial Property Performance Rankings*. Paper to the RICS Cutting Edge Conference, Aberdeen University, September 1995.

Rodney, W., Lasfer, M., Venmore-Rowland, P., Citron, D. and Axcell, A. (2001) *The Impact on Shareholder Value of Corporate Property Holdings*. Research Report. London: Trillium Land Securities & City University Business School.

Sayce, S. and Connellan, O.P. (2000) *The Valuation of Non-profit Orientated Leisure Property*. London: RICS.

Scarrett, D. (1991) *Property Valuation: The Five Methods*. London: E&FN Spon.

3 Property investment: placing property within the multi-asset investment spectrum

Aims of the chapter

- To provide a comparative analysis of investment media: gilts, equities and cash.
- To introduce property as an investment.
- To define and provide examples of return.
- To introduce discounted cash flow techniques: net present value (NPV) and internal rate of return (IRR).
- To examine the place of property within the investment portfolio.

3.1 Introduction

The main financial institutions include insurance companies, pension funds, unit trusts and managed funds who invest their funds in portfolios that comprise fixed interest securities such as gilts, debentures, corporate and local authority loans, equities in the UK and overseas, cash for liquidity and property investments. All the investment media compete for institutional funds.

The financial institutions are very important due to their high level of investment and ownership within the stock market and property market. For example, according to DTZ's *Money into Property 2003*, financial institutions invested £31 billion in property in 2001 and £17 billion in commercial property in 2002, with 21% coming from overseas investors (DTZ, 2003). In fact Investment Property Databank (IPD) held within their portfolio 10 811 properties valued at £105.072 billion at the end of 2003, representing some 90% of institutional property assets.

3.2 A comparative analysis of investment media

3.2.1 Fixed interest securities

Fixed interest securities such as bonds and gilts are a type of loan or IOU issued by a government, company or international institution that wants to borrow money. In return the lender will receive a series of pre-set fixed interest payments with the promise that the loan will be repaid on a fixed redemption date in the future. However, in contrast to other loans these securities are tradable on the secondary market without reference to the original borrower. In the UK, companies are now using bonds much more to finance their needs as the low rates of interest (3.5–3.75% in 2003) make this a very cheap form of finance. In the year 2000 bonds raised more than four times as much cash as equities (Winterflood and Diamond, 2002).

British government bonds are called 'gilt-edged bonds' as the certificates were originally edged with gold leaf, and the fixed interest payment is sometimes called a coupon. US government equivalent bonds are called Treasury bonds while the German Government issues 'bunds'. Corporate bonds (sometimes called debentures) are issued by companies and are a cheap form of finance when interest rates are low. The growth of corporate bond funds has been driven partly by the introduction of personal equity plans (PEPs) and subsequently individual savings accounts (ISAs). Both these vehicles enabled tax-free saving schemes, for which there has been much demand.

The face value price of a bond and the redemption price are known as par value and most bonds have a life of between five and 25 years. They are normally classified into categories according to their redemption dates – shorts mature in less than five years and mediums in five to 15 years, whilst longs have a redemption date of over 15 years. Bonds are usually described by the name of their issuer, maturity date, and coupon rate based on par value: for example, Exchequer, 2010, 8%. A few government bonds issued in the early 1900s to fund the First World War are undated.

Gilts and bonds offer a fixed income for a fixed term plus full capital repayment at redemption and are held for their security and stability, particularly by income seekers. Bond income is considered to be more secure than equities as payments must be honoured before shareholders can claim their dividends. Bond holders also get preferential access to assets if a company is wound up.

Bond prices will also change if the issuer is unable to repay the interest or loan, and creditworthiness is constantly assessed through agencies such as Moody's and Standard & Poor's. The highest security bonds offered by governments are given a rating of Aaa/AAA. Bonds which may fail are given ratings of Ba3 or BBB. The less reliable bonds are known as junk bonds or high yield bonds. The yields offered by bond issuers will rise as the credit rating of the borrower decreases since there is greater risk of default on the interest and loan payment.

However, with the onset of high inflation in the 1960s and 1970s the real value of the bond fixed income was quickly eroded. If inflation ran at 5% the real value halved in 15 years. As a result, investors demanded a higher yield and prices fell, so £1000 invested in 1970 was worth just £682 in real terms by 1980 (Barclays, 2001). In the 1990s the tide was turned, with government achieving low rates of inflation, and once again fixed interest securities became attractive, outperforming equities between 1999 and 2003.

Bond holders are not tied to their redemption date and can liquidate their investment holding at any time. Interest on gilts is subject to income tax, normally paid gross, and exempt from capital gains tax. Bonds held as PEPs and ISAs escape tax altogether providing they have five years remaining at the time of purchase.

Owners of bonds enjoy low dealing costs. Although bonds held in collective investment vehicles benefit from the expertise of a professional manager they also charge a management fee, which increases transaction charges.

3.2.2   Index linked gilts (ILG)

In the UK index linked bonds were introduced by the Government in 1982 to provide an income and redemption payment that were both index linked to the rate of inflation. The

Table 3.1 Bonds and the effects of inflation.

Year	Real (purchasing power) cash flow	Inflation index	Inflation rate p.a.	Nominal (monetary) cash flow
0	−£100	1.00		−£100
1	£4	1.035	3.5%	£4.14
2	£4	1.066	3%	£4.26
3	£4	1.093	2.5%	£4.37
4	£4	1.147	5%	£4.59
5	£104	1.23	7%	£127.68

Source: Hoesli and MacGregor (2000).

guaranteed income and final payment, if held to maturity, gave protection against inflation. The income from such bonds is therefore fixed in terms of real purchasing power but will vary in monetary (nominal) terms according to the rate of inflation. This is simply illustrated in Table 3.1 where the index linked gilts offer 4% interest; this rises with the annual rate of inflation.

3.2.3 Equities

Equities is another term for company ordinary shares, which are paper assets entitling the owner to a share in the capital and income of a company and voting rights in the management of the company proportional to the number of shares held. The dividend is the income paid twice yearly in arrears and is not guaranteed but depends on the company profits and the policy of its directors. The net profits after tax will depend on the success of the company and the state of the economy. The board of directors will decide how much profit will be distributed as dividends and how much is retained for future liabilities or investment. Over the long term, real profits and dividends have grown in line with real levels of economic activity, but dividends and profits tend to be higher in a buoyant economy. Equity investments are linked to levels of economic activity and provide protection against inflation.

Public companies have a defined amount of issued capital divided up into shares of nominal par value, such as £1 or 50p. However, the market value will not be the same as this and generally rises to reflect the growth of a company. Equities are very liquid and are traded on the stock market. Unlike bonds, however, their capital value is not guaranteed and indeed can be highly volatile, as was experienced in the late 1990s when high returns of 23.8% were achieved. This figure then fell to −22% in 2002 (IPD, 2003), halving the value of shares on the stock market. Equities involve risk as the dividend and market price are not guaranteed, so the investor will require a risk premium over and above the return on the 'safer' fixed interest securities.

3.2.4 Property investments

Property investments can range from indirect, which are based on paper assets backed by property, to direct property holdings such as the freehold or leasehold interest in commercial property – that is, offices, retail or industrial and warehousing property, or residential or leisure property. Freehold and leasehold interests give the owner legal rights over the property. The freeholder is subject to certain restrictions relating to building standards, land use, restrictive covenants or rights of way. A freeholder can occupy the property, or can treat the property as an investment by leasing the property and passing on their rights of occupation to a leaseholder for a term of years in exchange for a rental income.

In the UK commercial leases are usually from 10 to 25 years with periodic rent reviews, typically five-yearly. Unlike equities and fixed interest investments, rental income is received quarterly in advance, but it is vulnerable to inflation between rent reviews. Traditional leases tend to have upward only rent reviews, so at rent review a higher rent is negotiated if market rents are rising but the rent remains fixed if market rents are falling. At the end of the lease, possession may not revert to the freeholder due to the operation of statutory controls. In periods of high economic growth property owners will benefit from rising rents at review, while in periods of low growth or deflation the upward only rent review protects the investor from falls in income. Over the longer term property, like shares, should protect against inflation. With the promotion of a new flexible lease code (RICS/BPF, 2002), the long lease and upward only rent reviews are at risk and this adversely affects security of income for the investor. Evidence from IPD (Investment Property Databank) points to a very significant drop in lease lengths since 2002, so the protection given by long leases which has been enjoyed by investors for many years is now less of a reality.

The default risk depends on the quality of the tenant and their ability to pay the rent, and is similar to the default risk of a bond which depends on the issuer. Rental income is considered to be more secure than dividends as it is a contractual obligation, and a company will stop paying a dividend before it stops paying a rent. Even if a tenant defaults and there is a rental void the property can be relet, whereas if a company goes bankrupt the shareholder loses everything. Introduction of the new flexible lease code is an attempt to offer the tenant a more attractive lease term, shorter length of lease and upward/downward rent reviews.

Property investments, like equities, have no maturity date and can be traded on the secondary market, but their capital value can rise or fall depending on actual and future income and yield expectation. Whereas all equities in a company are the same, properties are heterogeneous, or unique, and will vary by size, location, use, age, construction and tenant. Although retail warehouses in a retail park will all have different capital values depending on the individual tenant and lease terms, they will all be affected by a change in yields or consumer expenditure.

Direct property interests come with a very high unit value of several hundred thousand pounds, whereas £100 will buy a gilt and shares can be purchased for just a few pounds. This makes it impossible for small investors to participate in the property market, and very large prime property investments, such as a shopping centre, require funding by several institutions. It also means that only large investment funds can afford to assemble a balanced and diversified property portfolio.

Property is a real asset comprising indestructible land and buildings with a long economic life expectancy, so property is viewed traditionally as a long-term investment with returns linked to the economy. Although it should be noted that individual properties may be traded to generate short-term performance in a competitive fund market, research by Collett *et al.* (2003) shows that institutions tend to hold commercial property for between eight and 12 years. Retail properties are likely to be held longer than industrial or office properties, whilst properties purchased in recession are traded more frequently.

Ownership of paper assets such as bonds and equities requires passive management whereas a real asset like property requires day-to-day management such as rent collection, rent reviews, lease negotiation and maintenance. Sometimes this gives an opportunity for pro-active management to refurbish, acquire adjoining sites or redevelop to release extra value to the property investment, and these activities can be timed to coincide with market conditions to give maximum benefit to value. It is not possible to add value to equity/bond portfolios in this way.

Illiquidity is a major disadvantage of a property investment compared with equities and gilts, which can be bought easily and quickly in an efficient market. Property transactions are expensive and time-consuming, involving complex legal interests, physical surveys, marketing and negotiation between buyer and seller to agree a price, arrangement of finance and the lack of a single trading market.

To maintain a quality of physical and environmental life for households and good relationships with neighbours in the housing and commercial property world, there is substantial government intervention in the UK. This takes the form of planning and environmental controls, building regulations, rent controls and landlord and tenant Acts (affecting commercial lettings), which add to management obligations and will also affect property value.

3.3   An introduction to investment analysis and pricing

Return and risk are fundamental to investment analysis. The measures of historical return are used to analyse risk and to compare the performance of different investment markets. Historic returns are also used to compare the performance of different funds with their competitors and with the market to see whether they have achieved above-average returns and as a basis for forecasting models to predict future expected returns. In the property market, returns can be measured at a local level to compare individual property performance or at sector and portfolio level to compare performance of properties in different locations.

Investment managers are concerned with the valuation of assets and strive to purchase assets worth more than their cost. The fund manager needs to assess the current market value of an investment, and in a well-functioning market like the stock market, where assets are frequently traded and all buyers and sellers have access to all relevant information, this will be similar to the true value. In a less efficient market like the property market, the market price may not equate to the true value of worth.

It is important first to understand how assets are valued, and the following section considers some simple measures of return and investment yields used in the pricing of assets.

3.4   Definitions and simple examples of financial return

3.4.1   Interest rates

The rate of interest on newly issued gilts will be determined by the level of interest rates, which relates closely to the minimum lending rate of the banks. Since 1998 the Bank of

England has operational independence to set interest rates through the Monetary Policy Committee (MPC) which meets monthly to determine whether any changes in the minimum bank lending rate are required in order to regulate the economy, influence the supply of money and maintain low levels of inflation. The minimum lending rate is then used as the basis upon which major commercial banks fix their interest rates for lending and borrowing in the money markets. These interest rates are reflected in the capital markets where stocks and shares are traded, and influence the long-term interest rates on mortgages. Interest rates thus also relate to the property market.

The rate of interest received by the bond holder is dependent upon the creditworthiness of the issuer, the economic climate and the length of the loan term. Interest is the compensation the lender requires for the loan of the money; the rate of interest reflects the risk that a borrower may go bust and be unable to pay the interest or the loan. The greater the uncertainty, the greater the interest demanded by the lender.

The prevailing level of central bank interest rates and the outlook for changes and inflation will also affect interest rates. Investors can place their money in safe bank deposits, so bonds need to offer competitive returns. Also if inflation is high the real value of money reduces over time, so investors will demand higher interest rates as compensation.

3.4.2   Income yields

The income yield is a simple expression of the relationship between a current income and the current purchase price in terms of a percentage. The income or flat yield is calculated by dividing the fixed interest income by the price: a bond purchased for £1000 yielding an income of £100 produces a yield of 10% p.a. It is expressed in the following formula:

$$\text{Yield} = \frac{\text{Income}}{\text{Price}} \times 100$$

$$\text{For example, } 10\% = \frac{100}{1000} \times 100$$

Yields rise as bond prices fall and yields fall as bond prices rise, so if the above bond were purchased for £2000 the yield would fall to 5%.

$$\text{Yield} = \frac{100}{2000} \times 100 = 5\%$$

The income yield in the gilt market is also known as the interest yield, running yield or flat yield. The interest received on fixed income securities is fixed in pounds and pence, but if the bond is traded on the stock market the yield will vary as the price of traded bonds changes according to the economic climate and stock market conditions. The tradable price will adjust to reflect rises or falls in the general level of interest rates, in order to remain competitive.

However, yield calculation is only that simple where there is no prospect of future change in price or income. It is the possibility of change that gives rise to the need to introduce other calculations and terms.

Table 3.2   Running yields.

Year	Investment A Fixed income Price £1000	Running yield	Investment B Variable income Price £1250	Running yield
1	100	10%	100	8.0%
2	100	10%	120	9.6%
3	100	10%	140	11.2%

3.4.3   Nominal yields

Bond yields as calculated in 3.4.2 are known as nominal yields and reflect an annual income. However, the coupons are normally paid twice yearly so there will be a difference between the nominal yield and the effective yield.

3.4.4   Running yield

The running yield reflects the income return as at a specific point in time, where the annual income is expressed as a percentage of the value or purchase price of a property (either gross or net of costs). For a fixed interest investment such as a bond the running yield at each point in time would be the same as the income yield, but for a variable income investment it would change from year to year. It is calculated in the same way as the income yield: income/price × 100.

Assume a fixed income investment A is priced at £1000 and investment B, producing a rising income, is priced at £1250. The running yields would be as shown in Table 3.2.

3.4.5   Dividend yield

A dividend yield is similar to the interest yield on fixed interest securities, except that it is calculated on a per share basis:

$$\text{Dividend yield} = \frac{\text{Dividend per share}}{\text{Market price per share}} \times 100$$

A dividend yield shows the relationship between the dividend payout per share and its market price. The dividend payout per share is arrived at by dividing the total dividend paid by a company by the total number of shares. The total dividend paid by a company will be determined by the company and is paid out from the profits or equity earnings of the company. The dividend may not be known in advance so the dividend yield normally refers to the previous year's interim and final dividend.

$$\text{Dividend per share} = \frac{\text{Dividend payment}}{\text{Number of shares issued}}$$

If a company has (i) equity capital of £10 million issued in 10m × £1 shares; (ii) equity earnings of £4 million; and (iii) £2 million is allocated as dividend payout:

$$\text{Dividend per share} = \frac{2\,000\,000}{10\,000\,000} \qquad \text{Dividend per share} = 20\text{p}$$

If each £1 share is currently trading on the stock market at £4, the dividend yield is:

$$\text{Dividend yield} = \frac{\text{Dividend per share}}{\text{Market price per share}} \times 100$$

$$\text{Dividend yield} = \frac{20}{400} \times 100$$

$$\text{Dividend yield} = 5\%$$

It should be noted that this has been simplified, as tax will affect the dividend yield. The above is a net of tax dividend yield and will need to be grossed up because gross of tax yields are used for comparison purposes on the stock market.

Prices of stocks and shares are determined by supply and demand. Changes in yields of stocks and shares will respond quickly to changes in supply and demand due to the high efficiency of the stock market. An efficient market can be defined as one where all information, including past, current and future expected events, is fully reflected in the prices for buying and selling and where the prices adjust quickly and accurately through the use of electronic communications. Investors are able to respond to short-term changes by switching or buying and selling investments quickly on the stock market. Property is considered to be a longer-term investment and investors tend to respond to longer-term trends in the yield.

3.5   Property yields and returns

3.5.1   Initial yield

In the property market the income yield is known as the initial yield. It shows the ratio of current rent passing to the current price.

A property investment produces a current income of £100 000 per annum and is valued at £1 600 000. The initial yield is:

$$\frac{£100\,000}{£1\,600\,000} \times 100 = 6.25\%$$

3.5.2   Reversionary yield

The open market rent is the best rent that property can fetch on the open market at that time. In the UK property market rents are fixed generally for five years before they are reviewed. In between reviews the market rent (MR) will adjust to changes in supply and demand, and with rising inflation will generally be above the contractual rent. The initial yield shows the relationship between the current rent passing and the current price while the reversionary yield is the MR divided by the current price on a property investment let at a rent below the MR.

If in the above example the MR is £120 000 per annum, the reversionary yield would be 7.5%.

3.5.3 All risks yield

If a property is let at market rent then the all risks yield is the MR divided by the price.

3.5.4 Capital return

It has already been noted that investors are concerned with the overall return they obtain from their money, and that this can take the form of either income return or capital return or both. In most cases investors will look to see their capital returned, with gilts held to redemption; this is secure, but in most media the return of capital (the original investment price) is not guaranteed as the price may rise or fall. The change in capital value of the investment over the holding period gives rise to the capital return. This may be positive if values rise or negative if values fall. The capital return, therefore, shows the relationship in percentage terms between any change in capital value and the purchase price or value at the beginning of the measurement period. It is expressed in the following formula:

$$\text{Capital return} = \frac{CV_1 - CV_0}{CV_0} \times 100$$

Where CV_0 is the capital value at the beginning of the measurement period
CV_1 is the capital value at the end of the measurement period.

Assume investor A buys the 9% Treasury stock in year 1 for £100 and is forced to sell to investor B for £60. The capital return to investor A is as follows:

$$\text{Capital return} = \frac{£60 - £100}{£100} \times 100 = -40\%$$

Assume that investor B sells the stock for £90. The capital return for investor B would then be:

$$\text{Capital return} = \frac{£90 - £60}{£60} \times 100 = +50\%$$

Although fixed interest securities are frequently considered to be risk free – that is to say, income is certain – the example above illustrates clearly that they are not. Losses and gains can be made on the capital value arising from change in the prevailing level of interest rates. The capital return is completely dependent on changes in the capital value of an investment resulting from movements in the level of interest rates. The capital return should therefore only be compared with the capital return of other investments.

3.5.5 Income return

This is the net income received over the measurement period divided by the purchase price or capital value at the beginning of the measurement period. The net income is net of any outgoings and costs.

$$\text{Income return} = \frac{\text{NI}}{\text{CV}_0} \times 100$$

Where CV_0 is the capital value at the commencement of the measurement period
NI is the net income received during the period.

3.5.6 Total return

It is well known that investors are therefore frequently – and rightly – more interested in the combination of both income and capital return, or total return. The total return is the percentage relationship between any capital gain or loss and income over the purchase price or capital value at the beginning of the measurement period. It is in fact the sum of income and capital return. It is the true return an investor receives on his money and is the only true means of comparing investments financially.

$$\text{Total return} = \frac{\text{CV}_1 - \text{CV}_0 + \text{NI}}{\text{CV}_0} \times 100$$

Where CV_0 is the capital value at the commencement of the measurement period
CV_1 is the capital value at the end of the measurement period
NI is the new income over the period.

For example, assume that 9% Treasury stock are issued in year 1 at £100. As the market interest rates change each subsequent year, the market price of the 9% Treasury stock also adjusts. If the 9% Treasury stock were bought by investor A at the time of issue in year 1 for £100 and sold in year 2 for £60 – when there was a general rise in the level of interest rates resulting in a fall in the market prices – the total return would be:

$$\text{Total return} = \frac{9 + 60 - 100}{100} \times 100 = -23\% = \text{loss}$$

Compare this loss of −23% with the capital loss of −40% in the previous example. It should be noted in the calculation of total return here that the loss in capital value is in part offset by the income return.

If the 9% Treasury stock were bought by investor B for £60 and sold for £90, and produced a fixed income of £9 each year, then the total return to investor B would be:

$$\text{Total return} = \frac{9 + 90 - 60}{60} \times 100 = 65\% \text{ gain}$$

Again, the total return has been enhanced by including the income return with the capital return, providing a better overall picture of how an investment is performing.

3.6 Yield and return distinguished

A yield usually reflects the relationship between a current income and the purchase price and does not take into account any capital loss or gain made. Return usually reflects any income, expenditure and/or capital gain or loss made on investments and gives a clear indication of the financial position of the investor.

A yield is used to estimate the market value of an investment while a return is used as a means of comparing the financial attractiveness of different investments to an individual investor and will be used in the investment decision process for the selection of investments. The total return is the return the investor receives on his or her money over time. It therefore has a historic dimension. Yield, on the other hand, is a 'spot' time figure. The timing of buy and sell decisions can be crucial in determining the return that an investor realises.

3.6.1   The reverse yield gap

For many years during the first half of the twentieth century, and in particular in the period of the 'Great Depression' during the late 1920s and 1930s, many businesses found it difficult to make profits and dividend payments and share prices were as likely to fall as to rise (Isaac, 1998). Inflation and interest rates were also very low, and in fact there were periods of deflation. The guaranteed income from gilts was therefore considered to be very secure and attractive compared to equities, particularly when the purchasing power of a fixed income would increase (rise in real terms) during deflationary conditions. As growth expectations were minimal, the total return investors received would only reflect income. During the inter-war years the income yield was therefore the same as the total return.

At this same period 'blue-chip' company ordinary shares were considered to be more risky than gilts as dividends and share prices could fall and, with the greater risk of bankruptcy, companies were more likely to default on payment of the dividend. Investors wanted to be compensated for this risk, requiring a higher dividend yield and total return than on gilts. The dividend yield on blue-chip ordinary shares was between 4% and 6%, a premium of at least 1.5% above the 2.5% Consols to reflect the extra risk. This difference in yields between gilts and equities is known as the yield gap. The all risks yield on prime property investments also stood around 3.5% above gilts, as property incurred management costs and the risk of tenant default. There was therefore a fairly clear yield structure reflecting levels of risk and management (Isaac, 1998).

During the 1950s, following reconstruction of bombed sites, there was a period of high employment, an increase in wealth and a booming economy. This resulted in rising salaries and increased disposable incomes, leading in turn to increased turnover in shops and subsequently more construction of shops within town centres. (See Dubben and Sayce, 1991, for a more detailed account of the history of the economy and property market.) In the 1960s people were able to think about future security through insurance policies and pension schemes. This led to the growth of the service industry, particularly in insurance and pension funds which in turn invested their funds in equities on the stock market. The profits made by public companies rose with reduced risk of company failure, so the shareholders benefited by receiving rising dividends.

The rise in the standard of living and higher disposable incomes led to rising prices and to a new phenomenon: inflation. As inflation rose, the value of the pound decreased. Fixed interest investments were no longer attractive as the fixed income was unable to keep up with inflation. However, dividend payments on equities were rising as the companies' profits rose, and the growth in dividends not only kept up with but often produced real growth above inflation. Equities now became attractive growth investments.

Table 3.3   Reverse yield gap.

	1930	1950	1961	1969
2.5% Consols	4.7	4.5	6.25	9
Blue-chip ordinary shares	6.1	5.5	4.75	4.5
Yield gap (reverse yield gap)	1.4	1.0	(1.5)	(4.5)

Source: Barclays de Zoete Wedd, as quoted in Fraser (1993).

Demand for gilts accordingly, decreased, causing a fall in prices; thus the gilt interest yield was forced up. For the first time the interest yield on 2.5% Consols rose to 6.25%, above that of blue-chip ordinary shares at 4.75%. This phenomenon was called the reverse yield gap. The 'risky' equities now offered a lower yield than the 'safer' gilts. Gilts were seen as a risky investment in the inflationary conditions. By 1970 the reverse yield gap was as high as 4% (Baum and Crosby, 1995) and it was accepted that growth investments were more attractive in times of rising inflation (see Table 3.3). As a result, the dividend yield and total return were now very different for equities. Subsequently, the yield on 2.5% Consols rose above the all risks yield on prime property as property yields fell.

So why should an investor be prepared to accept a lower yield on equities considered to be more risky investments than on a safer investment such as gilts? As companies prospered, the dividend payout rose and the equity prices on the stock market likewise increased due to demand. The demand for shares had tended to rise as a consequence of investor expectations of future performance and expected dividend. Investors will be prepared to accept a low dividend yield if they perceive increases in the future. This future gain can also be a reflection of the possibility of future sale price rises. So an investor could expect to make a gain on the sale of his shares which would be reflected in the total return. Thus the expectation of changing capital value was a root cause of the emergence of the reverse gap and the mark of a time at which yield and return could be distinguished.

An example of the distinction between yield and return on equities is given below. An investor purchases ordinary shares for £3.60, receives a dividend of 18p and at the end of the year sells the shares for £4. The dividend yield is:

$$\text{Dividend yield} = \frac{18}{360} \times 100 = 5\%$$

This yield is different from the total return as it does not reflect the capital gain made on the sale of the shares. The total return that the investor receives on his investment is greater:

$$\text{Total return} = \frac{18 + 400 - 360}{360} \times 100 = 16\%$$

It can be seen that the principle is exactly the same as that noted for the pricing of government stock. An investor would only accept a low dividend yield on equities if high growth rates on their dividend and share prices were expected and the investor was more interested in the return than the income or dividend yield as a financial indicator. Thus a low yield implies a high price in relation to the current income and vice versa, but the total return is the best measure for comparing different types of investments.

Following the reverse yield gap in the 1950s, rental levels in the commercial property market sector were expected to rise in the future so shorter leases with rent reviews were gradually introduced to enable landlords to enjoy some of the benefits of the rising rents (see, for example, Marriott, 1969; Scott, 1996). By 1970 rent reviews had become commonplace. At first this was on a seven-year cycle but by the 1980s a typical institutional lease was for between 20 and 25 years, with five-yearly upward only reviews. Although the all risks yield showed the relationship between the current rental value and market price, it also reflected the investor's expectations of future rental growth. Prime property was considered to be a growth-type investment like equities, and the lower all risks yield compared to gilts implied a high price. The total return was therefore different from the all risks yield. Investments with high capital and income growth potential produce a higher expected total return.

Investments in property tend to offer a total return of between 2% and 4% above gilts (Baum and Crosby, 1995). This return reflects the additional risks of, for example, illiquidity, management and maintenance costs, and tenant default as involved in investing in property. For prime property investments, prevailing yields have been below gilt yields most of the time since the 1970s. The exception has been the period in the early 1990s when property became the subject of investor disaffection, leading to a very significant rise in yields to well above those prevailing in the gilts and equity market (see Fraser, 1993; Ross Goobey, 1993).

During the late 1990s gilt returns decreased to very low levels of between 4.5% and 5% due to a sustained period of very low inflation of around 2.5%. The policy of the Labour Government at that time was to maintain low inflation in order to achieve price stability and real economic growth. During these low inflationary conditions the yield gap between gilts and growth-type investments reappeared and once again yields for equities and property were above those of gilts. An interesting difference between the inter-war period and the 1990s is that equities and property were showing real positive income and capital growth during the late 1990s.

3.7   Compounding and discounting

Simple interest is where the interest earned on invested capital is not reinvested but is spent, so the capital remains the same and the interest each year remains the same. For example, £100 earning interest at 10% will always earn £10 interest each year if the £10 is withdrawn from the investment so that the capital remains £100.

The theory of compounding assumes that when money is invested today it will accumulate interest at the end of a stated period, normally one year. The interest is added back to the capital and reinvested over year 2 and so on, thus the interest earns interest and the capital builds up more quickly than with simple interest. Thus £100 invested today earns 10% interest and becomes £110 at the end of the first year. This £110 then earns interest. This is illustrated in Table 3.4.

The Amount of £1 formula for calculating quickly the total accumulations is $(1 + i)^n$ where i is the interest rate expressed as a decimal and remains constant and n is the number of years. In the above example where £100 is invested for four years at 10%:

Table 3.4   Compound interest.

Year	Beginning of year	Interest at 10%	Total at end of year	Using the amount of £1 formula at 10%
1	100	10	110	$100 \times (1 + 0.10)$
2	110	11	121	$100 \times (1 + 0.10)^2$
3	121	12.1	133.1	$100 \times (1 + 0.10)^3$
4	133.1	13.31	146.41	$100 \times (1 + 0.10)^4$

$$\text{Total amount accumulated} = £100 \times (1 + 0.10)^4$$
$$= £100 \times 1.4641$$
$$= £146.41$$

Thus £146.41 is the future value of £100 receivable today.

The concept of time value of money is essentially that a given sum of money has a different value depending on when it occurs in time, even if inflation is zero. It is based on the assumption that money can be invested to earn interest, so in the above example the investor would have no preference between receiving £100 today or £146.41 in four years' time; £46.41 is the compound interest earned on the £100 investment, and interest represents the time value of money.

3.7.1   Theory of discounting – arriving at present value

This is the reverse process whereby a single sum of future money is worth less today, so in the previous example £146.41 receivable in four years' time is worth £100 today; £100 is the present value which, if invested over four years at 10%, will become £146.41. Discounting is, in effect, deducting over time the compound interest from a future sum to arrive at its present value.

The formula to convert future money into its present value is $1/(1 + i)^n$ or this can be written $(1 + i)^{-1}$. The present value of £146.41 receivable in four years' time discounted at 10% is:

$$£146.41 \times 1/(1 + 0.10)^4$$
$$£146.41 \times 0.6830$$
$$\text{Present value} = £100$$

3.7.2   Annual percentage rates and compounding

So far it has been assumed that interest has been accumulating annually in arrears, but in the case of bonds and equities interest is paid half-yearly in arrears and rental income on property investments is normally receivable quarterly in advance. If interest were quoted at 8% per annum but paid each quarter, it would be assumed that 2% would be receivable every quarter. However, if 2% is compounded every quarter it will accumulate to more than 8% per annum, as shown below:

$$(1 + r_{quarter})^4 = (1 + r_{annual})$$

$$(1 + r_{quarter})^4 - 1 = r_{annual}$$

$$(1 + 0.02)^4 - 1 = 0.0824 = 8.24\% \text{ p.a.}$$

The 8.24% is often quoted as the annual percentage rate (APR) on loan agreements. It is interesting to note the differences on annual interest rates charged by credit companies who claim interest on a monthly basis. A monthly rate of 1.25% accumulates to APR of 16.08% whereas 1.5% – just 0.25% different – accumulates to 19.56% p.a.

3.7.3   Effective interest rates

The effective rate of interest is the rate per period that, when compounded, equates to the annual percentage rate. If the annual rate of interest is 8% but interest accumulates quarterly, it is important to be able to calculate the true effective quarterly rate that will compound to 8% p.a. using the following formula:

$$r_{quarterly} = (1 + r_{anual})^{1/4} - 1$$

$$r_{quarterly} = (1 + 0.08)^{1/4} - 1$$

$$r_{quarterly} = 0.019426$$

$$r_{quarterly} = 1.943\%$$

3.8   Discounted cash flow (DCF)

The theory of discounting, as explained above, converts a future sum to its present value over one period. However, an investment will often produce a series of future incomes over a number of periods. Each income will need to be discounted and the results added together to arrive at the total present value. This is simply illustrated in the example set out in Table 3.5.

An investment produces an income of £1000 per annum for five years. If the required return is 9%, what is the total present value? Table 3.5 shows that if the investment is purchased for £3889.64, the investor achieves a return of 9%. This represents the worth to the investor at his required rate of return.

Table 3.5   Calculating gross present value by discounting.

Period	Income ×	PV £1 $(1 + i)^{-n}$	= Present value
1	£1000	$(1.09)^{-1} = 0.9174$	£917.43
2	£1000	$(1.09)^{-2} = 0.84167$	£841.67
3	£1000	$(1.09)^{-3} = 0.77218$	£772.18
4	£1000	$(1.09)^{-4} = 0.70843$	£708.43
5	£1000	$(1.09)^{-5} = 0.64993$	£649.93
		Gross present value	**£3889.64**

Table 3.6   Net present value.

Period	Income ×	PV £1 $(1+i)^{-n}$	= Present value
1	£1000	$(1.09)^{-1} = 0.9174$	£917.43
2	£1000	$(1.09)^{-2} = 0.84167$	£841.67
3	£1000	$(1.09)^{-3} = 0.77218$	£772.18
4	£1000	$(1.09)^{-4} = 0.70843$	£708.43
5	£1000	$(1.09)^{-5} = 0.64993$	£649.93
		Gross present value	**£3889.64**
		Less price	**£3750.00**
		Net present value (NPV)	**+£139.64**

3.8.1   Net present value (NPV)

If the price is less than the gross present value – let us say it is £3750 – then the investor makes a return of 9% plus an additional profit of £139.64, which is known as the net present value (NPV) (see Table 3.6). If, however, the investor has to pay *more* than £3889.64 then he or she would incur a loss, or negative NPV.

Where the NPV is equal to or greater than zero, there is a rational financial argument to say that an investor should buy. If the price equates to the present value and the NPV is therefore zero, the discount rate is known as the internal rate of return (IRR).

3.8.2   The internal rate of return (IRR)

Assuming the investor purchased the investment for £3750 in the above example, he would achieve a higher return than 9%. The IRR represents the actual return the investor will make at any given purchase price. That is to say, if the purchase price is 'given', the IRR is the rate of return that exactly equates the purchase price to the sum of all the discounted future cash flows.

For a price of £3750, the IRR has been calculated to be 10.42% (45p error due to rounding up) and is illustrated in Table 3.7. If the IRR is equal to or greater than the required target return, an investor should buy.

Table 3.7   The internal rate of return.

Period	Income	PV £1 $(1+i)^{-n}$ using 10.42%	= Present value
1	£1000	$(1.1042)^{-1} = 0.90563$	£905.63
2	£1000	$(1.1042)^{-2} = 0.82017$	£820.17
3	£1000	$(1.1042)^{-3} = 0.74277$	£742.77
4	£1000	$(1.1042)^{-4} = 0.67268$	£672.68
5	£1000	$(1.1042)^{-5} = 0.6092$	£609.20
		Gross present value	**£3750.45**
		Less price	**£3750.00**
		Net present value (NPV)	**£0.45**

Table 3.8   Finding the internal rate of return.

A	B	C	D	E	F
Period	Cash flow	PV £1 at 9%	DCF B×C	PV £1 at 11%	DCF B×E
0	−3750	1	−3750	1	−3750
1	1000	0.917431	917.4312	0.900901	900.9009
2	1000	0.84168	841.68	0.811622	811.6224
3	1000	0.772183	772.1835	0.731191	731.1914
4	1000	0.708425	708.4252	0.658731	658.731
5	1000	0.649931	649.9314	0.593451	593.4513
		+NPV	139.6513	−NPV	−54.103

The IRR is most accurately calculated on an electronic spreadsheet using a built-in function key; for example, in Excel the formula would be =IRR (target rate, cash flow cell range including negative cost in year 0). In fact the target return can be omitted from the formula entry but a negative cash flow must be included in year 0 as laid out in Table 3.8. In Excel the IRR on the above example is calculated to be 10.4248%.

The approximate IRR can be found by interpolation between two discount rates producing a negative and a positive NPV. The same cash flow has been set out in Table 3.8 assuming a price of £3750 and the cash flow has been discounted at 9% and 11% to produce +NPV of £139.65 and −NPV of £54.10, respectively.

The IRR can be calculated by interpolation using the following formula with the above NPVs.

$$\mathrm{IRR} = r_1 + \left[(r_h - r_1) \times \frac{\mathrm{NPV}_1}{(\mathrm{NPV}_1) - \mathrm{NPV}_h} \right]$$

Where r_1 is the lower trial discount rate
   r_h is the higher trial discount rate
   NPV_1 is the NPV at the lower discount rate
   NPV_h is the NPV at the higher discount rate.

Substituting the appropriate variables into the formula:

$$\mathrm{IRR} = 0.09 + \left[(0.11 - 0.09_1) \times \frac{139.6513}{(139.6513) - (-54.103)} \right]$$

$$\mathrm{IRR} = 0.09 + (0.02 \times 0.72076)$$

$$\mathrm{IRR} = 10.4415\%$$

Since the 1970s discounted cash flow (DCF) has been promoted in leading academic texts as an appraisal and valuation technique. In the UK the profession has been slow to accept the practical uses of discounted cash flow, particularly in the absence of formal guidelines. Nonetheless, it has steadily gained ground and a good knowledge of DCF is now an essential part of the appraiser's toolkit.

3.9   An introduction to the imperfections of the property market as compared with the equities and bonds market

Investments are supplied initially on the primary market by the issuer, and the purchaser can then trade with third parties on the secondary market. The stock market is a central secondary market where buyers and sellers of equities and gilts can trade electronically, allowing investors to exchange capital today for a future income and capital. Prices are based on the balance between supply and demand. An efficient market is one where prices reflect all information that could affect the price transacted between buyers and sellers quickly and accurately. However, there are different degrees of efficiency relating to the pricing of stocks and shares:

- *Weak form efficiency* – an investor receives a return based on a price that reflects all market information.
- *Semi-strong form efficiency* – share prices reflect all known publicly available information relevant to each company, such as new products and financing information.
- *Strong form efficiency* – the most efficient form of market where the share price reflects all published and other relevant information, whether generally available or known only to certain parties such as corporate insiders and specialists.

In respect of the stock market, Lumby and Jones (1998) claim that there is evidence to support semi-strong efficiency, where a company's share price will reflect business decisions that have been released to the stock market for the general public. The stock market is a central market where many buyers and many sellers interact for a homogenous investment – a share in a company or a specific gilt – to produce a market price.

Although formal tests of property market efficiency are limited, five studies identified by Gatzlaff and Tirtiroglu (1995) provide evidence to support weak form efficiency. Property returns as calculated on the basis of valuations consistently show serial correlation where returns or simply price movements in one period are correlated with returns in previous periods.

However, there is no central property trading market but separate investment, occupier and development markets and local markets requiring local knowledge. As property is heterogeneous, information on one transaction is not an exact proxy for the selling price of another property. In the stock market, transaction data is plentiful to allow for tracking price movements. In contrast, there is limited information available on transaction prices in the property market and the volume of transactions is low. An important difference is that valuations are used to track property movements. These valuations are estimates of likely selling prices and may lead to market mis-pricing (Hoesli and MacGregor, 2000:23).

In the property market it is difficult to increase supply quickly to meet any changes in demand. Creating new property investments through development activity is a lengthy process taking several years and involving land acquisition, finance, planning permission, construction time, marketing and the search for suitable tenants. An increase in economic activity can trigger development booms but by the time the new development is complete and comes onto the market the demand may have changed, so that there is an oversupply. This time delay in the supply coming onto the market can adversely affect rental growth and have consequences for property prices and hence returns.

In equity and bond markets, transactions can be conducted quickly with screen-based trading and e-commerce. In the property market there is an unwillingness to share information which involves lengthy transaction times, large lot sizes and high transaction costs. This situation is not helped by the impact of higher stamp duty as these are brought into line with the relatively higher costs of Eurozone countries. Despite recent moves to introduce property databases via the web, comprehensive property data is still not readily available to investors and the lack of a securitised property market adds inflexibility and illiquidity.

3.10   Property as an asset class compared with gilts and equities

Property, equities and gilts are all similarly affected by changes in interest rates, with falling interest rates leading to a rise in returns and rising interest rates causing a fall. However, returns on property tend to lag behind those of equity and gilts, with gilts leading the performance cycle and therefore peaking first before the top of the cycle (Fig. 3.1) (Fraser *et al.*, 2002).

Returns from property are driven by rental growth reflecting economic activity. This is strongly evidenced by the office and industrial market where an oversupply of space arising from a recession tends to continue into the recovery period, delaying any growth.

The supply of gilts will be affected by the Public Sector Borrowing Requirement while equities will depend on new issues by companies. However, the supply of property is greatly affected by the time lag in the development cycle.

Despite the boom/bust nature of property cycles, the property market performs more smoothly than the highly volatile stock market. This can be explained by the stable income arising from the traditional institutional lease and the impact of regular rent reviews, although this may well change with the introduction of the new lease code. The heterogeneous nature of property and the relative unreliability of indices based on periodic valuations due to a lack of transactional evidence will also cause a smoothing of returns. The imperfect and inefficient property market causes a lag in the pricing mechanism.

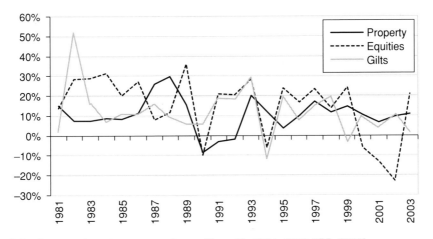

Fig. 3.1   Comparative returns: property, equities, gilts 1981–2003 (IPD, 2003).

3.11   The place of property within the multi-asset portfolio

Research carried out by Lee (2002) concluded that property included in a mixed asset portfolio can lead to an increase or a decrease in portfolio returns, depending on the performance of property relative to other investment media, but will always lead to reductions in risk, especially where allocations to property are at least 15–20%. Work by Sweeney (2004) also supports the argument that property can act as an effective risk reducer within the portfolio, and this is considered further in Chapter 11.

That property can offer diversification benefits to the mixed asset portfolio in the long run is indicated by a study carried out by Fraser *et al.* (2002). It showed that property offers low correlation with gilts and equities and that property returns lag behind those of equities, gilts and property companies, with gilts leading the cycle. This can partly be explained by the development cycle, which creates long time lags in the completion of development projects, reacting with economic cycles to generate the boom/bust cycles experienced in the late 1980s and early 1990s (Fraser *et al.*, 2002).

For any asset to act as a successful investment medium, it will need to out-perform the risk free rate. Performance is measured by total return, which is a combination of annual incomes and capital returns. For equities this is a combination of dividend and movements in the share price, while for bonds total return is derived from the coupon (interest) plus any stock price changes. Direct property investment returns are derived from annual rental income and changes in capital value. Property investors will want to achieve both rental and capital growth to generate adequate total returns. Income returns tend to be fairly consistent over time while changes in the capital value have a greater impact on fluctuations in total return. Property income also tends to be more stable than dividend growth and helped to maintain positive returns over the 1998–2002 period when equity returns were negative.

Institutional perceptions of how the property market will perform have great impact on UK property investment prices and values due to their dominance and substantial funding and tax advantages over other investors.

Value is based on an income stream, and appraisals of property investments use discounted cash flows techniques (DCF) which will become increasingly important. The calculation of worth (see Chapter 6) uses DCF techniques and involves establishing rental growth, risk premiums and forecasts. Many investors now require annual valuations based on worth, which will need forecasting advice, instead of open market values based on traditional, often inaccurate techniques, which are inadequate as investment appraisal tools.

There is a need for easily accessible and efficient property databanks for the sharing of comprehensible property information which can also be used to encourage funded research. Securitisation and derivatives should be used to create flexible property investment vehicles to overcome the illiquidity particularly of large, expensive, prime property investments. Institutions need property investment vehicles that offer greater liquidity and tax transparency. Investment bankers also need better information if they embark on joint ventures with property companies or participate in limited partnerships.

If property investments are to provide a secure income or to be used as security for corporate financing purposes, the operation of the investment markets will need to demonstrate greater economic 'efficiency'; at the same time there is a need for occupiers to be able to measure their satisfaction with the property in more rigorous terms. The UK leasing structure has for many years been geared to support the landlord through a stable rental income stream payable over long leases and upward only rent reviews. This has over time made UK property investments more attractive than their European counterparts. However, the institutional lease is now a memory of the 1980s and 1990s. Leases are reduced in length and offer break clauses and the future of the five year upward only rent review is currently under threat by the flexible lease code. Additionally, the introduction of more institution grade stock on UK-style leases is leading to harmonisation in investment opportunities.

The property market is renowned for its booms and recessions. The 1980s boom was a result of over-investment by UK and overseas banks funding surplus property developments, leading to a severe downturn in the property market. However, all cycles are different and are linked with economic events – not just domestically but now also globally, as evidenced by the 2003 economic slowdown. The Bank of England now sets interest rates independently, with the remit to contain inflation within a low band to maintain economic stability.

3.12 Summary

Compared with equities and gilts, property investments in freehold and leasehold interests are regarded as heterogeneous, with high unit values that are often only accessible to large investment funds. A major disadvantage of property investments is the high illiquidity due to the inefficient market and high costs of transactions. Property ownership is affected by statutory controls and requires management, but if this is pro-active it can lead to added value. Rental income is more secure than dividends but will depend on the quality of the tenant. The introduction of the new flexible lease code offers more attractive terms to tenants, with significant reductions in lease length together with the possible departure of the upward only rent reviews; this would reduce investor security of income. Over the long term, property has offered protection against inflation.

Income, dividend, nominal and running yields were distinguished with simple examples showing the relationship between current income and purchase price and its equivalence to the income or initial yield in the property market. This is a 'spot' measure used to estimate market value. Reversionary, equivalent and all risks yield are similar, showing the ratio of market rent to current purchase price. Return was distinguished from yield; it reflects the income, expenditure, and capital gain or loss over time, and is determined by the timing of buy and sell decisions. Measures of historical return are used to analyse risk and compare the performance of investment assets, investments funds and markets, providing the basis for forecasting.

Discounted cash flows (DCFs) are based on the principle that future money is worth less today. Discounting is deducting the compound interest earned from a future sum to arrive at its present value. When a series of future sums are discounted at a target rate of interest, the resulting total present value is known as the gross present value (GPV). The difference between the GPV and the price is known as the net present value (NPV) and this can be positive or negative. If the NPV is zero, the discount rate is known as the internal rate of return (IRR) and is most accurately calculated using Excel. A positive NPV and high IRR will increase the likelihood of an investor purchasing the investment. Appraisal of property investments using DCF is becoming increasingly important.

The property market is inefficient compared with the semi-strong efficiency of the stock market where there is plenty of transactional data using screen-based trading and one central marketplace. There is limited information available on property transactions with separate investment, occupier, developer and local markets, although some web site property databases have been introduced. Supply is slow to adapt to changes in demand due to the lengthy development process and this time lag in supply can affect rental growth and property prices, with adverse changes in economic activity.

Property, like equity and gilts, will be affected by changes in interest rates but lags behind them in the performance cycle. The stable income arising from the traditional institutional lease has explained the smooth performance of the property market compared with the highly volatile stock market, despite the boom/bust nature of property cycles. Property cycles are influenced by global economic events and overseas investment but are helped domestically by the Bank of England independently setting interest rates to maintain stability and low inflation.

Property can be an effective risk reducer in a mixed asset portfolio due to the low correlation with gilts and equities (Fraser et al., 2002). Property investors will, however, want to achieve both rental and capital growth to generate adequate total returns. The stable property income has helped to maintain positive property returns while the changes in capital value will greatly impact fluctuations in total return, although the impact of the flexible lease code has shortened leases and put upward only rent reviews under threat. Many investors want annual valuations based on DCF techniques which require forecasting advice. More information is now needed through an accessible databank in order to improve efficiency, and the introduction of more flexible investment vehicles is necessary to overcome illiquidity.

References

Barclays (2001) *Equity Gilt Study*. London: Barclays Bank Ltd.

Baum, A. and Crosby, N. (1995) *Property Investment Appraisal*, 2nd edn. London: Routledge.

Collett, D., Lizierim, C. and Ward, C. (2003) Timing and the holding periods of institutional real estate. *Real Estate Economics*, 31 (2): 205.

Dubben, N. and Sayce, S. (1991) *Property Portfolio Management*. London: Routledge.

DTZ Research (2003) *Money into Property 2003*, Edition 28. London: DTZ Tie Leung.

Fraser, W. (1993) *Principles of Property Investment and Pricing*, 2nd edn. London: MacMillan.

Fraser, W., Leishman, C. and Tarbert, H. (2002) The long-run diversification attributes of commercial property. *Journal of Property Investment & Finance*, 20 (4): 354–73.

Gatzlaff, D.H. and Tirtiroglu, D. (1995) Real estate market efficiency: issues and evidence. *Journal of Real Estate Literature*, 3: 157–89.

Hoesli, M. and MacGregor, B.D. (2000) *Property Investment: Principles and Practice of Portfolio Management*. Harlow: Pearson Education Ltd.

Investment Property Databank (2003) *IP Annual Index*. London: IPD.

Isaac, D. (1998) *Property Investment*. Basingstoke: MacMillan.

Lee, S.L. (2002) The implications for real estate portfolio management of changes in correlation. *Review of the Academy of Finance*, 2 (1): 36–45.

Lumby, S. and Jones, C. (1998) *Investment Appraisal and Financial Decisions*, 6th edn. London: International Thomson.

Marriott, O. (1969) *The Property Boom*. London: Pan Books.

Ross Goobey, A. (1993) *Bricks and Mortals: Dream of the 80s and the Nightmare of the 90s – Inside Story of the Property World*. London: Random House Publishers.

Royal Institution of Chartered Surveyors/British Property Federation (2002) *Code of Practice for Commercial Leases in England and Wales*, 2nd edition. London: RICS.

Scott, P. (1996) *The Property Masters*. London: E&FN Spon.

Sweeney, F. (2004) *Constructing an efficient real estate portfolio*. Paper to the IPD/IPF Property Investment Conference 2004, Brighton, 18–19 November.

Winterflood, B. and Diamond, R.A. (2002) *Guide to Bonds*. Bondscape.net.

Further reading

Boydell, S. and Clayton, P. (1993) *Property as an Investment Medium: its Role in the Institutional Portfolio*. London: Financial Times Business.

Brown, G. and Matysiak, G. (2000) *Real Estate Investment: A Capital Market Approach*. London: Pearson Education Limited.

Bryne, P. and Lee, S. (1995) Is there a place for property in a multi-asset portfolio? *Journal of Property Finance*, 6 (3): 60–83.

Fraser, W. (2004) *Cash Flow Appraisal for Property Investment*. Basingstoke: MacMillan.

RICS Commercial Market Panel (1999) What drives property investment today? *Chartered Surveyor Monthly*, June.

4 The market appraisal approach: rental value

Aims of the chapter

- To provide an explanation and definition of the different types of rent.
- To detail the influences on rental value.
- To provide information on how rent can be assessed in different circumstances.
- To explain the hierarchy of evidence when estimating rental values.
- To discuss the influences resulting in a shift from institutional leases to more flexible leases.
- To provide information on how to adjust headline to effective rents.

4.1   Introduction

Underlying the concepts of both value and worth is that of rental value, or the annual 'utility' of the property in the hands of the actual or hypothetical occupier. Without value in occupation, investment worth will not exist. Yet, strangely, many of the leading textbooks on property investment concentrate almost exclusively on the capitalisation of rents to form value or worth and do not address in any detail the factors that drive rents from the occupational perspective. In this chapter we seek to redress this balance by considering the nature of rent, the way in which it is established in the market place and the emerging occupational agenda which may influence rental performance.

4.2   Types of rent

At its simplest rent is the amount paid by a tenant to a landlord under a legal agreement made between the parties. It should be the last term that is finalised prior to completion of the agreement as it will be affected by the totality of the terms, such as lease length and tenant covenants. Only when these have been agreed between the parties should the level of rent be agreed. Commonly, however, rent is agreed prior to the other terms being finalised. In section 4.3 consideration is given to the effect on rent of the main clauses and covenants in a lease.

In modern commercial leases, rent will be 'reserved' as a payment to be made to the landlord normally quarterly in advance and payable whether or not demanded. However, despite this practice, market property appraisals are normally still formulated on the assumption that rent is paid annually in arrears. The reasons for this are historic in terms of the normal lease arrangements, but the assumption also relates to the ease of analysis of comparable transactions. For example, a capitalisation rate of 10% on the annual in arrears assumption produces a multiplier (or years purchase) of 10; if the annual in advance construction is taken, the multiplier becomes 10.38.

4.2.1   Rental value

In classical economics the term 'rent' was related to land as a factor of production (Balchin *et al.*, 1988; Ball *et al.*, 1998; Eccles *et al.*, 1999) in which the productivity of the land determined rent and with it the price of food. Under this theoretical approach rent would be a 'given', and the resultant product *price* would be derived from this. Such a theoretical stance was perhaps understandable and valid in a land market in which the remains of feudal command lines were still prevalent.

However, by the early nineteenth century, even before the process of urbanisation took place in western Europe, this approach was discredited, with Ricardo (1817; reprinted 1973) arguing that rent was not the determinant of price but instead was the residual or surplus that could be paid by a tenant to the landlord. To Ricardo, therefore, rent was a function of the demand for land for a given type of use. In his case of agricultural grain production, the fertility of the land would affect the productivity so that rental *value* would be highest for the land that had the highest crop-bearing capacity and lowest for that with the poorest capacity. However, such an explanation, whilst still holding true in many ways, does not fully account for the determination of rent within the current operation of commercial property markets.

In the Ricardian model supply was fixed (or largely so), which resulted in capacity and access to markets being the only determinants of the rent that the land would bear. To Ricardo rent was an economic function based on the ability to pay. However, to the later neoclassical economic movement, rent is a function not just of capability but of scarcity; therefore it is expressed in terms only of its market price as determined by the interaction of supply and demand. This point is important because, although the supply of *land* is relatively fixed, the supply of *property* within a given use and of a certain specification is not fixed over time. This gives rise to the dynamics of change within the rental markets and leads to the need to understand both the supply of property and its determinants, and the occupational demand for that property.

In determining rental value, both supply and demand factors will influence the level achievable. In relation to supply, the property market is in reality a second-hand market. It has been estimated that only 1–2% of the UK's building stock is replaced in any one year (Sayce *et al.*, 2004). Although the total level of stock can and does alter, it takes time for new or refurbished property to come on stream and supply change is dependent on numerous factors, most notably the availability of development finance and planning consents. Accordingly, in the short term supply to a would-be tenant is normally a function of the vacancy rate, so at times of high tenant demand a landlord may be able to set and achieve a rent that is in excess of the actual tenant's ability to pay. This is important when considering the establishment of rental value in a situation where an occupying tenant may not have the ability to 'walk away' from the deal – for example, when a rent is reviewed under a standard commercial lease.

However, although tenants may find themselves in a position in which, in the short term at least, the rental they have to pay is in excess of their economic ability to pay (or the 'worth' to them), the rent that a tenant will be prepared to pay in the open market will be a function both of ability to pay and level of supply. Where the level of supply is such that they do not have to bid up to their maximum level of 'worth' in order to secure the property, then rental value will be less than the maximum economic rent.

An appraiser who wishes to arrive at a market value of a property must understand the concepts of economic rental value in the hands of the occupier and of market rental value. If there is a divergence and the rent being paid is more than the tenant's economic rent, there must be an abnormal risk to the income flow; conversely, if rent is below the ability to pay there may be prospects for abnormal rental growth.

4.2.2   Market rent

The neoclassical approach to rent has been widely adopted and is recognised within the guidance provided by and to the international valuation community. The International Valuations Standards Committee (IVSC) has defined market rent (MR) as:

> The estimated amount for which a property or space within a property, should lease (let) on the date of valuation between a willing lessor and a willing lessee on appropriate lease terms in an arm's length transaction after proper marketing wherein the parties had acted knowledgeably, prudently and without compulsion.

Whilst use of this definition to undertake appraisals is only recommended by the IVSC, it is binding on members of the RICS (Royal Institution of Chartered Surveyors) under their practice statements (RICS, 2003: PS3.4) and departure can only take place in consultation with the client and for good reason. The RICS Appraisal manual goes on to provide further guidance in relation to interpretation of the definition. In particular the assumption must be made that both the parties are willing and that they have acted 'knowledgeably'. The latter point is particularly important as frequently a property rental transaction takes place in which one of the parties (normally the tenant) has not been well advised. This can often be the case when the property being considered is other than a large unit located in a prime position.

The assumption of 'appropriate terms' also needs some explanation. Within all established property markets a set of 'norms' will have evolved in terms of leasing practice. Over time these will change, but the challenge to the appraiser or valuer will normally arise when seeking to assess the rental value of a property let on non-standard – or 'inappropriate' – terms. As will be shown below, the notion of 'appropriate' and 'standard' is open to interpretation.

4.3   Assessing rental value

Rental value is normally assessed for the following purposes:

- grant of a new lease;
- rent review under an existing lease;
- lease renewal, either by agreement on by third-party determination; and
- assessment of the market rent of a let unit as part of an investment valuation or assessment of investment worth.

In all cases, as stated above, the rent will be assessed with reference to the existing or proposed lease. This may or may not define rent in accordance with the definition developed by the IVSC, but it is absolutely critical that the assessment does take place on the assumptions ascribed by the actual circumstances; otherwise the assessment of worth or value will be distorted. Before detailing the process of arriving at rental value, it is important to appreciate the relevance of this concept.

4.3.1   Grant of a new lease

When a new lease is to be granted, the transaction will normally be at 'arms' length', in accordance with the IVSC definition. However, the level of the rent will depend on the lease terms. Normally the terms that have a significant effect on rent are:

- length of the lease;
- presence and wording of the rent review clause;
- provisions regarding repair, alterations and improvement;
- provisions for alienation and parting with possession;
- user clause;
- service charge provisions (in the case of a multi-let property); and
- any onerous provisions – such as 'keep open' clauses.

It can be seen from the above that the rent should be agreed between the parties following negotiation of all the 'heads of terms'; in practice this is often not the case, with rent being agreed first and the terms of the lease agreed subsequently. (It is outside the scope of this book to explore these issues in depth; for that, readers are directed to texts on property asset management.)

The length of the lease may have a material effect on the rent to be paid but this will depend on whether or not there is a rent review, the possibility of lease renewal, the type of property and the market conditions.

4.3.2   Rent review

It seems inconceivable today that commercial properties were ever routinely let for very significant periods of time on leases containing no provision for adjusting the level of rent. Yet this was the case until the concept of the rent review was introduced following the period of post-war development in the late 1950s and 1960s. Early clauses were generally on a 14 year, then a seven year cycle linked to the then prevailing 28 or 42 year lease pattern. This long rent review cycle reflected the prevailing low levels of inflation in the economy and stable rental levels. (For a detailed history of the evolution of modern lease patterns in the UK see Dubben and Sayce (1991), Fraser (1993), Scott (1996) and Marriott (1969).)

However, by the early 1970s a combination of tight planning regulations on the supply of new stock, rapidly rising rental levels and double-digit retail price inflation pressures encouraged the new institutional investor landlords to modernise their rent review patterns. The growth in popularity of commercial property as an investment asset class gave rise to the so-called 'institutional lease', which was typically modelled on a 25 year term, containing full repairing and insuring terms and five-yearly upward only rent reviews. The upward only rent reviews provided a floor to the rent passing such that could not fall below the previously agreed rent. This floor provided property investments with

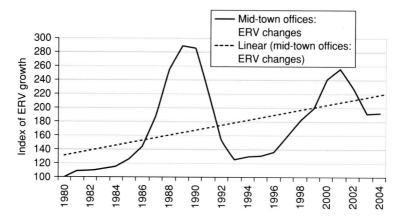

Fig. 4.1   Rental values for mid-town offices showing volatility.

bond-type characteristics, but with the benefit of a potential upside at each rent review. In section 4.8.5 consideration is given to the impact that different rent review patterns have and the rental equivalent that should be paid when a non-standard rent review pattern exists.

Rent reviews are a characteristic of the UK and Irish property markets. In contrast, rent review provisions are seldom found in Continental European leases, except in the Netherlands where longer retail leases will frequently have five-yearly rent review provisions; however, these are normally for the *average* of the previous five years' rental value.

In Continental European leases the norm is for there to be indexation provisions instead of rent reviews. These indexation provisions are usually for annual uplifts in the rent passing, with an increase linked to the rate of retail price or construction cost inflation. In section 4.10 consideration is given to the main provisions found in Continental European leases and their relative differences from those normally found in UK leases.

The market rental values in UK property markets have exhibited significant volatility since the mid 1970s. As an example, the graph in Fig. 4.1 shows the rental values for Mid-Town London, the Holborn area of London. This illustrates the importance to landlords of the upward only rent review, and the timing of the lease grant date. If this is fortuitously at the bottom of the rental cycle, the landlord can be expected to be able subsequently to lock into significant increases in rentals. If, in contrast, it is at the top of the cycle, the upward only provision provides a floor to the rents receivable.

In an effort to encourage landlords to consider the potential merits of annual indexation provisions as against five-yearly upward only rent reviews, Adams *et al.* (1993a,b) considered from an actuarial standpoint the different net present values of the cash flows where the rents rise annually in line with inflation, as against rents being fixed for five years then rising to the greater of the passing rent or the then open market rental level. They concluded that the impact of indexation on landlords' cash flows was greatly underestimated and that in the large majority of circumstances it produced superior net present worth. This work was extended to look at how the rental volatility of property could, from an actuarial standpoint, be incorporated into freehold valuations (Adams *et al.*, 1993c).

Table 4.1   Average lease lengths – main sectors 1997 to 2002.

	1997	1998	1999	2000	2001	2002
Unweighted						
Retail	10.5	9.6	9.9	9.4	9.6	9.2
Office	8.0	7.6	7.2	8.3	7.7	7.6
Industrial	9.8	8.9	8.4	7.5	7.8	6.9
All sectors (excl. other)	9.6	8.9	8.9	8.6	8.6	8.2
Rent weighted						
Retail	16.9	15.4	15.7	14.5	13.8	14.1
Office	14.8	12.7	12.5	13.4	12.5	11.0
Industrial	16.7	13.9	14.1	13.8	12.8	11.7
All sectors (excl. other)	16.2	14.2	14.4	13.9	13.1	12.6
Floorspace weighted						
Retail	17.7	17.1	15.7	15.5	14.4	16.1
Office	13.0	12.3	13.7	13.0	14.3	14.4
Industrial	16.5	13.2	13.1	12.9	12.7	10.8
All sectors (excl. other)	16.0	14.2	14.1	13.5	13.7	13.4
ERV weighted						
Retail	17.1	15.3	15.5	14.7	14.0	14.4
Office	15.8	14.5	13.8	14.4	13.1	13.7
Industrial	16.7	14.2	14.0	13.9	12.7	12.0
All sectors (excl. other)	16.4	14.8	14.6	14.4	13.5	13.8

Source: ODPM, 2004.

Indexation provisions are, at the time of writing, relatively infrequently used by UK landlords. However, the shortening of lease lengths and increasing flexibility in the UK were highlighted in the Investment Property Forum's response to the ODPM's paper on commercial property leases (IPF, 2004).

This shortening in lease length, ignoring break clauses, is shown in Table 4.1. When break clauses are incorporated into the figures, the weighted average lease length drops from 13.8 years as shown in Table 4.1 to 12.2 years as shown in Table 4.2.

From a practical perspective, it is the unexpired lease term that is of interest to landlords. The reduction in average lease lengths has come about thanks to a majority of new lettings being for terms significantly shorter than the traditional 25 year lease term, producing an average lease term in the low teens. As the traditional 25 year lease terms expire and new lettings are on shorter terms, it is reasonable to expect the weighted average figures to drop even further. However, even though lease length is shortening, the rent review pattern is tending to remain at five years, as shown in Table 4.3.

The IPF (2004) noted that there had been a significant change in the nature of lease terms. In 1990, 60% (not weighted by estimated rental value) of the properties in the IPD index had 20 to 25 year lease terms and had upward only rent reviews. By 2002 the position had reversed and 60% of the leases were either without a rent review or the tenant had a break option on or before the first rent review. This represents a very significant change in terms of market practice.

Table 4.2 Average lease lengths to first break – main sectors 1997 to 2002.

	1997	1998	1999	2000	2001	2002
Unweighted						
Retail	9.9	9.1	9.3	9.0	9.2	8.5
Office	6.8	6.7	6.1	7.4	7.0	6.2
Industrial	8.2	7.9	7.3	6.4	6.8	6.0
All sectors (excl. other)	8.7	8.2	8.1	7.9	8.0	7.3
Rent weighted						
Retail	16.2	14.9	15.4	14.1	13.5	13.0
Office	12.7	11.3	10.7	12.5	11.4	8.8
Industrial	15.0	12.7	12.6	12.9	11.5	10.0
All sectors (excl. other)	14.8	13.3	13.3	13.1	12.3	11.0
Floorspace weighted						
Retail	17.2	16.4	15.2	15.0	14.0	15.3
Office	10.7	10.9	11.2	12.0	13.7	12.5
Industrial	14.7	11.8	11.7	12.1	11.9	8.7
All sectors (excl. other)	14.4	13.0	12.8	12.8	13.1	11.7
ERV weighted						
Retail	16.4	14.8	15.2	14.3	13.7	13.3
Office	13.9	12.9	12.0	13.4	12.0	11.6
Industrial	14.9	12.9	12.7	13.1	11.5	10.4
All sectors (excl. other)	15.0	13.8	13.6	13.7	12.7	12.2

Source: ODPM, 2004.

Table 4.3 Frequency of different review periods – main sectors 2002.

	All property	Retail	Office	Industrial
Unweighted				
no review	22.6%	19.8%	22.4%	28.8%
1 yr	4.8%	5.6%	6.0%	1.5%
2 yrs	0.9%	0.7%	1.1%	1.0%
3 yrs	3.7%	1.9%	3.0%	8.3%
4 yrs	0.7%	0.5%	0.7%	1.1%
5 yrs	66.9%	71.0%	66.6%	58.3%
>5 yrs	0.5%	0.4%	0.2%	0.9%
	100%	100%	100%	100%
Rent weighted				
no review	11.2%	9.3%	11.9%	14.7%
1 yr	3.1%	2.9%	4.3%	1.4%
2 yrs	0.7%	0.5%	0.3%	1.9%
3 yrs	1.3%	0.7%	0.8%	3.2%
4 yrs	0.7%	0.1%	1.0%	1.5%
5 yrs	82.6%	85.8%	81.5%	76.6%
>5 yrs	0.5%	0.6%	0.2%	0.6%
	100%	100%	100%	100%
ERV weighted				
no review	11.4%	9.7%	11.9%	15.0%
1 yr	2.8%	2.9%	3.1%	1.9%
2 yrs	0.6%	0.5%	0.1%	1.6%
3 yrs	1.1%	0.8%	0.7%	2.8%
4 yrs	0.6%	0.1%	0.7%	1.5%
5 yrs	83.2%	85.6%	83.3%	76.7%
>5 yrs	0.4%	0.5%	0.2%	0.4%
	100%	100%	100%	100%

Source: ODPM, 2004.

4.3.3   Determining rent for lease renewal

Within England and Wales (but not Scotland) the provisions of the Landlord and Tenant Act 1954 (part 2) apply to business leases except where the parties have agreed to exclude them. Although exclusions under the Act are becoming increasingly common and have been made easier to achieve through amendments to the Act introduced in June 2004, many lettings of commercial premises come within its remit. The Act applies to premises let to an occupying tenant for the purposes of a business where the tenant remains in occupation. Under the protection afforded by the Act, subject to certain exclusions set out in section 30 to the Act the tenant is entitled to the grant of a new lease for a term of up to 15 years on terms agreed between the parties or, failing agreement, as assessed by the court or by an arbitrator acting on court terms. The PACT scheme (Professional Arbitration on Court Terms) was introduced in the later 1990s in an attempt to take pressure off the courts, but it is seldom used.

The basis on which rent is to be assessed under the provisions of the 1954 Act are set out in section 34, and although they are similar to the terms of market rent as defined by IVSC there are very significant differences. Under the Act the rent is to be:

> that at which the property might reasonably be expected to be let in the open market by a willing lessor, there being disregarded:
> (a) any effect on rent of the fact that the tenant has or his predecessors in title have been in occupation of the holding;
> (b) any goodwill attached to the holding by reason of the carrying on thereat of the business of the tenant (whether by him or by a predecessor of his in that business);
> (c) any effect on rent of an improvement to which this paragraph applies; and
> (d) in the case of a holding comprising licensed premises, any addition to its value attributable to the licence.

The Act then specifies that the improvements to be disregarded are ones that were carried out:

- by a person who at the time it was carried out was the tenant;
- otherwise than in pursuance of an obligation to his immediate landlord;
- *either*
   o it was carried out during the current tenancy; *or*
   o it was completed not more than 21 years before the application to the court was made; *and*
- the holding has at all times remained subject to a business tenancy to which the Act applies.

If these provisions are examined in detail, it can be seen that the rent a tenant will pay on lease renewal may be somewhat different from that which could be commanded had the tenant vacated and a new letting been achieved.

For example, a shop property is let for a period of 20 years and in year 11 the tenant carries out works that increase the rental value by say £50 000. At lease renewal the tenant takes a new lease for say 10 years. In this case the additional value will not fall to be rentalised at any time during the second lease. Further, in the event of another renewal under the Act the improvements will again be disregarded under the application of the 21 year rule.

Another difference in the section 34 rent is that there is no assumption as to a willing lessee. Such a lessee is not assumed as it is self-evidently the reality. It should be noted that the provisions of the 1954 Act have led to a significant number of cases of interpretation, and for this reason rents agreed under the Act or decided by the court may not form the best evidence of market rental value.

4.4   Establishing rental value

The main methods adopted for assessing rental value are with reference to:

- comparable transactions (the comparable method);
- trading potential (the profits or accounts approach); and
- cost.

Of the three methods listed, the preferred method and that which is applicable to all investment property is the comparable method, with reference to transactional data. This is considered in some detail below, but first the other two methods are considered.

4.4.1   Rent by reference to trading potential

The trading potential method has conventionally been used for trading properties, such as hotels and leisure properties which have normally been held in the owner-occupation sector. Accordingly, comparable rents have seldom been available and where a lease has been granted the rent has been established in relation to the trading potential of the property. In recent years institutional investment interest in leisure properties has grown (Sayce, 1998) and more evidence is now available, causing the comparable method to be used more frequently (Sayce, 2000).

The guidance to valuers contained in the RICS *Appraisal and Valuation Standards* states that trade-related appraisals will normally be undertaken for properties such as hotels, bars, restaurants and cinemas (RICS, 2003: GN1). In such cases the value is to be assessed in relation to fair maintainable trade. (For a fuller explanation of these techniques see, for example, Marshall and Williamson, 1996.) However, due to the rise in the number of lettings an appraisal with reference to direct evidence of similar transactions should always be undertaken wherever practicable.

A variant of the rent in relation to trading potential is the turnover lease. Widely used in the US for retail premises, turnover leases have not been widely used in the UK although they have had their advocates among shopping centre investors (see, for example, McAllister, 1996) and there is some evidence that their use is becoming more widespread (Edwards and Ellison, 2003).

Turnover rents in practice tend normally to combine a base rent, which may be around 85% of the estimated rental value, plus a turnover rent expressed as a percentage of the verified turnover. It is the base rent that is subject to periodic rent reviews. Leases with turnover provisions usually also contain a provision that enables the landlord to exercise a notice to determine the lease if the tenant's trading performance as measured by turnover is disappointingly low. The turnover percentage will vary according to the type of occupier and the occupier's gross sales margin. In shopping centres, anchor tenants may be subject to beneficial turnover percentages to reflect their importance to the well-being of the shopping centre as a whole.

4.4.2   Rent by reference to cost

Within the UK context valuations in relation to cost are normally only undertaken where the property is of a type, location or use that means that it will not normally be sold other than as part of the sale of a business or enterprise. Accordingly, cost-based rental valuations are seldom undertaken for anything other than management accounting purposes; even here they tend to be prepared only within the public sector using the methodology advised by CIPFA (Chartered Institute of Public Finance and Accounting).

Practice in other countries is not always the same, however. Adair *et al.* (1996) conclude that cost-based market valuations are a hallmark of markets in transition from control economies to market economies, and in the US cost approaches may be used to support evidence-based figures (Gelbtuch *et al.*, 1997).

4.5   The principle of rental value established through comparison

Underlying the practice of establishing the rental value of commercial property will normally be the principle of comparison. Put simply, the appraiser, in adjudging whether the rent that is actually passing in a given investment property is 'full' or not, will seek to compare the attributes of the property and the terms under which it is let with details of other property transactions that have taken place. In making this comparison, a number of issues must be addressed:

- size and configuration;
- quality and type of accommodation;
- condition;
- location;
- covenants of the lease.

Baum and Crosby (1995) make the case that the quantity and quality of comparable transactions is key to all comparable valuation and that 'when comparables cannot be applied directly, all adaptations are intuitive'. Scarrett (1996) suggests that the 'information available will be no more than indicative'. In practice, therefore, it will be down to the landlord's and the tenant's professional advisers to assess the available information and the impact of the lease terms on the figures and arrive at a mutually acceptable rental value, or to seek an independent determination via an arbitrator or independent expert.

4.6   Challenges in assessing with reference to comparison

Even when the market is active, the heterogeneity of property means that the perfect comparable will never be realised. Accordingly, the skill of the appraiser lies in making justifiable adjustments to reflect the quality of both the evidence and the characteristics of the property.

4.6.1   The nature of comparability

The key concept in establishing comparability relates to evidence. As stated above, this is often a probem. Given that property is heterogeneous and that leases are normally individually negotiated, the quality of the evidence is all-important. Evidence must be:

- recent;
- relevant;
- accurate, reflecting the full position; and
- capable of analysis.

Given that all property is more or less heterogeneous, it follows that no evidence will be an exact match for the property to be valued. Having accepted this, the criteria discussed below are usually used in practice to assess the limits of comparability.

Location is assessed in terms of both physical proximity and the quality of the location. For retail premises location is a key factor, with some traders having a requirement to locate close to other traders of a complementary nature. In some instances the requirement is to be close to competing brands; for example, retailers of comparison goods, such as ladies fashion shops, jewellers and shoe retailers, prefer to locate close to competitors. For other retailers, the presence of similar traders close by is less important.

Within retailing it is not just the proximity factor that is important but also the level of visibility of the location, so measures such as pedestrian footfall are important in assessing whether a location is to be regarded as prime, secondary or tertiary. With the growth of eating out and drinking out, many towns and cities have developed 'leisure quarters' in which bars and restaurants have clustered together. For such businesses the quality of location may depend less on immediate visibility, so the differentiation in rental value from the high street to a side street may be less than for fashion goods retailers.

Other users, such as offices, may be less location-dependent, and comparability of location may depend upon the proximity to transport nodal points such as public car parks, railway links, etc.

4.6.2   Sources of evidence

Within the UK there is no central register of property rental transactions that the appraiser can access in order to obtain details of comparable transactions. Accordingly, the search for evidence on which to base an opinion of value may be an exercise in detective work! Within the UK, unlike many European countries, the appraiser or valuer may well be operating within the agency market and undertaking lettings. In this case the most reliable source of evidence will be transactions in which the valuer has been personally involved, as this will provide an assurance that the full details are known. There may of course be an issue as to whether client confidentiality will prevent the public use of this information, but it can still be used to help inform views.

Given that the valuer may well not have direct personal knowledge, other sources can be consulted. Today, most large consultant firms will hold databases of transactions with which they have been involved and they will also log other deals of which they are aware. The *Estates Gazette* and its online service EGi (www.egi.co.uk) provides a useful source for valuers and the FOCUS database (www.focusnet.com) is an extensive listing of published information. The Land Registry holds details of all property transactions with a lease length of six years or longer (www.landreg.gov.uk).

Other sources of evidence may include lease renewals and rent review settlements, arbitration awards, and sale and leaseback transactions. Such information has to be treated with some caution as other factors may distort the evidence. However, in markets where there have been few new lettings this information may be the best available.

4.6.3   The hierarchy of evidence

It is clear from the analysis above that not all sources of evidence will be equally valid when forming an estimate of rental value. Yet it is important that it is all assessed appropriately so that the valuer can have as much confidence as possible in the figures that will be adopted for the appraisal. The common practice is to adopt what is termed the 'hierarchy of evidence' in order to place appropriate weighting on the information gathered.

Under this convention, the best evidence will always be that which relates to open market lettings between unconnected parties. After this, the next best evidence is that achieved by negotiation at lease renewal and, after that, rent review. Lease renewal evidence is generally regarded as more reliable than rent review as the tenant, though not necessarily the landlord, has the ability to walk away from the deal. However, unlike a new letting, a tenant who is renewing a lease will normally have an established business and the costs of moving, should the renewal not proceed, could skew the rental bid they are prepared to make (see, for example, McAllister, 2001). With rent reviews, even though the term may be agreed by negotiation, neither party can walk away from the deal so again the evidence may be skewed. Within England and Wales, unless the landlord has granted a 'contracted out' tenancy, the tenant will have the right to take a new lease at a market rent unless the landlord can prove one of a limited number of grounds set out in section 30 of the Landlord and Tenant Act 1954.

Of lower reliability are rents settled by a third party. In these cases additional factors have to be taken into account: first, who makes the decision; and second, on what basis? In the case of a court decision on lease renewal, the ultimate decision may be taken by a judge who, whilst an expert in law, is not necessarily well versed in valuation matters. For a rent settled by arbitration, the arbitrator is obliged, under the terms of the Arbitration Act, to decide on the evidence produced by the parties, although recent cases (*Warborough Investments Ltd* v. *S. Robinson & Sons (Holdings) Ltd* (2003) and *Checkpoint Ltd* v. *Strathclyde Pension Fund* (2003)) have upheld the ability of the arbitrator to use his or her own expertise in valuation matters in certain circumstances. Nonetheless, the rent awarded is likely to be significantly influenced by the strength of the representations made by the parties to the dispute. For this reason, arbitration awards are not regarded as good-quality evidence. This view is supported by the case of *Land Securities* v. *Westminster City Council* (1993) in which evidence from a rent review arbitration award was refused as admissible evidence in another arbitration hearing. Whilst the passing of the Civil Evidence Act 1995, which provided that any evidence is admissible, would prevent such a situation happening again, it is likely that similar evidence would be given a very low weight.

Rental evidence from an award by a third party acting as an independent expert can be regarded as potentially more reliable as the expert can and will rely on his or her own judgement. However, such awards may be idiosyncratic and do not necessarily represent market opinion. They are therefore not good-quality evidence as to prevailing market rental value.

The least reliable evidence is that from sale and leaseback transactions as these may not be at 'arm's length' and are frequently part of a portfolio restructuring deal in which the rent is set to facilitate a larger corporate financing deal. Where evidence that relates to finance leases is available, it should be remembered that the rent payable under such leases bears no relation to market rental levels.

4.6.4   Assessing rental value in a thin or distorted market

As indicated above, the quality of evidence may be insufficient to achieve good comparability due to the heterogeneous nature of property. However, the quantity of evidence also becomes an issue when the marketplace is 'thin' and there are few transactions. This normally coincides with a period when deals, if they are concluded, show falling values. In such circumstances, conditions of uncertainty are deemed to exist. This should be reported to the client, but simply reporting does not solve the problem of what rent should be agreed.

When the marketplace is thin, the appraiser will have to use evidence that is either older, less comparable in nature (for example, the comparable property differs significantly from the property to be valued) or in a different location. Adjustments are then normally taken on an intuitive basis. Where evidence is completely missing, the valuer may have to make a subjective assessment based on, for example, alternate use. Alternatively, the valuer may resort to a cost-based approach. Within the commercial property markets in the UK there is an extreme reluctance to adopt a cost approach, though in the US and parts of Europe it is more common.

4.6.5   Zoning: a crude measure of comparison

It is a convention that when assessing the rental value of shop units the rent is expressed in terms of zone 'A' equivalent (ITZA). For large retail stores and retail warehouses, a rent on a per square metre basis is applied.

Historically, the zoning units were 20 feet for shops, except those in the prime locations of the West End of London, such as Oxford Street and Regent Street, where 30-foot zones were used. Post metrication, some professionals still work in imperial units whilst others work in metric figures. It is therefore important to determine the exact zoning figure used in calculating the ITZA figure.

The concept of zoning is straightforward, as shown in Fig. 4.2. In zone A the rents are x per square metre or foot, in zone B they are x/2, zone C x/4 and zone D x/8. The remainder of the space and the basement and upper-floor retail accommodation is normally put in at a

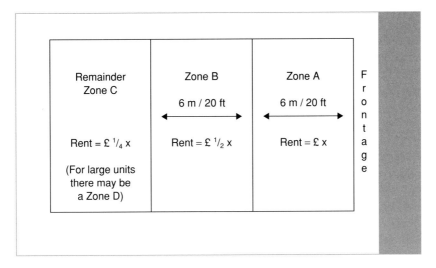

Fig. 4.2 Zoning retail units.

per square metre or square foot basis. One complication is where there is a return frontage. In this case it will be down to the experience of the valuer to determine the appropriate zoning of the space with the return frontage.

4.6.6   Retail floor areas

Retail units are normally let on a 'shell' finish basis. The rentalisable floor area will therefore include all the accommodation in the demise; for example, outside the front door/ window and staff toilets will be included in the lettable floor area on which the ITZA rent is calculated. In contrast, offices floor areas are calculated for rental purposes on net lettable space, and industrials may be on a net internal or gross external basis according to their general location. The measurement codes are periodically updated by the RICS, and can be found on their web site (www.rics.org).

4.6.7   Alternative approaches to establishing rental value

In section 4.3.2 consideration was given to the shortening of the lease length and in section 4.10 we consider the typical terms to be found in Continental European leases, where the indexation of rents is common.

In reality, the rent negotiation between landlord and tenant is subject to the relative negotiating strength of the parties, the state of the market and their relative demands and desires. Landlord and tenant legislation in the UK provides the parties with significant flexibility in setting out the terms of the rent review. In addition to market rents, indexation or a percentage of the index increase, turnover rents and fixed rental increases may be inserted into the lease.

In the public sector, where properties may be specialist (for example, doctors' surgeries), rent reviews may be written such that they are to the higher of the market rental value or say a 2% per annum increase. The market rental value may be with reference to a neighbouring town, or to a particular class of property. Such a situation is not restricted to the public sector. When retail warehouses were first developed in the mid to late 1980s, it was common for their rent reviews to be to the higher of market rent as a retail warehouse or 125% of prevailing industrial rents in the locality. Similarly, many cinemas also contain 'fall-back' use provisions and indexed increases.

The flexibility the parties have to write in a variety of rent review arrangements produces a number of non-standard rent review provisions. Where the provisions are particularly onerous on the tenant – that is, where the rent they are paying, and will continue to pay after subsequent rent reviews, is significantly greater than that evidenced in the open market – the valuer will have to have due regard to the tenant's financial covenant and the unexpired lease term when valuing the property.

4.7   Non-standard leases

For approximately 30 years the UK commercial property market was dominated by the so-called institutional lease of 20–25 years with rent reviews at standard five-yearly intervals. This comparative homogeneity in the marketplace meant that appraisers had the ability to compare like with like. However, the pattern of homogeneity has increasingly broken down and commercial leases are now shorter and more variable in terms of covenant, hence the ability to compare has been reduced. The reasons behind this and the consequences for assessing rental value are now considered.

4.7.1   The decline of the institutional lease and the move to flexible leases

The institutional lease has changed over the years. Prior to 1995 the lease length was 20–25 years with five-yearly upward only rent reviews for many types of commercial property. Although this gave security of income, it presented some difficulties for land-lords who needed to refurbish more frequently, say every 15 years for a shopping centre. Overseas investors were attracted not only by the assurance of a rising income but also because if the tenant defaulted it was possible to pick and choose any previous tenant and sue the one with the best covenant under the privity of contract clause (Hall, 2003:2).

In the early 1990s, during the economic downturn when occupiers struggled to meet their costs, retailers pressurised the government to promote flexibility in the property market. The government preferred to encourage a voluntary industry code of practice rather than legislate and in December 1995 the first Code of Practice for Commercial Leases was published. The government agreed, however, to monitor the effectiveness of the Code.

Leases granted prior to January 1996 included a provision that the original tenant was liable during the whole of the lease even if it had been assigned several times (privity of contract) but the Landlord and Tenant (Covenants) Act 1995 ended this situation on leases granted after 1 January 1996. After the Act, the landlord inserted an express provision requiring the tenant to sign an authorised guarantee agreement (AGA) guaranteeing the performance of the assignee (Vivian, 2002:36). The landlord could impose further conditions restricting the tenant's ability to assign, such as a profit test which was subjective.

In 1998 research carried out by Reading University and commissioned by the RICS (RICS, 1998), showed that 40% of occupiers still found UK leases unsatisfactory, and pointed to lease lengths, break clauses, rent reviews, repairs and insurance as areas of particular concern. Landlords and investors argued that reducing lease lengths, offering break options to tenants without compensation to the landlord and abolishing upward only rent reviews would remove certainty of income and devalue their property investment. (Cockram, 2001:39).

However, the research findings showed that the average lease length had become shorter, reducing from 24 years in 1990 to 12 years by 1995 (Crosby *et al.*, 2005) but the use of break clauses and rent free periods were a function of a weak lettings market. The British Property Forum reported at the 5th Annual Lease Review 2002 that the average lease length for offices was less than 13 years, for retail 16 years and for industrial property 13.4 years (Creasey, 2002) but that tenants were opting for the old-fashioned structure which was cheaper. The voluntary Lease Code of 1995 was deemed to have failed because not enough had been achieved in terms of creating a flexible property market: increases in flexibility were the result of market forces, not the code.

In April 2002 the second edition of the *Code of Practice for Commercial Leases in England and Wales* was launched, recommending good practice in landlord and tenant negotiation over leases offering flexible terms including lease length, break clauses and up and down rent reviews (RICS, 2002). It recommends that landlords should offer prospective tenants a choice of lease terms, with a range of appropriate rents and including break clauses. To operate a break clause the tenant must comply with any condition that materially affects any obligation such as payment of rent and to carry out all repairs, however minor. In *Osbourne Assets* v. *Britannia Life* (1997) a tenant lost his right to break as he had redecorated using two coats of paint instead of three as required by the lease (Vivian and White, 2003). The average first break clause in commercial leases has reduced from 11.3 years in 1992 to 4.6 years in 2002, while only 10% of retail leases have break clauses (Creasey, 2002).

The new Code recommends that landlords should offer price-adjusted alternatives to upward only rent reviews and funders should not insist on upward only rent reviews. The higher risk of up/downward rent reviews would be reflected in a higher initial rent. To prevent legislation being passed to force this issue, the profession need to show that tenants select their preference from a range of options to illustrate the impact of the Code.

The government consultation paper released in July 2004 offers five possible options for replacing the upward only rent review:

- an upward only review ban;
- a ban conceding that rents do not fall below the initial rent;
- an automatic break clause if the rent ought to decrease under market conditions but does not due to the upward only system;
- strict rules on a priced menu of different lease terms; and
- encouraging or forcing tenants to take leases of less than five years, so making rent reviews obsolete.

If a ban is introduced on new leases, some practitioners believe fixed or index-linked rent rises will be introduced. CB Richard Ellis estimate that such leases comprise 5% of the London office market and are growing in popularity (Jansen, 2004).

The new Code also recommends that tenants' repairing covenants should reflect the length of term and condition of the property. The Code recommends that alienation should not be over-restrictive, and landlords are recommended to seek guarantee agreements to bind subsequent tenants only where the financial standing of the assignee is lower than the outgoing tenant as at the date of assignment. Further, the code requires that this must be justified through the retention of agents' correspondence and records of negotiation, otherwise the only restriction is requiring the landlord's consent (Dowden, 2004).

Whilst the Code is voluntary, the government has been monitoring its application. If this is judged to be unsatisfactory, the government will consider legislation despite the objections of many in the property industry (IPF, 2004).

In practice, landlords have to date succeeded in maintaining upward only rent reviews but at the expense of shorter leases. There is a new generation of landlords (for example, British Land plc) who actively manage their buildings and treat their tenants as customers. Inclusive rents and short-term tenancies can give landlords more control and an immediate cash flow with benefits for enhancement. Flexible accommodation and flexible leases allow businesses to expand and contract and should ideally provide a sustainable cash flow. Shorter leases may not hinder long-term loan facilities provided the characteristics of property, tenant quality and management are sound. Single-let trophy buildings or warehouses may be let for a 15 year lease term while five year leases with different expiry dates are appropriate for multi-let offices.

The effect of the greater flexibility and diversity that is now working its way through to the property markets will have great implications for valuers seeking to rely on the comparable method of valuation, as true comparables may simply not exist.

4.8   Establishing rental value where headline rents are used

The rent terminology detailed above can produce confusion amongst non-property professionals. The starting point from a rent analysis point of view is the rent passing, which is the rent that the tenant is paying under the terms of the lease. The issue is: what is the true position in terms of the rental value when the tenant pays a rent that is higher than that prevailing in the market? Such rents are known as 'headline' or 'face' rents.

Investors will often gain a financial advantage by keeping their rents as high as possible. The high rent passing will be beneficial in terms of their bank lending ratios if debt has been used to help finance the property purchase and, in the case of long leases and an occupier of excellent financial standing, will assist in keeping up the valuation of the asset.

For a tenant to pay a rent in excess of the open market, some benefit will need to have been offered. Such benefits are set out in sections 4.8.3 to 4.8.9. The value of the benefit to the tenant can be calculated in financial terms, and the headline rent can then be adjusted to provide an effective rental value.

Before reading the finance sections below, readers are advised to ensure they have grasped the DCF techniques set out in Chapters 3, 5 and 6 and are familiar with the risk terminology introduced in Chapter 8.

4.8.1 Traditional methodology

The traditional methodology for such calculations has been a net present value model, which equates the cost to the tenant of the cash flows predicated under the terms of the lease with those of a lease let on normal market terms. The effective rent is adjusted to the point where the NPVs of the two sets of cash flows are equal. The two key variables in this calculation are the rental growth and the discount rate.

The second approach is a 'finance-driven' approach, which uses a net present value model but also takes due consideration of the different risk profiles of the cash flows. Referring to Fig. 4.1 and the position relating to Mid-Town London rents, the average rental growth for the period 1980 to 2004 is seen to be 2.2% per annum. In the traditional DCF model a current estimate of rental growth with due regard to this growth figure would be incorporated into the model. However the *average* rental growth figure does not carry any information in it relating to the volatility characteristics of the market.

Consider the position of tenant A who takes a new 15 year lease granted in 1985 with five-yearly rent reviews and an upwards only rent review (UORR) clause. The first rent review would have coincided with the top of the market and the second would have been waived due to the adverse nature of the market. From 1985 to 1990 rents more than doubled.

Now consider a lease granted to tenant B in 1987, on similar terms. At the first rent review in 1992 the top of the market would have been missed, and at the second review in 1997 little change in the rent would have occurred.

The net effect of this is that the total rent payable over the lease period is a lottery for both the landlord and the tenant and depends on wider movements in the property market, and indeed the wider economy.

4.8.2 Incorporating the pricing of risk transfer

The changes in the market place have provided a spur to new finance-driven approaches which incorporate the concept of risk transfer. In volatile rental markets tenants will pay for flexibility as it could save them from unanticipated shocks, as was the case with tenant A above.

The principle of a risk transfer model approach is that, in a volatile and unpredictable marketplace, break options provide tenants with a financial get-out when the market is very buoyant and they wish to avoid paying a significantly increased rent, opting instead to re-locate to a cheaper location.

The two main models used under the finance approach are:

- *Real option pricing models* which draw on the then groundbreaking (and almost not passed for publication by the editorial board) paper by Black and Scholes (1973). The mathematics behind the Black and Scholes model is relatively challenging and the minutiae make their application to property more difficult. For example, the model assumes no income payouts, and that the underlying prices follow a geometric Brownian motion with constant volatility. Those interested in the mathematics and theory behind option pricing might like to refer to books on the subject, such as Focardi and Fabozzi (2004), or van Deventer *et al.* (2004).

- The second model is a *discounted cash flow simulation model* with probability distributions assigned to each of the key variables. This model is simpler in mathematical terms and is therefore likely to be used in preference to real option pricing models. Gemmill *et al.* (1998) contrasted the use of real option pricing against DCF simulation, and found the results of the two methods to be broadly similar.

Gemmill *et al.* (1998) and McAllister (2000) address the issues relating to the application of such models. In practice these models have at the centre the traditional DCF model which matches the net present cost of the net cash flows of the headline payments with those of the effective payments.

In particular it is the simulation of the rental growth figure with due regard to a standard deviation or a triangular distribution that is important (see Chapter 8 for more on this topic). For the example set out in Fig. 4.1, the standard deviation of the estimated rental value for the period 1980 to 2004 was 16.0%. So on the basis of an average rental growth rate of 2.2% per annum and on the basis of a 95% confidence limit (representing plus or minus 2 standard deviations), a range of rental growth for between −28.8% p.a. and 35.2% p.a. is generated.

The scene has been set in terms of the methodologies that can be utilised to enable the calculations that identify the difference between headline and effective rents for different lease and other linked contractual agreements to take place. The main inducements that a tenant might receive are set out in sections 4.8.3 to 4.8.9.

The mathematics and discounted cash flow calculations behind each of these are available via spreadsheet downloads from the web site, details of which are given in Appendix B. When downloading, please refer to the boxes giving details of the spreadsheet name. It should be noted that if the reader wishes to undertake the simulation calculations then an Excel Add-In will be required. Suggestions for these are set out on the spreadsheets in question.

For each of these examples it is possible to use either the traditional or the 'finance-based' DCF simulation approach. The latter can produce significantly different figures, which are often sensitive to the input figures.

4.8.3   Adjusting for rent free periods

The first cash flow to be constructed is that for the actual lease which incorporates the rent free period in question. The rent is inserted into the cash flow on the basis that it is payable, and the rent review dates are identified. The length of the cash flow is normally to the lease term or the first break option date, whichever is the shorter. (If there is a break date the costs of exercising the break need to be incorporated. If they are penal then a second calculation for the full length of the lease should be calculated.) Incorporating a rental growth rate and an appropriate discount rate for the tenant, the net present cost of the rent cash flows is calculated. A second cash flow for a similar length of time is constructed. At the start of the cash flows a normal rent free period is incorporated to reflect that which an incoming tenant might expect in normal market conditions. (For offices this is often taken as between three and six months.) Any rent is then inserted into the cash flows at the first rent receipt date, and the rent is then adjusted at the rent review dates in line with the stated rental growth figure. From this a net present cost figure (NPC) is produced.

Using Excel's Goal Seek function or DCF Analyst's Calculate Again function (www.i-analysis.com), the NPC of the second cash flow is set to equal the NPC of the first cash flow by altering the initial rent payable for the effective rent cash flows. The spreadsheet calculates by iteration the required effective rent and this can then be compared with the passing headline rent.

> Please see Spreadsheet 2 for a working example of a traditional discounted cash flow calculation and a DCF simulation, which show how to calculate the percentage difference between the headline and effective rent adjusting for different rent review patterns.

4.8.4   Adjusting for capital inducements and reverse premiums

A capital inducement is payable by the landlord normally to assist the tenant with fitting out costs. In some instances it is simply an inducement to get the tenant into the property and to pay a higher rent than might otherwise be the case.

A reverse premium is often payable when a tenant assigns a lease to another tenant where, for example, the passing rent under the lease is greater than the open market effective rent.

The discounted cash flow calculations incorporate the capital inducement and the effective rent is calculated following steps similar to those set out in section 4.8.3 above.

The tax position in respect of the payment received should be considered. Rents are a tax deductible expense whereas capital inducements can attract a tax charge, and consideration should be given to this.

> Please see Spreadsheet 3 for a working example of a traditional discounted cash flow calculation and a DCF simulation, which shows how a capital inducement or reverse premium may be incorporated into an appraisal.

4.8.5   Adjusting for lease take backs

A lease take back is where the landlord takes on board the liability of the accommodation costs of the property from which the prospective tenant is moving. The total occupation costs of the property from which the tenant is moving should be calculated for the period for which the tenant has a contractual obligation. The net present cost is calculated and the figure can then be treated as if it were a capital inducement as in section 4.8.4 above.

The rental growth figures for the building from which the tenant is moving may be different from those for the building into which they are moving.

> Please see Spreadsheet 4 for a working example of a traditional discounted cash flow calculation and a DCF simulation, which show how to calculate the percentage difference between the headline and effective rent adjusting for lease take backs.

4.8.6   Stepped rents

A stepped rent occurs when a tenant agrees a lease with a rent that goes up in pre-agreed 'steps', which may or may not result in the tenant paying above a market rent at review.

In the case of stepped rents the tenant is contractually bound to pay fixed and not open market rental increases. The cost or benefit to the tenant can be calculated, using a model similar to that used in the above examples. The key will be whether the fixed increases are perceived to be higher or lower than those forecast for the market.

> Please see Spreadsheet 5 for a working example of a traditional discounted cash flow calculation and a DCF simulation, which show how to calculate the percentage difference between the headline and effective rent adjusting for stepped rents.

4.8.7   Adjusting for profit share on sale

In many lease renewals the landlord will recognise that the building is worth more with the tenant renewing their lease rather than vacating. The landlord's strategy may be to renew the lease and then sell the property. In such cases there may be a side agreement whereby the tenant on renewing the lease is granted a percentage of the profit on the subsequent sale of the property, or a percentage of the sale proceeds.

The prospective figure receivable by the tenant is contingent on a sale, and therefore is not certain. However, with advice from a valuer and an investment surveyor, a relatively certain sale figure may be estimated, together with the time it might take to complete the transaction. A percentage of the potential net proceeds may be incorporated into the cash flows to determine the effect this would have on the difference between the effective and headline rents.

The potential figures involved can be significant, and the tax position of the sum receivable on a sale should also be considered. The DCF simulation approach is better suited to dealing with the probabilistic nature of the profit share and the amount potentially receivable.

> Please see Spreadsheet 6 for a working example of a traditional discounted cash flow calculation and a DCF simulation, which show how to calculate the percentage difference between the headline and effective rent adjusting for the profit share on sale.

4.8.8   Adjusting for different rent review patterns

The traditional method, and the one that is commonly used, equates the net present costs of the cash flows with the different rent review patterns. In these calculations the rental growth figure and discount rate are the key variables. The starting point usually is to take a standard lease term for the type of building in that location.

However, different rent review patterns will pick up different sections of the rental cycle. On this basis, the traditional method does not address the risk transfer differences between short and long rent review patterns. Whether or not the rent reviews are subject to upward only rent reviews is a significant point. Upward only rent reviews lock in rental uplifts and thus make the shorter rent review patterns potentially more onerous for the tenant. Accordingly, the DCF simulation approach can produce different figures from the traditional approach.

Please see Spreadsheet 7 for a working example of a traditional discounted cash flow calculation and a DCF simulation, which show how to calculate the percentage difference between the headline and effective rent adjusting for different rent review patterns.

Table 4.4 The exercise of lease break clauses in 2003.

Percent of leases*	Over-rented	Reversionary and rack-rented
Break not exercised	67	78
Break exercised	33	22
Re-let	7	14
Vacant at year-end	25	8

* Results are weighted according to ERV of lease at end 2002.
Source: Strutt & Parker/IPD (2004).

4.8.9 Pricing break clauses

The trend towards shorter leases has been assisted by the increasing incorporation of break clauses into leases. However, of key interest when considering break clauses is what percentage of tenants, in terms of rents receivable, exercise their break option.

- Is the property as at the break date over- or under- or rack-rented? If it is under-rented, the exercise of the break may offer an active management opportunity to add value by reletting the property at an increased rent. In this context Strutt & Parker/IPD's annual report (Strutt & Parker IPD, 2004) provides interesting figures relating to the percentages of breaks exercised during 2003 (Table 4.4).

   For properties let at below market rent, just over three-quarters of the tenants did not exercise their break option but for over-rented properties the figure was two-thirds. Break options provide the tenant with flexibility, and in normal market conditions a relatively small proportion of breaks are exercised. However, in severe recessions they will be of great value to the tenant as they give the ability either to quit the property or to renegotiate lease terms.
- What period of notice is the tenant required to give? The longer this is, the more opportunity the landlord has to find a suitable alternative tenant.
- What is the cost to the tenant of exercising the break? In many instances the tenant will pay between six months' and one year's rent for exercising the break option. This provides the landlord with cash flows in advance. If the property can be relet at a similar or higher rent and becomes income-producing during this period, the landlord gains financially.

Please see Spreadsheet 8 for a working example of DCF simulation, which shows how to calculate the percentage difference between the headline and effective rent adjusting for break clauses.

4.9 The comparative approach: a reservation

As has been set out above in some detail, rental value is normally established as an evidence-based exercise, having regard to other deals struck in the vicinity and in the recent past. Only where such an approach is not tenable due to lack of evidence is any other method (trading accounts or cost) advocated. Seldom is the market comparison approach questioned; yet such an evidence-based approach does have some deep flaws.

The criticisms that can be levelled again the comparable evidence approach relate to the backward looking nature of the method, the lack of true comparability within the market-place and its disconnection with the ability to pay.

4.9.1   A backward analysis

Of necessity, rental evidence is outdated: sometimes the length of the deals and the thin nature of the market means that an appraiser will be using transactional data that is a year or more out of date. Yet what is being sought is a rent on the basis of assumed *future* occupation. Hence the influences that may affect a market into the future are often dis-counted even if they are considered, and the rent is agreed by reference to yesterday's occupier agenda – not tomorrow's.

In a stable market that may not be regarded as too serious an issue, but in a situation of rapid change it is a serious flaw. For example, work recently undertaken in relation to sustainability criteria for commercial property (Sayce and Ellison, 2000a,b) points to a developing agenda of issues that should be included in the calculations from the tenant and landlord perspective. These include sharply rising energy costs and the need to insure against pollutant incident risks which will significantly affect the occupational costs of buildings and should impact on rents. However, there is currently no evidence that such matters are having any influence on rental value (Pett *et al.*, 2004). As long as this con-tinues to be the case, and rental negotiations concentrate on the past instead of the future, investors will be at risk of misconceived rental flows.

4.9.2   A mis-match with the ability to pay

As argued at the beginning of this chapter, the concept of rent has been refined in economic terms from something directly related to the surplus arising from production to an amount determined by the laws of supply and demand. However, the principle of the market pric-ing mechanism is that if the ability to pay is reduced, demand will fall and so will price. In theory there should be a clearly recognisable follow-through. If there is not, and the rent is more than the tenant can justify on economic grounds, there is a potential for default, with all the attendant costs to the investing owner. It is therefore important for a landlord to be aware of the tenant's level of ability to pay, in order to judge whether or not there is a likelihood of default.

In the case of office and industrial property, the ability to pay may be difficult to estimate as there is a large body of evidence to suggest that in the past corporate occupiers have looked on rent very much as a fixed business cost without due consideration of either the property's strategic importance to the company or its ability to contribute to performance (see, for example, Bootle and Kalyan, 2002). However, as Edwards and Ellison (2003) argue, the situation is changing fast and the advent of benchmarking and performance measurement, facilitated by increasing data flows from organisations such as OPD (Occupiers Property Databank), is enabling corporate tenants to gain a much clearer indication as to what would be a reasonable cost to bear in the way of rent for any particular buildings.

Increasingly, occupiers now want to ensure that their assets are working for them and are not a drain on their balance sheets (Nelson Bakewell and OPD, 2004). As tenants become better informed and as leases become shorter and more diverse in their terms, so the occupier's ability to measure performance is likely to become more influential in determining rents. It looks likely that in the future tenants will have an increasing ability to make their rental bids not just with reference to the market but with a confident reference to their projections of ability to pay.

Whilst the relationship between rent and occupational costs attributable to an individual property and the value of that property to the business may not yet be very transparent for offices and industrial property, this is not the case with retail and leisure properties. For these the relationship is much easier to establish.

4.10   Continental European leases – an overview of the differences

The nature of Continental European property is outside the scope of this book. However, in the case of lease agreements, a concise summary of the differences between lease terms in the UK and Continental Europe has merit. This is because in Continental Europe lease lengths tend to be much shorter, and have a range of terms different from those found in the UK.

The trend for UK leases is that they are becoming shorter (Crosby *et al.*, 2005), and it should be of interest to see what the differences are for countries with shorter leases. The usual French or Belgian office property lease is for a nine year term with three-yearly break clauses. In the Netherlands, Germany and Spain five and ten year leases are common. In Sweden three and five year leases predominate. Further afield, US leases are often for five or ten year periods. With these shorter lease lengths and the frequency of break clauses, the key differences in the 'heads of terms' shown in Table 4.5 should be considered in relation to UK leases.

Table 4.5   Broad comparison of lease terms.

Continental European leases	UK leases
Internal repairing obligations	Full repairing obligations
Non-recoverables may include non-repair related items	Non-recoverables are infrequent in institutional-style leases
Indexation of rents	Five-yearly rent reviews
Break clauses common for leases of over five years	Break clauses becoming more common in leases of over 15 years
Tenant's right to renew at lease expiry very common; however, the new rent is not always the open market rent and may be the prevailing rent plus a continuing link to inflation	Tenants have right to a new lease, but the new rent will have due regard to the existing lease terms and the open market rental values

In Chapters 1 and 2 there was a discussion about the impact shorter leases will have on valuation methods. In Continental Europe shorter leases give rise to higher levels of void risk; indexation to some extent removes the short- to medium-term link to prevailing open market rental levels, and internal repairing obligations pass structural plus plant and machinery risks across to the landlord. The implicit cash flows from a valuation perspective are considerably harder to pin down. It is perhaps not surprising that the initial yield method of valuations is a favoured approach across much of Continental Europe, and that alongside the initial yield approach DCF is used as a valuation method.

4.11   Summary

When undertaking a property valuation or a discounted cash flow appraisal the calculation and estimation of the effective rent is of key importance. The effective rent is the open market rent and has had due regard to any inducements that the tenant may have received.

For valuations, the net effective rent is used to consider whether the property is over-, rack- or under-rented, and this is reflected in the valuation methodology used, in particular in the context of the reversion.

In DCF analysis it is the effective rent to which the rental growth rate is applied, and not the headline or passing rent.

For both valuations and appraisals, the correct determination of the effective rental value is a key skill of a property adviser, whether they be advising the owner or an occupier.

References

Adair, A.S., McGreal, W.S. and O'Roarty, B.A. (1996) The rental assessment of retail property in the United Kingdom. In: *Megatrends in Retail Real Estate: Research Issues in Real Estate,* Vol. 3 (ed. J.D. Benjamin). Boston: Kluwer Academic Publishers.

Adams, A., Booth, P. and Venmore-Rowland, P. (1993a) An actuarial approach to property valuations. *Proceedings of the RICS Cutting Edge Research Conference 1993.*

Adams, A., Booth, P. and Venmore-Rowland, P. (1993b) *An Actuarial Approach to Property Valuation.* Working Paper 93.2. Edinburgh: Centre for Financial Markets, University of Edinburgh.

Adams, A., Booth, P. and Venmore-Rowland, P. (1993c) Theoretical volatility measures for freehold property investments. *Journal of Property Research*, 10 (3): 153–66.

Balchin, P., Kieve, J. and Bull, G. (1988) *Urban Land Economics and Public Policy.* Basingstoke: Macmillan.

Ball, M., Lizieri, C. and MacGregor, B.D. (1998) *The Economics of Commercial Property Markets.* London: Routledge.

Baum, A. and Crosby, N. (1995) *Property Investment Appraisal*, 2nd edn. London: Routledge.

Black, F. and Scholes, M. (1973) The pricing of options and corporate liabilities. *Journal of Political Economy*, 81 (3): 637–54.

Bootle, R. and Kalyon, S. (2002) *Property in Business: A Waste of Space?* London: RICS.

Cockram, A. (2001) On very bad terms. *Estates Gazette*, 14/04/2001: 39–41.

Creasey, S. (2002) BPF: leases are shorter but must be flexible. *Property Week*, 11/02.

Crosby, N., Hughes, C. and Murdoch, S. (2005) *Monitoring the 2002 Code of Practice for Commercial Leases.* London: ODPM.

Dowden, C. (2004) Legal briefing code of practice for commercial leases – proving compliance. *Journal of Property Investment & Finance*, 22 (3).

Dubben, N. and Sayce, S. (1991) *Property Portfolio Management: An Introduction*. London: Routledge.

Eccles, T., Sayce, S. and Smith, J. (1999) *Property and Construction Economics*. London: International Thomson.

Edwards, V. and Ellison, L. (2003) *Corporate Property Management: Aligning Real Estate with Business Strategy*. Oxford: Blackwell Publishing.

Focardi, S. and Fabozzi, F. (2004) *The Mathematics of Financial Modelling and Investment Management*. London: Wiley.

Fraser, W.D. (1993) *Principles of Property Investment and Pricing*. Basingstoke: Macmillan.

Gelbtuch, H.C., Mackmin, D. and Milgrim, M.R. (eds) (1997) *Real Estate Valuation in Global Markets*. Chicago: Appraisal Institute.

Gemmill, G., Rodney, W., Matysiak, G. and Venmore-Rowland, P. (1998) *Pricing of break clauses*. Research Paper, City University Business School, London.

Hall, S. (2003) *The demise of the institutional lease?* Property Review issued by D J Freeman, 11/03 (36): 1–2.

Investment Property Forum (2004) *Response to the ODPM Paper on Commercial Property Leases: Options for Deterring or Outlawing the Use of UORR Clauses*. London: IPF.

Jansen, M. (2004) Reports of their demise. *Special Report Property Week*, 13.08.04: 62.

Marriott, O. (1969) *The Property Boom*. London: Pan Books.

Marshall, H. and Williamson, H. (1996) *The Law and Valuation of Leisure Property*. London: Estates Gazette.

McAllister, P. (1996) Pricing short leases and break clauses using simulation methodology. *Journal of Property Valuation & Investment*, 14 (2): 6–23.

McAllister, P. (2000) *Pricing short leases and break clauses using simulation methodology*. Research Paper, University of Reading.

McAllister, P. (2001) Turnover rents: comparative valuation issues. *Journal of Property Investment & Finance*, 19 (4): 361–74.

Nelson Bakewell and OPD (2004) *Occupational Flexibility and Corporate Strategy 2003*. London: Nelson Bakewell/OPD.

Office of the Deputy Prime Minister (2004) *Commercial Property Leases: An Interim Report*. London: ODPM.

Pett, J., Guertler, P., Hugh, M., Kaplan, Z. and Smith, W. (2004) *Asset Value Implications of Low Energy Offices*. London: Association for the Conservation of Energy.

Ricardo, D. (1973) *The Principles of Political Economy and Taxation*. London: Dent.

Royal Institution of Chartered Surveyors (1998) *How Are Lease Structures Changing in Commercial Property Markets?* RICS Research Findings, No. 21, May 1998.

Royal Institution of Chartered Surveyors/British Property Federation (2002) *Code of Practice for Commercial Leases in England and Wales*, 2nd edition. London: RICS.

Royal Institution of Chartered Surveyors (2003) *Appraisal and Valuation Standards*. London: RICS.

Sayce, S. (1998) An investigation into leisure property as an institutional investment vehicle. Unpublished PhD thesis, University of Reading.

Sayce, S. (2000) Leisure property. In: *Valuations: Principles into Practice* (eds W. Rees and R. Hayward). London: Estates Gazette.

Sayce, S. and Ellison, L. (2003a) *Towards sustainability indicators for commercial property occupiers and investors*. Eighth Annual International Sustainable Research Conference, Nottingham, 24–25 March.

Sayce, S. and Ellison, L. (2003b) *Integrating sustainability into the appraisal of property worth: identifying appropriate indicators of sustainability.* American Real Estate and Urban Economics Association Conference, RICS Foundation Sustainable Development Session, Skye, Scotland, 21–23 August 2003.

Sayce, S., Walker, A. and McIntosh, A. (2004) *Building Sustainability in the Balance: Promoting Stakeholder Dialogue.* London: Estates Gazette.

Scarrett, D. (1996) *Property Valuation: The Five Methods.* London: E&FN Spon.

Scott, P. (1996) *The Property Masters.* London: E&FN Spon.

Strutt & Parker/IPD (2004) *Lease Events Review Summary.* London: IPD.

van Deventer, D., Imai, K. and Mesler, M. (2004) *Advanced Financial Risk Management.* London: Wiley.

Vivian, J. (2002) Consent shift is a sign of the times. *Property Week*, 13/12: 36.

Vivian, J. and White, G. (2003) Breaking all the rules. *Estates Gazette*, 21/11/02.

Further reading

Benjamin, J.D. (ed) (1996) *Megatrends in Retail Real Estate, Research Issues in Real Estate*, Vol. 3. Boston: Kluwer Academic Publishers.

Enever, N. and Isaac, D. (2002) *The Valuation of Property Investments*, 6th edn. London: Estates Gazette.

Goodchild, R. and Crosby, N. (1992) Problems with over-renting. *Journal of Property Valuation & Investment*, 11 (1): 67–81.

Hendershott, P.H. (1995) Real effective rent determination: evidence from the Sydney office market. *Journal of Property Research*, 12 (1): 127–35.

Hoesli, M. and MacGregor, B.D. (2000) *Property Investment: Principles and Practice of Portfolio Management.* Harlow: Longman.

Isaac, D. and Steley, T. (2000) *Property Valuation Techniques.* Basingstoke: Macmillan.

O'Roarty, B., McGreal, S. and Adair, A. (1997) The impact of retailers' store selection criteria on the estimation of retail rents. *Journal of Property Valuation & Investment*, 15 (2): 119–30.

O'Roarty, B., McGreal, S., Adair, A. and Patterson, D. (1997) Case-based reasoning and retail rent determination. *Journal of Property Research*, 14 (4): 309–28.

Rees, W. and Hayward, R. (eds) (2000) *Valuations: Principles into Practice.* London: Estates Gazette.

Reeves, D. (1985) Valuing large stores at rent review. *Rent & Lease Renewal*, 5 (1): 5–15.

Teale, M. (1995) Reviewing retail rent reviews by audit. *Journal of Valuation & Investment*, 13 (1): 66–81.

Thomas, H. (2003) D-Day for landlords. *Property Week*, 28/11/03.

5 Assessing capital value: analysing discount rates

Aims of the chapter

- To explain the construction of property valuation yields and of years purchase multipliers.
- To place property yields into the context of the bond and gilts markets.
- To discuss the relationship between gilt and property yields and the drivers behind the shape of the gilts yield curve.
- To discuss the components of property's risk premium and how it might be deconstructed.
- To consider the different discount rates used by investors in the context of the risk adjusted discount rate.
- To compare the risk adjusted discount rate approach with that of certainty equivalence.
- To introduce the pay back and discounted pay back methods.
- To review the valuation methodologies used for rack-rented, under-rented and over-rented properties.

5.1 Introduction

As part of a commercial property transaction, it can be expected that the purchaser and seller will each undertake a valuation of the property, and/or will instruct a consultant valuer to undertake a valuation of the property. Furthermore, if a bank is involved in lending money to finance the transaction it will require an independent valuation to be carried out by a valuer on its approved valuers list. Thus for a single property transaction between two and five valuations may be undertaken. Part of each valuation will be the choice of a valuation yield.

This chapter considers what is meant by the term valuation yield and what is implied by it. This is put in context with Chapter 1 in which the methods of valuation were discussed, Chapter 2 which considered the valuation process from the position of the consultant valuer, and Chapter 4 which looked at the process of calculating rental values. Thus this chapter takes a step back to consider the property yield and the years purchase valuation multiplier, and to answer such questions as: how is the valuation yield derived? what is implied in to the yield? what is a years purchase multiplier? and what methodologies do valuers use for valuing rack-rented, over-rented and under-rented properties?

5.2 The valuation yield

The valuation yield is derived from comparable evidence gained from recent transactions involving similar properties. Using contacts within the property industry, in-house data, and online information providers such as FOCUS, the valuer gathers information on comparable transactions and analyses them such that rental values and yields for these properties are obtained. (Focus holds a vast database of information on property deals,

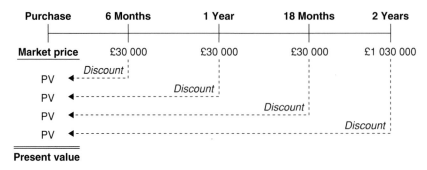

Fig. 5.1   The effect of discounting on price.

news and published information, which acts as a frequent starting point for valuers; see www.focusnet.co.uk for further information.) The valuation yields obtained provide the valuer with information for an open market view of comparable yields.

In the property market the term yield is in effect an income ratio. It relates the income receivable to the capital value. This is different from the concept of yield used in the other capital markets. For example, in the bond market the gross redemption yield is an internal rate of return (IRR)-based yield, which incorporates both the income and capital gains or losses elements.

The calculation of a bond yield thus looks at the income flows to its maturity (also known as the redemption date) and incorporates the return of capital. This is known as the yield to maturity, the calculation of which is set out in Fig. 5.1.

The yield to maturity is the yield that discounts the future cash flows, such that their net present value equals the market price of the bond. The nature of UK bond cash flows is precisely known: with a very few exceptions the incomes, known as coupons, are receivable half-yearly in arrears, and the capital is redeemed at a specified date in the future. The capital value at redemption is usually looked at in terms of £100 units and this is known as the nominal value. The price in the market is known as the face value. (US and Japanese bonds also pay half-yearly (semi-annually) in arrears, but Eurobonds pay annually in arrears.)

As the future cash flows of a bond are precisely known, and where the issuer is the UK Treasury/Government, this form of investment can be described as a risk-free rate of return, in that the cash flows are guaranteed by a borrower of the highest quality. Bonds issued by the UK Government are known as gilts. (From the days when they were bearer certificates printed on gilt-edged paper.)

However, in the property market there are a number of different yields, and consideration first needs to be given to what they all are. They can then be placed into a bond market yield context.

The variety of property yields used include:

- initial, equivalent and reversionary yields;
- gross and net of costs yields;
- gross and net of outgoings or repairs yields;
- true equivalent and nominal yields;
- effective and nominal yields;

- accumulative and remunerative yields as used in dual rate years purchase valuations;
- sinking fund rates or yields.

These are income ratios, which relate incomes with the capital value. The one property yield that is equivalent in terminology to a bond yield is the equated yield. This is the expected or implied rate of return for a property investment.

These property yields are ways of describing the attributes of a valuation such that the valuer and client can gain an insight into how a valuation or a price is constructed. Thus behind the above terminology is an array of financial formulae. These formulae, together with descriptions of the terms used, are a topic in themselves and, with relevant examples, are set out in Appendix A.

5.3   The years purchase multiplier

In property valuations the assumption is that the net rental income being valued, or each tranche of net rental income being valued, is constant and the rent is receivable annually in arrears. The passing rent and the estimate of rental value are taken as at the valuation date. If there is a rent review or reversion (lease expiry) it is, in traditional valuations, today's estimate of the rental value that is used to determine the rent that will become receivable following the rent review or a new letting.

As valuations are therefore dealing with fixed or constant income streams, it is possible to arrive at a formula that is a multiplier, which when applied to the rent produces the capital value of that rental stream. This is the role of the years purchase multiplier.

The years purchase multiplier is thus the sum of the present values for each of the years for which the rent is assumed to be receivable. Thus, for example, if the years purchase (YP) valuation yield was say 10%, and the valuer assumed that the rent in effect was receivable in perpetuity, then the YP multiplier equals the sum of all the present values of each of the years to perpetuity, as shown in Table 5.1 below. Mathematically the present

Table 5.1   Demonstration of the YP in perpetuity.

Yield =	10.00%	Present value of £1 multiplier
Year	1	0.9090909090909090000
Year	2	0.8264462809917350000
Year	3	0.7513148009015780000
Year	4	0.6830134553650710000
Year	5	0.6209213230591550000
Year	6	0.5644739300537770000
Year	7	0.5131581182307060000
Year	etc.	
Year	etc.	
Year	99	0.0000798222874916297
Year	100	0.0000725657159014815
Year	101	0.0000659688326377105
Year	etc. to	
Year	infinity	
YP in perpetuity @ 10% =		10.0000000000000000000

value figures into perpetuity are a geometric series that can be summed and simplified to produce the years purchase in perpetuity formula, which equals 1 divided by the yield. This and the other YP formulae are set out in Appendix A. The same methodology is used for the calculation of the YP single rate formulae.

Consideration has been given to what the years purchase multiplier represents. The focus of the next section of this chapter is on what the yield figure represents and what is implied into it.

5.4   Gilt yields

Property is part of the capital markets, along with equities and bonds. As discussed in section 5.3, bonds are fixed interest investments. (Consideration will be given later in this chapter to index linked bonds, which have cash flows linked to the rate of inflation.)

The yield to maturity on bond investments, particularly on gilts (government issue bonds), is used as a benchmark against which the pricing of other asset classes and assets are priced. The gross redemption yield on gilts is seen as a risk-free rate of return. It is this performance figure that property and equities are measured against.

In simple terms, the starting point is the risk-free rate of return – a benchmark gilt yield – plus an adjustment for the risk profile relative to gilts of the investment in question. Thus the required rate of return consists of the relevant gross redemption yield on a gilt plus a risk premium:

Required return of an investment = Risk-free rate of return + its risk premium.

If this equation is considered in the context of a property yield and into perpetuity it becomes:

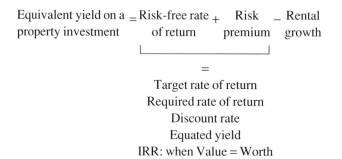

The rental growth rate that is deducted from the target rate of return is the average growth rate into perpetuity. If a shorter analysis period is used then growth will incorporate rental and capital growth over the period in question.

As this equation relates gilts yields (the risk-free rate of return) to property valuation yields, it is important to gain an understanding of the factors that drive the shape of the gilts yield curve. The gilts yield curve as set out in Fig. 5.2 shows the gross redemption yield for bonds of different maturities. Four different shapes of the gilts yield curve are depicted:

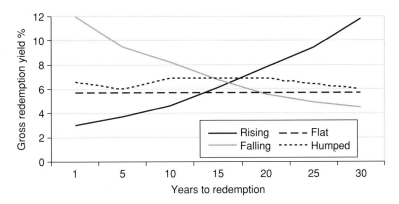

Fig. 5.2   The gilts yield curve.

- upward sloping (rising);
- humped;
- flat;
- downward sloping (falling).

The gilts yield curve is a graphical representation of the average discount rate to be used when valuing gilts of different maturity dates. Consideration therefore needs to be given to why the discount rates change for different holding periods, particularly since these are used as a benchmark in the construction of property yields and also are part of the target rate of return in discounted cash flow analysis. Thus for a five or ten year DCF analysis due regard is given to the gross redemption yield of five or ten year gilts respectively.

For valuations it is less straightforward to pick a benchmark gilt gross redemption yield. Some postulate that as valuations use years purchase in perpetuity the yield on undated gilts should be used. Others say that long-dated gilts should be the appropriate benchmark as property is a long-term asset, whilst another group argue that, as the average holding period for property investments is in the order of seven to ten years and lease terms are shortening, medium-term gilt yields should be used. Finally there are those who, having read the equity investment and finance text books, see the risk-free benchmark rate for equities as being three month treasury bills, and would like to apply this figure.

The tendency currently is to use long-dated gilts. However, as occupational leases shorten, it may be expected that the shift will be towards using medium-term gilt yields. Of the four choices, undated gilts are problematical because there is a very thin (small) market in them; the bid ask spread reflects this and is abnormally large. Treasury bills on the other hand are very short term, and three months in the context of a property invest- ment is an unrealistically short holding period.

Gilts provide the property market with the risk-free rate of return benchmark. What then drives gilt yields?

There are five main factors that influence the gilt redemption yields:

- liquidity preference;
- expectations hypothesis;
- segmentation theory;

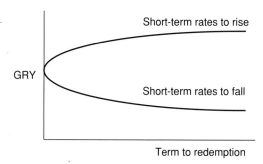

GRY

Short-term rates to rise

Short-term rates to fall

Term to redemption

Fig. 5.3   The effect of expectations on the gilts yield curve. GRY: gross redemption yield.

- unexpected inflation risk premium;
- sentiment.

Liquidity preference recognises that long-dated gilts are more volatile and sensitive to interest and inflation rate changes than short-term gilts. Long-dated gilts are therefore more risky and thus should offer investors a higher rate of return. All other things being equal, the gilts yield curve should be upward sloping.

Expectations hypothesis places liquidity preference to one side and considers that investors are indifferent as to whether they invest long or short term. However, it focuses on the fact that a long-term investment comprises a series of short-term investments and thus the future movement of interest rates will influence the shape of the yield curve. If short-term interest rates are expected to rise, by a majority of investors, the yield curve will be upward sloping; if interest rates are expected to fall then the curve will be downward sloping, as shown in Fig. 5.3.

Segmentation theory considers the influence of supply and demand for each element. It recognises in particular that different investors have different liability profiles and regulatory constraints. Thus, for example, life insurance companies and pension funds are investors at the long end of the market; in contrast, banks and building societies have a preference for the shorter end of the market. The demand side therefore focuses on the short and long ends of the market, often leaving less demand for medium-term gilts, particularly in the five to ten year range. The result is a humped yield curve. However, the position is compounded by the Treasury's requirement to sell gilts to fund its budget shortfall. (In buoyant periods of the economic cycle the government can be a purchaser of gilts when it has surplus revenues.) In addition, the Treasury is a proponent of the Private Finance Initiative (PFI), which uses real yields derived from long-dated gilts as the discount rate to determine the viability of PFI projects. A significant amount of the gilt issues have not been at the long end of the market, which has kept long gilt yields relatively low. (This has prompted life insurance companies to be big players in the commercial property mortgage market, offering 20+ year mortgages.) Also, with the majority of the Group of 8 countries running large deficits, it may be expected that there will be additional pressure on government bond issues in the future.

Unexpected inflation risk premium reflects the fact that gilts offer investors fixed income returns with no protection against unexpected inflation risks. Expected inflation is priced into the interest rate structure. If inflation unexpectedly increases it will in particular adversely affect the price of long-dated gilts, as the discount rate (or required rate of return) will rise. During the period 2000–2005, inflationary pressures ranged from negligible to very modest, and the market did not incorporate a significant unexpected risk premium into gilts prices. (For gilts and bond prices and yield curves see www.bloomberg.com.) The unexpected inflation risk premium compensates the investor for any unexpected increase in inflation rates and the risk this imposes.

Sentiment is a major factor behind all markets. The weight of money and expectations of where the money will be going can influence investors. During the share market recession of 2000–2002 there were many investors who found themselves over-exposed to equities and this started a shift in investment policy away from equities into the 'safe haven' of the gilts market. Sentiment is fickle, and with the gilts and fixed interest markets the expectations of interest rates and inflation are the two main ingredients that are considered first.

Thus there are a number of theories that suggest how the gilts yield curve is influenced. It can be helpful to understand these influences. They can assist the property valuer to understand the link between shifts in gilts yields and property yields. For example, if gilts yields rise at the long end by say 2%, a property investor argues that property yields should rise to reflect the higher return available on gilts. If the rise was due to a sudden burst of government borrowing at the long end, this could make sense. However, if the reason behind the rise in long-dated gilt yields was the expectation that inflation was to rise sharply, then as property is perceived as a hedge against inflation it might reasonably be expected that rental growth would increase, and thus property yields might well stay unchanged.

One final point to remember is that the gilts yield curve has a number of names:

- term structure of interest rates;
- gilt or bond yield to maturity;
- gross redemption yield;
- the gilt or bond internal rate of return;
- the geometric mean of the forward rate structure of interest rates.

For more on the pricing of bonds and the mathematics that lies behind this and other markets, please refer to Adams *et al.* (2003).

5.5   Index-linked gilts and strips

For a number of investors, their liability profiles are linked to future inflation rates. In consequence assets with inflation hedging characteristics are sought to counter inflation risk. In the financial markets there are index-linked gilts, which pay a coupon linked to the retail price index. The gross redemption yield on these gilts provides a better benchmark for such investors.

By applying a 'real' coupon to the principal amount, an index-linked bond protects the investor from unexpected changes in the retail price index. As property is a 'real' asset, the yield to redemption on long-dated index-linked gilts is selected as the basis for the real risk-free rate plus an allowance for expected inflation which can be sourced from long-term economic forecasts, or assumed to be the government's inflation target.

Long-dated issues should be selected to reduce the impact of the redemption of principal on the yield. To be more accurate than using published real yields at arbitrary rates of inflation, the real yield should be calculated on the index-linked gilt using the forecast of inflation.

There can be issues with using UK Government bonds as a proxy for the risk-free rate when their values may be influenced by factors other than the time value of money, such as varying levels of issuance, and suitability in meeting investment requirements of certain types of investor for liability matching and taxation purposes. In these cases it can be helpful to look at real yields in other countries where governments issue consumer price index-linked gilts. It is then possible to see if UK yields deviate significantly and to consider whether any adjustment might be appropriate.

In Appendix A the formula for converting a real rate of interest to a nominal (before inflation) rate of interest is shown. In practice the two figures are simply added together, which slightly understates the position.

However, index-linked gilts yields are seldom used as a benchmark for the risk-free rate of return. If they were, it should be remembered that the risk premium for property would rise when compared to that for fixed interest gilts as property's relative inflation hedging benefits would no longer be a plus factor.

The gilts yield curve is also known as the geometric mean of the forward rate structure of interest rates. It is possible to look at fixed interest gilts as a series of zero coupon gilts. In 1985 the US introduced a scheme whereby US Treasury bonds could be exchanged for stripped (zero coupon) bonds. (Strips is an acronym for Separately Traded and Registered Interest and Principal Securities.) The UK Treasury followed suit in the 1990s. However, in the UK the gilt strips market remains relatively thin with small trading volumes, so determining spot rates from the stripped gilts is not very reliable (Adams *et al.*, 2003).

5.6   Property yields relative to gilts yields: the risk premium calculation

In the above section consideration was given to the relationship between gilts and property yields. This section examines yield construction by building a required return for a subject property reflecting elements of market and specific risk and simple ways to price them. For the purposes of the example, the property is assumed to be rack-rented with an income yield of 7%.

5.6.1   Risk-free rate

As discussed above, the risk-free rate is a theoretical interest rate at which an investment may earn interest without incurring any risk. Because the British Government is reckoned to be one of the least likely entities in the financial environment to default on a loan, the gilts yield is believed to be about as close to risk-free as you can get for sterling investments. To the risk-free rate is added the property risk premium.

5.6.2   Property risk premium

The property risk premium is the amount by which property returns should exceed the expected returns from the risk-free asset. It is effectively the reward investors get paid for taking the risk of investing in property.

The traditional view has been that 2% should be adopted, based on the historical relationship between prime property yields and gilts yields prior to the reverse yield gap. From 1970, the margin in returns has been 1.1%, although over the last ten years it has expanded to almost 4%. Bond returns have benefited from a significant reduction in inflation expectations over this period. The historic differential between property and gilt returns understates the current required risk premium as property's risk premium is likely to have increased over recent years as investors have become increasingly aware of property's shortcomings against other asset classes, such as lack of liquidity and increased transaction costs.

Property's required risk premium is priced into its yield structure and comprises a wide variety of components such as asset liquidity, transaction costs and management. In order to isolate the risk premium priced into property investments, the premium has been broken into the following components:

- property management;
- tenant renewing lease risk premium;
- tenant default risk premium;
- allowance for quarterly in advance cash flow;
- illiquidity premium;
- transaction costs.

Each component is analysed and estimated below.

Property management costs

Property is a management-intensive asset with ongoing costs – such as property management/rent collection, rent review and lease renewal fees – incurred to keep the property income-producing.

Based on a single tenant property currently let and renewed on ten year leases, the assumptions in Table 5.2 produce management expenses totalling an average of 1.5% of rent passing per annum. To build a required return, these costs are shown as a deduction from the current income yield. Rent review fees are assumed to be incurred on every tenth year on a ten year lease following the first review in five years' time.

The risk-free rate derived from government bond yields will implicitly include an allowance for portfolio management costs. For a passively managed bond portfolio this could be a very low figure, so for simplicity no assumption has been made.

Table 5.2 Construction of a net income yield.

Gross income yield		7.000%
Basic management (% rent) annually	1.000%	
Rent review fees (% ERV) every other 5th anniversary	5.000%	
Total as % Income	1.500%	
Total deduction from income yield (7.000% × (1−1.500%))		0.105%
Income yield net of management costs		6.895%

Table 5.3   Income yields adjusted to reflect possible renewal costs.

Net income yield		6.895%
Tenant renewal fees (% ERV)	7.500%	
× 50% probability	3.750%	
Loss of income (after mgt costs)	100.000%	
Repairs and insurance (% ERV)	12.000%	
Void rates (20% ERV) after 3 Months	15.000%	
Reletting fees (% ERV)	15.000%	
Sub total	142.000%	
× 50% probability	71.000%	
Total as % income	74.750%	
Divide total by 10 to get annual premium	7.475%	
Total deduction from income yield		0.515%
Income yield net of probable renewal costs		6.380%

Tenant renewing lease risk premium

This is the risk that the tenant will interrupt the income flow from the property by not renewing the lease or by operating a break option. This is an allowance for the greater volatility attached to property income compared to income from bonds, as is shown in Table 5.3.

To provide the risk premium, a probable annual cost is calculated and deducted from the income yield. This cost is based on an assumed 12 month void period with loss of rental income plus costs of the void period (maintenance, insurance and void rates) and the costs of reletting.

Quite obviously not every tenant will want to vacate their premises at the end of the lease so for the purposes of this example it is assumed that there is a 50% chance of the tenant renewing. Accordingly there are two separate costs for renewal fees, assumed at 7.5%, and reletting costs such as instructing a letting agent to find a new tenant. As the example is based on a ten year lease, the costs are spread over a ten year period.

Tenant default-risk premium

This is the risk that the tenant will interrupt the cash flow by defaulting on the obligation to pay rent, such as when their business fails. The costs are priced on a similar basis to the tenant renewing lease risk premium, namely the costs of having the property empty plus the costs of reletting and the loss of rent. Default ratings supplied by ratings agencies on corporate bonds could be used as a guide to default, although bonds are different from property as when a bond issuer defaults the recovery rate is only around 30–40% whereas a property can be re-let.

To provide the risk premium the assumption that the property is vacated is multiplied by a default rate assumed to be 2% per annum for the grade of tenant occupying this property; that is, 2% of rent is lost through default per annum across all properties let to tenants of this default grade. Of course default rates will change year by year and will increase in a recession, so the rate used here should be considered as a long-term average. The requirement to adjust for these assumptions is shown in Table 5.4.

Table 5.4 Income yield reflecting adjustments for possible voids.

Net income yield		6.380%
Loss of income (after mgt costs)	100.000%	
Repairs and insurance (% ERV)	12.000%	
Void rates (20% ERV) after 3 months	15.000%	
Reletting fees (% ERV)	15.000%	
Sub total	142.000%	
× 2% probability	2.840%	
Total deduction from income yield	0.181%	
Income yield net of probable default costs		6.198%

Table 5.5 Income yield adjusted to reflect cash flow timing.

Net income yield		6.198%
Quarterly in advance IRR based on income yield	6.446%	
Half-yearly in arrears IRR based on income yield	6.294%	
Total addition to income yield	0.152%	
Income yield net of income pattern adjustment		6.350%

Allowance for quarterly in advance cash flow

Gilt coupons are paid half-yearly in arrears whereas commercial property rents are received quarterly in advance. For a given annual income, a quarterly in advance cash flow is more valuable than one received half-yearly in arrears so we have reduced the risk premium by the difference between the quarterly in advance and the half-yearly in arrears adjusted income yield to reflect this benefit.

A simple way to calculate the added value is to compare the IRR from a quarterly in advance income with a half-yearly in arrears income stream using a simple spreadsheet calculation. Alternatively effective capitalisation rates can be calculated using the quarterly in advance and biannually in arrears conversion formulae. The requirement to adjust for this is shown in Table 5.5.

Illiquidity premium

This is the additional return required by investors for the uncertainty of both how long it will take to convert the investment into cash and what price will be received.

The settlement period on gilts is one day and on UK equities it is three days, so how would it be possible and what would it cost to put property onto the same liquidity basis as securities, where you can sell instantly at the current valuation? A theoretical solution to indicate the price of achieving this is to borrow an amount equal to the sales proceeds short term in a bridging loan. For the purposes of this example three months is assumed to be the average time from the decision to market a property until completion although this will depend on the type, size and market conditions when the sale decision is made. Market terms can be sourced for the margins above LIBOR (London Interbank Offered Rate) that are currently offered for 100% bridging loans and their arrangement costs, such as valuations for the lender, to price the costs of the loan, which can be offset against rental income received until sale.

Table 5.6   Income yield adjusted to reflect illiquidity.

Net income yield		6.350%
3 month LIBOR	5.000%	
Margin over LIBOR	3.000%	
Total interest rate	8.000%	
Over three months	2.000%	
Loan security valuation (% of capital value)	0.100%	
Loan arrangement fees (% of capital value)	0.100%	
Total costs	2.200%	
Divide by five for annual premium	0.440%	
Net income yield after illiquidity premium		5.910%

Of course, the property could sell for above or below the current valuation due to market movements or the inaccuracy inherent in valuations, so the method outlined arguably overstates the premium by ignoring this potential upside. A purely theoretical approach to valuing this upside could be the cost of hedging the downside loss at sale to the upside gain using a 'collar strategy' of a long put and a short call. Of course there are no counter-parties in the market for these derivatives but the fair net value of the two options could be calculated.

It is assumed that the cost is spread over a five year holding period. Table 5.6 shows the effect of these costs on the income yield.

Transaction costs

The transfer costs for property are higher than those for bonds so these need to be reflected in the required rate of return. The costs of stamp duty, conveyancing fees and agents' fees on sale and purchase ('round tripping') of 7% are assumed to be incurred in every five year holding period. These are not inconsiderable and their amortised costs over the assumed five year holding period are shown in Table 5.7.

Total risk premium

Adding up the above components of risk gives a total required return of just under 8.0% of which the risk premium is 2.5% over the risk-free rate. Amongst investment professionals

Table 5.7   The effect of transaction costs on income yield.

Net income yield		5.910%
Stamp duty	4.000%	
Purchase legal fees	0.500%	
Purchase agent's fees	1.000%	
Sales legal fees	0.500%	
Sales agent's fees	1.000%	
Total costs	7.000%	
Divide by five for annual premium	1.400%	
Net income yield after transaction cost adjustments		4.510%

Table 5.8 Summary of income yield construction.

Risk-free rate	3.000%
Expected inflation	2.500%
Property management costs	0.105%
Tenant renewing lease risk premium	0.515%
Tenant default risk premium	0.181%
Quarterly in advance adjustment	−0.152%
Illiquidity premium	0.440%
Transaction costs	1.400%
Total	7.990%

the rule of thumb for the property risk premium is 2% for institutional quality property. Since the 1970s this figure has varied but has broadly been between 1% and 4%, depending on prevailing tax and market conditions. Table 5.8 demonstrates the summarised 'build-up' of the investor's required return.

The decision on whether to buy, sell or hold this asset will depend on whether the expected return from the asset exceeds the required return. If the equivalent yield plus the expectation of rental growth and/or an inward yield shift exceeded 8% then the property would appear to be a buy or continued hold.

This discount rate can be considered 'all risks' in that it implicitly reflects the risks in the cash flow it is discounting, just as the equivalent yield will do. However, if a cash flow model for the property were constructed it would be likely to reflect management costs, void periods/costs and quarterly in advance cash flows. Accordingly, using a required return already reflecting these costs will double count them in the net present value.

While this type of required return construction is intuitive it has a number of drawbacks so is only really a rule of thumb. The main drawbacks are as follows:

- Costs are averaged so an extra premium is not generated for events in the short term, such as lease expiries.
- Just as bond investors require compensation for the inflation they expect plus the risk that inflation could increase during the term of their investment, investors in property are exposed to the risk that the reversion they expect will fall from today's values. Obviously, the longer the period to the next review or lease expiry, the greater the rental growth risk premium that would be required.
- Other risks such as taxation – each 1% rise in stamp duty would add 0.2% to the required rate. There are also legal risks which may force a change in lease structure plus sector and planning risks which may detract from the appeal of the property to tenants.

Simulation models using software such as @Risk and Crystal Ball can help to answer some of the failings. However, these models require a lot of judgemental inputs: can a property manager really assign a probability to the chance of a tenant renewing at the end of their lease in ten years' time? Accordingly these models can get bogged down in the 'garbage in – garbage out' trap, although they are very useful for indicating exactly how shifts in certain factors can impact on future returns and current net present values.

Table 5.9   Deconstructing the IPD equivalent yield and comparing with the equity analyst's approach.

Yield component	%	Comment
Risk-free real benchmark	+2.4%	Index-linked bonds with a 10 year maturity
Tenant risk premium	+2.9%	Moody's Baa 10 year corporate bond spread
Depreciation	+1.2%	Building depreciation absorbed by the landlord
Transaction costs	+0.8%	Legal, agent and stamp duty amortised over 10 years
Management costs	+1.0%	Annual cost of outsourcing management costs
Rents payment profile	−0.3%	Advantage of quarterly in advance cash flows
Impact of rent reviews	+0.3%	Five yearly steps, rent monetised at review
Liquidity adjustment	−0.1	Property – gilt returns over a one month transaction period
Void adjustment	+0.5%	Impact of tenant delinquencies and voids at lease expiries
Long term rental growth	−0.0	Deduct real growth at portfolio level
SSSB implied equivalent yield	8.6%	Theoretical yield basis (rounded)
IPD equivalent yield	8.4%	Assumes quarterly in advance rents
Difference	+0.2%	SSSB relative to IPD

Source: Schroder Saloman Smith Barney estimates.

5.7   Property equity analysts' approach

The above approach can be compared with that of the equity analysts' approach as set out in Table 5.9.

5.8   Risk adjusted discount rate

The use of a risk adjusted discount rate (RADR) in a discounted cash flow analysis is a frequent approach amongst property analysts and investors. The technique is relatively easy and intuitive to use and points the user in broadly the right direction (although in extreme circumstances it can be excessively misleading if used without a clear under-standing of the timing of the risks – for example, high discount rates penalise long-term cash flows and place the focus on the short-term cash flows). It does, however, suffer from three main limitations:

- One discount rate – namely a risk adjusted rate – is applied to all the net cash flows, and thus it fails to distinguish those elements of the project that are risky from those that are less risky.
  - o This will necessarily require subtle adjustments to the rate to compensate for the weighting of risky to non-risky elements (a mathematical problem).
  - o It also fails to flag the risky elements properly (for purposes of controlling, shifting, hedging, etc.). This problem can be partially overcome by dividing the asset into its component parts (defined by risk) and discounting at differing rates.
  - o This is the approach adopted in traditional valuations. In a modified form it is explored in the Sliced Income Approach (Baum and Crosby, 1995).

- It relates risk to time in a somewhat myopic manner. This arises because the risk premium tends to be based on the assumption of an annual rate and therefore offers a very weak reduction in discounted values to near (risky) cash flows, whilst acting severely on distant cash flows. Whilst it may be said that, in general, the more distant the cash flow, the more risky it is likely to be, and hence the impact of discounting is in the right direction, it might also be said that the growth in risk is unlikely to be at exactly the same exponential rate as the growth inherent in the risk premium. The mathematics are not simple, especially when comparing projects of unequal length but similar types of risks.
- There is a potential problem with double counting of risk. Where risks are explicitly taken account of in the cash flows being analysed in the DCF (for example, potential voids), the RADR should not also be increased to take into account these same risks.

An alternative to using one discount rate is the sliced income approach where the net cash flows are disaggregated into sets of cash flows with different risk profiles and to which different discount rates are applied. This methodology is rarely used in the property investment market, but it does have merit in that the net cash flows from rents are secured under the terms of a lease. In contrast, the future exit value is subject to the cyclical nature of the market. In property valuations a hardcore top slice or split income approach is used when the risk profile of the net rental income changes significantly at a future date (for example, following a lease expiry of an older property). It should be noted that, in the analysis of bond investments, bond analysts acknowledge that interest rates and returns on bonds vary over time. The analysts unbundle the bond yield curve and thereby calculate a series of forward interest rates, which can be used as the basis for discount rates for future cash flows.

However, the use of a risk adjusted discount rate provides a helpful starting point for those using DCF as an investment appraisal tool in their quest to determine whether an investment is fair value or is over- or under-priced. As pointed out above, the RADR has its limitations but is nevertheless widely used by practitioners.

5.9   Unbundling a valuation yield to derive the implied rate of rental growth

In Appendix A the formula for the calculation of the implied rate of growth is set out. The rate of growth is dependent upon the rent review pattern and the required rate of return. From this the required rate of rental growth (the average rate into perpetuity) for different valuation yields can be calculated.

5.10   The individual investor's required rate of return or choice of discount rate

As discussed above in the sections on risk premiums and on RADR, these form the starting point for many investors in their quest for the appropriate discount rate to use in their discounted cash flow analysis, and the background to their valuation yield structure. However, it should be noted that different players in the property investment market have different approaches for arriving at their discount rate or target rate of return.

- *Institutions*: life insurance companies and pension funds make use of the concept of opportunity cost. They consider the risk/return profile of suitable alternative investments and place property into this context. Their starting point is the return on gilts (government bonds) for a comparable holding period. To this is then added a risk premium that reflects the different risk profile of property. For example, property suffers from illiquidity, tenant default risk, location and structural risk, taxation and legislation risks. Against these, property is perceived to be a hedge against unexpected inflation: an attribute that bonds do not have. So in calculating the risk premium there are a series of factors that make the risk premium positive, from which can be deducted the benefits of being an inflation hedge. The long-term rule of thumb is that for prime property investments the risk premium is 2%. In the low inflationary environment of the late 1990s and where equities were sought after, the prime property risk premium drifted up to some 4%. The weight of money in the 2004 property investment market brought it back down to around 2% for many institutional investors.

  Institutions frequently start their analysis of valuation yields by considering the risk-free rate of return plus a risk premium. As mentioned in the section above on RADR, care should be taken with double counting of risks where risks are accounted for explicitly in the net cash flows being used for the DCF analysis.

- *Open end funds and property unit trusts*: these property investment vehicles predominantly attract investment moneys from private investors who generally perceive cash deposits or short-term bonds as the alternative investment. For the fund managers of these funds, short interest rates are frequently seen as the necessary income hurdle that must be achieved to make their property funds competitive. In consequence, these fund managers often focus on initial yields that exceed those on short interest rates, sustainable incomes (portfolios with strong tenants and long leases) and properties that are readily saleable. As their benchmark is cash returns driven, a number of these players do not seem to use DCF approaches.

- *Core plus investors*: these investors seek to achieve higher returns (10–14%) by using a combination of gearing and adding value through active management strategies. They may well take on board an element of reletting risk or refurbishment, and a level of gearing, in order to achieve their required returns.

  Again, care should be taken in checking that double counting of risks does not occur in the discount rate and again explicitly in the net cash flows.

- *Property companies*: the aim of the directors running property companies is to maximise shareholder wealth. To do this they need, just like all other companies, to beat their weighted average cost of capital (Brealey and Myers, 2002). Unlike institutional investors, property companies have no long-term liabilities other than their debt commitments and thus have flexibility in their investment approaches.

  The yardsticks used by property companies vary. Some may (erroneously) use the marginal cost of debt; others set target rates of return according to what the Board of Directors perceive as an achievable hurdle level of return; and some use weighted average cost of capital, which is a net of tax discount rate.

Private property companies may in practice not explicitly set required rates of return. Rather, they are seeking to service their debt payments and have the anticipation of owning an unmortgaged property at a date in the future. For such investors DCF analysis is seldom used.

- *Corporate occupiers*: the tendency for larger corporate occupiers is to consider the activity that the property assets support, and to consider the worth to the business of their property assets using a weighted average cost of capital approach. In addition to financial considerations, flexibility is an important issue. In Chapter 9 consideration is given to corporate occupiers and the role of property assets.

    Smaller corporate occupiers may consider property assets a safe haven for surplus cash and an asset that can be used as collateral at a future date, should the business require additional funding. For some of them the financial analysis may be simplistic.

5.11   Pay back and discounted pay back

In the case of high-risk investments, the investor may perceive that there are excellent potential returns but that there are risks and unquantifiable uncertainties that make the modelling of the cash flows required to undertake a full DCF analysis very difficult or impossible. In such circumstances the pay back or discounted pay back method can be used.

The pay back method calculates how many months or years it will take for the estimated net cash flows from the investment to recoup the initial capital outlay. In the discounted pay back approach the cash flows are discounted (often using a high discount rate of 20% or more) to reflect their potential increasing uncertainty going into the future. The discounted net cash flows are deducted from the initial outlay and the time taken, in months or years, to recoup this sum is calculated.

5.12   Certainty equivalent

An alternative approach is not to consider first what the required discount rate should be, but rather to consider the investment in a risk averse manner. Certainty equivalent looks at the investment's prospective secure net cash flows and determines these by taking on board the use of the standard deviations of the variable input to the DCF model to adjust the expected cash flows to, for example, a 95% certainty level (two standard deviations).

Certainty equivalent methodology is not often used in the property investment market. Dubben and Sayce (1991), Baum and Crosby (1995) and Isaac (1998) all discuss its application in depth. The certainty equivalent approach has its uses in that it gets the investor to focus on the downside risks inherent in the property investment. In practice, the alternative and conceptually broadly similar approach that is used is the application of scenario testing, whereby a pessimistic or bearish scenario is constructed and analysed.

5.13   Risk adjusted discount rate v. certainty equivalent

These two approaches should produce similar net present values if the figures have been adjusted in an appropriate manner, as shown in Fig. 5.4. However, the use of certainty equivalent in the market is limited and so professionals are unaccustomed to making the necessary adjustments.

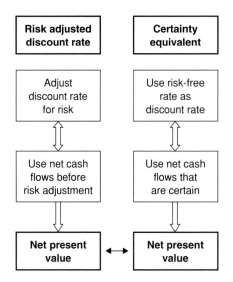

Fig. 5.4   Risk adjusted discount rate (RADR) v. certainty equivalent.

5.14   Freehold valuation approaches

In this next section consideration is given to how the yields are applied in the context of the various valuation methodologies used in the market by consultant valuers.

The three main groupings of freehold valuations are:

- properties let at the open market rental value;
- properties that are under-rented;
- properties that are over-rented.

The valuation approaches for each of the above reflect the fact that the net rental streams being valued have different profiles. In each case the assumption is that it is today's passing rent and today's estimate of the open market rental value that are used. Thus growth (and risk) is implicit in the valuation yield.

In the UK valuation yields are usually quoted on a net of costs basis, whilst in Continental Europe they may often be quoted on a gross basis. Appendix A sets out the calculation of gross and net yields. The costs relate to the purchaser's acquisition costs, which at the time of writing are generally taken to be 5.7625% for direct property purchases of more than £500 000. The costs are broken down, as set out in Table 5.10.

In the examples below the sample valuations have been done on a before costs basis. Appendix A sets out examples of gross and net of costs yields as applied to valuations. In these valuations the term years purchase is abbreviated to YP.

5.14.1   Rack-rented investments

A rack-rented property investment is one where the net rent passing for the property equals the market rental value. The assumption in the valuation formula is that the rental income flows to perpetuity. However, the valuer will adjust the yield to reflect the length of the unexpired term on the lease. Set out in Table 5.11 is a typical valuation structure. In this

Table 5.10   Analysis of typical purchase costs.

Costs	%
Stamp duty	4.00%
Agents fee on purchase	1.00%
Legal fees on purchase	0.50%
VAT on fees at 17.5%	0.2625%
Total	5.7625%

Table 5.11   Valuation of rack-rented freehold property investment.

Net rent receivable	650 000	
Years purchase in perpetuity @ 6.75%	14.8148	
Value		9 629 630
	Say	9 630 000

Table 5.12   Valuation of rack-rented freehold property investment where lease term is short and comparable evidence limited.

Net rent receivable	650 000	
Years purchase in perpetuity @ 7.25%	13.7931	
Value		8 965 517
	Say	9 000 000

example the property is let on an FRI (full repairing and insuring) lease with an unexpired lease term of 20 years, and the valuation yield is 6.75%.

We can now take the example where the property is again let at the open market rental value, but in this case the unexpired term of the lease is five years. There is limited comparable evidence available which suggests that a 0.5% increase in the yield to 7.25% would be appropriate. The valuation figure is then adjusted downwards as shown in Table 5.12.

The valuer decides that an alternative method of valuation would be appropriate to cross check the above valuation. The valuer perceives that the tenant is likely to vacate and that, on becoming vacant, the property will require a minor refurbishment, which it is estimated in today's terms will cost £225 000 after taking into account a dilapidations sum expected from the tenant. The valuer estimates that there will be a nine month void period followed by a three month tenant fitting-out period and a six month rent free period. The landlord's improvements to the property at the expiry of the lease, which the valuer calculates, increase the rental value of the property in today's terms to £680 000 p.a. The letting fees are estimated at £68 000, and the valuer estimates 7.5% to be an appropriate discount rate for the cost of the letting fees. These assumptions are shown diagrammatically in Fig. 5.5. If these assumptions are built into the calculation it results in the valuation shown in Table 5.13. This valuation backs up the valuation arrived at using limited comparable evidence.

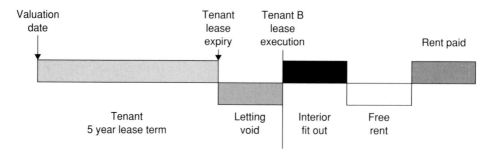

Fig. 5.5   Typical valuation assumptions for valuing a reversionary investment.

Table 5.13   Valuation of a reversionary investment showing treatment of a void period.

Net rent receivable	650 000	
YP single rate for 5 years @ 6.75%	4.1278	
		2 683 064
Rent on reletting	680 000	
YP in perpetuity @ 6.75%		
Deferred 6.5 years =	9.6896	
		6 588 915
		9 271 979
Less		
Letting fees	68 000	
Present value £1 for 5.75 years @ 7.5%	0.6598	
		44 865
Refurbishment costs		250 000
Value		8 977 113
	Say	9 000 000

5.14.2   Under-rented investments

The valuation of under-rented properties occurs when the passing rent receivable for a property is less than the open market rental value. The under-rented nature of the property may be either because the property is part vacant, or because of rental growth which has resulted in the property becoming under-rented even while fully let.

For under-rented properties, two main methodologies are adopted:

- layer method;
- term and reversion.

In the investment marketplace the layer method using one equivalent yield tends to be the preferred method, the reason being that as only one valuation yield is used it makes the analysis of comparable evidence and other market transactions simpler. From an academic standpoint the term and reversion method treats the rentals according to their risk and growth characteristics and is thus a preferred method.

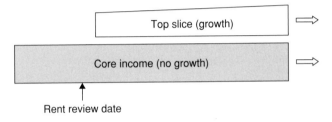

Fig. 5.6   The layered method applied to a reversionary investment.

Table 5.14   A reversionary freehold investment valued by the layer (hardcore) method.

Net rent receivable	830 000	
YP in perpetuity @ 7.25%	13.7931	
		11 448 276
Open market rental value	920 000	
Less rent passing	830 000	
Uplift on rent review	90 000	
YP in perpetuity @ 7.25%		
Deferred 2 years	11.9913	
		1 079 220
Value		12 527 496
	Say	12 530 000

5.14.3   Layer method

The structure of the layer method is shown diagrammatically in Fig. 5.6. A property is let at £830 000 per annum on an FRI lease with 17 years unexpired. The open market rental income is estimated at £920 000 per annum, and the next rent review is due in two years' time. Comparable evidence points to an equivalent yield of 7.25% being appropriate. The result is shown in Table 5.14.

5.14.4   Term and reversion method

The term and reversion method treats the term income as being a secure non-growth income. Its security is reinforced by the under-rented nature of the property and, were the tenant to default, a reletting at a higher value would be beneficial to the owner. The income after the rent review is viewed as being growth income but is riskier. The yield adopted for the term is typically reduced by some 0.5–2.0%.

The structure of the term and reversion method is shown diagrammatically in Fig. 5.7. The valuation, using the same assumptions and information, is shown in Table 5.15.

It can be noted that, if the same yield is used for the term and reversion, the result is the same as the for layer method. However, if an adjustment is made to either the term yield or the top slice yield, the two methods yield slightly different results (see Table 5.16).

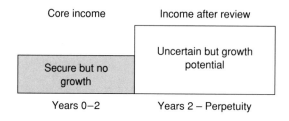

Core income

Income after review

Uncertain but growth
potential

Secure but no
growth

Years 0–2

Years 2 – Perpetuity

Fig. 5.7   The term and reversion method applied to reversionary investments.

Table 5.15   A reversionary investment valued by the term and reversion method (term yield adjusted).

Net rent receivable	830 000	
YP single rate, 2 years @ 6.5%	1.8206	
		1 511 120
Open market rental value on review	920 000	
YP in perpetuity @ 7.25%		
Deferred 2 years	11.9913	
		11 032 025
Value		12 543 144
	Say	12 540 000

Table 5.16   A reversionary investment valued by the term and reversion method (no yield adjustment).

Net rent receivable	830 000	
YP single rate, 2 years @ 7.25%	1.8018	
		1 495 471
Open market rental value on review	920 000	
YP in perpetuity @ 7.25%		
Deferred 2 years	11.9913	
		11 032 025
Value		12 527 496
	Say	12 530 000

5.14.5   Over-rented investments

Where a property was let at a rent greater than the open market rental value, the traditionally adopted method sought to split the incomes into the hardcore growth element and the non-growth risky top slice. The shortcoming with this method is that the top slice income was usually taken to the expiry of the occupational lease. An alternative method was put forward (Baum and Crosby, 1995), which took into account the implied rental growth rate to calculate at what point in time the property would return to being rack- or under-rented. From this point in time the property's rental incomes would revert to having growth potential. This new method has been described as the 'short cut DCF'.

Table 5.17 An over-rented property investments valued by the hard core top slice method.

Full market rent	900 000	
YP in perpetuity @ 7.0%	14.2857	
		12 857 143
Top slice		
Rent receivable	1 200 000	
Market rental value	900 000	
Over rent top slice	300 000	
YP single rate 18 years @ 12.0%	7.2497	
		2 174 901
Value		15 032 044
	Say	15 030 000

5.14.6 Hard core top slice

In the example set out in Table 5.17, a property is let at £1 200 000 per annum on an FRI lease, with 18 years unexpired, and the benefit of five-yearly upward only rent reviews, with the next rent review due in three years' time. The current estimate of the rental value is £900 000, and the yield on the core income is 7.0%.

This method is convenient but inherently inaccurate as the top slice (the over rent) will erode over time as rental values recover and increase. Therefore it is often inappropriate to make the assumption that the over rent persists until lease expiry.

5.14.7 Short cut DCF

The valuer considers that a target rate of return of 9.0% is appropriate. From this it is possible to calculate the implied rental growth rate, using the formula set out in Appendix A (p. 324).

$$k = e - (SF \times p)$$

Where k is the market yield
     e the equated yield
     SF the annually in arrears sinking fund formula
     and p the rent review pattern.

Setting this up in a spreadsheet, using Excel's Goal Seek function, or DCF Analyst's Calculate Again wizard, the implied rental growth can be calculated to be 2.3%.

The process now is to identify at what point the market rental value will exceed the rent passing. The term slice is then valued to that rent review date at the equated yield (target rate of return), and thereafter the reversion is valued using a growth and risk implicit yield and discounted at the equated yield. Hence this method is named the short cut DCF.

In Table 5.18 the same property is valued again using a short cut DCF. This reveals that the hard core method has over-valued the property by failing to recognise the eroding nature of the over rent.

Table 5.18   An over-rented property valued using a short cut DCF approach.

	Current rent passing	1 200 000	
	Estimated rental value	900 000	
	Implied rental growth	2.30%	
	Growth	**ERV**	**Status**
Current ERV	0.0%	900 000	Over-rented
Rent review in 3 years' time	7.1%	963 539	Over-rented
Rent review in 8 years' time	20.0%	1 079 562	Over-rented
Rent review in 13 years' time	34.4%	1 209 555	Under-rented
Valuation			
Rent receivable		1 200 000	
YP 13 years @ 9.0%		7.4869	
			8 984 285
Reversion to ERV			
At review in 13 years' time		1 209 555	
YP in perpetuity @ 7.0%	14.2857		
Deferred 13 years @ 9.0%	0.3262		
		4.6597	
			5 636 157
Value			14 620 442
		Say	14 620 000

5.14.8   Short cut DCF versus full DCF

The short cut DCF valuation method has made a useful addition to the tools available to the valuer. However, the implied rental growth rate may not reflect the short-term rental growth or falls that professional advisers expect in the marketplace. The graph in Fig. 5.8 shows the long-term rental figures for mid-town London offices. The average rental growth since 1980 was 3.2%. However, the growth rates have varied significantly.

Between the 1985 and 1989 inclusive the rental growth rate was 20% p.a.; in contrast, the five years ending 31 December 1994 produced negative rental growth of −15% p.a., and for the period 1992 to end 1996 the growth rate was −9%.

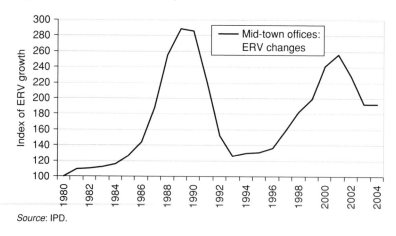

Source: IPD.

Fig. 5.8   Mid-town office rents showing changes to rental growth patterns.

The implicit rental growth rate may not be the same as the estimated rental growth rate for the period of the unexpired term of the lease. When short cut DCF was proposed (Baum and Crosby, 1995) the use of spreadsheets was still in its infancy and full DCF appraisals were rarely used. Now that spreadsheets have become part of the valuer's and appraiser's tool kit, it seems reasonable that a full DCF should be undertaken alongside the short cut DCF to check the reasonableness of the respective numbers.

5.15   Summary

In this chapter consideration has been given to the construction of the years purchase valuation formulae and the deconstruction of valuation yields to identify their constituent parts. This was followed by a review of the main valuation methodologies used for valuing rack-, under- and over-rented properties.

References

Adams, A., Booth, P., Bowie, D. and Freeth, D. (2003) *Investment Mathematics*. Wiley Finance.

Baum, A. and Crosby, N. (1995) *Property Investment Appraisal*, 2nd edn. London: Routledge.

Brealey, R. and Myers, S. (2002) *Principles of Corporate Finance*. Irwin: McGraw Hill.

Dubben, N. and Sayce, S. (1991) *Property Portfolio Management*. London: Routledge.

Isaac, D. (1998) *Property Investment*. London: MacMillan.

Further reading

Baum, A., Mackmin, D. and Nunnington, N. (1996) *The Income Approach to Property Valuation*, 4th edn. London: International Thomson Publishing.

Butler, D. (1987) *Applied Valuation*. London: MacMillan.

Darlow, C. (1983) *Valuation and Investment Appraisal*. London: Estates Gazette.

Davidson, A.W. (1989) *Parry's Valuation and Investment Tables*. London: Estates Gazette.

Enever, N. and Isaac, D. (1995) *The Valuation of Property Investments*, 5th edn. London: Estates Gazette.

FOCUS www.focusnet.co.uk

Gane, D. (1995) A DCF analysis of market price for leasehold investments. *Journal of Property Valuation & Investment*, 13 (3).

Isaac, D. and Steley, T. (1991) *Property Valuation Techniques*. London: MacMillan.

Richmond, D. (1994) *Introduction to Valuation*, 3rd edn. Basingstoke: MacMillan.

Royal Institution of Chartered Surveyors (1997) *Commercial Investment Property: Valuation Methods: An Information Paper*. London: RICS.

Scarrett, D. (1993) *Property Valuation: The Five Methods*. London: E&FN Spon.

Trott, A. (1986) *Property Valuation Methods Research Report*. London: RICS/ Polytechnic of the Southbank.

6 Issues of leasehold appraisal

Aim of the chapter

- To detail the nature of leasehold interests and introduce the concept of the wasting asset.
- To explain the need for the replacement of capital and demonstrate how interest includes return on and of capital.

- To provide an explanation of how leaseholds can be appraised using both conventional and DCF approaches.
- To analyse the reasons why conventional approaches to leasehold appraisals are outmoded.

6.1 The nature of leasehold interests

The previous chapter considered the valuation of freehold interests where the income is assumed to continue into perpetuity. However, there are other property interests, known as leaseholds, in which the income is only receivable for a certain number of years until the lease ends. A leasehold interest is time limited and is created when the landlord grants a lease for a specific term to a lessee or tenant who may occupy the premises for the period of the lease. The tenant will pay a rent to the landlord for this right and has to return the property to the landlord when the lease terminates, which may be after the lease has been extended by statutory occupation rights.

6.1.1 Terms of a lease

Two of the principal terms are the length of the lease and the rent review periods. During the 1980s a typical institutional lease on commercial lettings would have a term of 20 or 25 years with upward only rent reviews every five years, allowing the landlord to benefit from rising rental values while being protected from any downturns. However, during the 1990s property recession commercial premises lettings became more difficult because of an oversupply of property and a decreasing demand from tenants. Accordingly, tenants held greater negotiating power and, with the introduction of new lease codes in 1995 and 2000, the typical term of years was reduced to ten years or less for offices, with break clauses allowing either tenant or landlord to end the lease after a specified term. The upward only rent clause is currently under review, thus threatening the landlord's security of income.

The lease should also specify who is responsible for the repairs and insurance of the property. For valuation purposes, gross rents may have to cover repairs and/or insurance and should always be converted to net rents before a capital valuation is produced; any expenses not recoverable from a sub-lessee should be deducted from the gross income.

6.1.2   Subletting or assignment

If an occupational tenant no longer needs to occupy the premises but does not wish or cannot terminate the lease, he has the choice of either subletting or assigning his property interest to another tenant, assuming the lease allows it. In both cases the permission of the landlord will usually be required.

The tenant can sublet the premises by granting a sublease to a new occupying tenant for a term of years less than the lease. In this case the original tenant is known as the head lessee (or lessor) and the new occupying tenant is called the sub-lessee. The sub-lessee will pay a sub-rent to the head lessee who in turn will continue to pay his rent – the head rent – to the freeholder.

By assigning the leasehold interest, the tenant will transfer all rights to the property to the assignee (incoming tenant) for the full remaining term of years. The assignee will then be directly responsible to his landlord (the freeholder). All leases granted prior to 1 January 1996 are covered by a privity of contract clause whereby the assignor (original leaseholder) will still remain liable to the freeholder – his or her landlord – under the terms of the lease if the assignee defaults. This provides a measure of security for the landlord but disadvantages the head lessee. However, under the Landlord and Tenant (Covenants) Act 1995 assignors will cease to be liable to the landlord on assignment on leases granted after 1 January 1996, and the sub-lessee is responsible directly to the landlord. Nevertheless, in these leases both landlords and tenants now tend to accept an authorised guarantee agreement (AGA) where the assignor agrees to guarantee the rent if the assignee defaults, thus protecting the landlord's income.

6.2   Leasehold value: the profit rent

Where an occupying tenant pays a rent below the market rent (as defined in Chapter 4), the tenant is said to enjoy a 'profit rent', which is the difference between the higher market rent and the rent paid. This difference in rental levels gives the leasehold interest some value. If a head lessee receives a sub-rent which is greater than the head rent he pays to the freeholder or higher landlord, that is a profit rent. Where the two rents are the same, no profit rent exists.

A profit rent can arise from a number of situations. For example, rents may have risen since the start of the lease because of an increase in occupational demand resulting, perhaps, from a booming economy or a period of rising inflation, or the tenant may have paid a capital sum (known as a premium) at the beginning of the lease. A profit rent can be intermittent and its level can change depending on when rent reviews take place, or it can be related to a percentage of the sub-rent or full rental value, such as a geared ground rent (explained below).

During a period of property recession such as in the 1970s and 1990s when rental values fell, many tenants were paying rents in excess of the open market rental value, giving a negative profit rent. This makes the lease very difficult to assign or sublet and reflects the high risk nature of a leasehold interest in times of falling rental levels. Profit rents can therefore give great complications in analysis and valuation.

There are two basic types of leasehold investments: long and short leaseholds. Long leaseholds are over 25–30 years, originating from a ground lease in which land has been

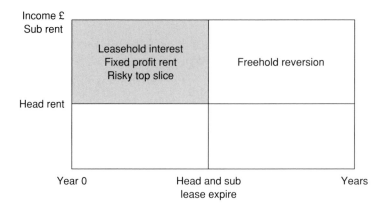

Fig. 6.1   A fixed profit rent.

leased to a leaseholder who subsequently constructs a building on the land and then either occupies the premises or sublets the premises as an investment. The leaseholder will pay a ground rent to the freeholder for the use of the land only. However, at the end of the ground lease both the land and the building will revert to the freeholder.

Prior to the 1950s ground rents were fixed for the whole lease, which in periods of zero inflation maintained their value. However, since the 1960s, when the reverse yield gap arose (see Chapter 3), rent reviews have been incorporated into modern ground leases and ground rents are often geared to an agreed fixed percentage of the market rental value.

Short leaseholds of less than 25 years are created by a subletting, as explained above.

There are also two types of profit rent: a fixed profit rent and a with-review profit rent. The fixed profit rent is derived from a sub-rent and head rent which both have the same expiry date and there are no rent reviews in either the head or the sublease (Fig. 6.1). This profit rent is considered to be more comparable to fixed income investments such as gilts, but whereas the income from gilts is very secure in that the government is unlikely to default, there is a risk attached to the profit rent dependent upon the covenant strength of the sub-lessee.

The with-review profit rent arises from a fixed head rent and a sub-rent that is capable of upward review, leading to a rising profit rent situation as illustrated in Fig. 6.2. The cash flow becomes complex particularly if the dates of head lease reviews do not coincide with those of the sublease; additionally, the levels of growth for both will probably be different, giving differing ratios of rent received to rent paid over the relevant period.

6.3   Inherent disadvantages of leasehold interest compared to freehold interest

A leasehold interest has a number of disadvantages:

- It is a more risky investment because the profit rent is a top slice and is more sensitive to changes in market rents. Changes in rental levels can arise from a change in occupier demand, inflation or deflation, or oversupply of property, and may result in negative

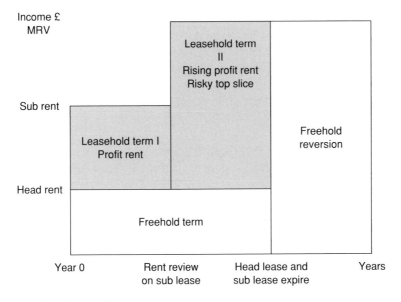

Fig. 6.2   A 'with review' profit rent.

profit rents. The strength of the sub-lessee's covenant (their ability to pay the rent) is critical in determining the risk element.

● There is inconvenience in having a superior landlord in addition to restricting lease terms.
● There can be difficulty in re-letting if a tenant vacates before the end of a lease. A new tenant has to be found, giving rise to expense and perhaps a temporary void in occupation, and then may only agree to concessionary terms which may produce a reduced profit rent. If no tenant can be found, there will be a negative profit rent (as the head rent still has to be paid by the head lessee).
● A leaseholder is liable for dilapidations at the end of the lease and this can be a substantial financial liability if the cost cannot be recovered from the sub-lessee.
● Management expenses may be a liability if the head and sub-lease terms are different.

An appropriate method of valuing a leasehold investment should be able to cope with valuing complicated cash flows and should reflect the inherent disadvantages mentioned above.

6.4   A wasting asset and the need for replacement of capital

In a freehold interest the owner is entitled to receive an income into perpetuity; alternatively, there is the option to sell the freehold interest and receive a capital sum. The freeholder will therefore always have the ability to retrieve the original capital. If sentiment in the market has improved towards the sector and yields have fallen during the period of ownership and/or the rent passing has risen then the sale of the freehold interest may realise a larger sum than was originally paid, resulting in a capital gain. Most institutional investors hold property investments for about seven years before selling them on.

However, the value of a leasehold interest gets progressively less towards its expiry date when the income will cease and the property will revert to the superior owner – either the freeholder or a lessee with a longer lease. Once the lease ends and after any statutory protection has been applied, the occupational leaseholder will have to vacate the premises. With no income or interest to sell, the leaseholder will lose the original capital sum that may have been invested at the start of the lease, by way of say a premium that reflects buying a lease with a substantial profit rent, or in carrying out works to the premises as a condition of the lease.

This type of investment is known as a wasting asset. The value of the leasehold interest will diminish over time until it has no value at all when the lease ends. Even if the profit rent is the same as the freeholder's, it is time limited by the length of the lease and therefore will command a lower capital value. The profit rent must not only be able to compensate the leaseholder for the loss of his capital but must also provide the investor with an adequate return, reflecting the inherent disadvantages of a leasehold investment and the burdens of obligations faced by the leaseholder, even if the premises are sublet to an occupying lessee on good terms.

6.5 Establishing capital value for a leasehold interest

In establishing the appropriate capital value for a leasehold interest, there are two main approaches:

- the conventional or historic approach using an all risks yield; and
- a DCF.

Whilst the DCF approach has been advocated by academics since the 1980s (Baum and Crosby 1995), the market approach is still often based on the all risks yield approach, despite numerous studies pointing to its mathematical inaccuracies (Trott, 1986). However, the DCF approach is being increasingly adopted and is exclusively used for investment worth calculations, as opposed to the estimation of a market transaction price. In this book the DCF approach is advocated as being the only defensible approach that can be adopted. For completeness, however, an analysis of the historic method is supplied below in section 6.6.

A contemporary appraisal using a DCF technique will treat the profit rent as a cash flow like any other type of investment, but the required equated yield for the leaseholder should be above that of a similar freehold investment in order to reflect the additional risks involved. In this case the investor will expect a higher income to offset the capital loss and achieve the same desired return as any other investment. Similarly, in a leasehold interest there is no need to allow for replacement of capital if the profit rent is sufficient to provide the investor with the required rate of return.

6.5.1 Simple leasehold profit rent

The profit rent in a leasehold investment is discounted by the required rate of return and should be large enough to compensate the leaseholder for the lack of capital at the end of the lease. There is therefore no need for an allowance for the replacement of the capital purchase price. However, the choice of the target rate of return will depend upon the individual investor's requirements, and it is argued by Butler (1995) and Baum and Crosby (1995) that an extra risk premium above a freehold equated yield would be logical to reflect the inherent extra risks and characteristics of a leasehold investment, in particular the covenant strength of the sub-lessee. An illustration of the valuation of a simple fixed profit rent is given in Example 6.1.

Example 6.1

A property is held on a head lease with four years remaining at a fixed head rent of £10 000 p.a. The head lessee has sublet the premises on a co-terminus sublease (expires a few days before the head lease) at £110 000 p.a. with no further reviews. Assuming the freehold equated yield is 11%, an extra 5% risk premium is added so the leasehold equated yield is 16%.

Table 6.1   DCF layout for appraisal of a head leasehold.

Year	Rent received	Rent paid	Profit rent	PV £1 at 16%	DCF
1	£110 000	£10 000	£100 000	0.86206	£86 206
2	£110 000	£10 000	£100 000	0.74316	£74 316
3	£110 000	£10 000	£100 000	0.64066	£64 066
4	£110 000	£10 000	£100 000	0.55229	£55 229
				Capital value	**£279 817**

The DCF approach in Table 6.1 can be shortened to a more traditional layout using the YP single rate at the same equated yield. Note that the YP is simply the addition of the PVs so where a constant income is being valued the simple shortcut layout below can be used to produce the same answer.

Short cut layout:

Rent received	£110 000
Less head rent	£10 000
Profit rent	£100 000
YP for four years at 16%	2.7982
Capital value	£279 818

An illustration of how the DCF approach allows for interest or a return of 16% on the original purchase price plus the replacement of the capital purchase price by investing a portion of the profit rent each year into an accumulating fund, or sinking fund, is given in Example 6.2. It is assumed that the profit rent is received at the end of each year (annually in arrears) so the annual sinking fund investments can only start at the end of the first year. The first investment will therefore only accumulate interest for three years and the second for two years while the final payment is added into the fund but receives no interest at all.

The profit rent thus provides the investor with a return of 16% per annum on the purchase price and allows for a replacement of capital by investing in a sinking fund in other similar investments yielding 16%. In practice, however, the investor is more likely to reinvest the whole of the profit rent.

Example 6.2

The head lease of a property held on a head lease with four years remaining at a fixed head rent of £110 000 p.a. has just been sold for £280 000. The head lessee is subject to a subletting which is co-terminus (expires a few days before the head lease) at £210 000 p.a. with no further reviews, thus giving a fixed profit rent of £100 000 p.a. Assuming no liability on the head lessee for potential dilapidations or other outgoings, demonstrate that the purchaser will receive a return of 16% on his investment over the period.

Table 6.2   Appraisal of a leasehold interest showing return on capital and return of capital.

Year	A Profit rent	B Return on purchase price at 16%	C (A–B) Annual sinking fund payments	D Amount of £1 at 16% $(1+0.16)^n$	E (C×D) Annual sinking fund accumulations
1	£100 000	£44 771*	£55 229	1.5609	£86 207
2	£100 000	£44 771	£55 229	1.3456	£74 316
3	£100 000	£44 771	£55 229	1.1600	£64 066
4	£100 000	£44 771	£55 229	1.000	£55 229
				Capital replaced by ASF	**£279 818**

*£44 771 is 16% of £279 818.

6.5.2   Geared leasehold profit rent

A geared profit rent arises where the head rent is fixed (often a ground rent) and the premises are sublet on a modern lease with regular rent reviews. The profit rent has therefore great potential for growth and is geared for upward growth. The profit rental growth or gearing is reflected within the actual cash flow while the growth rate is only explicitly applied to the full rental value achieved upon review. The cash flow is illustrated in Example 6.3.

Example 6.3

A retail shop is held on a ground lease with 15 years unexpired at a fixed ground rent of £10 000 p.a. net. The head lessee has just sublet the shop at MR of £200 000 p.a. on a modern lease with five-yearly rent reviews (see Fig. 6.3). Assume the freehold all risks yield is 6%.

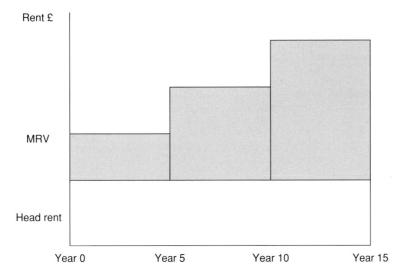

Fig. 6.3   A geared leasehold profit rent.

The market rent growth rate is a constant long-term average found by a formula based upon the mathematical relationship between the all risks yield and the freehold equated yield. The growth rate is determined by supply and demand for all comparable properties in that location and is not affected by the nature of the legal interest that is being valued. The growth rate applied to the full rental value will be the same for both the freehold and leasehold interest in the same property. The growth formula as explained in Chapter 7 is used here to calculate the growth rate for the full rental value and is based on the freehold all risks yield of 6% and freehold equated yield of 11%. The growth rate is calculated to be 5.57%, as shown below.

$$(1 + g)^5 = \frac{\text{YP perp at k\% − YP five years at e\%}}{\text{YP perp at k\% × PV five years at e\%}}$$

Applying this formula, the solution becomes:

$$(1 + g)^5 = \frac{\text{YP perp at 6\% − YP five years at 11\%}}{\text{YP perp at 6\% × PV five years at 11\%}}$$

$$(1 + g)^5 = \frac{12.9708}{9.8916}$$

$$g = \sqrt[5]{1.31128} - 1$$

$$g = 0.0557 = 5.57\%$$

In the example set out above an equated yield of 11% has been assumed for the freehold plus 5% extra risk margin for the leasehold, giving an equated yield of say 16%. The MV is increased at each future review by multiplying by the amount of £1 formula $(1 + g)^n$ to reflect the gearing nature of the investment where g is the annual expected growth rate and

Table 6.3   Appraisal of a rising profit rent.

Years	Rent received	Growth at 5.57%	Rent received	Rent paid	Profit rent	YP 5 years at 16%	PV £1 at 16%	DCF £
1–5	200 000	1.000	200 000	10 000	190 000	3.2743	1.000	622 117
6–10	200 000	1.3113	262 260	10 000	252 260	3.2743	0.4761	393 247
11–15	200 000	1.7195	343 902	10 000	333 902	3.2743	0.2267	247 850
							Capital value	1 516 843

Table 6.4   The effect of tax on a leasehold appraisal.

Years	Profit rent as before	Profit rent net of tax at 40%	YP for 5 years at 9.6%	PV £1 at 9.6%	DCF
A	B	C	D	E	C × D × E
1–5	190 000	114 000	3.8298	1.000	436 597
6–10	252 260	151 356	3.8298	0.6323	366 473
11–15	333 902	200 341	3.8298	0.3998	306 753
				Capital value	1 109 823

n is the number of years prior to the review. The profit rent is capitalised using the equated yield at 16%. The years purchase capitalises each five year tranche of income which is then deferred by the present value of £1 for the relevant number of years in the previous terms. Table 6.3 gives an appraisal of a rising profit rent.

As suggested by the RICS Information Paper on commercial property valuation methods (RICS, 1997) an explicit net of tax approach can be used. Both the profit rent and the leasehold equated yield have been adjusted for tax at 40% so that the net of tax yield is $16\% \times 0.6 = 9.6\%$. The effect of tax on a leasehold appraisal is shown in Table 6.4.

6.5.3   Complicated cash flows where sublease and head lease reviews do not coincide

Complex cash flows on leasehold investments can often arise. For example, rent reviews on subleases and head leases may not coincide, thus producing a mixture of positive and negative profit rents during the holding period of the investment. In such cases the conventional approach to calculating a capital value cannot readily be applied. However, an explicit DCF can cope with the situation and Example 6.4 illustrates how such an investment can be appraised using a DCF.

Example 6.4

Value the leasehold interest in a retail shop that is currently sublet to an occupying tenant on a standard lease with five-yearly reviews and has 18 years unexpired. The current sub-rent is £45 000 p.a. and is due for review in three years. The head lease also has 18 years unexpired but is let on a seven year rent review basis, the next review being due in four years' time. The head rent currently payable is £38 000 p.a.

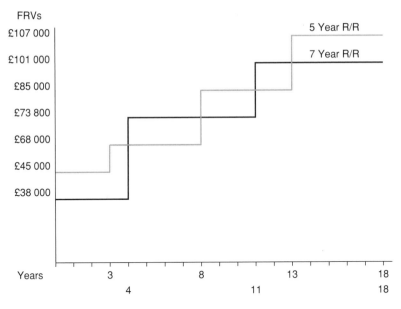

Fig. 6.4   A complicated leasehold interest arising from non-coinciding rent reviews.

Market evidence indicates an all risks yield of 7% for this type of property and a full rental value of £60 000 per annum on a five year review whilst seven-yearly reviews have a 3% uplift. Assume a freehold equated yield of 11% and a 2% extra risk premium for a leasehold equated yield.

The growth rate is found using the growth formula applying a freehold equated yield (e) of 11%, all risks yield of (k) of 7%, and n is the five year rent review to produce a growth rate of 4.55% per annum.

The unusual cash flow is illustrated in Fig. 6.4. Table 6.5 sets out the complicated rent review patterns.

6.5.4   Valuation of a short leasehold investment

An advantage of using an explicit DCF approach is that a short leasehold interest can be valued to reflect the timing of income, such as on a quarterly in advance basis incorporating all relevant outgoings including rent review fees, repair and maintenance liabilities or costs that are non-recoverable from the sub-lessee. Inflation on costs can also be built into the DCF and expected growth on any future reviews on rent receivable or payable can be incorporated. Thus the DCF can give a much more accurate valuation of a realistic cash flow and can be easily programmed on a computerised spreadsheet as shown below in Example 6.5.

Example 6.5

Value a short leasehold interest of five years' unexpired term with a fixed head rent of £40 000 p.a. The sub-rent passing is £100 000 but the full market rent on a three year term is estimated at £125 000. See Table 6.6.

Table 6.5   Valuation of a complex head leasehold.

Sublease

FRV on five year rent review pattern	£60 000
Rent passing	£45 000
Years to review	3
Unexpired term	18

Head lease

FRV on seven year rent review pattern	£62 000	£60 000 plus 3% uplift for seven year review
Rent passing	£38 000	
Years to review	4	
Unexpired term	18	
All risks yield	7.00%	
Freehold equated yield	11.00%	
Growth rate	4.55%	
Leasehold equated yield	13.00%	

NB Rent received in year 4 = £60 000 × (1 + 0.0455) ^ 3
Rent paid in year 5 = £60 000 × (1 + 0.0455) ^ 4 + 3% uplift

Year	Rent received (five year R/R)	Rent paid (seven year R/R)	Profit rent	PV £1 at 13.00%	DCF
1	£45 000	£38 000	£7 000	0.8850	£6 195
2	£45 000	£38 000	£7 000	0.7831	£5 482
3	£45 000	£38 000	£7 000	0.6931	£4 851
4	£68 568	£38 000	£30 568	0.6133	£18 748
5	£68 568	£73 839	−£5 271	0.5428	−£2 861
6	£68 568	£73 839	−£5 271	0.4803	−£2 532
7	£68 568	£73 839	−£5 271	0.4251	−£2 240
8	£68 568	£73 839	−£5 271	0.3762	−£1 983
9	£85 653	£73 839	£11 814	0.3329	£3 933
10	£85 653	£73 839	£11 814	0.2946	£3 480
11	£85 653	£73 839	£11 814	0.2607	£3 080
12	£85 653	£100 821	−£15 168	0.2307	−£3 499
13	£85 653	£100 821	−£15 168	0.2042	−£3 097
14	£106 995	£100 821	£6 174	0.1807	£1 115
15	£106 995	£100 821	£6 174	0.1599	£987
16	£106 995	£100 821	£6 174	0.1415	£874
17	£106 995	£100 821	£6 174	0.1252	£773
18	£106 995	£100 821	£6 174	0.1108	£684
				Capital value	**£33 991**

Table 6.6 sets out the valuation of the short leasehold investment in Example 6.5. However, a problem with using this explicit DCF approach to arrive at a market valuation is the same as with the freehold and lies in the choice of a market accepted rate of return and reliable forecasts for rental growth and yield changes.

6.6   The conventional or historic perspective

The historic approach to valuing a leasehold interest was to capitalise a net profit rent using a yield 1% or 2% higher than the freehold all risks yield on a similar comparable

Table 6.6 Valuation of a short leasehold interest using DCF and spreadsheet.

Sub Lease

MRV on 3 year review pattern	£125 000 per annum payable quarterly in advance
Rent passing	£100 000 per annum payable quarterly in advance
Years to review	2 years
Unexpired term	5 years

Head Lease

Rent passing – fixed	£40 000 per annum payable quarterly in advance
Unexpired term	5 years
Non-recoverable costs	£8000 per annum payable quarterly in advance
Inflation	3.00% per annum reflected on costs
All risks yield	6.00% analysed from local freehold transactions
Freehold equated yield	10.00%
Leasehold equated yield	13.00% 3% extra risk premium
Growth rate	4.23% p.a. derived from formula using 10%, 6% & 3 years
Expected FRV at review	£135 799 per annum payable quarterly in advance
Rent review fees	7.00% of expected FRV payable in two years

Year	Rent received	Rent paid	Costs incl. review fees	Profit rent	PV £1 13.00%	DCF
0	£25 000	£10 000	£2 000	£13 000	1.0000	£13 000
0.25	£25 000	£10 000	£2 015	£12 985	0.9699	£12 594
0.50	£25 000	£10 000	£2 030	£12 970	0.9407	£12 201
0.75	£25 000	£10 000	£2 045	£12 955	0.9124	£11 820
1.00	£25 000	£10 000	£2 060	£12 940	0.8850	£11 451
1.25	£25 000	£10 000	£2 075	£12 925	0.8583	£11 094
1.50	£25 000	£10 000	£2 091	£12 909	0.8325	£10 747
1.75	£25 000	£10 000	£2 106	£12 894	0.8074	£10 411
2.00	£33 950	£10 000	£11 628	£12 322	0.7831	£9 650
2.25	£33 950	£10 000	£2 138	£21 812	0.7596	£16 568
2.50	£33 950	£10 000	£2 153	£21 796	0.7367	£16 058
2.75	£33 950	£10 000	£2 169	£21 780	0.7146	£15 563
3.00	£33 950	£10 000	£2 185	£21 764	0.6931	£15 084
3.25	£33 950	£10 000	£2 202	£21 748	0.6722	£14 619
3.50	£33 950	£10 000	£2 218	£21 732	0.6520	£14 168
3.75	£33 950	£10 000	£2 234	£21 715	0.6323	£13 732
4.00	£33 950	£10 000	£2 251	£21 699	0.6133	£13 308
4.25	£33 950	£10 000	£2 268	£21 682	0.5949	£12 898
4.50	£33 950	£10 000	£2 285	£21 665	0.5770	£12 500
4.75	£33 950	£10 000	£2 301	£21 648	0.5596	£12 114
					Capital value	**£259 581**

property, to reflect the inherent disadvantages of a leasehold interest. This yield was known as the remunerative yield and represents interest on the purchase price to the leaseholder.

In addition, it was assumed that the leasehold investor would allow for a sinking fund, which is a portion of the annual net profit rent invested in a fund. Within the method, this is assumed to accumulate at very low safe yields, normally between 2% and 4% net of tax, to ensure that at the end of the lease the fund accumulations will be sufficient to replace the original purchase price. This is a historical assumption based on insurance policies which then offered 2–3%.

The dual rate approach was introduced in texts written by various academics during the first half of the twentieth century but according to Baum and Crosby (1995:63) it was not until after the Second World War that the dual rate untaxed method was used in practice. At that time rental levels were assumed to remain fairly constant with little expected rental growth; thus profit rents were expected to remain fixed until lease expiry. The sinking fund accumulations allowed the investor to purchase another leasehold interest for the same monetary value at the end of the lease, which equated a wasting leasehold investment with a perpetual freehold.

The historic approach to the valuation of leasehold interests is based on the use of a dual rate years purchase where the return on capital is represented by the remunerative yield and the annual sinking fund allows for the replacement of the capital that was the original purchase price. Before explaining the application of the years purchase dual rate, it is important to describe the derivation of the annual sinking fund formula.

6.6.1   The amount of £1 per annum

The amount of £1 per annum calculates the future accumulations from the investment of £1 at the end of every year accumulating at compound interest. It is particularly useful in estimating the future sum due under a regular savings plan or endowment policy. It is derived from the addition of the compounding formula amount of £1 which is $(1 + i)^n$. It adds up the amount of £1 multipliers for n years less 1 and adds 1 to the total. This can be rather tedious and is simplified into the following formula.

$$\text{Amount of £1 per annum} = \frac{(1+i)^n - 1}{i} \quad \text{or} \quad \frac{A - 1}{i}$$

6.6.2   The annual sinking fund

The annual sinking fund calculates the small annual sum that should be invested in order to accumulate to £1 at the end of a given period of n years. The annual investment sum is referred to as a sinking fund and is assumed to accumulate at compound interest.

The purpose of this formula is to calculate how much should be saved (the sinking fund) at the end of each year in order to accumulate to a specific required sum in the future. Where the amount of £1 per annum formula calculates the future total from an annual investment of £1, the annual sinking fund formula calculates the amount of annual investment necessary in order to accumulate to £1 in the future. The future fund will comprise the annual savings plus interest and, like the amount of £1 per annum formula, assumes that the final payment is made at the end of the investment period but earns no interest. The annual sinking fund is the reciprocal of the amount of £1 per annum formula, as seen below.

$$\text{Annual sinking fund (ASF)} = \frac{1}{\text{Amount of £1 per annum}} \quad \text{or} \quad \frac{i}{(1+i)^n - 1} \quad \text{or} \quad \frac{i}{A - 1}$$

It is particularly relevant to the valuation of a leasehold investment using the historic approach as the sinking fund is the portion of the profit rent invested each year in order to accumulate to replace the purchase price.

6.6.3   The years purchase dual rate – valuation and analysis

As explained earlier, when valuing a freehold investment the basic approach is:

Rental income $\times$ YP = Capital value

The same principle applies to a traditional leasehold valuation where the income is the profit rent and the YP multiplier incorporates two separate rates of interest. The investor in a wasting asset seeks to obtain an income representing the return on the investment comparable with a freehold but must also re-invest an annual sum into a sinking fund. The profit rent is therefore split into two parts:

- The spendable income is the return for the risks attached to the investment. The rate applied to the spendable income is known as the *remunerative rate* and is derived from the freehold all risks yield. It is in fact the simple rate of return expected by the investor on the original loan and is represented by the symbol **i**.
- The sinking fund is the annual investment into a fund to allow for replacement of the purchase price of the leasehold interest at the end of the lease. The rate applied to the sinking fund is the low risk-free *accumulative rate* of return of capital and is represented by the symbol **SFi**.

When the rates on the above two differ, the YP dual rate formula is used. If the accumulative and remunerative rates are the same then either the years purchase dual rate or single rate formula can be used to produce the same answer, as follows:

$$\text{YP dual rate} = \frac{1}{(i + SF)}$$

Where   i = remunerative rate
SFi = accumulative rate

$$\frac{1}{i + \dfrac{SFi}{(1 + SFi)^n - 1}}$$

When the sinking fund accumulates at a lower safer yield than the remunerative yield, the two yields are incorporated into the dual rate YP as illustrated in Example 6.6.

Example 6.6

A freeholder has let a shop on lease with ten years to run at a ground rent of £2000 p.a. The new lessee has sublet the premises for £12 000 p.a.

(a) Value the head lessee's interest for sale in the open market assuming comparable evidence indicates a freehold all risks yield of 6%.

(b) Show how both a return on and return of capital are achieved.

To reflect the additional risks of a leasehold interest a remunerative yield of 7% is adopted and a sinking fund of 4% (Table 6.7).

Table 6.7   Valuation of a leasehold interest using traditional methodology.

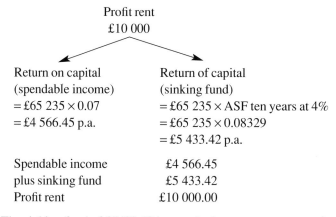

Net income received	£12 000
Less ground rent payable	£ 2 000
Profit rent	£ 10 000
YP for 10 years at 7 + 4%	×6.5235*
Capital value	£65 235

$$*\text{YP for 10 years at } 7 + 4\% = \cfrac{1}{0.07 + \cfrac{0.04}{(1.04)^{10} - 1}} = 6.5235$$

The following analysis shows how a return on and return of capital are achieved:

Profit rent
£10 000

Return on capital
(spendable income)
= £65 235 × 0.07
= £4 566.45 p.a.

Return of capital
(sinking fund)
= £65 235 × ASF ten years at 4%
= £65 235 × 0.08329
= £5 433.42 p.a.

Spendable income	£4 566.45
plus sinking fund	£5 433.42
Profit rent	£10 000.00

The sinking fund of £5433.42 is exactly the correct amount to be invested each year to accumulate to the original purchase price and can be proved to be sufficient as follows.

Annual sinking fund × amount of £1 p.a. 10 years at 4%   £5433.42 p.a. × 12.006

Capital recouped   £65 234*

*£1 error is due to rounding off

6.6.4   Reasons for rejection of the years purchase dual rate approach

As has been said above, the dual rate approach was predicated on the notion that rental values and yields would remain static, or fairly static, throughout the period of the lease. It was also put into practice during a time before rent reviews became common, again reflecting the lack of expected rental growth. With the emergence in the 1960s and after of both inflation and upward only rent reviews, the ability of investors to reinvest at the end of the term on comparable terms vanished and with it the rationale for the dual rate approach. In particular, a number of technical difficulties were revealed.

Much research has taken place into the adequacy or otherwise of traditional techniques. The first major report was the Trott Report (1986), which was commissioned by the RICS to examine the issues. This report, like those of later writers, concluded that the techniques then adopted were flawed and should be either mathematically adjusted or replaced by the use of DCF. Below is a summary of the issues.

Sinking fund

- The low yield is unrealistic and borrowers are also unlikely to accept 3% when they are paying probably twice as much on their loan (Gane, 1995).
- The sinking fund only recoups an original historic purchase price, and in times of rising inflation the accumulated sinking fund will not be adequate to replace the value in real terms. This does not make the leasehold interest equivalent to a freehold and therefore fails to comply with the rationale of the YP dual rate approach.
- However, a consolation is that in times of inflation the rental value in the example above would have risen from £12 000 per annum to £16 127 per annum over five years (assuming growth at 3% per annum), so where there is a review in the sublease and a fixed head rent there is potential for high short-term rental growth far exceeding that achieved in a freehold investment.

Investment behaviour

- Where the term to be valued was an occupational lease, the initial purchase price was normally regarded as an investment into the business to be recouped out of business profits, and not as a property investment.
- Investors normally purchase a number of property leasehold and freehold investments and a sinking fund is rarely taken out as the whole of the profit rent will be reinvested in other similar property investments.
- Borrowers will have a loan with an interest rate in excess of the low accumulative rate and therefore would be extremely unlikely to set up a sinking fund.
- Another problem with the low sinking fund rate is that the investor may apply a lower remunerative rate than the gross sinking fund return. For example, if 7% remunerative yield were used with a net 4% sinking fund and tax at 50p, then the gross accumulative yield would be 8%, which is greater than the remunerative yield so the investor would be better advised to invest in the sinking fund only.

Comparable leasehold evidence

- There are fewer leasehold transactions (Gane, 1995) available for use as comparable evidence with the same locational and physical qualities, unexpired term, reversionary date and ratio of rent to full rental value. The extra 1% or 2% increase on the freehold yield reflects these differences but may not be adequate, as a leasehold interest is a top slice investment with different growth potential and characteristics from a freehold investment (Baum and Crosby, 1995).
- The RICS Research Report (Trott, 1986) highlighted the difficulty in a full analysis of the combination of the variables used in the YP dual rate (remunerative rate, annual

sinking fund rate, tax rate). For example, a YP multiplier of 8.1 could be 7% and 3% (tax 30p), or 7.5% and 4% (tax 30p) or 9.3% and 5% (gross fund) or 10.75% single rate (Darlow, 1983:273).

Frequency and timing of payments

- The YP dual rate assumes that the profit rent is receivable and the sinking fund payable annually in arrears, whereas most modern leases are let on quarterly in advance terms. If the head rent is paid annually in arrears and the sub-rent is receivable quarterly in advance, then greater errors are made in the above valuation.

Occupiers as purchasers

- According to the RICS Research Report (Trott, 1986) it is inappropriate for an occupier to replace the capital value by an ASF because occupiers regard the purchase price as a rental paid in advance and it is a deductible expense for income tax purposes.
- In taking an assignment, many occupiers base their bids on the potential profitability of that location and pay 'key' money for prime sites, which makes valuation and analysis particularly difficult as the bids cannot often be reconciled to àny normal valuation method.
- The length of lease term is often irrelevant for occupiers as under the security of tenure terms in the Landlord and Tenant Act 1954 the tenant has the prospect of renewing his lease, although there is the risk that the landlord may succeed in recovering possession.

Profit rents and gearing

- If there are more rent reviews on the sublease than the head lease, then the profit rent has the potential to grow and is highly geared. The traditional YP dual rate is unable to reflect the gearing nature of some leasehold investments, as is illustrated in Example 6.7.

Example 6.7

Two leasehold investments each produce a profit rent of £45 000 p.a. and are held on ten year head leases. Both are sublet for ten years at MRV but there is a rent review on the sublease in five years' time.

A traditional approach can only value the current profit rent for ten years and is unable to reflect the different growth potential of both investments, as illustrated below:

Investment A	£	Investment B	£
MRV	50 000	MRV	250 000
Less fixed head rent	5 000	Less fixed head rent	205 000
Profit rent	45 000	Profit rent	45 000
YP for 10 years at 11% and 4%	×5.1735	YP for 10 years at 11% and 4%	×5.1735
Capital value	£232 808	Capital value	£232 808

Both investments are valued at £232 808, but if rents are growing at 5% p.a. over the next five years, then the growth in the profit rent for each investment shows a very different picture.

Investment A		**Investment B**	
MRV	£50 000	£250 000	
× Amount £1 five years at 5%	× 1.2763	× 1.2763	
Estimated MRV at review	£63 815	£319 075	
less fixed head rent	£5 000	£205 000	
Profit rent	£58 815	£114 075	

Increase in profit rent

Investment A: $\dfrac{13\,815}{45\,000} \times 100 = \mathbf{30.7\%}$

Investment B: $\dfrac{69\,075}{45\,000} \times 100 = \mathbf{154\%}$

Annual rate of growth

Investment A: **5.49%**

Investment B: **32.4%**

Investment B therefore has the most growth potential and is at most risk if rents should fall, but the traditional approach is unable to distinguish between the two investments. Highly geared investments tend to have a different growth profile from freehold investments and that growth rate will depend upon the ratio of rent received to rent paid.

If we use a shortcut DCF approach to value the same leasehold investments, a different set of results occurs.

Assuming an equated yield of 16% and an annual rental growth rate of 5%:

Investment A		**Investment B**	
Term I		*Term I*	
Rent receivable	£50 000	Rent receivable	£250 000
less head rent	£5 000	less head rent	£205 000
Profit rent	£45 000	Profit rent	£45 000
YP for five years at 16%	3.2743	YP for five years at 16%	3.2743
CV of term	£147 344	CV of term	£147 344
Term II		*Term II*	
MRV today	£50 000	MRV today	£250 000
× amount £1 five years at 5%	1.2763	× amount £1 five years at 5%	1.2763
Expected MRV	£63 814	Expected MRV	£319 075
less head rent	£5 000	less head rent	£205 000
Profit rent	£58 814	Profit rent	£114 075
YP for five years at 16%	3.2743	YP for five years at 16%	3.2743
PV five years at 16%	0.4761	PV five years at 16%	0.4761
CV term II	£91 685	CV term II	£177 831
CV of leasehold	£239 029	CV of leasehold	£325 175
say	£240 000	say	£325 000

Leasehold investments can also produce very complex patterns of rental growth, particularly where review dates on head and subleases do not coincide. The top slice can be very sensitive to just small changes in the growth of full rental value and the profit rent is therefore very highly geared. This complex gearing is not reflected by the use of all risks yield derived from freehold analysis by adopting the all risks yield plus + 1% or 2%.

Rising profit rents

Rising profit rents will occur when the rent receivable is below the MRV and there is a review on the sublease in five years' time. There is an over-provision of the capital by the two separate sinking funds set up over terms I and II. The first sinking fund will continue to accumulate over term II so when the lease ends there will be an over-replacement of capital by the sinking fund resulting in an under-valuation of the investment. All that is needed is a single sinking fund.

This problem has been overcome by a number of alternative traditional approaches including the double sinking fund, annual equivalent or sinking fund methods which are detailed in Baum *et al.* (1996). However, all methods involve rather tedious calculations, which produce varying answers and are rarely used in practice. The hardcore approach does, however, minimise the problem of valuing varying profit rents.

6.7 Summary

The RICS and Polytechnic of the Southbank Research Report on property valuation methods (Trott, 1986) and other subsequent study papers including research by Baum and Crosby (1995) consider the use of the years purchase dual rate in some detail. The general conclusion is that this approach is not only mathematically inaccurate but has many inherent flaws. The use of the traditional YP dual rate approach was logical during a period of zero inflation, but today so many problems arise, producing great errors in the valuation of leasehold investments, that most valuers have now adopted growth explicit methods involving the use of DCF. A defensible modern approach to the valuation of leaseholds should address the problems related not only to the sinking fund but also to gearing and other fluctuations in the profit rental pattern.

There is therefore a need for a modern professionally acceptable pricing technique to value leasehold interests, and it should be able to reflect the special and different characteristics inherent in a leasehold investment. It would appear that an explicit DCF approach overcomes many of the problems arising from the use of a historic approach. A DCF approach can deal with complicated cash flows and provides an essential analytical tool in the investment decision process for the investor. Whether it is an accepted market approach to leasehold valuation depends upon the practitioner's attitude to choice of a market rate of return, confidence in incorporating realistic rental and yield projections into the cash flow, and total rejection by the profession of the historic approach.

References

Baum, A. and Crosby, N. (1995) *Property Investment Appraisal*, 2nd edn. London: Routledge.

Baum, A., Mackmin, D. and Nunnington, N. (1996) *The Income Approach to Property Valuation*, 4th edn. London: International Thomson Publishing.

Butler, D. (1995) *Applied Valuation*, 2nd edn. Basingstoke: MacMillan.

Darlow, C. (1983) *Valuation and Investment Appraisal*. London: Estates Gazette.

Gane, D. (1995) A DCF analysis of market price for leasehold investments. *Journal of Property Valuation & Investment*, 13 (3): 42–52.

Royal Institution of Chartered Surveyors (1997) *Commercial Investment Property: Valuation Methods. An Information Paper*. London: RICS.

Trott, A. (1986) *Property Valuation Methods Research Report*. London: RICS/Polytechnic of the Southbank.

Further reading

Brown, G. and Matysiak, G. (2000) *Real Estate Investment: A Capital Market Approach*. London: Pearson Education Limited.

Davidson, A.W. (2000) *Parry's Valuation & Investment Tables*, 12th edn. London: Estates Gazette.

Enever, N. and Isaac, D. (1995) *The Valuation of Property Investments*, 5th edn. London: Estates Gazette.

Hoesli, M. and Macgregor, B.D. (2000) *Property Investment: Principles and Practice of Portfolio Management*. Harlow: Pearson Education Ltd.

Isaac, D. (2000) *Property Investment*. London: MacMillan.

Isaac, D. and Steley, T. (1991) *Property Valuation Techniques*. London: MacMillan.

Richmond, D. (1994) *Introduction to Valuation*, 3rd edn. Basingstoke: MacMillan.

Royal Institution of Chartered Surveyors (1995) *Code of Practice for Commercial Leases in England and Wales*. London: RICS.

Royal Institution of Chartered Surveyors/British Property Federation (2002) *Code of Practice for Commercial Leases in England and Wales*, 2nd edition. London: RICS.

Scarrett, D. (1993) *Property Valuation: The Five Methods*. London: E&FN Spon.

7 Structuring investment appraisals to determine investment worth

Aims of the chapter

- To develop and explain the meaning of investment worth in a property context.
- To introduce readers to the methodology used in appraising property investments.
- To place value and worth into the context of market efficiency.
- To explain the factors that drive a DCF worth calculation.

- To consider the structure and components of a DCF and analyse the inputs and outputs to the cash flows.
- To examine the exit period assumptions and practice.
- To consider the checks and balances to be incorporated within the DCF calculation.
- To detail the professional (RICS) guidance on worth and its rationale.

7.1 Introduction

The concept of investment worth has come to the fore within the real estate professional literature and practice in recent years. It is distinguishable from a market valuation in that it takes as its concern an individualist and subjective approach.

In Chapter 1 consideration was given to the distinctions between value, worth and price. If markets are pricing future expected returns correctly, then valuations using comparable evidence and valuation methodologies should equal worth derived by appraisal of future expected cash flows and returns.

Within earlier chapters of the book the determinants of market valuations have been considered. In essence, where property is to be valued for the purposes of determining a likely transaction price, the chief consideration for the valuer will be to ensure that the figure produced takes cognisance of only those factors that would be included within the valuation of the potential purchaser(s). It is, in reality, an exercise in interpretation, through experience and expertise and careful analysis of transactional data, of the comparable evidence and 'mood' of the market at a given point in time.

However, the position of the appraiser is different where the instruction is for the purposes of advising on the worth of a property for a specific instructing client, either to inform a possible purchase decision or as part of ongoing management. In these circumstances, the process is introspective and focused only on the specific circumstances and needs of the instructing client organisation. It is with the latter set of circumstances that this chapter is concerned.

7.2   The efficient market hypothesis

The pricing of an investment within an investment market is said to be efficient where value equals worth. This is known as the efficient market hypothesis. Levy explores this in a capital markets context in his book on the essentials of investment (Levy, 2002). Considerable research on this area has been undertaken in relation to the stock market, but there has been less attention to it in relation to property.

For market efficiency to prevail a number of key tenets need to be present. The application of these ideas is explored further when we consider portfolio risk, but they are introduced here. They can be grouped under four headings.

- *Information efficiency*: this has three levels:
  - o For a truly efficient market, a strong form of efficiency is where *all* information is publicly available and is in the price of investments.
  - o Below this is the semi-strong form of information efficiency, in which all publicly available information is in prices, but 'insider information' is not.
  - o Finally there is the weak form of efficiency in which information relating to past price movements is encapsulated into market prices such that abnormal profits cannot be gained by identifying price trends.
- *Good analysts*: there is an assumption that those operating in the markets are good analysts and are able to understand and apply appropriate valuation and appraisal methodologies.
- *Ability to deal on price anomalies*: where price anomalies exist there is the ability in the market to undertake buy/sell transactions quickly and cheaply to remove the price anomaly.
- *Taxation free*: there is an (unrealistic) assumption that there are no taxes in the market place that could give rise to pricing differentials.

If a market is inefficient then price or value will not be equal to worth. If this is the case then assets within the market may be under- or over-priced. This gives the potential for investments to out- or under-perform the returns that otherwise might be expected.

DCF analysis provides a framework whereby the analyst can seek to identify mis-priced investments, and thus identify buy and sell strategies.

7.3   The efficient market hypothesis in a property market context

In the context of the above four elements required for value or price to equal worth, how does the property investment market stand? Consideration is given to each of these points individually in the following.

- *Information in the commercial property market.* The commercial property market, unlike the stock market, has no central market place. Detailed information about and details relating to transactions are only available to those involved in the deal and to those who through their network of contacts can gain access to this information.

  The publicly available information on property sales and letting transactions is available to subscribers through Property Intelligence's Focus service (www.focusnet.

co.uk) and EGi (www.egi.co.uk). These services provide information that has been published in the trade press, annual accounts, via press releases, and so forth. However, whilst this information is a good starting point for valuers and appraisers, it is not subject to verification. In practice, the levels of information held by parties and potential parties to a transaction may be significantly different.

o The calculation of the effective open market rental value, as against the headline rent, may differ according to the information gathered by the respective parties. It is not uncommon for the publicly available information about a letting deal to not tell the full story; for example, the amount paid as a capital inducement or information on lease take backs may be omitted.

o Off-market transactions, where agents have not been involved, currently form a growing section of the investment market and details of these deals frequently are not disclosed.

o Specialist properties often require specialist valuation methods, which may not be generally understood.

o Good valuers and appraisers develop a wide network of contacts, such that they can gather in reliable information on deals. This point is recognised in the RICS Valuation Manual, which states that valuers must have knowledge and experience of the market in which they operate.

- *Good analysts in the commercial property market.* The UK property industry has developed a sophisticated range of valuation techniques, as set out in Chapters 1 and 2. However, the discounted cash flow appraisal method is still not widely used nor fully understood by a significant number of players.

o The DCF analysis methodologies used in other capital markets to analyse expected future cash flows and returns are not generally used in conjunction with valuations in the UK. This is the case, in particular, outside the major property markets.

o Property professionals in the main have little experience of forecasting techniques as these generally do not form part of their professional or academic training. The future cash flows on which their DCF analysis is based may not always be robust.

o Property investors in the UK look in the main at investments on a single asset basis, and rarely from a portfolio diversification perspective. Properties with diversification benefits may as a result be mis-priced. Chapter 12 considers this in more detail.

- *Ability to deal on price anomalies in the commercial property market.* Unlike equities and bonds which are readily tradeable on the stock market, property is complicated and expensive to transact. At times during a property recession (as in 1973–75 and 1990–92), transactions across the market may be difficult to complete. For specialist properties, or properties with structural, locational or legal problems, it may be difficult to undertake transactions quickly. High transfer costs and the inability to buy/sell property quickly leads to what a number of academics call sticky pricing.

- *Taxes are ignored.* In the efficient market hypothesis, taxes are ignored. For investors in bonds and equities, the tax consequences of investing in the asset can be calculated in a relatively straightforward manner, and are usually similar for all listed companies. When investing in direct property, however, the tax position can vary from property to property.

Capital allowances and other taxes relating to property, in particular when property is held by a corporate vehicle, are a complex area. Property analysts tend to undertake their appraisals on a before tax basis, leaving their clients to add in details relating to their tax position. A small number of players in the market are very sophisticated in this area, whilst the majority tend not to be.

Given the above, market efficiency for the commercial property market is less easily achieved than for the equities and bond markets. It is possible for buyers and sellers to identify mis-priced properties, and to undertake transactions accordingly.

The potential benefits thus lie with those investors who have access to excellent levels of information, high-quality analytical skills, the ability to work with leading agents, good solicitors who can transact deals quickly, and access to good tax advice. For these investors there can be opportunities to identify property investments where value or price and worth are not the same. In this context Baum *et al.* (1996) considered the way in which prices were formed in the property market, the occurrence of mis-pricing and the important role of DCF-style investment analysis techniques.

7.4   The worth approach – discounted cash flow analysis

Previous chapters have discussed the scope of value, price and worth, and identified the areas of overlap. It was concluded that discounted cash flow analysis in the UK was predominantly used as an investment appraisal tool. In a historical context, explicit DCF analysis has been used by leading institutional investors since the 1960s to calculate rates of return to aid investment decisions in equity and fixed interest markets.

In contrast, the application of growth-explicit DCF approaches in the UK property market only really started to be considered by a few leading players in the mid to late 1980s. However, it was the recessionary market of the early 1990s that encouraged most leading investors and their investment advisers to undertake DCF analysis in addition to valuations.

The publication of Brown's book, *Property Investment and the Capital Markets*, provided a starting point for the practitioner to consider alternative approaches to appraising property investments (Brown, 1991). Practitioners were encouraged by the limitations of the conventional valuation techniques to consider alternative methodologies used by analysts in the competing asset classes.

In particular, rapidly changing rental values and uncertain prospects for rents prompted a growing number of investors to make explicit their views about the future movement of rental value, rather than to rely on constant rental growth figures implied into the valuation yields. The publication of Baum and Crosby's book on property investment analysis (Baum and Crosby, 1995) provided practitioners with a much-needed analytical framework. Peto *et al.* (1996) added to the debate, as did a joint Investment Property Forum/RICS Information Paper on the calculation of worth (IPF/RICS, 1997). By 2000, the commercial property industry had latched onto DCF methodologies, though the debate over the calculation of investment worth continued (Hutchison and Nanthakumaran, 2000), and has been placed into a Continental European context (McParland *et al.*, 2000).

Whilst the valuer is seeking to determine a single point estimate of value, the property investment analyst using DCF methodology is seeking to identify worth in terms of the best estimate of the property's worth, and a range of possible outcomes around the best estimate. As will be discussed in Chapter 8, DCF provides the wherewithal for the analyst to put the prospective performance and returns into a risk context by identifying a range of possible figures for the worth of the property.

One of the perceived strengths of traditional valuations is their simplicity. There are relatively few components in a traditional property valuation: passing rent, unexpired term of the leases, estimate of the market rental value (MRV), purchaser's selling costs and valuation yield. In practice a number of these are known variables; those that the valuer has to determine using comparable evidence are the valuation yield and the MRV.

In contrast, DCF analysis includes many more variables and data inputs. In the main DCF is used as an appraisal tool to determine whether the price for the property in the market fairly reflects its worth from the investor's perspective. Thus these inputs are viewed from the investor's perspective, not that of the market place.

DCF analysis requires the property analyst to:

- reflect the components of all anticipated cash flows;
- have cash flows based on comparables and reasoned forecasts;
- reflect investors' market perceptions;
- reflect debt finance;
- reflect taxes; and
- reflect risk to future net incomes and capital flows.

DCF should be complementary to market valuations. DCF calculations should be carried out in a professional manner, with the adoption of standard definitions and standardised layouts. The growing usage of debt to finance property purchases (Kingfisher Property Finance, 2004) has encouraged many investors to consider not just the property returns but also the returns on equity. Traditional valuations, unlike DCF analysis, are ill equipped to deal with this. The requirement to take a return on equity approach, combined with the increasing usage of spreadsheets within the property industry, has significantly increased the use of DCF analysis.

Discounted cash flow calculations can arrive at a single figure or a range of figures for worth by reflecting all anticipated cash flows, based on analysis of comparables or indirect evidence and expectations of the future derived from forecasts or estimates. In contrast, the inputs to valuations are derived from current market evidence, and there is no forecasting of rents. In a valuation, if there is a rent review in say three years' time, it is current rental value that is applied as at the rent review date and not forecast rental value. This is because any rental growth is implied into the valuation yield. Implicit within the valuation yield are all the factors influencing the property and its returns in the future. The valuation yield used in the valuation is derived from evidence of comparable deals done.

DCF analysis, unlike implicit valuations, unbundles the key variables and makes them explicit. Given that more variables are involved, it is good practice to include as part of a DCF appraisal a statement that follows the practical guidelines for preparing worth calculations as suggested by the IPF/RICS. This should include a statement that establishes and confirms the client's needs; limitations as to use; caveats covering assumptions, extent of liability and restriction on publication; and the form and content of the report including the basis of the discount rate, time scale, mathematical calculations and factual and estimated data.

A number of countries, such as the US and Australia, use DCF widely to the point that it has become a recognised and approved explicit valuation tool. In fact the Australian Institute of Valuers and Land Economists goes further and has drawn up industry standards for DCF appraisals. These cover a comprehensive range of items including layout styles, required information, such as whether the cash flows are conventional or non-conventional, mathematical conventions, software used and its underlying assumptions, and an explanation and glossary of terms.

7.5   Introduction to property discounted cash flows

The creation of a DCF appraisal model for a property with a single tenant, and let on a long FRI lease with upward only rent reviews, is relatively straightforward. However, increasing complexity is brought on board with multi-let properties and where there is one or more of the following: non-recoverable outgoings, indexation of rents, short leases and void potential, gearing, tax issues, and intricate structures.

In essence, the worth calculation requires the appraiser or property analyst, in consultation with the client (the owner or potential bidder), to develop a DCF model. The IPF/RICS (1997) in particular highlighted three primary areas of a DCF calculation:

- *Cash flows.* Throughout the holding period the cash flow must be estimated; this requires knowledge of actual cash flows and estimation of future cash flows which will be based on estimates of rental growth; potential voids; and depreciation and estimates of outgoings (such as refurbishment costs). Of particular importance is the terminal value and the exit yield used to arrive at the exit value. At the end of the holding period, the assumption is that the property will be sold. It is therefore important to determine the terminal value, which represents the worth of the cash flows after the exit/sale date.
- *Time horizon.* This is the estimated holding period. All DCFs must be carried out over a specific period. In contrast, a traditional valuation will assume a holding period of perpetuity for freeholds and the unexpired term for leaseholds. In a DCF (worth) appraisal, a holding period of between five and 15 years is normally adopted.
- *Discount rate.* The discount rate will represent an individual investor's required return for the property, including an allowance for both specific and market risk. (Issues relating to the discount rate were discussed in Chapter 3 in the context of competing asset classes, and looked at in more detail in Chapter 5.)

DCF should be viewed as complementary to market valuations, and there is merit in having standard definitions and standardised layouts. In a DCF, each net cash flow, including the term income, the income expected following rent reviews and the value of the property in the last cash flow period, is discounted at either a target or required rate of return to produce a net present value (NPV), or at the internal rate of return (IRR), which produces an NPV of zero.

The discounting process should also reflect the actual timing of the payment of rent (normally quarterly in advance) and interest payments (usually quarterly in arrears). In consequence a DCF approach is more accurate in comparing the timing of all costs and benefits to arrive at the NPV or IRR. The DCF appraisal involves a 'forecast' of rents, outgoings, debt service costs and capital expenditures over the holding period, together with a 'forecast' of the exit value as at the end of the cash flows.

DCF is not necessarily a solution to producing a more accurate market valuation, but has the advantage of accounting explicitly for growth for each period of contracted and expected income; for instance, by use of different growth rates for each year, and provision for rental voids (provided that market-derived yields do not already allow for voids). In essence a DCF unpicks the implicit assumptions of a traditional valuation, and thereby enables the property analyst to consider whether these implicit assumptions are in line with the client's expectations for the property.

7.6   Discounted cash flow analysis in practice

Before embarking on the structure of a DCF model, it is important to recognise that the valuer is seeking to determine a single point estimate of value. In contrast, the property investment analyst using DCF methodology is seeking to identify worth in terms of the best estimate of the property's worth, and is seeking to place this into a range of possible figures for the worth of the property. This use of a range of figures for the property's worth is explored in more detail in Chapter 9, which considers risk analysis.

It is the wide range and number of different variables that are or can be incorporated into a DCF model that can put off many property users. Thus for some players in the commercial property market this requirement for significant amounts of data and forecast information is seen as a weakness and a flaw in DCF appraisals. To others, however, it is seen as a strength and an opportunity to identify mis-priced investments. It is worth remembering that the investment analysts in the equities markets use DCF as a valuation technique, and they are accustomed to dealing with forecasts and large numbers of variables.

When building a DCF model, the skill is to identify the known inputs and the variables, and to create a series of cash flow figures for each period over which the analysis is being undertaken from which the required outputs can be calculated. The framework of a DCF model, as set out in an Excel worksheet, is described in Table 7.1.

Table 7.1   Framework for a DCF.

Ref., author, checked by		Analysis date and client	
Known values	NPVs IRRs Exit ratios		Data table for sensitivity analysis
Assumptions			
Periods and frequency of cash flow (quarterly or monthly)			
In flows (rent, recoverable expenses, parking fees)			
Out flows (fees, void expenses, refurb costs)			
Net cash flows for the property investment			
Borrowings and debt service cash flows			
Net cash flows on the equity investment			
Tax cash flows (allowances, grants, subsidies)			
Net cash flows on equity investment after tax			

Please see Spreadsheet 9 for a worked example of how a DCF appraisal model can be set out for a property investment with a single tenant.

The components of a DCF model can be split into specific components. Different players have developed different layouts for their DCF models but the calculation methodology for the different models is intrinsically similar; the differences are in the complexity in construction of the cash flows and the underlying forecasts.

The DCF appraisal model, thus, comprises a number of elements:

- *Background information*: relating to the property, the client, the author of the analysis, the analysis date and the name of the individual who has checked the spreadsheet.
- *Known values*: for example, the passing rent, the date of the next rent review(s), the floor area. In some instances the purchase price and the purchaser's costs will be known.
- *Variables*: for example, the rental growth rate, the exit valuation yield, the required rate of return, the estimate of the open market rental value, non-recoverables, growth rate for non-recoverables.
- *The analysis period*: will the period over which the analysis is taken be one year, five years, ten years or even longer? Clearly the longer the period of analysis, the greater the degree of uncertainty that arises.
- *The cash flow periods*: under traditional valuation methods, there is an assumption that rents are received annually in arrears; in reality, they are normally paid quarterly in advance. The DCF will require to be set up with due regard to assumptions as to the cash flow periods.
- *The net cash flows*: the in flows minus the out flows. The net cash flow may also be known as the property's net operating income.
- *The debt cash flows*: to produce the net cash flow for the equity investor, being the net property cash flows plus the money borrowed minus the debt service costs.
- *The tax, grants and subsidies cash flows*: to produce the net cash flows for the equity investor after tax and debt service costs.

Using the above, or a similar, framework it is possible to incorporate the property analyst's and the client's views on what numbers are appropriate for the key variables. The main variables that usually need incorporating into the DCF model are discussed below.

7.6.1   Timing of the cash flows

The convention with DCFs is to allow for future cash flows in equal periods of time, reflecting the actual receipt of income. Most rents are receivable on a quarterly in advance basis. The DCF can be adapted to reflect this, and so can provide a realistic calculation of IRR and NPV that also allows comparison with other non-property assets.

There is no recommended layout for an explicit discounted cash flow although many organisations have developed their own individual approach on a spreadsheet. However, the model is attempting to forecast a future cash flow, and an advantage of an explicit discounted cash flow is that it can assess the cash flows as and when they occur.

For long cash flows, it is sometimes viewed as being simpler and more convenient to use annual periods. However, this will produce different figures for the IRRs and NPVs as compared to quarterly or monthly cash flows. When gearing is involved this difference can be significant and will usually produce underestimates of the IRR and NPV figures.

Where the cash flow is expressed not on an annual basis but, for example, quarterly, the IRR produced using the standard Excel function =IRR(values, guess) will be a quarterly IRR and thus will need to be compounded up to the annual figure. Excel's =XIRR(values, dates, guess) function can be used to produce an annual IRR or, alternatively, the =ANN_IRR(values, periods_pa, guess) function using the Excel Add-In, DCF Analyst can be used. There are similar functions for the NPV calculations.

> Please see Spreadsheet 10 for a worked example showing the effect that the timing of cash flows has on IRR and NPVs.
>   This worked example also highlights the need in Excel's NPV function to initially ignore the period zero cash flow, and to add it back in at the end of the calculation.

Timing of cash flows could be in advance at the beginning of the period (BOP) or in arrears at the end of the period (EOP). Excel assumes all cash flows are receivable at the end of the period, so adjustments need to be made for in advance cash flows, for example, an in advance cash flow receivable at the beginning of period 1 would be entered into Excel as being receivable in period 0.

7.6.2   Length of analysis or holding period

DCFs require cash flow forecasts over a specified future holding period rather than valuing to perpetuity. Commercial real estate tends to have a much longer holding period than equities, partly due to the relatively high transaction costs and illiquidity issues. As will be demonstrated below, the choice of a benchmark/risk free interest rate with an appropriate maturity date may be determined by the holding period. (This is also detailed in Chapter 5.)

Research has shown that a median holding period for commercial property as a sector is between eight and 12 years (Collett *et al.*, 2003). Retail property was shown to have a longer holding period than small office and industrial property. Research by Buck (2003) at Kingston University in conjunction with IPD/DID also confirmed that the holding period for offices by UK institutional investors had a median of ten years, whilst in Germany this was significantly longer at 23 years. Buck also found that the age of property and the return were key factors influencing the holding period and that transaction costs had a minimal effect. The holding period reduces for properties acquired in a recession in order to increase fund performance.

Holding period time is normally specified by the client requirements. A number of different holding periods can be incorporated into the analysis. In the UK an analysis period of five years is commonly used as this ties in with the prevailing rent review pattern. In the US ten year analysis is more common, and in the Netherlands 20 years is not uncommon. Property traders may use shorter analysis periods, and those using long-term finance may use a longer analysis period in line with the debt repayment period. There is no hard and fast rule that determines the analysis period. However, if the analysis of property is being undertaken in conjunction with that of other asset classes, then a similar time horizon should be used. It is this that has prompted a number of UK institutional investors to use five year analysis periods.

It is a useful 'rule of thumb' that the shorter the analysis period, the more sensitive the IRR and NPV will be to the exit valuation, while for longer cash flows rental growth will become a key variable. In addition, time horizons may be chosen that will be influenced by the timing of, for example, lease expiries, break clauses and refurbishment/redevelopment. Clients may alternatively, require a specific time frame for strategic, budgeting or business management purposes.

7.6.3   Rental growth

An important difference between traditional valuation/capitalisation methods and DCF analysis is the treatment of rental growth expectations. Capitalisation models bundle expected rental growth into the yield. DCFs show rental growth explicitly in the future income stream. Rental growth is applied to the current estimate of the open market rental value and not the passing rent.

Analysis of a market yield can reveal the implied rental growth rate. This is a useful reference figure, but in a DCF assumptions should be made in light of the analyst's and the client's expectations for the property's rental growth prospects. Thus the task of forecasting future income growth involves a consideration of local area and sector characteristics, individual lease terms and conditions, probable lease renewals dates or break clauses, maintenance schedules and the impact of capital expenditures.

Consideration should be given to whether a single constant compounding rental growth rate should be used or whether it is more appropriate to use separate annual, short-term and long-term rates. Performance data (IPD, 2004) shows that, historically, rents have a cyclical tendency.

Where the property analyst or client has access to a research/forecasting team, annual rental forecasts are often used. An alternative is for the analyst to use a short-term (two to three year) rental growth rate to reflect the current market supply and demand conditions and the current position relative to the property rental cycle. Jones Lang LaSalle produce each quarter, a property rental clock (see Jones Lang LaSalle, 2004) which depicts the state of local rental markets, and indicates whether:

- rents are falling – the first quadrant of the clock (from midnight to three o'clock);
- rents are bottoming out – the second quadrant;
- rental growth is accelerating – the third quadrant; or
- rental growth is slowing – the fourth quadrant.

A short-term rental growth forecast can then be followed by a long-term forecast giving a constant rental growth rate, with due regard to the property's location, design, specification, environment, tenure and the terms of the lease(s).

Rental growth forecasts are often a combination of an explicit interpretation of professional judgement and knowledge of the local market, combined with a formal rental growth model. In this context, Matysiak and Tsolacos (2003) identified a number of short-term indicators for real estate rental performance. For additional discussion on forecasting, please refer to section 7.9 and to Chapter 12.

7.6.4   Inflation

It is necessary to be consistent in the treatment of the cash flows and the discount rate. Both should be expressed in either real or nominal/monetary terms. Hoesli *et al.* (1997) considered the short-term inflation hedging characteristics of UK real estate and concluded that the data showed there was no statistical relationship between inflation and property performance. The normal market practice is to use nominal terms.

7.6.5   Exit valuation yield

Incorporated into the final cash flow is an exit valuation, which reflects the value of the net rents receivable after that date to perpetuity, or the expiry of the interest in the property.

A variety of different approaches are adopted in the market, for example:

- The forecast rent receivable as at the end of the analysis period is capitalised on an initial yield basis. It should be noted that such initial yield valuation approaches imply in the capitalisation rate the under- or over-rented nature of the property as at the exit valuation date.
- The forecast net rental income for the year following the end of the analysis period is capitalised on an initial yield basis (US practice). In the US, the exit valuation yield is often referred to as the 'kick out' or 'going out' cap rate.
- The forecast rent receivable as at the end of the analysis period, plus the expected uplifted rack rent as at the next rent review, are valued using either an equivalent yield, or a term and reversion, or a hardcore top slice method.
- Where a long (ten years plus) holding period is used, or where the property is nearing the end of its economic life, a site value, or vacant possession value, may be adopted.

The exit yield adopted may reflect the general anticipated trends in fixed interest rates and property yields. However, the forecasting of property yields is recognised to be an extremely difficult task.

The exit valuation yield used should be adjusted to reflect the unexpired term on the lease(s), the increased age of the property, and relative changes in the location, desirability of its design, specification and environment. Double counting of risks should, where possible, be avoided. For example, if the exit valuation yield used is higher than the investment yield at purchase to reflect the effect of obsolescence during the holding period, does the risk premium in the risk-adjusted discount rate applied to the net cash flow during the holding period also include an allowance for obsolescence? The exit valuation yield should be put into the context of the valuation at purchase, and the initial, equivalent and reversionary yields derived from the purchase price.

In the UK the tendency is to use nominal valuation yields (annually in arrears) as opposed to true yields that reflect the quarterly in advance nature of property rents. The Investment Property Forum is strongly recommending the use of true yields as these show the income characteristics of property relative to bonds. In Appendix A the relevant formulae are set out together with a description of the differences between nominal, effective and true yields.

It is important that a proper and explicit rationale is given for the selection of the exit yield, taking into account all the circumstances and assumptions such as length of the holding period, basis of the discount rate, provision for preventative maintenance or refurbishment and growth prospects, and what elements in this context have been incorporated into the risk adjusted discount rate.

7.6.6 Landlord's repairs and non-recoverable outgoings

In the UK the majority of commercial property investments have the benefit of full repairing and insuring leases, in consequence of which landlords receive net rental incomes and have few non-recoverable outgoings.

In Continental Europe and the US, occupational leases tend to be shorter than in the UK. With such leases the tendency is for the landlord to be responsible for a range of the repairing and property services, and not to be reimbursed by the tenant(s).

Traditional valuations adjust the net rents for the costs of landlord's repairs and non-recoverable outgoings. However, the implicit assumption is that rental and repairs growth rates will be similar. In practice this is not necessarily the case. For example, a brand new property may be expected to have good short-term rental growth prospects and few repair costs; in contrast, a 30-year-old building may have poor short-term rental growth prospects but growing repair costs. DCF analysis has the wherewithal to pick up these differences.

Where the landlord is responsible for repairs and non-recoverable outgoings, these need to be included in the cash flows. The growth of these costs needs to be put into the context of the condition of the property and expected building cost inflation trends.

Where the costs of repairs or non-recoverable outgoings are expected to be significant at a future date (for example, the lift will need replacing), the tendency is to set up a sinking fund to meet the cost over the period of the expenditure. This has the advantage of smoothing the cash flows, a desirable feature when using debt finance (see Chapter 9).

7.6.7 Depreciation and obsolescence

Depreciation can be affected by location and by the building's specification and design. Location can lead to a rise or a fall in value through the economic prosperity of a town/region or site specific factors; for example, the development of a new shopping centre affecting the pedestrian flow of a nearby high street shop.

However, buildings will be affected by technological changes rendering them obsolete for a particular use whilst they remain still physically sound; for example, perhaps office workers require increased natural day light, as specified by a new (but unforeseen) EU directive. Some depreciation/appreciation/obsolescence such as wear and tear can be forecasted, but unforeseen technological or legislative changes are difficult to predict. A number of studies (such as Baum, 1991) have shown that the present life cycle of buildings can be used for assessing the life of buildings and reduction in rental growth.

Within a DCF framework, rental income flows tend to be subject to depreciation whilst capital values can be depressed by obsolescence. These factors can be shown either explicitly in rental growth and exit yield adjustments, or implicitly in the risk premium in the required or target rate of return.

7.6.8 After gearing/equity returns

A benefit of DCF analysis is its ability to factor in financing of the property, using borrowings and other financial instruments. This differentiates DCF analysis from traditional valuations. For the equity investor in particular, it is the return on equity (IRRs and NPVs) that is important. Chapter 9 considers the use and impact of debt finance on the returns of an equity investor.

7.6.9 Post tax and grants

A calculation of worth is an appraisal of a real estate investment from a particular investor's viewpoint. It is appropriate in these circumstances to show the after tax cash flows, calculating the impact on net incomes and on capital gains.

Anticipated change in the incidence and level of tax should be considered. The appraisal could also use finance rates or borrowing rates to reflect the impact of gearing, tax allowances and liabilities. In the UK the tendency is for the property analyst/appraiser working for the agent to calculate the equity cash flows before tax and for clients to incorporate the net of tax cash flows into their calculations.

7.6.10 Fees

Fees in respect of rent reviews, new lettings, lease renewals, the deemed sale as at the exit of the cash flows, the raising of finance, management and other fees should be incorporated into the cash flows. Increases in these fees should also be considered.

7.6.11 Contamination and deleterious materials

Discovery of contamination or deleterious materials (for example, blue asbestos, calcium chloride, wood wool slabs, high alumina cement) can have serious financial implications. In particular, exposure to third party liabilities must be considered. Where the risks are high, it is not uncommon for analysts to resort to a pay back or discounted pay back method of cash flow appraisal.

Environmental audits should be undertaken before a transaction price is agreed and warranties obtained from the current owner. Former uses of the building, site or adjacent land might suggest potential contamination. If the real estate is being held as an investment, liability for clean up may have to be accounted for irrespective of the identity of the actual polluter.

7.6.12 Sustainability

A small but growing number of corporate occupiers and institutional investors have placed sustainability high up on their corporate agendas. This has been in response to government and supra-government initiatives and shareholder activism, and there is also a growing recognition that corporate social responsibility, which incorporates a positive stance to both social and environmental issues, can be good for business. This has been witnessed in the performance of companies listed on, for example, the Dow Jones Sustainability Index and the FTSE4Good. There is as yet no firm knowledge as to the way in which this can be incorporated within a DCF; however, work by Sayce and Ellison (2004) provides a possible way forward.

7.7   The DCF appraisal outputs

DCF appraisal models seek to inform the investor as to the expected or prospective returns they would earn by investing in a specific property investment at a specified price. The key outputs are:

- Internal rate of return:
    o on the investment, without debt, known as the property or project IRR;
    o on the investment after incorporating debt, known as the equity IRR;
    o on the investment after incorporating debt and tax, known as the post tax equity IRR.
- Net present value:
    o on the investment, without debt, known as the property or project NPV, using the required or target or risk adjusted rate of return as the discount rate;
    o on the investment after incorporating debt, known as the equity NPV (in this case the investor's before tax or gross weighted average cost of capital (Brealey and Myers, 2002) can be used as the discount rate);
    o on the investment after incorporating debt and tax, known as the post tax, equity NPV (in this case the investor's weighted average cost of capital (Brealey and Myers, 2002) can be used as the discount rate, as this is a net of tax discount rate).

A detailed discussion relating to the application and interpretation of IRRs and NPVs is covered in Levy (2002) and is considered in Chapter 5.

7.8   A summary of factors affecting cash flow data

A summary of issues that should be considered when undertaking a DCF analysis is set out in Table 7.2. These are separated into known current data, and data of variables that will require forecasts or projections so that they can be incorporated into the cash flows at future dates.

7.9   Forecasting the variables

Discounted cash flows can be complementary to a market valuation, using the best available forecasts. As the number of assumptions increases, so do the range of values of worth; but as assumptions are explicit they can be questioned both within the calculation and by the client. DCF needs input from the client reflecting his or her risk/return requirements but will include assumptions on, for example, rental growth, exit yields, depreciation rates, redevelopment costs.

Table 7.2 Factors affecting cash flow data.

Cash flow data	Known current data	Forecast
Tenure	Freehold or leasehold details; rents payable and receivable; other liabilities, including repairs; rent review and expiry dates.	
Physical qualities	Data on floor areas; storage; car parking; building specifications, such as air conditioning; tenants' improvements. Environmental quality including contamination.	Future planned changes to areas/parking.
Lease/sublease and occupational interests	Number of tenants and tenancy details; lease expiry dates, detail and dates of break clauses; review provisions.	Possible future voids in cash flows. Structure and timing of future leases.
Value	Current rents passing.	Future local market rents. Future rents for the clients' property. Future exit yield.
Costs of property ownership	Current voids; unrecoverable service charges or management charges; estimated letting and review costs, and purchase and sale costs.	Inflation on maintenance charges.
Redevelopment/ refurbishment	Current redevelopment or refurbishment costs; potential dilapidations claims.	Inflation on building costs. Timing of redevelopment or refurbishment.
Finance	Agreed loan details and break costs. Costs of finance should be reflected in a worth calculation if so instructed by the client, but it may be necessary to adapt the discount rate to reflect the effects of a geared investment.	Changes in interest rates.
Taxation	Income tax; capital gains tax; VAT and capital allowances. It should be noted that market valuations are normally carried out to gross of tax values, but a calculation of worth can allow for clients' specific tax liabilities. It may be appropriate to carry out both a with and a without worth calculation.	Can include anticipated tax liabilities.

Forecasts are normally based on econometric modelling of the economy and property market which identify relationships in variables in the past and use forecasts of each variable to produce an estimate or forecast. Forecasts are usually national/regional or local and are not normally carried out for individual properties. National and regional forecasts are easier than local forecasts due to the availability and quality of data upon which to base the econometric modelling. Property market forecasts therefore need to be subjectively adjusted using available local information as price movements can vary greatly within cities and from town to town.

According to the RICS Information Paper (1997), true forecasting involves the construction of econometric models based on the property market and financial and economic market models, and requires specific skills. The complexity of undertaking growth explicit cash flows raises the issue of whether valuers are equipped to undertake appraisals of worth, although the information can be purchased through organisations such as IPD (Investment Property Databank) or provided by specialist consultancies or in-house research departments. In its advice on worth the RICS also differentiates between a forecast and market expectation based on market sentiment (RICS, 1997). For example, a growth rate derived from a market all risks yield and an assumed equated yield using Stracey's tables is based on a mathematical relationship between the variables; it shows the average long-term growth rate that the current market expects and reflects market sentiment. Valuers who do not have access to specific formal forecasts should make informed comments on prospects for growth, but the basis of the assumptions should be made clear to the client. A sensitivity analysis using several growth rates may be worth producing to aid the client's decision-making process.

In a property investment DCF appraisal, rental growth and exit valuation yields tend to be two of the key variables that require forecasting or assessing as at a future date. There has been a substantial amount of applied work in real estate markets investigating rental performance. There are a variety of quantitative models and variables used in modelling and forecasting work. These models offer a variety of choices in terms of methodologies that can be applied to property forecasting.

The forecaster can use single equation models that include exogenous variables such as output, employment and combinations of financial variables to model and forecast rental growth, returns or yields. More general, simultaneous models can also be estimated in which all segments of the market (such as demand or absorption, supply and prices) are modelled. Such models are interactive: that is, the various component parts of the market are allowed to interact, thereby jointly providing a dynamic description of the property market. These types of models may broadly be described as 'structural' or 'behavioural' models (Matysiak, 1997).

Other methodologies offer a framework to model property performance based purely on past performance information and past disturbances. Disturbances will usually capture random events affecting performance, their duration lasting for only a few periods. For example, foot and mouth disease was a disturbance that impacted on tourism attractions and countryside hotel performance in the UK in 2001. An important task is to apply the various methodologies and seek to identify those that provide superior forecasts.

Modelling is a task that takes time and knowledge of the conditions required for the application of the various methodologies in different situations. The characteristics of the data (for example, strongly trended or non-trended) can also determine the extent to which various methodologies can be used. Moreover, due to lack of data the application of all methodologies may not be feasible in some markets.

Another task of the forecaster is to seek sources of information about the economy and property markets that will improve forecasting performance. Such sources of information for the general economy and business conditions are provided by series that are updated frequently and provide early signals for economic variables such as output, employment, consumer spending and so forth. For example, it can be argued that the share price index, dividend yields, swap rates, the futures markets in interest rates, housing starts and changes in inventories contain signals about the near future direction of the economy.

Economists have carried out extensive work to identify series that provide early signals in industrialised economies. An interesting question concerns the extent to which such series contain information that may be used in property forecasting. After all, these series provide indications of where the economy is heading, and consequently where the property markets are heading, assuming there are proportional relationships between the property markets and the wider economy. Therefore the property forecaster should seek to identify such 'leading' indicators and explore ways to incorporate the information these series contain into property forecasting models.

Many studies have sought to identify key variables that affect rent variation through time. The set of explanatory variables varies by sector. In the office sector, for example, the gross domestic product, output and employment in financial and business services, unemployment, interest rates and operating expenses are the indicative economic variables assumed to capture the effect of changing economic circumstances that are likely to have an impact.

Despite issues of definition and measurement, the vacancy rate is considered to play an important role. It is assumed that these variables affect the vacancy rate, which in turn affects rental growth. In particular, it is the gap between actual vacancy rate and structural vacancy rate that matters. In the retail sector expenditure, retail sales and the gross domestic product seem to be the most successful demand side indicators. In the industrial market the gross domestic product and manufacturing output seem to be the most significant variables in the UK literature (Thompson and Tsolacos, 1999). Attempts have also been made to incorporate supply side variables in the models. In the context of the UK, these variables, which are not always successful, are mainly new orders and output series such as the floorspace stock. Official publication of floorspace statistics has been discontinued, and floorspace needs to be estimated if stock is to be included in estimated relationships.

In conclusion, the forecasting of the variables is a specialist activity, and one which is frequently brought on board by the property analyst through an in-house research team, or via a third party provider.

7.10 Cash flow modelling: useful practical pointers

Cash flow modelling uses either 'black box' software packages or spreadsheets as the framework for analysis. Spreadsheets and bespoke 'black box' models can be complex in nature, and when constructing and/or using them there are a number of guidelines that should be considered:

- *Transparency*: the spreadsheet or software package and its contents/calculation methodologies and the underlying assumptions should be transparent. When using a spreadsheet, it should be straightforward to see and find out what is being analysed and how the calculations work. The inputs, cash flows and outputs, plus the assumptions relating to these, should be simple to find and understand.

The use of complex functions – for example, lengthy nested IF statements in Excel – should be avoided. These may be understandable to the programmer, but tend to be opaque to most end users.

Alongside transparency goes 'the ability to audit'. Opaque spreadsheets are time-consuming and difficult to audit. They can thus be counterproductive. Cynics might argue that the growth of complex DCF spreadsheet models provides the specialist Excel programmers with job security. However, this is at the risk or cost of an unforeseen error creeping into the calculations.

- *Flexibility*: spreadsheets should be flexible, such that changes in the inputs should flow through to the cash flows and the outputs. Hard coding (typing numbers straight into the cash flows) should be avoided. This flexibility will enable the use of 'what if' and risk analysis techniques, such that outputs (answers) can be easily obtained for differing inputs. Further details of this are given in Chapter 8.

- *Consistency*: the methodology used in one spreadsheet and in others should be consistent. This applies to individuals and individuals working in teams and firms. Clients and end users are not impressed by widely differing approaches to similar problems or property investment analyses.

  With increasing use of software to undertake valuations and DCF appraisals, the transferability of data has become of key importance. This has given rise to PISCES compliancy standards for bespoke packages.

The property valuer and investment analyst owes a duty of care to his or her client and thoughts frequently turn to professional indemnity insurance. As a consequence, transparency and auditability of valuations and DCF models have become very important. Also the underlying thought processes and numbers that underpin these methods have become opened up to scrutiny.

7.11   The DCF appraisal report

The growth in the use of DCF models promotes questions regarding their acceptance as a recognised method within the professional standards. The RICS has now increased the codification of valuations within its standards (RICS, 2003) but it seeks to stand apart from methodology. However, in some areas it does stray into method, as in the valuation of specialised property. It also published some years ago initial information about worth calculations (RICS, 1997), but practice now has moved on and this requires recognition within the issued advice. It is the authors' view that such advice would support new appraisal methods and information bases and would reduce the valuer's dependence on traditional valuation methods.

Traditional methodology was appropriate when occupational leases were long and on FRI terms, with upward only rent reviews, but it has limitations and is insufficiently flexible to handle the needs of sophisticated investors such as finance driven investors or those looking at investments with non-standard cash flows.

The issue is not a new one. The report of the Mallinson Committee (Mallinson, 1994) recommended, *inter alia*, the more extensive use of DCF; the Committee also highlighted the need for valuers to gain a deeper knowledge of, and be more responsive to, their clients' requirements. The subsequent debate has led to calls for the development of investment valuation methodology – see, for example, French (1996); Crosby *et al.* (1997) and Mackmin and Emery (2000) subsequently considered the need for standards in the assessment of worth and concluded that confusion over the meaning of worth and the use of DCF would continue if international standards were not agreed. Traditional valuation approaches have a role to play as they are based on market determined assumptions, but these are implicit within the all risks yield and therefore cannot be unbundled.

The profession overhauled its mandatory instructions to valuers in 1993 (RICS, 1993), but it has not issued guidance notes specifically relating to DCF methodologies and their potential use in appropriate circumstances. Given that the standards require valuers to establish their clients' needs, clarification of best practice in the calculation of worth would be beneficial. It is argued that this needs to address the following issues:

- Choices relating to discount rates, timescale, mathematical calculations, factual and estimated data (such as inflation, growth and interest rates), non-conventional cash flows, mutually exclusive projects, apportioning IRRs, the treatment of capital expenditures, and valid approaches for determining the exit valuation.
- The appropriate caveats relating to assumptions that are implicit within DCF calculations. These should address the status of information given in the report and state that the resultant worth value will vary if the assumptions are changed. The report should confirm that the calculation of worth is not a market valuation, should not be published and is not for use by third parties. The current guidance to valuers does contain a caveat as follows:

> No responsibility can be held by the Valuer for the use of his calculation of worth, which incorporates assumptions about the future which may or may not prove to be correct.

> (RICS, 1997:33)

It is our view that this is in need of updating. In Australia, in contrast to the UK, practice standards have been developed and published (Parker and Robinson, 2000). The valuer is called on to follow a method, whilst disclosing the specific assumptions. However, a number of considerations remain to be finalised, such as the application of the term cash flow to net operating income, income after finance, and income after finance and tax. Parker and Robinson conclude that the preparation of standards is an evolutionary process; this would indeed appear also to be the case in the UK.

7.12 Summary

Recent years have witnessed a growing use of DCF calculations to enable investors to appraise what a property is *worth* to them. In a truly efficient market, the views of all investors would be the same or very similar as they would all be working from the same information.

However, it is acknowledged that the efficient market hypothesis is not realistic, at least not as applied to property. For this reason, if for no other, there must be an acceptance that such a figure is not necessarily the same as the market value. Currently, therefore, the worth calculation is seen to be complementary to the market value; it is provided to aid investment decision-making.

This chapter has explored the inputs to a typical DCF and concludes that there are some key elements in the calculation; for example, if the calculation being undertaken is to produce a net present value (NPV), the choice of the discount rate is very important. Likewise when using IRRs it is important to know the hurdle rate of return above which an investment is deemed a buy and below which it becomes a sell.

Unlike UK government bonds, where the exact timing and amount of the cash flows are known, property's prospective cash flows do not have such certainty. Thus there are elements of risk to be considered in the appraisal of property investments. In Chapter 8 consideration is given to a number of risk analysis techniques that can be employed with DCF. These include sensitivity analysis, data tables, scenarios and simulation techniques.

However, each investor will consider the returns of a property investment in the context of a risk/return tradeoff. The more risk an investment has, the higher the return investors will wish to see to compensate them for taking those risks on board. In Chapter 12 consideration is given to the benefits of portfolio diversification which enables a number of risks to be diversified away.

A real benefit of undertaking worth/DCF appraisal calculations is that they provide clients with an understanding of the investment and its characteristics and performance possibilities, and this can be used as a comparison tool with regard to other properties and non-property investments. Increasingly, most investment valuations are (or should be) done on an investment yield basis (that is, an implicit all risks approach) supported by a discounted cash flow appraisal, as is the practice in Australia and the US.

It has been argued that in the UK property, as an industry, has been slow in adopting the analytical techniques used in other property markets, and the suggestion is made that a positive lead by the RICS in the form of further guidance would be timely.

References

Baum, A. (1991) *Property Investment Depreciation and Obsolescence*. London: Routledge.

Baum, A. and Crosby, N. (1995) *Property Investment Appraisal*, 2nd edn. London: Routledge.

Baum, A., Crosby, N. and MacGregor, B.D. (1996) Price formation, mispricing and investment analysis in the property market: a response to 'A note on "The initial yield revealed: explicit valuations and the future of the property market"'. *Journal of Valuation & Investment*, 14 (1): 36–49.

Brealey, R. and Myers, S. (2002) *Principles of Corporate Finance*, 7th edn. London: McGraw Hill.

Brown, G. (1991) *Property Investment and the Capital Markets*. London: E&FN Spon.

Buck, O. (2003) Holding periods of offices in institutional real estate portfolios in the UK and Germany: a comparative study. Unpublished dissertation, Kingston University unpublished.

Collett, D., Lizierim, C. and Ward, C. (2003) Timing and the holding periods of institutional real estate. *Real Estate Economics*, 31 (2): 205.

Crosby, N., Newell, G., Matysiak, G., Rodney, B. and French, N. (1997) Client perception of property investment valuation reports in the UK. *Journal of Property Research*, 14 (1): 27–47.

French, N. (1996) Investment valuation developments from the Mallinson Report. *Journal of Property Valuation & Investment*, 14 (5): 48–58.

Hoesli, M., MacGregor, B., Matysiak, G. and Nanthakumaran, N. (1997) The short-term inflation hedging characteristics of UK real estate. *Journal of Real Estate Finance & Economics*, 15 (1): 27–57.

Hutchison, N. and Nanthakumaran, N. (2000) The calculation of investment worth. *Journal of Property Valuation & Investment*, 18 (1): 33–51.

Investment Property Databank (2004) *Investment Property Databank, Property Indices* at www.ipdindex.co.uk

Investment Property Forum/Royal Institution of Chartered Surveyors (1997) *Calculation of Worth: An Information Pap*er. London: RICS Business Services.

Jones Lang LaSalle (2004) *Property Rental Clocks*, available at www.joneslanglasalle.co.uk

Kingfisher Property Finance (2004) *Property Lending Statistics,* available at www. kingfisherpropert.finance.co.uk

Levy, H. (2002) *Essentials of Investment.* London: FT Prentice Hall.

Mackmin, D. and Emery, R. (2000) The assessment of worth: the need for standards. *Journal of Property Valuation & Investment*, 18 (1).

Mallinson, M. (1994) *Report on Commercial Property Valuation.* London: RICS.

Matysiak, G. (1997) Modelling and forecasting in commercial property. Editorial. *Journal of Property Finance*, 8 (4).

Matysiak, G. and Tsolacos, S. (2003) Identifying short-term leading indicators for real estate rental performance. *Journal of Property Investment & Finance*, 21 (3): 212–32.

McParland, C., McGreal, S. and Adair, A. (2000) Concepts of price, value and worth in the United Kingdom: towards a European perspective. *Journal of Property Valuation & Investment*, 18 (1): 84–102.

Parker, D. and Robinson, J. (2000) A brief history of the Australian discounted cash flow practice standard. *Journal of Property Investment & Finance*, 18 (2): 196–211.

Peto, R., French, N. and Bowman, G. (1996) Price and worth: developments in valuation methodo-logy. *Journal of Property Valuation & Investment*, 14 (4): 79–100.

Royal Institution of Chartered Surveyors (1993) *Appraisal and Valuation Standards.* London: RICS.

Royal Institution of Chartered Surveyors (1997) *The Calculation of Worth: An Information Paper.* London: RICS.

Royal Institution of Chartered Surveyors (2003) *Appraisal and Valuation Standards.* London: RICS.

Sayce, S. and Ellison, L. (2004) *Sustainability and commercial property investment – understanding the impact of direct effects and policy development on asset values.* Paper to the IPD/IPF Conference, Brighton, 18–19 November.

Thompson, R. and Tsolacos, S. (1999) Rent adjustments and forecasts in the industrial market. *Journal of Real Estate Research*, 17 (2): 151–68.

8 Risk within the appraisal and worth process

Aims of the chapter

- To consider the role of risk analysis in a property investment appraisal context.
- To consider approaches for dealing with risk and uncertainty.
- To contrast the role of qualitative and quantitative risk analysis approaches.
- To explain how SWOT analysis can be used as a risk analysis framework.

- To examine the use of the '3 Ss' (sensitivity analysis, scenarios and simulation) as risk analysis tools.
- To explore how risk analysis techniques can be used to determine the key variables in the DCF analysis of a property investment.

8.1 Introduction

This chapter considers how risk analysis can be explicitly incorporated into a property discounted cash flow analysis or development appraisal. In Chapter 5, consideration was given to the implicit incorporation of risk within the capitalisation process through an adjustment to the discount rate. The response to risk was taken to be a requirement for a higher return and this was reflected in either the risk adjusted discount rate or a higher target rate of return. In this chapter such an approach is questioned and alternative methods of dealing with risk in the appraisal process are examined.

It will be argued that, in order to ensure that there is not double counting, where identified risks are explicitly incorporated into the net cash flows of an investment or development the impact of these identified risks should not also be included in the risk adjusted discount rate. To illustrate this point, let us consider a property investment subject to a lease that expires in two years' time. The impact of a void can either be incorporated into the net cash flows or be reflected in the risk adjusted discount rate. It should not be included in both.

The property analyst or appraiser uses risk appraisal techniques to quantify the impact that identified risks will have on the prospective performance of a property investment. At their simplest, prospective returns are estimated in terms of a spot figure or best estimate of the IRR or NPV.

The role of risk analysis is to provide the investor or developer with an insight into the range and distribution of these estimated returns. In particular the analyst or appraiser seeks to identify the exposure that the investor or developer has to downside (and upside) risk. This is an important element of the skills base of the analyst or appraiser.

Thus risk analysis forms part of the arsenal of analytical tools that the property investment analyst can bring to bear. In contrast, such tools often have limited appeal to the valuer who will normally utilise comparable evidence which incorporates risk and uncertainty, implicitly, into the valuation yield.

Risk analysis is part of the analysis of a property to determine whether its price (or value) in the market place is similar to its worth as perceived by the owner (seller) and the purchaser. Valuations and prices are spot figures, whereas worth reflects the net present value of expected future cash flows using an individually constructed set of assumptions. Worth, in contrast to price or value, is not a spot figure unless the future cash flows are known with 100% certainty. Thus worth can be expressed as a best estimate, with there being an anticipated range of outcomes around this best estimate.

In this chapter we will look at the methods of creating and putting figures on the anticipated range of outcomes. This will enable risk to be incorporated into the appraisal methodology, and facilitate a more considered approach when contrasting price (value) with the worth of an investment.

In the property industry the terms risk and uncertainty are frequently used in a misleading manner; furthermore, the context in which many people use the term risk is frequently imprecise and addresses only part of the issue. It is important to differentiate between risk and uncertainty, and definitions are given below.

- *Uncertainty* is where an expected outcome is either unquantifiable or not able to be estimated with any degree of accuracy, and where the expected range of outcomes can only be estimated within a very wide range.
- *Certainty* is where a single value is expected, or the expected outcome is known, and the probability of the outcome occurring is perceived as being 100%.
- *Risk* is where a range of possible outcomes is expected, some of which are desirable (upside potential) whist others are undesirable (downside risk). It provides a quantifiable array of possible outcomes (probability distribution and standard deviation).
- *Objective probabilities* are based on past outcomes (often assumed to be good guidelines to future outcomes) or are capable of being modelled on reliable data.
- *Subjective probabilities* are not based on observed or recorded data but may rely on past experience or expert judgement. As a method of approaching uncertainty, subjective probabilities are generally assumed to be inferior to objective probabilities. Nevertheless, they are an operationally valid way of incorporating or making explicit intuition or professional opinion and combining it with such market data as is available. In a marketplace where data and even research and forecasting skills are frequently limited, subjective probabilities become in many instances the 'best available' approach for many.

As can be seen from the definitions above, uncertainty and risk are not the same: it is the ability to apply a probability distribution to the expected outcomes – even if the accuracy of the distribution is not precise – that makes an uncertain investment into a risky investment.

Other markets also have to deal with risk. In particular, the insurance industry has risk at the centre of its activities. Approaches relating to how the insurance market deals with risk assessment and risk management (Vaughan and Vaughan, 2003) can be helpful for property analysts considering property risks, as can the approaches for companies (Brealey and Myers, 2002) and capital market investors (Alexander *et al.*, 2001).

To put this chapter into context, it must be placed with other chapters in the book. In Chapter 2 we considered the purchase decision and defined the terminology: price, value and worth. In Chapter 12 we will consider the relationship between price (value) and worth and how, in an efficient market, price (value) equals worth. In a portfolio context, the use of probability distributions as part of the characteristics of a risky investment becomes an important feature in shaping the risk/return features of a property portfolio.

8.2   Quantitative v. qualitative risk approaches

The emphasis on risk analysis techniques has, in recent years, been concentrated on quantitative techniques and these are discussed in this chapter. However, it is important, first, to give due consideration to the role that qualitative analysis can play in providing an underlying framework that can assist in informing the property analyst.

8.2.1   Qualitative risk analysis approaches

In market places where property data and historic performance data are scarce, qualitative approaches can be used to help provide a methodology for incorporating professional views into the analysis process. Such techniques are used in the UK, but, given the abundance of performance data (see, for example, IPD indices, www.ipdindex.co.uk) many players frequently have a tendency to rely more on quantitative methods of analysis. However, it is possible to extract valuable background information from qualitative approaches, which can then usefully inform the inputs into the quantitative analysis.

Thus qualitative analysis can be seen as part of the spectrum of risk analysis. It precedes the quantitative analysis; it may be undertaken in a structured and methodological manner, or it may rely primarily on professional experience and judgement.

In the UK the role and expertise of the chartered surveyor in the property investment markets has resulted in a professional judgement approach being widely adopted. In contrast, in the Continental European markets, where no such profession exists in any significant form, a more structured approach may be found. This structured qualitative approach is derived from business school teaching and has been adapted to the property market, in particular to assist cross-border investors who are operating in markets where their experience is limited.

The qualitative methods look at the relative merits of one property against another or within a series of alternatives: it is relative ranking that becomes important. Also, the framework that enables the ranking to be undertaken can provide a valuable insight into the drivers of investment performance, which can then be picked up in the subsequent quantitative analysis. Several techniques are now considered.

8.2.2   PEST analysis

A PEST analysis considers the relative merits and disadvantages of competing property investment markets under four headings: political, economic, social and technological. Examples of items that can be incorporated into this qualitative approach when considering which country to invest into are set out below.

- *Political*
  o Who could come into power or who has influence?
  o Their impact on property's performance drivers: GDP, employment, inflation.
  o Their stance towards wealth and property: property specific taxes.

- *Economic*
  - o State of the economy.
  - o Breakdown of the GDP numbers: which sectors will growth come from, how large are these sectors in the country, are they private or public enterprises, and where are they located?
  - o Relationship with other economies as a whole.
  - o Leader or laggard in the economic cycle?
- *Social*
  - o Social support: education, health and retirement provisions.
  - o Importer or exporter of labour?
  - o Attractiveness or otherwise of living and working in the country.
- *Technological*
  - o Top end of the spectrum: the competitive nature of high tech businesses, and are they world class?
  - o Depth of technology: is technology used across the sectors or it is only piecemeal?
  - o How well educated are the employees in IT related matters?
  - o IT spine: is it based on fibre optics or copper, and which areas may be left out of the IT revolution with poor band width or benefit from the advent of good telecommunications?

A PEST analysis provides a valuable starting point when an investor is considering, for example, different use classes (retail warehouses v. high street shops v. out-of-town shopping centres) or cross-border investments (Paris v. London v. Moscow offices).

8.2.3   SWOT analysis

To follow on from a PEST analysis, a SWOT analysis, which considers the investment in more focused context, can be undertaken. This is a comparative approach, identifying the drivers of performance. SWOT analysis is particularly useful when dealing with markets where there is little data. It looks at the investment in terms of its relative:

- strengths;
- weaknesses;
- opportunities; and
- threats.

A SWOT analysis should be undertaken from the perspective of the occupier as a key component of the driver of rental growth, and also from the perspective of the investor in terms of, for example, the drivers of current yield structures and the ability to get in and out of the market at realistic prices.

In undertaking a PEST and a SWOT analysis, the property analyst needs to decide upon the timescale (investment holding period) and the ranking and weighting of the key factors. On completion of the analysis, the property analyst should be able to put the properties/their locations into performance bands:

Very attractive ◄————————► Unattractive

These rankings can be used alongside the performance figures (IRRs and NPVs) produced by DCF models.

> Please see Spreadsheet 11 for a working example of how a PEST and SWOT analysis may be constructed, including the ranking of results to provide league tables.

An advantage of starting with a PEST and a SWOT analysis when considering one or more property investments or developments is that these techniques provide the analyst or appraiser with a context into which the investments can be placed. The process also draws out many of the key issues and may even identify a number of performance drivers.

Referring to equities investment decisions, Oxelheim (2003) considers the macro-economic variables in the context of identifying corporate performance, and identifies the requirement for corporate managers and analysts to pay more attention to changes in macroeconomic drivers and the resultant 'noise' (riskiness) that these fluctuations cause in the context of corporate performance. PEST and SWOT analysis frameworks help provide real estate analysts with a clearer view of the drivers of performance, and provide a starting point for quantitative analysis.

8.2.4   Quantitative risk analysis

Quantitative analysis focuses on the future expected cash flows that an investment or development will produce. At the heart of quantitative analysis is the use of discounted cash flow models, where the key variables that influence the prospective performance are identified and drive the future expected net cash flows.

8.3   Quantitative risk analysis: building a risk analysis continuum

When analysing risk it is advisable to consider the following questions:

- What are the risk items?
- How significant is their potential impact?

Understanding risk begins with a process of estimating the expected range of outcomes around a point estimate. The undertaking of risk analysis is a step-by-step approach, often known as the '3 Ss' approach. The '3 Ss' are:

- sensitivity analysis;
- scenarios; and
- simulation.

These are described simply below and considered in more detail later in the chapter.

8.3.1   Sensitivity analysis

This is not strictly a risk analysis technique as it does not consider the relationship between the expected returns in terms of their expected distribution (that is, no probabilities are incorporated). It is, however, the first step on the road to undertaking risk analysis. Sensitivity analysis can be of two types:

- Single variable sensitivity analysis, where the IRR or NPV of an investment is considered in the context of:
  - o a set percentage change for each variable;
  - o realistic changes for each variable;
  - o identifying the break even value for each variable.
- Two variables (data tables) sensitivity analysis, where the IRR or NPV of an investment or development is considered in the context of the changing values of two key variables.

8.3.2   Scenarios

Scenarios identify the key variables in a discounted cash flow analysis that are expected to influence the performance of an investment or development. These key variables are changed to reflect, for example, different views of the future (such as an optimistic, a pessimistic and a best estimate, or the tenant stays v. the tenant quits). Each of these differing views can then be evaluated and weighted according to their probability of occurrence.

8.3.3   Simulation

Simulation is used in conjunction with a discounted cash flow analysis such that for each key variable a range of expected values are identified and systematically put into the DCF model, and the performance results (IRR or NPV) are collected and tabulated. Two main forms of simulation are used:

- Monte Carlo
- Latin Hypercube

8.4   Risk analysis in a practical context

Before exploring the '3 Ss' of risk analysis further, we will seek to place risk in a practical context and relate it to the current DCF analysis methods used by market practitioners.

The 2002 IPF-sponsored Risk Report (Matysiak *et al.*, 2002) usefully summarised how and why risk should be considered. The report reiterated the need for risk appraisal and argued that real estate investment analysis and development appraisals should be forward-looking processes and should not rely on past transactions.

Anticipating future outcomes is complex because a number of inputs to the discounted cash flow analysis are not precisely known. For example:

- *Rental growth* is uneven over time. In property valuations the assumption is that rental growth is constant over time, whereas in practice, and as reflected in DCF analysis, it may be cyclical.
- *Depreciation* can cause divergence of asset growth from sector growth and result in exit valuation yields shifting from investment to investment.

- *Irregular expenditures* may be incurred (such as maintenance and refurbishment) and the estimation of these costs may not be straightforward. When dealing with leases where the landlord bears the responsibility for structural repairs (as is predominantly the case in most European countries), this becomes an important issue.
- *Yields change* over time due, for example, to changes in the opportunity cost of capital, changing investor preferences and weight of money, and a changing investment environment.

These issues raise the question of whether or not a straightforward DCF model is likely to be of sufficient assistance in the analysis process. It will explicitly allow for any variables considered necessary, whilst retaining a mathematical simplicity. The cash flow items tend to average expected values, but there is a requirement to test the impact of different outcomes occurring.

A method commonly employed by practitioners to incorporate risk into a DCF is through the discount rate used. In Chapter 5 the term risk adjusted discount rate (RADR) was discussed, and it was concluded that a risk adjusted discount rate provided a useful starting point for those using DCF as an investment appraisal tool in their quest to determine whether an investment is fair value, or is over or under priced. But, as pointed out, the RADR approach has its limitations and, whilst it is widely used in business (Melicher and Norton, 2003), these limitation must be recognised. It is in the context of the limitations of RADR that the '3 Ss' become valuable additional analytical tools for the investment analyst or appraiser.

8.5   Sensitivity analysis

Sensitivity analysis is operationally valuable. It is seen by some as a first step in the process of risk analysis, and by some as a complete method of risk analysis in itself and the point at which the investment analysis process stops!

Sensitivity analysis involves several steps:

- The decomposition of the drivers of the performance of an investment into their component parts (the number is dependent upon the availability of information, the analyst's time, the client's requirements and computer programming constraints). Sensitivity analysis is easy to undertake with either property investment appraisal packages or spreadsheets.
- The identification of the critical variables in the project through testing by trial and error.
- The calculation of the impact of changes in the critical variables on the outcome of the project.
- Altering combinations of critical variables to explore their joint impact on projects.

Sensitivity analysis can take a number of forms: single variable, break even and two-variable analysis. Each will now be considered.

8.5.1   Single variable sensitivity analysis

This is the most commonly used form of sensitivity analysis. It involves:

- *Altering each variable by a fixed proportion* (say 10%) of the expected outcome, whilst holding all other variables constant, and testing the impact of this on returns/profit. The

Table 8.1   DCF Analyst sensitivity report.

	Best estimate	Best estimate plus 10%	Best estimate minus 10%	Top realistic estimate	Bottom realistic estimate
Rent	38	41.8	34.2	40	37
Outputs					
IRR	9.00%	13.74%	3.24%	11.60%	7.60%
Sensitivity		52.74%	−63.95%	28.88%	−15.54%

weakness of this form is that it can be misleading because it assumes a symmetrical range around the best estimation. Upside and downside risk are seldom symmetrical.

- *Testing for the impact of each variable over a realistic range* of possible outcomes, whilst holding all other variables constant. This can be considered as a quasi-probabilistic approach as it draws out judgements on the best and worst values for each variable.

Please see Spreadsheet 12 for a working example of how to undertake sensitivity analysis on single variables using Excel's single variable data tables and DCF Analyst's sensitivity analysis wizard for use in Excel.

Table 8.1 looks at the impact that changes in rental value have on the IRR of a property investment. In this example, the best estimate of the rental value is £38 psf. A sensitivity analysis of plus or minus 10% shows that the rental value figures have a significant impact on the IRRs. When realistic estimates are used for the rental value estimates, the sensitivity analysis table shows that there is more upside than downside potential.

8.5.2   Break even sensitivity analysis

Break even sensitivity analysis identifies the level of break even for the investment for each variable. It is also helpful in indicating the level of change necessary to erode profit completely. It can be calculated in the same way as for single variable sensitivity but the use of Excel's Goal Seek function or DCF Analyst's Calculate Again function makes the calculation of the break even figure simple.

Please see Spreadsheet 13 for a working example of how to calculate the break even in a sensitivity analysis.

8.5.3   Two variables sensitivity analysis (data tables)

Two variable sensitivity identifies a matrix of outcomes by combining two risky variables together at differing values. An important step forward in demonstrating that change is likely to be a complex mixture of counter movements in variables: for example, rents might increase, but so might obsolescence.

In Excel a two variable sensitivity analysis can be constructed using the data table function. Table 8.2 shows the effect on the IRR of changes in the interest rate and changes

Table 8.2   Equity investment IRRs.

Interest rate (%)	Exit value yield (%)				
	6.25%	6.50%	6.75%	7.00%	7.25%
5.00	24.8	22.6	20.3	18.1	15.8
5.25	24.0	21.8	19.5	17.3	15.0
5.50	23.2	21.0	18.7	16.4	14.1
5.75	22.5	20.2	17.9	15.6	13.2
6.00	21.7	19.4	17.1	14.8	12.4
6.25	21.0	18.7	16.3	13.9	11.5
6.50	20.2	17.9	15.6	13.1	10.7

in the exit valuation yield for a property investment. This table can be converted into a graph using the DCF Analyst graph wizard.

> Please see Spreadsheet 14 for a working example of how to construct a data table showing a sensitivity analysis with two variables. This Spreadsheet also contains an example of the DCF Analyst data table wizard and graphing wizard, which speeds up the process.

A weakness of all types of sensitivity analysis is that they consider the impact of one or two variables, and the changes to those variables, at a time. No understanding is gleaned of how they all interact, thus the full picture is not provided. In addition, no probabilities are used in sensitivity analysis. For this reason, whilst sensitivity forms a useful start in the risk analysis process, in itself it is not a risk assessment technique. The erroneous perception amongst many in the property investment market is that sensitivity analysis and the use of a data table is an all-encompassing risk analysis method for a property investment.

8.6   Scenarios

Scenarios are an extension of sensitivity analysis. They involve undertaking a number of different DCF analyses, each based on different assumptions, and then calculating the outputs (IRRs and NPVs). The key skills of an investment analyst undertaking scenario analysis are the identification of the key variables that change the prospective cash flows and of outputs (that is, the performance measures).

A useful starting point when building scenarios is to consider the figures that come out of the sensitivity analysis, in particular the testing for the impact of each variable over a realistic range on the performance measures (IRR and NPV). This helps to identify those variables that have a significant bearing on the DCF Analysis. For an investment property, the key variables that usually drive the investment performance are drawn from:

- valuation yield on exit;
- rental growth rate;
- cost of finance (if debt is used);
- non-recoverable outgoings and their growth over the analysis period;
- void periods and associated rent free periods.

> Please see Spreadsheet 15 for a working example which shows the identification of the key variables using sensitivity analysis with realistic ranges for each variable, in the context of constructing a scenario.

Inflation is frequently observed as an underlying driver of real estate and its performance. Pyhrr *et al.* (1990) considered inflation and inflation cycles to have been a major underlying reason for the financial successes and failures of real estate investors in recent history. These cycles, he concluded, have complex impacts on cash flow variables and thus on real estate returns and investment values. This study adopted a scenario approach to ascertaining the impact of inflation and inflation cycles.

To conduct a scenario approach it is first necessary to identify the different scenarios that could realistically occur in the future; for example, the identification of best estimate, bullish and bearish scenarios for the property. Next, for each scenario a separate DCF analysis is carried out with the key variables being changed to reflect the scenario adopted.

For properties where there are break clauses or short leases, DCF analyses could accommodate the following scenarios:

- tenants renew their leases;
- tenants break or do not extend their leases, but the rental void periods are relatively short;
- tenants break or do not extend their leases, but the rental void periods are relatively long;
- a percentage of leases are renewed and a weighted average void period is applied.

Other considerations for the use of scenario calculations include:

- properties where amortised finance is being used;
- properties where a refurbishment is in prospect at the reversion, with a subsequent letting at an enhanced rent;
- properties with an exit value to site value.

The use of scenarios usually incorporates the changes to each variable as follows:

$$\text{HIGH} \longleftarrow\longrightarrow \text{REALISTIC} \longleftarrow\longrightarrow \text{LOW}$$

Scenarios can be very helpful, but their use does raise a number of questions:

- How practical is it to establish each scenario?
- What is the probability of each possible outturn, or is each one equally likely?
- Should confidence limits be set and, if so, at what levels?

Set out in Spreadsheet 16 is a scenario report for a property investment where four key variables have been identified and seven outputs are considered in the context of the analyst's expectations for three views of the future: the best estimate, an optimistic view and a pessimistic view.

> Please see Spreadsheet 16 for a working example of how to construct a Scenario Report in Excel. In this spreadsheet there is also an example of the DCF Analyst scenario wizard. Excel's Scenario Report is static, whilst the DCF Analyst scenario report is dynamic, just like a data table. Inputs can be changed and the output can be recalculated simply and quickly.

Table 8.3 DCF Analyst scenario report.

	Best estimate	Bullish	Bearish
Variables			
Rental growth	2.50%	4.00%	1.00%
Exit valuation yield	6.75%	6.00%	7.50%
Interest rate	5.50%	5.00%	7.00%
Outgoings	4.00%	3.00%	4.00%
Outputs			
Project IRR	8.94%	12.65%	5.68%
Project NPV	156 765	832 215	−362 611
Project: income ratio	27.9%	26.5%	29.6%
Project: exit ratio	72.1%	73.5%	70.4%
Equity IRR	18.7%	31.0%	0.0%
Equity: income ratio	39.2%	38.7%	29.7%
Equity: exit ratio	60.8%	61.3%	70.3%
Probability	100.00%	40.00%	20.00%
Expected (probability weighted)			
Project IRR	9.77%		
Project NPV	323 070		
Project: income ratio	27.70%		
Project: exit ratio	72.30%		
Equity IRR	19.91%		
Equity: income ratio	37.11%		
Equity: exit ratio	62.89%		

The outputs, or results, are significantly different. To arrive at expected outcomes, the analyst has incorporated probabilities for the three different scenarios. In this case the probability weighted outcomes are above the best estimate as the analyst is more bullish than bearish. (See Table 8.3.)

Spreadsheets enable this form of analysis to be carried out very easily (for example, by using a Scenario Manager in Excel, or DCF Analyst's Scenario wizard). Although the scenario analysis technique can be considered an improvement on sensitivity analysis, it so far does not incorporate probabilities. Put simply, without the application of probabilities it does not move into the realms of risk analysis.

The application of a probability to the outcome of each scenario will result in a probability adjusted or expected return (IRR, NPV, developer's profit), but this is not strictly a full probability analysis. Nevertheless, it is a helpful means of showing a preference or relative weighting for the likely alternative outcomes, and the impact that this has on the probability weighted outcome.

The use of scenarios is still relatively uncommon within the property investment industry. However, they are straightforward to construct and, when used with an appropriate understanding of the drivers of the investment's performance, they can provide a valuable insight into the prospective performance characteristics of the investment. They have the additional advantage that they can provide a useful starting point for putting property into the context of actuarial asset/liability models.

Please see Spreadsheet 17 for a working example of how to incorporate probabilities into a scenario analysis, using Excel's Scenario Manager or DCF Analyst's Scenario wizard.

Table 8.4   DCF Analyst scenario report.

	Best estimate	Amortised debt	Interest only debt	Mixture of debt
Variables				
Amortised: initial LTV %	0.0%	75.0%	0.0%	35.0%
Amortised: terminal LTV %	0.0%	70.0%	0.0%	30.0%
Interest only LTV %	80.0%	0.0%	75.0%	35.0%
Amort. interest rate	5.50%	5.50%	0.00%	5.50%
Interest only rate	5.50%	0.00%	5.60%	5.50%
Outputs				
Equity IRR	18.7%	16.0%	16.4%	14.7%
Equity: exit ratio	60.8%	70.6%	63.8%	72.2%
Equity income return	10.93%	6.98%	9.74%	6.76%

In Chapter 10 property finance is considered, and it will be shown that the addition of gearing increases the sensitivity of the performance measures (IRRs and NPVs) to the key variables. Scenarios are a useful analytical technique for capturing the impact of different levels of gearing under each scenario. Dynamic scenarios as created by the innovative DCF Analyst Excel Add-In software provide the ability to consider different types of gearing side by side in terms of the performance figures (IRRs and NPVs). The input variables can be changed (just as in data tables) and the outputs simply recalculated in the worksheet.

In Table 8.4, a scenario is used in the context of analysing the returns profile of a property investment where different types of gearing are used.

A further use of scenarios comes in the context of actuaries' asset/liability modelling exercises. In these models, the cash flows of the investment fund's assets and liabilities are stress-tested for the impact of key economic drivers on each of the main variables. Property assets are often not included in these complex models. However, a simple way to show property's ability (or not, as the case may be) to match the liability profile of an investment fund is to use economic scenarios.

An objective of the property analyst or appraiser is to identify properties that have the wherewithal to outperform, and those that are potential underperformers. Risk and uncertainty are common ingredients in such appraisal models. Wilson (2003) stipulated that the valuation of hyper-growth or high-uncertainty companies poses difficulties for the traditional present value (DCF) model, particularly because of the model's sensitivity to the discount rate. Wilson proposed that the combination of adjusted DCF analysis with scenario analysis could mitigate some of the problems.

8.7   Simulation

Simulation is a major leap forward in terms of the application of risk analysis in that it is much more sophisticated. However, this sophistication is accompanied by complexity, and with this additional complexity come problems of poor results leading to the so-called GIGO syndrome (garbage in, garbage out). Thus an understanding of where the inputs come from and how they are determined is important.

Simulation analysis tests permutations and combinations of change for the variables that have been identified as key drivers of the investment appraisal outputs (IRRs and NPVs). In the context of a DCF analysis, the simulation process runs a series of DCFs with each one drawing on new figures for each variable in accordance with pre-set probability distributions. The relationship between the variables (correlations) can be incorporated into this process.

Incorporating simulations into spreadsheets sounds rather difficult and time-consuming. However, there are now at least two excellent Excel Add-Ins that provide the extra tools to enable the property analyst to undertake simulations of discounted cash flows relatively quickly, simply and reliably.

Whilst it is possible to set up a DCF simulation using Excel's paste functions, this requires relatively complex programming and can be a lengthy process. Technically, one might argue that Excel's random number generator is not truly random in that there is some relationship to the seed number used to start off the random number generation sequence. However, it is in their simplicity of use and the quality of their outputs that the bespoke Excel simulation Add-Ins come to the fore.

Once a discounted cash flow analysis has been set up for the analysis of a property investment or development, it is a relatively straightforward task to incorporate the simulation process so as to obtain additional information on the risk/return profile of the investment or development. Just as when undertaking a scenario analysis, the property analyst is required to identify the key variables and outputs (performance measures). However, whilst in scenarios individual values for each variable are chosen in the context of the scenario in question, in simulation the analytical methodology moves on a step. The same key variables and outputs are chosen, but this time thought is given to the realistic range and probability distribution that relates to each variable, and the relationship (correlation) between the variables.

There is no doubt that the sheer range of variables to be considered does raise issues about the complexity and validity of the exercise, with a possible potential for GIGO (garbage in, garbage out). Whilst this is acknowledged, it is also true that the world of the property investment analyst is not one in which investors are excellent forecasters and have a clear view of what the future holds.

Simulation provides a framework whereby it is possible to gain a clearer picture of the risk/return profile of the property in question, in that it provides a large number of DCF calculations which provide a mass of data for analysis and consideration.

One of the skills required in undertaking a simulation is the choice and specification of each probability distribution assigned to each key variable. These probability distributions are tools by which to describe and quantify each variable more effectively.

8.7.1 Setting up a simulation

The simulation process is set out diagrammatically in Fig. 8.1 and Table 8.5. The first step is to build the DCF model which analyses the property in question and includes as inputs the

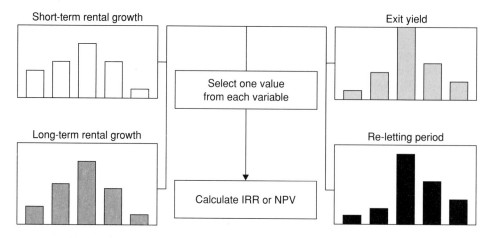

Fig. 8.1   Identifying variables for a SWOT analysis.

Table 8.5   Simulation input.

Variable	Value	Probabilities	
		%	**Cumulative**
Short-term rental growth	0.00%	15.00%	0–14
	2.50%	60.00%	15–74
	5.00%	20.00%	75–94
	7.50%	5.00%	95–99
Long-term rental growth	2.50%	5.00%	0–4
	5.00%	75.00%	5–79
	7.50%	15.00%	80–94
	10.00%	5.00%	95–99
Valuation yield	6.50%	5.00%	0–4
	7.00%	5.00%	5–9
	7.50%	70.00%	10–79
	8.00%	20.00%	80–99
Letting void (months)	3	10.00%	0–9
	6	45.00%	10–54
	9	25.00%	55–79
	12	20.00%	80–99

key variables that are expected to drive the investment's performance (or lack of it). In a straightforward DCF, a best estimate is chosen for each variable, and the resulting answer – IRR or NPV – is used as the determinant of whether the property is a buy/hold/sell.

In simulation there is a recognition that one is dealing with future events, and that the figure for each variable is unlikely to be a single input but will be one of a range of possible figures, with some figures being more likely than others. We will see at the end of this section that one of the strengths of simulation is that it assists in identifying the variables that produce the riskiness of the property. In practice, it may be possible to remove certain individual risks (at a cost); for example, opt for fixed rate borrowings rather than variable

Table 8.6

Key variable	Random number	Number inserted into the DCF model
Short-term rental growth	45	2.5%
Long-term rental growth	13	5.0%
Yield	89	8.0%
Voids (in months)	56	9 months

rate; go for a pre-let rather than have a speculative scheme; extend a tenant's lease several years before expiry to improve the financing and exit yield.

In simulation we therefore need to determine the range and expected values for each key variable (Table 8.6). Once this has been done, one value is selected from each distribution via a random number, which over a large number of runs provides for each variable input numbers that are in line with the underlying probability distribution for that variable.

In the simple example set out in Table 8.6, four random numbers will be generated for each run. Let's say that 45, 13, 89 and 56 are produced as the random numbers, so that for short-term rental growth, long-term rental growth, yield and voids (in months) the numbers shown in Table 8.6 will be inserted in to the DCF model and a calculation will be undertaken. In the case of short-term rental growth, for example, the random number 45 lies within the range 15–74, so the value 2.5% is inserted into the DCF model. The same process is repeated for the other variables.

In each run of the simulation a number is picked for each variable. These numbers are put into the DCF model, the answer or output (IRR or NPV) is saved, and the process is repeated. So in overall terms the simulation process is as shown in Fig. 8.2.

Simulation randomly generates thousands of what-if scenarios. Each scenario is captured, aggregated and presented in a frequency chart, or output distribution. This process is repeated many times such that 5000 or more runs and results (IRRs or NPVs) are calculated and collected.

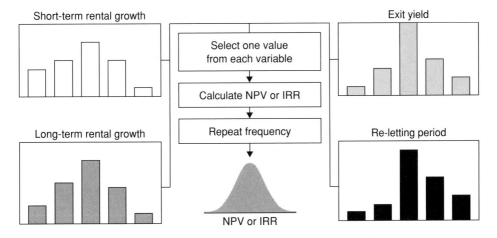

Fig. 8.2 Single-variable sensitivity showing commonly used variables.

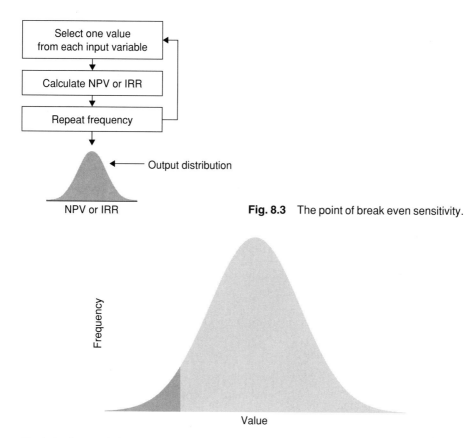

Fig. 8.3   The point of break even sensitivity.

Fig. 8.4   A normal distribution of values showing (shaded) the area of likely downside risk.

The above inputs for the variables are discrete numbers, this is a simplification and in practice it is usually more appropriate to use continuous distributions.

These results (IRRs or NPVs) are put into a frequency distribution, so that one can see the range of returns (Fig. 8.3). It is then for the property investor to consider what is their minimum threshold IRR or NPV.

This minimum required IRR or NPV forms a critical level below which the investment is 'bad news' and above which it is 'good news'. This can be represented in probabilistic terms. The area under the graph in Fig. 8.4 represents 1. The area of the graph to the left of the critical level represents approximately 5% of the total area, and consequently there is a 5% chance of the property underperforming the required minimum return.

Using this overview as a simplified starting point, consideration is now given to each of the above stages and the method by which they would be incorporated into a full-scale simulation process.

8.7.2   Building a simulation model

Before specialist Excel Add-In packages became affordable and easily available, the few using simulation resorted to building their own simulation model in Excel, using the *fx* paste function RAND( ), combined with macros that collected the results and placed them into a distribution table. (RAND( ) returns a random number greater or equal to zero, and less than one. This number is to 14 decimal points, and is evenly distributed, and changes on each recalculation of the spreadsheet.) As these models were complex and not always robust, it is is not surprising that the technique was not widely adopted. However, there are now a number of specialist simulation packages which, just like the DCF Analyst software, are Excel Add-Ins. This means that simulation technique is now within the scope of most analysts and professionals.

Please see Spreadsheet 18 for a working example of an Excel-based simulation model for a property investment, which incorporates the RAND( ) function and macros.

NB: if you are using Excel XP and you can not get the spreadsheet to run, you will need to go to Tools ⇒ Options ⇒ Security ⇒ Macro Security ⇒ reset at Medium.

Please see Spreadsheet 19 for a summary of the characteristics of a couple of the Excel Add-In simulation models, together with web links to the software developers' web sites.

Using specialist simulation Add-In software speeds up the process such that, once the main DCF model has been built and the key variables have been identified, the whole process of getting the simulation to run and produce output distributions (of IRRs and NPVs) can take a matter of a few minutes.

Two examples of the outputs of a DCF simulation are illustrated here: Fig. 8.5 shows the probability distribution of the IRRs for an investment, whilst Fig. 8.6 shows that the same data could be portrayed, alternatively, as a cumulative probability distribution.

In order for simulation to be really worth while, however, a number of factors must be considered:

• distributions for each key variable;
• relationship between the variables (correlations);

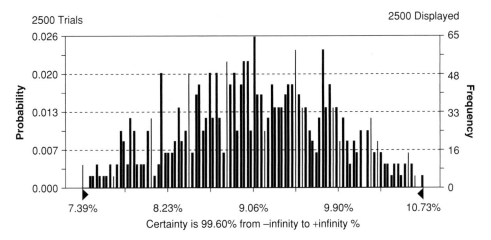

Fig. 8.5   Forecast: project IRR frequency chart.

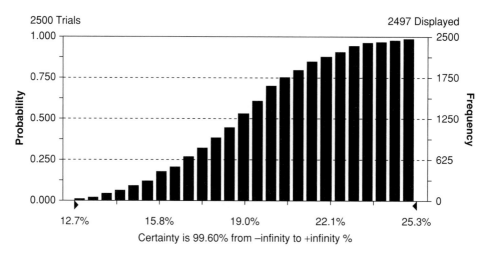

Fig. 8.6   Forecast: equity IRR cumulative chart.

- sampling methodology of the simulation model;
- number of runs (trials) of the simulation;
- interpretation of the outputs.

These are discussed separately below.

8.7.3   Distributions for each key variable

A practical starting point is to cut down the number of distributions offered by the specialist Excel Add-In Simulation programmes to the number most applicable to property investment analysis and development appraisals. These are as follows:

- normal distribution;
- triangular distribution;
- uniform distribution;
- non-uniform customised distribution.

Each distribution has on the x axis the values relating to the variable being used in the DCF model, and on the y axis the expected probability of each value being achieved. The sum of the probabilities must equal one; alternatively, this can be expressed such that for the area under the graph the probability distribution equals one.

Normal distribution

The normal distribution frequency curve provides information on expected figures about a mean. The range of returns about the mean is expressed in terms of standard deviation; in simulation analysis of a property investment, for example, one of the key variables is rental growth.

The distribution of the rental growth over the analysis period will have a mean (an average) and range of expected figures. This range will be measured in terms of standard

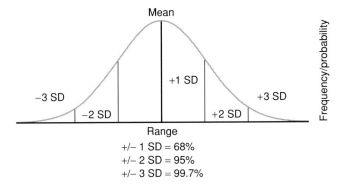

Range
+/− 1 SD = 68%
+/− 2 SD = 95%
+/− 3 SD = 99.7%

Fig. 8.7   The qualities of the standard deviation in a normal distribution.

Table 8.7

Number of standard deviations about the mean	Percentage of expected figures that will be included within this section of the probability distribution
1	68.26
2	95.44
3	99.73
4	99.99

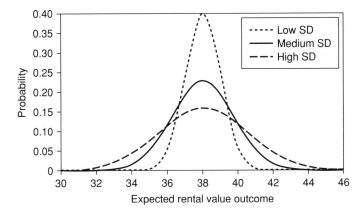

Fig. 8.8   Normal distributions.

deviations, and Fig. 8.7 provides an illustration of a normal distribution showing where standard deviation falls in relation to both the mean and the distribution of the total results around the mean. The figures are set out in more detail in Table 8.7.

The smaller the standard deviation figure, the more peaked the distribution. The larger the standard deviation figures, the flatter the distribution, as shown in the Fig. 8.8.

Let us now put some figures relating to a normal distribution into a property context. If the mean expected rental value is £38, and one standard deviation equals £1, then the

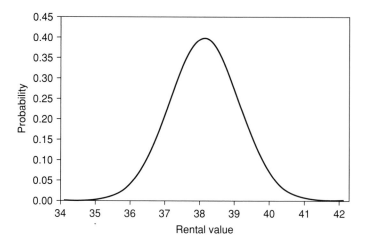

Fig. 8.9   A peaked normal distribution showing a small standard deviation of rental values around the mean.

Table 8.8   DCF Analyst sensitivity report.

	Best estimate	Best estimate plus 10%	Best estimate minus 10%	Top realistic estimate	Bottom realistic estimate
Rent	38	41.8	34.2	40	36
Outputs					
IRR	9.00%	13.74%	3.24%	11.60%	6.13%
Sensitivity		52.74%	−63.95%	28.88%	−31.92%

Table 8.9

Number of standard deviations either side of the mean rent of £38	Gives a range of rents as follows	Percentage of rents that may be expected to be included within this rental range
1	£37 to £39	68.26%
2	£36 to £40	95.44%
3	£35 to £41	99.73%
4	£34 to £42	99.99%

probability distribution can be represented by the graph in Fig. 8.9. This distribution should bear a relationship to the figures incorporated in the sensitivity analysis, as set out in Table 8.8. Being a normal distribution, it has the characteristics shown in Table 8.9.

The question the property analyst has to ask is: 'is the distribution of the expected values for the variable in question going to be a normal distribution – that is, bell-shaped and symmetrical about the mean?' If it is the conclusion that a normal distribution is appropriate, then when using the bespoke simulation Excel Add-In packages you will be asked to input the following data:

- *Mean (average) expected value for the variable in question.* The mean figure is straightforward, in that it will be your best guess for the variable – in this case, the rent (£38).
- *Standard deviation for the variable in question.* This is a little more difficult to deal with, in that you are dealing with future values for the variable in question – in this case future rental levels. A useful approach is to consider what the likely range of the figures that would capture the vast majority of expected figures might be; say a range that captures approximately 95% of the expected values. For rents in the above example, one might think in terms of a rental range of £36 to £40. This represents a range of £4, which represents £2 above and £2 below the mean. In a normal distribution, two standard deviations either side of the mean represent 95% of expected outcomes, so in this case one standard deviation equals £2/2, namely £1.

Normal distributions are symmetrical about the mean. Thus in those instances where the distribution is skewed or not bell-shaped, the normal distribution is inappropriate.

Triangular distributions

In the property market the availability of data series for the variables that drive DCF investment analysis models is often limited. Accordingly, the determining the probability distributions for each key variable at a future date requires a combination of the analyst's market knowledge and research skills.

The use of normal distributions as above is one approach. However, another approach is to use triangular distributions. For this, three pieces of information are required:

- the mode (the value with the highest probability of occurring);
- the top figure;
- the bottom figure.

The analyst should consider the figure for the mode as being their best estimate for the value of the variable.

The top and bottom figures tie in with the figures adopted in the earlier sensitivity analysis (see Table 8.8) where the top and bottom realistic estimates of the variables were incorporated. This information can be incorporated into a triangular distribution as shown in Fig. 8.10.

In the above case, the top realistic estimates and bottom realistic estimates are evenly distributed about the mean, with a top realistic value of £40 and a bottom realistic value of £36. These realistic estimates should look to include the vast majority of expected figures (around 95%, or similar to two standard deviations as for the normal distribution). When adopting this approach the property analyst is required to focus on that which is perceived as being realistic. The danger in incorporating unrealistically large ranges is that the property analyst will arrive at inputs into the DCF model that cease to bear much relationship to the property and the market in which it is located.

However, as shown in Fig. 8.11, in some instances the figures and distributions for the key variables may be skewed. In this case the mode future rental value is £21; however, the property analyst perceives that there is potentially more upside than downside,

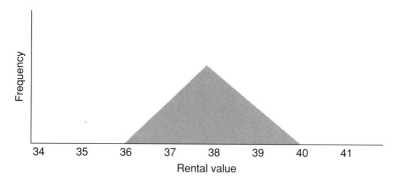

Fig. 8.10   Triangular probability distribution evenly distributed.

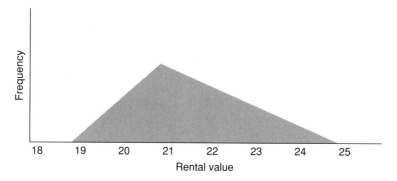

Fig. 8.11   Triangular probability distribution showing downward skew.

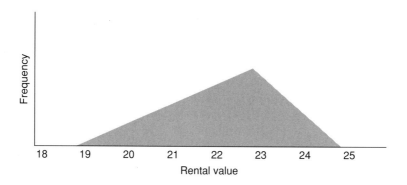

Fig. 8.12   Triangular probability distribution showing upward skew.

with the top expected rent being £25, and the bottom £19. This produces an upside skewed distribution.

The opposite, as shown in Fig. 8.12, can occur when the triangular distribution is downside skewed, where there is a higher probability that the result will be lower than the mode rental value.

The ability to use triangular distributions for the inputs for the distributions of the key variables makes the setting up of the inputs for a simulation relatively straightforward.

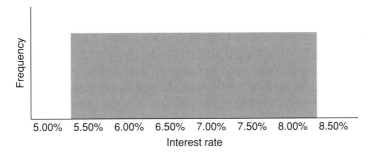

Fig. 8.13   Uniform – equal probabilities.

Uniform distribution

Fig. 8.13 depicts a uniform distribution where each figure has a similar expectation of occurring. Where a range of values are thought to be equally likely, or where the analyst finds it difficult to come up with an alternative probability distribution, or where there is little information early in the project and the analyst cannot determine a 'most likely' figure, a uniform distribution is often used. For example, if finance costs are being included within the DCF model, and these finance costs incorporate a floor and a cap such that the minimum interest cost will be 5.50% and the maximum will be 8.50%, and the analyst believes that there is little to choose between them in terms of which the figure will actually be, the use of a uniform distribution is appropriate.

Non-uniform customised distribution

In some cases the distribution may be polarised and non-uniform. For example, where there is a break clause in a falling market, if the tenant does not break the rent will be say £22; in contrast, if the tenant exercises the option to break, and the property has to be relet in a weak and falling market, the estimated rent is £19. Two distinct answers are possible due to the terms of the lease, as shown in Fig. 8.14.

Brown and Matysiak (2000) consider the distributional characteristics of real estate returns, and stress the importance of identifying the statistical characteristics of these returns and the underlying performance drivers when carrying out real estate analysis.

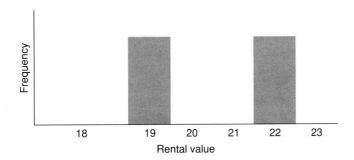

Fig. 8.14   Twin peaks.

8.7.4   Relationship between the variables (correlations)

Traditional simulation models assumed the independence of each of the variables in a simulation. This was in part to keep things simple, but was also a significant weakness of simulation relative to scenario approaches of risk analysis. The advent of specialist Excel Add-In simulation models has corrected this shortcoming. They make provision for correlation between the variables: the analyst can identify appropriate correlation figures, and the specialist software adjusts for correlations in its sampling methodology.

In the property market, data series are not easy to gather. Thus when one seeks to incorporate the correlation between the data series for different variables into the simulation, matters get even more difficult – particularly in the eyes of the sceptical practitioner who believes that a simple DCF will encompass every investor's needs. Significant additional research is needed in this area so that users of simulation have empirical evidence on which to base their assumptions on the correlations between the variables.

If identifying the correlations is a problem, then a pragmatic approach with property investment appraisals is to consider which of the key variables could be correlated. With property investment analysis, unlike development appraisals, a relatively small number of key variables will be used. The two main variables will normally be the rate of rental growth and the exit valuation yield. The pragmatic approach is first to assume that the variables are uncorrelated, then to rerun the figures on the basis that the variables are perfectly positively (+1) and perfectly negatively correlated (−1). Consideration can be given to how the extreme correlations impact on the output distribution.

In Fig. 8.15, the property investor has the ability to finance the property with senior debt (geared) or senior debt and mezzanine finance (highly geared). (See Chapter 9 for more on senior debt and mezzanine finance.) The introduction of debt increases the risk of the investment, as seen by the wide range of expected returns.

When considering risk, the conventional view is that an appropriate measure of risk of a property investment is the dispersion of the returns. Risk can be both upside and downside risk (underperforming a critical benchmark or rate of return). However, from the investor's perspective it is usually downside risk that needs to be avoided or limited as far as possible. It is therefore the impact on downside risk that needs to be considered carefully.

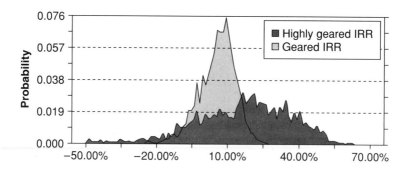

Fig. 8.15   Nil correlation.

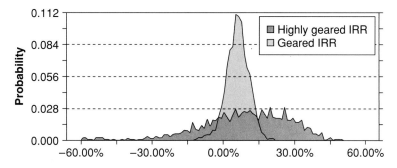

Fig. 8.16   Perfect positive correlation.

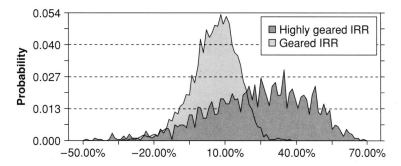

Fig. 8.17   Perfect negative correlation.

The nil correlation simulation, which has rental growth and exit yield with nil correlation, shows the highly geared results with a long downside tail, counterbalanced by higher upside potential than the geared investment (Fig. 8.15).

The perfectly positive correlated simulation (Fig. 8.16), which has rental growth and exit yield with perfect positive correlation, has pulled together the geared probability distribution, making it more peaked, whilst flattening and spreading out the results of the highly geared analysis.

The perfectly negative correlated simulation (Fig. 8.17) in this case provides an interesting set of results, in that it increases the risk profile of the geared analysis to a larger extent than those of the highly geared analysis.

The above three correlation analyses show the analyst that it is the negative correlations that will adversely influence the results. At this point, the analyst needs to consider what correlations are appropriate and within what range the correlations should be tested. In practice, when these three forms of correlation analysis are undertaken it is not uncommon for each set of results to show that the property being appraised clearly produces an acceptable or unacceptable risk/return profile. For simulation to become a fully robust method of risk analysis, the correlations between the key variables in the property DCF analysis require additional research by the real estate industry.

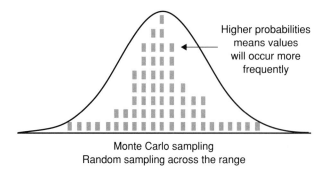

Fig. 8.18 Monte Carlo sampling: random sampling across the range.

Monte Carlo sampling
Random sampling across the range

Higher probabilities means values will occur more frequently

8.7.5   Sampling methodology of the simulation model

Samples from probability distributions are chosen randomly across the range. The probability distribution gives the probability of outcomes at each point in the range. However, once the distribution has been decided upon, the property analyst then needs to consider which is the appropriate sampling methodology to be used by the simulation model.

In the Excel Add-In simulation software, the two main methods of sampling offered are:

- *Monte Carlo*: this method, as shown in Fig. 8.18, samples across the probability distribution for each trial run. Accordingly, if relatively small numbers of trial runs are undertaken, the output may contain either too many or too few outlying results.

  For many people, Monte Carlo is synonymous with simulation. It is simpler and faster than the alternative Latin Hypercube. However, with specialist simulation software and the advent of PCs with good processing power available to all at relatively low cost, the advantages of the speed and simplicity of the Monte Carlo sampling methodology become less important.

- *Latin Hypercube*: this is more complex in its sampling methodology and requires more computer processing power. Its merit is that it deals with outlying results in a more consistent manner. The sampling methodology splits the probability distribution for each variable into vertical slices, and these slices are systematically sampled during the trial runs, as shown in Fig. 8.19.

  With modern computers, the days of setting up a trial run using Latin Hypercube, and then disappearing off for a long coffee break whilst the computer crunches through all

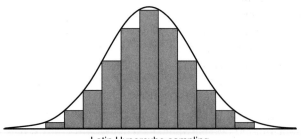

Latin Hypercube sampling
Slower, but preferable. Stratifies range into sections then randomly samples within each range, according to its probability

Fig. 8.19 Latin Hypercube sampling: slower, but preferable. Stratifies range into sections then randomly samples within each range, according to its probability.

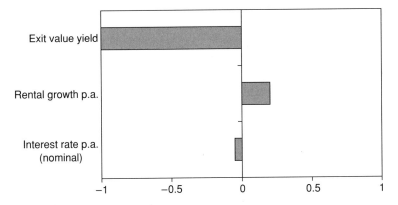

Fig. 8.20   Target forecast: project IRR.

the calculations, are gone. In short, advances in technology mean that Latin Hypercube is now a practical option for simulation, and it does offer advantages over Monte Carlo.

8.7.6   Interpreting the results of the simulation model

Tornado charts are one of the outputs available in simulation software packages. They show the contribution to variance that each variable makes to the outputs. This is calculated by regressing each output, with each of the key variables for each of the trial runs undertaken. The output identifies how significant each variable is in influencing the variability of the outputs; that is, its contribution to risk. Tornado charts enable the analyst to see which of the key variables is driving the outputs (IRR or NPV) and causing the variation in the numbers, and to rank the key variables in the order of their contribution to risk within the project.

Fig. 8.20 shows that, for the investment in question, it is the exit valuation yield that is predominantly driving the riskiness of the investment. After a first run has taken place and the results of the tornado chart have been considered, it should prompt the property analyst to review the probability distribution outputs for each of the key variables that have been identified as the drivers of the investment's risk profile.

8.7.7   Number of runs (trials) of the simulation

The number of trial runs to be undertaken is a function of the time available. Often, property analysts initially tend to undertake relatively modest numbers of trial runs (say 1000–5000) for each set of inputs. This enables them to glean a picture of the results. 'What if' adjustments can be tried, changes can be incorporated and the impact of the key variables can be considered.

Once the property analyst has run a series of exploratory trial runs, and is comfortable with the inputs into the simulation model, a larger number of trial runs should be undertaken. The number of runs can be set at a high number (say 25 000+), or it can be set up such that the simulation software stops as soon as the simulation calculations and

Table 8.10   Statistical output.

Forecast (statistic)	NPV (value)	Forecast (statistic)	IRR (value)
Trials	100 000	Trials	100 000
Mean	£936 983	Mean	19.72%
Median	£930 390	Median	19.74%
Standard deviation	£448 130	Standard deviation	5.42%
Skewness	0.09	Skewness	−0.02
Kurtosis	2.89	Kurtosis	2.89
Coeff of variability	0.48	Coeff of variability	0.28
Range low	−£804 667	Range low	−3.06%
Range high	£2 795 875	Range high	40.52%
Range width	£3 600 542	Range width	43.58%
Mean std error	£1 417.11	Mean std error	0.02%

outputs provide no additional information to the output distribution. The latter is a useful and time-saving facility offered by the better simulation packages.

8.7.8   Interpretation

The simulation software packages provide substantial amounts of statistical analysis on each of the simulation trial runs. This, coupled with good graphing facilities, provides property analysts with a valuable resource to enable them to describe and communicate the simulation results to their colleagues.

Table 8.10 shows an example of the type of statistical analysis available when using simulation Add-Ins. The elements can be summarised as follows:

- *Skew* calculation uses cubed deviations from the mean (magnifying the effect of the sign) and shows whether the output distribution is normal or has a skew to either side.
- *Kurtosis figure* (see Fig. 8.21) indicates whether the output distribution has a peaked or flat nature. A normal distribution has a kurtosis value of 3. A fat (long)-tailed distribution implies that extreme values are probable and that there is a greater probability of market extremes. A peaked distribution clusters values around the mean.

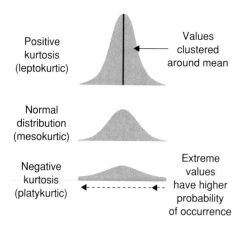

Positive kurtosis (leptokurtic) — Values clustered around mean

Normal distribution (mesokurtic)

Negative kurtosis (platykurtic) — Extreme values have higher probability of occurrence

Fig. 8.21   Kurtosis.

- *Coefficient of variation (%)* measures dispersion relative to the mean: (Standard deviation $\div$ Mean) $\times$ 100%
- *Audit trails* enable the property analyst to step through each of the calculations of the DCF model. A simulation with 5000 trial runs will produce 5000 DCF analyses. Information on which combinations of key variables have produced the outlying results (particularly those that are causing downside risk) can provide those making the purchase/sale decisions with something concrete to focus on when considering their stance towards risk and returns.

Whilst the use of simulation may for a number of practitioners be over and above what is expected or required, those with a business school or specialist property undergraduate degree or post-graduate education should be relatively comfortable with these statistical outputs. The latter are a growing force within the ranks of property analysts or appraisers. For those who would like to consider this topic in more detail, Adams (2003) provides a user-friendly approach to the subject.

8.7.9   A comparison of projects

A feature of simulation analysis is that it enables the property analyst to consider one property's output distribution relative to another's. Furthermore, the more sophisticated simulation software packages have the facility to combine the results of individual investments to provide the investor with portfolio-based information. Portfolio risk is considered in more detail in Chapter 12.

8.8   Prioritising the key variables for risk management

Simulation analysis enables the analyst to prioritise the risky elements (key variables) for risk management. This enables judgements to be made at various stages of the analysis. It is important for all judgements/assumptions to be well documented. In particular, it is important to:

- Define all project risks and state all assumptions clearly.
- Justify the values, probabilities and risk exposure period.
- State the sources of data used.
- List unquantifiable risks and their qualitative assessment.
- Outline the steps to be taken to manage retained risks.
- Provide evidence of discussions with the clients.

Historical data can provide a baseline, but is the future expected to be different? This is particularly important in development appraisals and, despite the advent of qualitative techniques, a significant element of the property risk analysis will continue to be judgmental. In part this is because the property analyst is frequently operating with only modest historic data series and with the knowledge that it is future trends that are being modelled.

Risk analysis in property is likely always to include an element of uncertainty. Historical data may be misleading, as changes in future economic circumstances, demand characteristics and planning regimes influence the property market. This is particularly important in development. It is frequently necessary to quantify and incorporate 'gut feel'.

The views of an experienced letting agent may produce figures different from those of the research department. The views of the latter should be carefully considered in the context of the agent's views.

Once the key variables that drive the risk profile of the property have been established, it is possible to consider how practical measures can be taken to remove a number of the risks whilst also looking at the cost implications of removing the individual risks. For example, such decisions could relate to:

- Moving from variable rate finance to fixed rate finance, by entering into a SWAP contract.
- Bringing on board caps and collars alongside the bank finance in order to reduce interest rate risk.
- Entering into pre-lettings for a development as against undertaking a speculative scheme.
- Undertaking a forward sale of a development, rather than refinancing or selling the property at a later date.
- Where a property investment has short, unexpired terms on the occupational leases, and there is no short-term refurbishment or redevelopment potential, negotiating with the main tenants to extend their leases in return for a reduced rent or capital sum now.

8.9   Geared property investments

Simulation provides a breakdown of the key drivers in the model and can easily incorporate the impact of gearing (see Chapter 10). In the context of gearing, which increases volatility, simulation provides better understanding of sensitivities of the bottom line performance measures and gives decision-makers a clearer presentation of the return and risk profile of properties.

The comparison of different levels of gearing can be made more transparent using simulation techniques. Fig. 8.22 shows a property financed using senior debt (geared) and

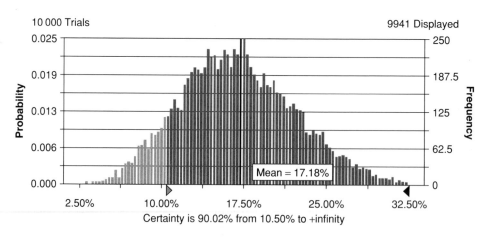

Fig. 8.22   Forecast: geared IRR frequency chart.

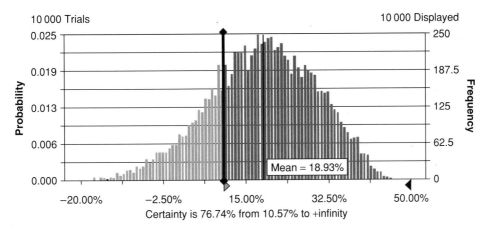

Fig. 8.23   Forecast: highly geared IRR frequency chart.

can be compared with Fig. 8.23 where both senior debt and mezzanine finance are used. The use of mezzanine finance increases the mean IRR for the investor from 17.2% to 18.9%, but also increases the risk profile of the investment significantly on three measures:

- The expected probability of getting a greater than 10.5% return for the geared investment is 90%, whilst it is only 77% when mezzanine finance is introduced.
- The downside risk profile changes. With the geared investment the worst expected return is an IRR of 2.5%, but with mezzanine finance added the at worst IRR becomes minus 20%.
- The upside risk profile for the geared investment shows the highest possible return of 32%, whilst with mezzanine finance it is 45%. But the probability of outperforming is not very large. Is the investor a gambler at heart?

In some instances the use of the overlay charting facility provides revealing results. In Fig. 8.24 the addition of low cost fixed rate gearing increases risk, as measured by the range of returns (14–25%), whilst the ungeared investment has a far smaller standard

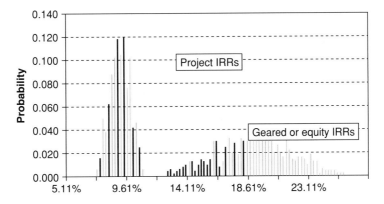

Fig. 8.24   Simulation: project v. equity returns.

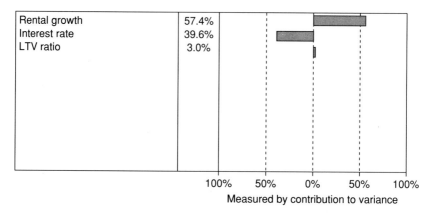

Rental growth	57.4%				
Interest rate	39.6%				
LTV ratio	3.0%				

100%   50%   0%   50%   100%

Measured by contribution to variance

Fig. 8.25   Sensitivity chart target forecast: highly geared IRR.

deviation of returns; if risk is considered in terms of downside risk then the geared investment offers better returns and a lower downside risk profile.

When dealing with gearing, tornado charts can be informative. For example, Fig. 8.25 shows rental growth as the key risk driver, followed by the interest rate, and then to a small extent the bank's view of the loan to value ratio (LTV).

8.10   Decision trees and associated sensitivity analysis

The application of decision trees provides the analyst with the ability to allocate probabilities against events that might occur in the future. The decision tree comprises a number of nodal points. At each node one or more events might occur. For example, at a lease expiry: branch one – the tenant vacates; and branch two – the tenant continues in occupation. For branch one there is say a 30% probability, while there is a 70% probability associated with branch two. From these, a probability weighted result can be obtained.

Decision trees are also known as binomial or polynomial lattices and enable the user to evaluate decision possibilities under uncertainty. Once a decision tree model has been built using bespoke software, it is often useful to carry out sensitivity analysis on the variable inputs to identify those variables that drive the performance of the investment or development. Some useful software is available that enables the analyst to set up a decision tree model and undertake the required calculations is available. These models provide a number of informative outputs. Please refer to Spreadsheet 20 for further details and screen shots of a worked example using the decision tree software.

Decision trees are particularly useful to developers who have, for example, a number of sites for which planning consent is being sought and wish to appraise the overall prospects for returns. A site may have a 10% chance of getting high density housing and a 90% chance of the planning application being refused. If refused, the developer may consider there is a 60% chance of getting planning consent for a lower density scheme linked to a road improvement, and a 40% chance of refusal. If refused again, the view might be that there is a 100% chance of getting planning consent for two houses. The prospects for the site on a probability weighted basis can be aggregated to provide an overall figure.

In addition, this figure can be viewed in the context of the prospects for other development schemes.

Alternatively, the decision analysis can assist in showing which routes through the decision tree will offer the best expected returns. Bespoke decision analysis software enables the analyst to calculate the returns for different probabilities and timings associated with the decision tree.

Furthermore, the decision analysis software enables the user to build interactive decision trees, with settings that include:

- probability or max/min decision nodes;
- multiple branches – up to nine per node are available;
- automatic recalculation when values are changed;
- links to other cells or worksheets or workbooks;
- exponential utility function;
- statistical analysis.

When working with decision trees, sensitivity analysis can be carried out on one or two variables at a time, and a wide range of outputs can be accessed, for example:

- Decision value tables, showing the value selected for each step variable.
- Strategic region table showing which decision was made for each step variable.
- One or two dimension chart showing expected monetary value for each step variable.
- Tornado and spider charts.

Decision analysis provides the property analyst with a useful risk appraisal tool that comes into its own when risky investments are being considered, in particular developments where there are significant uncertainties as to what planning consent may be granted.

Please see Spreadsheet 20 for an example of a decision tree analysis, and reference to web links for the decision tree software.

8.11   The analysis continuum

In this chapter consideration has been given to a range of risk assessment and appraisal techniques. These activities can usefully be considered as part of a continuum, such that one analytical process leads on to another, as described below.

- *Step one – a valuation of the property*: this provides the reference point, and the market's view of the transaction price that can be expected.
- *Step two – qualitative analysis*: this can be undertaken by a PEST or/and SWOT analysis and provides a framework for the relative ranking of competing investments using a number of categories by which the investments can be assessed.
- *Step three – quantitative analysis*: a discounted cash flow analysis can be undertaken to produce the expected or best estimate of the IRR and NPV. Initially, risk adjusted discount rate (RADR) methodology can be used to accommodate elements of risk. The analysis can then be broadened to include sensitivity and scenario analysis.

- *Step four – risk analysis of the property*: when the DCF has been carried out, a number of techniques based on probability weighted IRRs and NPVs can be used. These techniques include:
  - o probability weighted scenarios;
  - o decision analysis for uncertain schemes;
  - o simulation techniques, such as Monte Carlo and Latin Hypercube.
- *Step five*: the conclusion of step four provides the data that enables the individual property to be placed within a portfolio risk context, as will be discussed in Chapter 12.

8.12 Data handling

No consideration of risk within property appraisal would be complete without consideration of the data issue. One of the discussion points amongst analysts undertaking DCF analysis in the property industry is where do the future figures for the variables come from?

Should historic data series be used? Or should the analysts and researchers' views of future forecasts be used? Are the figures derived from number crunching or 'gut feel'? And how are the probability distributions to be dealt with?

Point estimates are not sufficient when dealing with DCFs and future returns. Scenarios incorporating probabilities for each scenario are a useful and straightforward way of undertaking a risk assessment of a property investment.

8.13 Summary

In this chapter we have considered ways in which risk can be analysed and evaluated in a property investment context. Risk analysis has a valuable role to play in assisting vendors and purchasers in their decision-making process and in helping property investors track the performance of their assets. In the past the development and utilisation of risk appraisal techniques have been hampered by the complexity of some of the mathematics. However, the development of Excel Add-Ins and the growth of greater computing skills amongst analysts have opened the door to the greater use of risk analysis techniques. Increasingly, practitioners will recognise that accounting for risk through a risk adjusted discount rate will not give a full picture, and more explicit measures will be required routinely.

However, whilst the property investment industry is beginning to adjust its practices to incorporate single asset risk analysis techniques, this will not be sufficient to meet the needs of large-scale investors. For them, the consideration of risk extends beyond that of the single asset decision: they require an understanding of the effect of risk at a portfolio level. Risk is considered within the portfolio context in Chapter 12.

References

Adams, A., Booth, P., Bowie, D. and Freeth, D. (2003) *Investment Mathematics*. London: Wiley Finance.

Alexander, G., Sharpe, W. and Bailey, J. (2001) *Fundamentals of Investments*. London: Prentice Hall.

Brealey, R. and Myers, S. (2002) *Principles of Corporate Finance*, 7th edn. London: McGraw Hill.

Brown, G. and Matysiak, G. (2000) *Real Estate Investment: A Capital Markets Approach*. London: Prentice Hall.

Investment Property Databank Indices: *Investment Property Databank UK and International Property Performance Indices*, www.ipdindex.co.uk

Matysiak, G., Booth, P. and Ormerod, P. (2002) *Risk Measurement and Management for Real Estate Investment Portfolios*. London: Investment Property Forum.

Melicher, R.W. and Norton, E.A. (2003) *Finance: Introduction to Institutions, Investments and Management*. New York: John Wiley & Sons Inc.

Oxelheim, L. (2003) Macroeconomic variables and corporate performance. *Financial Analysts Journal*, 59 (4): 36–50.

Pyhrr, S.A., Born, W.L. and Webb, J.R. (1990) Development of a dynamic investment strategy under alternative inflation cycle scenarios. *Journal of Real Estate Research*, 5 (2): 177–93.

Vaughan, E. and Vaughan, T. (2003) *Fundamentals of Risk and Insurance*. New York: John Wiley & Sons Inc.

Wilson, B.H. (2003) Valuing hyper-growth/high-uncertainty companies – a practical approach. *AIMR Conference Proceedings*, Association for Investment Management and Research.

9 Occupational property: decision-making and appraisal

Aims of the chapter

- To explain the emerging interest in property as a corporate asset and the importance of this to the investing owner.
- To explore the criteria that affect the decision to rent or own property.
- To discuss the criteria for individual building selection by corporate occupiers.
- To define the terms 'specialised' and 'non-specialised' property and their significance to valuations for financial accounts.
- To explain in outline the framework within which property valuations are carried out for the balance sheet.
- To explore methods of appraisal used for corporate decision-making.

9.1 Introduction

The emphasis within this book is upon the evaluation and appraisal techniques used by those advising investors in real estate. To the institutional investor the primary concern is to achieve homes for available funds that will be secure, will provide a competitive rate of return at an acceptable level of risk and can be compared in a meaningful way with other investment media. For the corporate property investor, the objective is the maximisation of shareholder wealth along with an optimum debt equity ratio for their investment portfolio.

The pursuit of these objectives has provided the dominant driver for developments in appraisal techniques since the 1960s. This, combined with the prevailing system of landlord and tenant relationships within the UK, is responsible, at least in part, for a 'lacuna' in understanding between investing landlords and occupying tenants. The dominant lease structure during the years from 1965 to 1995 assured the landlord of a rent that could not fall in actual money terms for periods of up to a quarter of a century from the date of grant of the lease; it also resulted in the passing of all liability for insurance, repair and upkeep to the tenant.

These factors, combined with the need for the institutional investor to analyse property income flows and returns in relation to equities, have led to property being viewed primarily as a financial asset. The financial nature of property was underpinned by the security of income, and for some 15 years up to the end of the 1990s this was reinforced by a property market in which for most years occupational demand outstripped supply. For the corporate property investor the object has been to look at real estate returns relative to the company's cost of capital, and in particular to beat the weighted average cost of capital (Brealey and Myers, 2002).

Sometimes investors have paid only scant consideration to property's functionality to the tenant and its relationship with the changing corporate environment. A property, once let, becomes a secure income stream; therefore, given an inflationary environment, any decrease in occupational attractiveness in real terms tends to be shielded behind rising overall levels of rents and prices.

This was the model until the early 1990s when a slump in tenant demand and a loss of interest in property investment as a home for funds forced a radical re-examination of the practice of investment choice and appraisal methodology. In turn, this sparked off a realisation that the underlying requirement of property to meet *occupier* needs both in terms of physical space and in terms of lease arrangement was fundamental to achieving successful investment. (For a full discussion and analysis of the property marked crash, see Scott (1996) and Ross Goobey (1992).)

Over a period of little more than a decade, the focus within the leading investor community has shifted to the development of understanding of both current and emerging occupational requirements. Changes to stamp duty charged on the granting of new leases (Finance Act 2004), the prospect of occupational leases coming on balance sheet (see section 8.6), market pressures and pressure from government – including the threat of legislation unless landlords offer tenants more flexibility – have resulted in very significant changes to leasing arrangements. An analysis of average length of lease, as tracked by IPD (Investment Property Databank), shows that these have fallen to less than ten years, and even less if break clauses are factored into the analysis (BPF IPD, 2004).

For these reasons, any consideration of appraisal and worth of investment property must be accompanied by an understanding of the role of property for the corporate occupier. Within the UK a very significant percentage of property lies within investment hands. However, the corporate owner-occupied sector represents probably a larger proportion of the national estate.

Whilst the focus of this book is on the investment markets, some consideration must nonetheless be given to those properties that are owner-occupied. Thus this chapter looks at the rationale for owner-occupation and the appraisal methods that are used for the calculation of worth of such properties.

9.2   Property as a corporate asset

Back in 1991 it was estimated that, on average, between 30% and 40% of the value of all corporate assets was represented by real estate, and that real estate formed the single largest input to the balance sheet (Currie and Scott, 1991). For this reason alone, it follows that any business needs to take due care over its property occupation decision-making process. This had been advocated by some for many years (see, for example, Zeckhauser and Silverman, 1983; Veale, 1989). However, research by the University of Reading in 1989 indicated that this was far from the case, with many companies being almost unaware of the extent of their property estate (Avis *et al.*, 1989). Since then, a series of other research projects during the 1990s have found similar results (Debenham Tewson Research, 1992; Gibson, 1994, 1995; Arthur Andersen, 1995).

Despite the inertia demonstrated by the findings of the research projects, the 1990s did witness enormous change, at least within the literature, with a growing realisation both of the importance of property as a corporate asset (see, for example, Apgar, 1995; Weatherhead, 1997) and of the relationship between occupational worth and investment value (Krumm *et al.*, 1998; Krumm, 2001). Such awareness was prompted to a large extent by the economic downturn of the early 1990s which resulted in many companies undertaking downsizing strategies and a series of corporate takeovers.

Research at City University Business School by Rodney *et al.* on the impact on shareholder value of corporate property holdings also highlighted the role of real estate in a corporate context (Rodney *et al.*, 2001). This research examined 4500 UK quoted and unquoted companies' financial statements for the period 1990–2000. Four principal areas were addressed:

- The value of property in the UK corporate market.
- Why companies hold leases on their balance sheet.
- Property holdings and shareholder value.
- The impact of size and industry.

The research concluded that in 1998 UK corporates reported a total of £212 billion gross book value of property (£175 billion net of depreciation). This represented 18% of total assets (or 45% of fixed assets, or 47% of tangible assets). Over the decade to 2000, the average gross property holdings for the corporate sector was £200 billion. Where Rodney and his research team's findings made particularly interesting reading was in relation to the property holdings of the corporate sector relative to other owners of property, as shown in Table 9.1.

Not included in the figures in Table 9.1 were private property investors, private property companies and overseas investors. Taking the government and local authorities as owner-users of real estate, the above gives a total of £564 billion of real estate in the hands of owner-occupiers. Thus when one considers corporate property holdings, one should not forget government property holdings.

Rodney's research identified that, over the analysis period, the combined corporate balance sheets showed 68% as freeholds and 32% as capitalised leases. Over the decade analysed, an increasing number of companies expanded their exposure to leaseholds, such that by 1999 around 40% of property was held on balance sheet as capital (finance) leases. It was noted that these corporate real estate figures give an approximation of the open market value of the property holdings, since property was often stated in the balance sheet at historic cost, and where it was valued it was to existing use with vacant possession (see section 9.6). Thus, the £212 billion for corporate holdings in real estate is, in open market value terms, likely to be an under estimate.

Table 9.1 Reported value of corporate property in context.

Property owner type	Value (£ billion)	Source
UK corporates (excluding property investment companies)	212	City University Business School (2004)
UK government	274	National Audit Office
UK local authority	78	Local authority statistics
UK institutional investors	95	IPD Digest 1999
UK quoted property companies	70	IPD Digest 1999

Section 9.8 considers in more detail the reasons why corporates hold leases on balance sheet and discusses whether the way property is held has an influence on the creation of shareholder wealth.

Bootle and Kalyan (2002) concluded that, even in 2002, property was still for many corporate organisations a wasted asset, with something in the order of £18 billion being wasted each year as a result of inefficient property management. However, although inefficiencies undoubtedly still exist, most companies are now far more aware than ever before of the need to align their property needs with their corporate strategy (Edwards and Ellison, 2003). As companies become aware of the need to manage their assets, so the potential attractiveness of property and, more significantly, the ability of property to *sustain* attraction in the hands of a corporate occupier, takes on added importance. This will affect both their policy towards property acquisition and disposal and the way in which they measure its performance and contribution to the company. In terms of the latter, it is recognised that a paucity of appropriate tools exists (Nourse, 1994), but as these are developed there will inevitably be an impact on investment performance.

Property does not play a major role in the operation and asset base of all companies: the nature of the business will dictate whether or not property is a key criterion. For example, restaurateurs and hoteliers are completely dependent on their property in order to carry out their business, despite property not being their core activity; retailers, too, have traditionally had a great reliance on their outlet space. Conversely, other companies are 'footloose' in their use of space or, in some cases, they may have little need for space at all (the dot.com companies of the 1990s are perhaps the classic example of this). When a downturn in activity takes place, businesses that are fully dependent on property must still continue to occupy – but their ability to pay rent is diminished. Those that are less dependent may well seek to dispose of space or shift activity to another location where costs are lower; this may of course mean a move to another country or continent.

Thus the type of business is fundamental to the relationship between corporate enterprise and property and to its performance as an investment asset.

9.3   Criteria for purchase or lease

In Chapter 2 the decision-making process of corporate occupiers was introduced and it was stated that the first key decision to be undertaken was whether to purchase or to rent.

This decision will be influenced by a number of factors.

9.3.1   Needs of the business and the anticipated holding period

The first of the decision factors will be the type of business. Where property is fundamental to the delivery of the core business, it is more likely that a decision will be taken to purchase. Within a large and complex company the business needs for property may well be split between *core* and *periphery*. Where the property services the core needs of the business, the space will probably be needed over a long period of time and this may prompt a decision to purchase, whereas activity that is peripheral to the business may be better suited to the acquisition of space on a short-term basis. Thus a short anticipated hold

Table 9.2   Lease length by sector type.

Sector	Lease length in years at date of grant			
	1999	2000	2001	Difference 1999–2001
Computers and high tech	12.3	11.7	11.2	−9%
Manufacturing	11.9	11.5	11.1	−7%
Business services	12.2	11.3	11.6	−5%
Government and other services	13.0	12.0	11.2	−14%
Telecoms	12.5	11.9	11.8	−6%
Construction	11.9	11.6	11.1	−7%
Retail	14.3	13.7	13.5	−5%
Financial services	12.4	12.0	11.8	−5%
Distribution	12.4	11.8	11.7	−5%

Source: Nelson Bakewell and OPD (2003), quoting IPD statistics.

period will prompt a lease decision. Given that business planning cycles are seldom more than five years, a decision to purchase may well not fit the corporate strategic position.

Nelson Bakewell and OPD (2003) found that businesses are increasingly wishing to develop a 'flexible relationship' with their property portfolio, and this has resulted in very considerably shortening leases where the decision to lease is taken. However, this varies markedly between sectors, as shown in Table 9.2. Although the findings show a very significant fall in lease lengths compared to those prevailing in the mid 1990s, they are still significantly in excess of the business planning cycle and for some types of property may well fall further. This is particularly likely given that companies operating on a global basis will be familiar with short terms in most other countries.

9.3.2   Financial constraints

Budget, too, is a major influence. Property that is owned freehold ties up capital that potentially could be used elsewhere in the wealth-creation process. If property can be released from the asset base, and the cash redeployed into the business, this will have an effect on and will potentially improve the investment analysis ratios (for example, the return on capital employed, return on equity and earnings per share could be enhanced). The receipts from property disposals are likely to have an impact on the company's gearing ratio, and also on the corporate weighted average cost of capital (Brealey and Myers, 2002).

To the occupier, however, such moves will lead to a reduction of flexibility in that the terms of the lease will control alterations and usage, and it may be far more difficult to time disposals as there are few purchasers for 'fag-ends' of leases. Frequently, of course, the inability to raise sufficient funds to purchase will dictate a policy of leasing when new space is required. This will be the case particularly when a company is in the early stages of development and does not have a proven creditworthiness. The impact of financial structuring on the purchase decision is considered in more detail in section 9.9.

9.3.3   Fiscal, financial and accounting considerations

The decision whether to buy or lease will be influenced by a number of factors. The top two factors viewed as key drivers of corporate property strategy are business flexibility (see below) and the cost control of accommodation (Rodney *et al.*, 2001). In the control of costs, it is the after tax costs that are considered, thus the structure of the prevailing tax regime becomes an important component in the decision-making process. Rent is tax deductible when property is leased. Likewise, interest costs associated with the cost of holding owner-occupied property are also tax deductible. Tax issues, by themselves, generally do not push the corporate in the direction of being an occupational lessee or an owner-occupier. In contrast, finance leases, which can release capital allowances, often result in tax-efficient finance, and lower costs of debt can be used advantageously. Capital allowances is a complex area of tax, the rules relating to it change periodically, and it is beyond the scope of this book.

From a business management and financial perspective, the nature of the ownership of property holdings has an influence on the well-being of the company. This relates to the financial structure of the company. Back in the 1980s Professor Richard Taffler developed Z-score models for the prediction of company bankruptcy and recovery; these are now widely used in the City and elsewhere. The Z-score models are regression based and use a number of key accounting ratios to identify bankruptcy probabilities (Taffler, 1997).

The accounting ratios that have the greatest predictive ability relating to prospective bankruptcy risk are cash or cash flow measures. It is in this area that the way in which property is held has an important influence. This was evidenced in the Telecoms sector post-2000 as a consequence of the bursting of the 'dot.com' bubble. Telecoms companies large and small suffered reduced liquidity and cash flow. Their credit ratings slid and their ability to borrow was constrained. How was their liquidity shortfall to be financed? Fixed asset sales became the order of the day. Freehold property represented a significant proportion of their fixed assets, and property sales through sale and leasebacks/outsourcing became a feature of this market (for example, both British Telecom and Deutsche Telekom undertook such programmes).

The third and related element that has an impact on how property is held relates to the prevailing accounting conventions. Changes to UK and international accounting standards are resulting in changes to the way in which occupational leases are treated in the balance sheet. Occupational leases will move from 'off' to 'on' balance sheet.

In March 2000 the international group of accounting standard setters (known as G4 + 1) published a discussion paper entitled 'Leases: Implementation of a New Approach', which was very similar to the UK Accounting Standards Board (ASB) discussion paper of the same title published in December 1999. The key principle set out in these papers is that lessees should record in their balance sheets the 'fair value' of the rights and obligations that are conveyed by leases, be they operating or finance leases. As the ASB stated:

> How leases are classified has important implications, for example, for reported levels of indebtedness, gearing ratios, return on assets employed and interest cover . . . The comparability (and hence usefulness) of financial statements would be enhanced if the present treatment of operating leases and finance leases were replaced by an approach that applied the same requirements to all leases (ASB, 2000).

Currently, finance leases are accounted for as 'on' balance sheet items, whereas operating leases (any lease which is not a finance lease – for example, an occupational lease) are 'off' balance sheet items, and effectively invisible from an accounting perspective. Changes to the UK, European and international accounting standards will result in operating leases being brought on balance sheet from 2005/6 onwards and will have a significant effect on the operation of property markets (see, for example, Eccles and Holt, 2002; Holt and Eccles, 2003).

9.3.4   The impact of leases moving 'on' balance sheet

Apart from at the start of the lease, the value of the occupational or operating lease will always be less than the value of the corresponding liability (Imhoff *et al.*, 1991). This is because while the asset is usually depreciated on a straight line basis, the liability is reduced each year by the amount of capital deemed to be repaid out of that year's rental. In the early years the amount of capital repaid will be small since the bulk of the rental is considered to be interest payment, as is the case with amortising debt (Rodney *et al.*, 2001).

Example 9.1 shows the effect of accounting conventions on leasehold interests.

Example 9.1

A company has 40 units of equity, 20 of debt and 60 of assets, and it owns all its property assets (15 units) freehold. The debt to equity or gearing ratio is 50%. Assume all the property assets are subject to a sale and lease back.

- With an 'off' balance sheet accounting convention:
  - *Following the transaction, the balance sheet will have 60 units of assets and 60 of liabilities.*
  - *The gearing ratios will not change.*
- With an 'on' balance sheet accounting convention:
  - *Following the transaction, the balance sheet will have on the liabilities side an additional liability of say 12, representing the present value of the rents due under the occupational lease, and on the assets side the 15 units of property will have been replaced with cash of 15 plus the new operating leases with a value of say 12.*
  - *The debt to equity gearing ratio with the occupational leases being on balance sheet will have changed from 20:40 to 32:52, a rise from 50% to 62%.*

The bringing on balance sheet of occupational leases is expected to have a profound impact on gearing ratios for the hotel, retail and leisure sectors. These may be expected to at least double in some cases (Rodney *et al.*, 2001), and in some quarters this has been anticipated. The main credit rating agencies, such as Standard & Poors and Moody's, already treat occupational leases as on balance sheet assets and liabilities in their corporate credit ratings and make prudent estimates for these figures.

The anticipation is that bringing occupational leases on balance sheet will encourage corporate finance directors to opt, where feasible, for shorter leases.

9.3.5   The need for specialised equipment

Another factor that will drive the lease or buy decision will be the anticipated usage. Where the proposed use involves investment in considerable specialised fixtures, fittings and equipment, as will be the case for many manufacturing processes and some leisure and tourism users, the size of expenditure may dictate the need for security over a timescale sufficient to amortise the cost. The lower the rate of return required for amortisation, the longer this timescale will be. Thus either a freehold or a long lease will be required.

For example, a property to be occupied as a multiplex cinema will require such significant investment by the operator that a lease of less than 25 years is seldom acceptable; conversely, a simply fitted-out office needs little time to amortorise costs, particularly if on any subsequent move the equipment can be re-utilised. This aspect is of growing importance as the costs of waste disposal grow.

9.3.6   Image, corporate identity and policy

Linked to the concept of anticipated holding period is that of company policy and corporate identity. As Weatherhead (1997) and Edwards and Ellison (2003) identify through case studies, the culture and policy of a company will have a significant effect on the decision. Although the disciplines of corporate real estate have grown, many companies do not have significant property representation at board level so their approach has been driven more by a conditioned behavioural response than a pure analysis of financial advantage.

However, it is not simply a matter of company culture. The need to establish a specific company 'image' will often result in the commissioning of headquarters buildings that will result in a match with the brand values of the organisation.

9.3.7   Availability of stock

The final identified factor driving the lease/purchase decision will be the availability of appropriate stock, in the context of the corporate business plan. Where the premises required are of standard specification, the option to lease may be available. However, where specialised premises are needed, few developers or investors will be prepared to fund and own, respectively, property for which, in the event of default, there would be few if any other potential occupiers.

In the case of multi-let and integrated schemes, such as retail parks and shopping centres, the necessity is for leasehold occupation. Indeed, it was the growth of the out-of-town and edge-of-town shopping schemes in the 1980s that for the first time resulted in Marks & Spencer reversing their previous policy of freehold ownership. Hence availability is related to property type, size of unit and location.

9.4   Criteria for building selection

It has been estimated (Bootle and Kalyan, 2002) that, after staffing, premises are normally an organisation's chief cost. It follows that 'the primary aim of real estate in organisations is to provide appropriate working environments for the least overall cost' (Johnson Controls, 2001).

Whatever decision regarding tenure is made or enforced by circumstances, Apgar (1995) argues, every dimension of the building choice decision is driven by considerations affected by costs. Whilst there is truth in this notion, cost considerations must be balanced against the benefits to the business. A simple policy of cost reduction will be disadvantageous to the business if competitive advantage is thereby lost. As argued in Chapter 2, the decision will be driven by 'five Ls': location, layout, lease cost, loose fit and low energy. These will now be developed in a little more detail.

9.4.1   Location

The old adage that 'location, location, location' is a chief driver of value has been promoted on many occasions. Indeed, it has spawned an entire literature of location theory, based mainly on the work of economists such as Van Thunen, Christaller, Alonso and Muth, all of whom seek mathematical models for location choice.

However, even if the theories of agglomeration and central location were ever sufficient to explain location choice, they are now under considerable strain due to changes in the way many companies use their real estate (see, for example, Ball et al., 1998). The internet and modern telecommunications system now render it possible for service departments in remote locations or other countries to back up product sales within the home country. In such situations, the decision as to where to locate has flexibility, and the cost and availability of cheap labour will be the main determining factors. Despite these reservations, the main determinants of location choice will be:

- *Type of business*: some businesses (for example, shoe shops) require to be located close to their competitors. For others close proximity to facilities is far more important (for example, hotels often require to be close to airports or central business districts). For such businesses the need is for accessibility, high levels of visibility and ease of communication.
- *Size of business*: in their research into the decision-making behaviour of office occupiers, Leishman and Watkins (2004) concluded that size as well as type of business was a critical factor.
- *Access to markets*: following on from the type of business is the proximity to markets. For a retailer this can be critical, though the growth in internet access changes the dynamic.
- *Accessibility*: for many occupiers accessibility is as key a consideration as actual location. With the advent of measures that attempt to curb private car use, easy access to public transport nodes is likely to become of increasing importance. However, to be accessible by public transport alone is likely to reduce attractiveness to the occupier and render such a solution untenable in social and economic terms even if it is attractive on grounds of environmental concern (Sayce and Ellison, 2004).

9.4.2   Layout or configuration

Layout refers to the amount of space and how it is arranged. During the 1990s the pressures to reduce costs led many organisations to re-engineer their business practices, particularly in relation to office space requirements. Although research undertaken at the time did not find that this was creating structural change in the likely demand for space

(Lizieri *et al.*, 1997), it is now becoming clear that office occupiers are seeking to gain efficiency in their space requirements per person, with estimates of up to 12% reduction taking place (Warren, 2003). Similarly, modern retailing practices and more reliable automatic monitoring systems have reduced the amount of stock that must be held at the premises and changed the nature of space requirements, so that a demand for distribution space has replaced the need for on-site storage in many cases. Also, web retailing has the potential (even if this is not yet the actuality) for generating change in the use of the high street unit, which for some commodities is turning into a showcase to heighten awareness of the brand image while actual transactions increasingly take place on line. Such changes have not, and will not, affect the requirements of restaurant and entertainment venues, where the personal experience is the product being marketed.

Work by Baum (1991) found that configuration is a critical factor in determining the potential for obsolescence. More recent work by Baum *et al.* (2004) confirms that susceptibility to depreciation varies according to property type and location, with offices being more prone to value loss than either industrial or retail units. These findings support the argument that, to office occupiers, the adaptability of space to changing working practices translates readily to the amount of rent that they are prepared to pay and to the capitalisation rate. MacGregor and Then (1999) make the case that space is very much linked to business success, so that issues such as configuration, floor plate size and general building quality and attributes are critical success factors.

9.4.3   Costs of leasing or occupation

Leasing or occupational costs are the third factor, although Apgar (1995) stresses that leasing costs should correlate with changes in the occupier's revenue in a competitive economy. Where the decision to lease is taken, the cost incurred will be dependent not just on rent but on the entire package including the estimated costs of outgoings, both in annual terms and in terms of amortised capital expenditure. Although some companies use whole-life cost analysis as a predictive tool within the occupation decision, it is believed that this is more commonly undertaken when a new building is being procured rather than when a standing property is purchased.

The occupier will want to achieve the most favourable lease or purchase terms through effective negotiation for the property that most suits the business needs. In terms of lease term negotiation, the major players within the property industry have published a Code of Practice covering both lease negotiation and the management of leases (Commercial Leases Working Group, 2002). This is aimed at providing the flexibility that business occupiers both want and need. However, research has shown that many landlords are not implementing its provisions (University of Reading, 2004). This may not be a one-way issue: a recent survey by Gerald Eve (*Estates Gazette*, 2005) pointed to fewer than a third of landlords offering flexible terms under the Code but in half these cases tenants refused the terms in favour of a lower rent.

Occupational leases

Accordingly, the critical issues under discussion at the point of occupational lease grant will be:

- *Length of term*: where it is anticipated that there will be large fit-out costs and the space is likely to be demanded over the long term, a long lease in excess of 15–20 years may be required. Peripheral space or that which is meeting a transient need will be required on short-term arrangement.
- *Rent and rent review*: the rent will always be reserved within the lease, but in most agreements, unless the terms is five years or less, there will need to be arrangements for review of rent. Whilst there is considerable pressure from government for review clauses to allow for rents to fall as well as rise, most commercial arrangements are locked into an upward only structure to provide security of cash flow for the landlord.
- *Repairing covenant and/or service charge arrangements*: most commercial leases place full repairing liability on the tenant, either directly where the building is single let or as a service charge in the case of multi-let buildings. This practice, which is not replicated in most other countries, can add a very significant revenue and capital expenditure to the occupier, and in some cases a sinking fund against possible dilapidations claims at the end of the term is also required. Unless tenants are well advised to limit their liability via the imposition of a schedule of condition, the potential repair liability can extend to putting in repair that which is not in repair at the commencement of the term. With the reduction in lease lengths that is being observed, the pressure to move to limited liability for repair and the transfer of this risk from tenant to landlord is increasing.
- *Covenants against unauthorised assignment, changes of use and alterations*: it is common practice for leases to contain covenants against changes of use or the undertaking of alterations without the landlord's consent. Whilst such clauses may be qualified in terms of consent not being unreasonably withheld, a wealth of litigation points to these clauses being matters of contention between a landlord and a tenant. They also restrict the ability of the occupier to exercise flexibility in the use of the premises and any planned disposal of them.
- *Surrender and break clauses*: in corporate strategy terms, one of the most critical factors will often be the presence, or otherwise, of a break clause or surrender clause. The exit strategy position is critical for any corporate occupier so most occupiers are increasingly resistant to taking leases of longer than ten years in which there is no possibility of early termination. Frequently break clauses will tie in with rent review clauses, but to provide greater flexibility some occupiers will wish to have the option to break at any time after say the fifth year.

From the above it can be seen that in terms of leasing cost it is not just the face rent that matters but the entire financial package.

Finance leases

An alternative to taking an occupational lease is taking a finance lease, where the property is sold to a financial institution and the company retains occupation rights and pays fixed or stepped lease payments. Where the company is considering a finance lease, the considerations will be different from those for an occupational lease and will include:

- *Money to be raised*: in loan to value terms, a company with a good credit rating may be able to secure finance of up to 110–140%.

- *Amortisation*: the basis on which the capital is repaid. Is there any amortisation holiday? Is straight line or accelerated amortisation proposed?
- *Interest cost*: what is the interest rate going to be, and will it be hedged or a fixed rate of interest?
- *Tax position*: usually the lessor takes the benefit of the capital allowances and passes a proportion back to the lessee by offering a reduced interest rate.
- *Ownership*: is the lessor willing to grant a buy back option, and if so at what cost? A small percentage over the money outstanding after a specified number of years may be appropriate.
- *Default provisions*: the lessor's right to possession and sale if the finance lease payments are not met should be addressed.
- *Accounting implications*: the impact on the company's cash flow, its gearing and return on equity ratios.
- *Property specifics*: this covers such items as repairing obligations, insurance, the state in which the building is to be delivered up at the end of the lease, the process of seeking permission to alter/improve the property, and the lessor's rights to refuse such requests.

The advent of accounting changes, the new stamp duty changes and potential government intervention are shifting the position such that finance leases can now offer the corporate better financial costs and the flexibility to repurchase the property at a later date. Traditional sale and lease backs have a keen competitor in finance leases.

When considering overall occupancy costs, there now exists a series of benchmarking services that provide detailed and useful comparable data for corporates on the costs of occupancy broken down into key categories (OPD service run by Investment Property Databank).

9.4.4 Loose fit or building flexibility

The point has already been made that whilst the original 'three Ls' of location are crucial to the building choice decision, other factors are beginning to gain importance too. The changes in working practices noted above have led to a greater need for flexibility. This is often taken to refer to flexible working patterns such as the ability of workers to operate in various locations and the advent of hot-desking arrangements. However, this is only one aspect of the need for loose fit buildings. By this term we mean that space is able to be used in a variety of ways and can be adapted at low cost. The space will remain usable in the hands of the occupier for longer, and will thus become redundant less quickly and require less radical refurbishments.

The ability of a user to adapt the configuration of the property for changing uses over time has been highlighted by Brand (1997) and Kincaid (2002), both of whom promote the reuse of existing buildings. Sayce *et al.* (2004) argue that building adaptability is a critical factor in the retention of occupier satisfaction and hence economic life. This aspect is broken down further by Sayce and Ellison (2003) who take building adaptability to refer to:

- *Adaptability within user*: this is where premises are capable of being used in differing ways that will meet the continuing and changing needs of the particular occupier. For example, an office with a cellular structure based on a small grid pattern cannot adapt to open plan – so if the occupier decides to change the way in which they wish to operate their business they will have to move; whereas if they were occupying a building with a larger floorplate and greater width between structural columns they could adjust their working patterns in ways that suited the business unconstrained by the building shape and configuration.

- *Adaptability within use*: here, even if the premises are no longer appropriate for the original user, they are still capable of beneficial use by a similar user without major adaptation.
- *Adaptability across use*: this last form of adaptability, in which the building is sufficiently flexible in structure that with minor adaptation it can accommodate a different use, is not only a protection against depreciation but helps to ensure saleability of the asset.

It follows that buildings whose structural components have the quality and design to allow for alterations within a 'loose fit' envelope are more likely to retain their economic value over time than those that are limited in the scope of users they can attract.

9.4.5   Environmental considerations

The growth of the 'green agenda' has now become important to all property occupiers, for economic reasons if for no others. As governments at all levels from intra-national to local have begun to embrace the principles of sustainable development (see, for example, WCED, 1987), so the financial case for moving towards buildings that can be regarded as 'environmentally friendly' becomes more convincing (Edwards, 2003). Despite this, research has concluded that environmental considerations have until recently had little impact on the building choice of occupiers, with the exception of some forward-looking companies who wish to promote a brand image of environmental awareness (Sayce *et al.*, 2001). However, there is now anecdotal evidence that some environmental considerations are beginning to affect corporate decision-making in relation to property.

The main environmental considerations that are of relevance to property occupiers are:

- *Energy consumption*: as carbon reduction policies develop further and are associated with financial consequences, so low-energy buildings are likely to become more sought after (Pett *et al.*, 2004). Additionally, the recent EU Directive on Energy Efficiency in Buildings (Commission of the European Communities, 2002) will result in energy 'labelling' of buildings; this is turn will make energy data for commercial buildings commonly available and will affect the building choice. This is expected to be the case particularly for high-energy building users such as leisure operators.
- *Pollutants*: apart from carbon, the main pollutants likely to be emitted by commercial buildings are CFCs from the coolants in air conditioning systems. Since these coolants are now banned in new systems, and will in time be banned in the servicing of equipment, any building that is still reliant on them will require substantial capital expenditure.
- *Waste management*: waste is now a very significant business expense. It is a focus for government legislation and the Environment Agency has estimated that businesses in England and Wales produce more waste than is produced by construction and demolition. The impact on society of the environmental costs of waste is reflected by the escalator imposed on landfill tax as an incentive to business owners to adopt waste

minimisation strategies. It is reasonable to assume that, over time, buildings that have waste facilities and are designed to minimise the production of waste will become increasingly sought after by occupiers.

9.4.6   The impact of corporate social responsibility on building choice

The rise of corporate social responsibility (CSR) within the boardroom agenda has been swift. With it have come growing property implications for both investors and corporate occupiers (Sayce and Ellison, 2003). The notion of CSR is essentially very simple. It requires that consideration be given by corporate organisations to both the social and environmental dividends as well as the economic. Another way of describing this is as a triple bottom line approach (TBL), in which the company seeks to balance its quest for economic return with the social and environmental pressures placed on the wider society.

The notion of CSR has been taken up widely within the business community and the publication of the FTSE4Good (http://www.FTSE4good.com) provides an indication of the growth of interest in the area. The corporate case for CSR can be measured at least externally and many companies report on the steps they are taking to ensure compliance with the principles. For companies there is no obligation to adopt CSR principles; however, pension funds are now under a regulatory obligation to have such a policy (Occupational Pension Schemes (Disclosure of Information) (Amendment) Regulations, 2000).

How these factors can be translated into property requirements policy is harder to see. The Sustainable Construction Task Group (2000) argued that adopting good TBL principles will provide companies with:

- *Strategic benefits*, such as enhanced reputation leading to the ability to improve their credit rating, attract high-quality staff and reduce the risks associated with non-compliance with environmental legislation.
- *Operational benefits*, such as reducing liability for climate change levy and landfill tax.
- *Revenue-generating benefits*, such as the ability to attract more clients or – in the case of investors – more funds, and the production of more flexible and attractive properties.

There is currently little firm evidence that corporate occupiers who espouse CSR are adopting these criteria for building selection; however, there are early signs that this is the case (Sayce and Ellison, 2003) and with time this can only increase. Those who do will seek buildings that meet with the principles set out above and that can also be argued both to meet employee needs and to minimise any adverse effects on their surroundings (Sayce *et al.*, 2004).

9.4.7   Evaluation of occupier satisfaction

The issue of occupier satisfaction is increasingly important and forms a significant element within the pursuit of CSR policies. With the growth of strategic facilities management techniques, such as pre- and post-occupancy evaluations, becoming commonly used, property occupiers are more alert to the need to provide working environments that will enable them to retain their staff. Evaluation of social performance is not an easy task as it tends to be lengthy and subjective. However, good design is known to reduce the incidence of sickness absence, and a growing body of research points to the need to take employee efficiency into account when selecting space.

Economic performance is more readily measured through a variety of performance indicators (see, for example, Weatherhead, 1997; OPD, 2004) including:

- Property costs as a percentage of business costs and on a per capita basis.
- Cost in relation to size of the estate.
- Return on physical capital employed compared with overall return on capital.
- Future liabilities – particularly in relation to repairs.
- Productivity and/or profit related to size.
- Total occupancy costs.

9.4.8   Summary on building selection

In summary, as occupiers become more aware of the role of property both on their balance sheet and as an expression of their corporate brand, so they are becoming more critical in their demands for space.

Not only are issues such as size and location important; the ability of a building to adapt and its potential to comply with future environmental and social legislation all point to more stringent occupational requirements being developed. Additionally, better data on the financial and physical performance of assets, ranging from OPD's total occupancy cost facilities to attempts to quantify the sustainability credentials of buildings, are assisting clients to became better informed.

Furthermore, the flexibility that is gradually emerging within lease structures prevailing in the UK is pointing to the need for investors to develop a deeper engagement with their tenants, both at the point of letting and thereafter.

9.5   Appraising property for corporate decision-making

Once a buy or lease decision has been taken, the corporate occupier will need to monitor the asset performance in order to ensure that it continues to satisfy corporate needs. The physical performance of the asset will be monitored and evaluated as part of the facilities management or building management function; the performance of the asset to the organisation in asset value terms will be the function of a value. The appropriate appraisals may be done 'in house' by a qualified valuer if the figures so produced are to be used solely for internal purposes (RICS, 2003a, 1: 5.5.1), but where the values produced are to be included in any documents to which a third party has access (for example, the company accounts), the professional code is explicit that the work must be carried out by an independent valuer (RICS, 2003a).

The appraisals are normally conducted for two distinct purposes:

- To advise on the value to be entered within the accounts for financial reporting purposes, or even for stock exchange prospectuses.
- To advise on the hold/sell decision or on redevelopment potential when a higher alternative use value is to be reported.

It is important that the two are dealt with separately, as the 'book value' may or may not be useful information for management purposes due both to the method adopted and the status of the valuation produced.

9.6   Appraising for financial statements

Chapter 2 introduced the basic requirements of the RICS *Appraisal and Valuation Standards*; in this section their application to financial statements is developed in greater detail. The standards are also considered in the context of the wider international standards (IVSC, 2003).

The RICS requires that, for the purposes of valuations for financial statements, properties are classified as falling within one of two classes: specialised or non-specialised. The IVSC, on the other hand, accepts that some properties lie somewhere between the two. These are limited market properties which, whilst they are capable of sale on the open market, require a longer marketing period due either to market conditions or to their unique features or to other unspecified 'factors' (IVSC, 2003:110). Although the concept of limited market property is entirely rational, there is currently no recognition of such property within the bases of valuation in either the IVS or the RICS standards. A tenuous connection may be found in the standards under the provisions for special assumptions and marketing constraints, but for all practical purposes it is only the distinction between specialised and non-specialised that has relevance in terms of valuations for financial statements.

9.6.1   Non-specialised property

Non-specialised properties comprise the vast majority of properties under consideration. They are those that are commonly bought and sold on the open market and include the bulk classes of offices, retail and warehousing, and residential property. They also include specialist trading properties, such as bars, hotels and petrol filling stations, which are normally valued with reference to their trading accounts (see Chapter 1).

9.6.2   Specialised property

Specialised properties are defined in both the RICS and the IVSC standards. They are those that:

> are rarely, if ever, sold in the open market, except by way of a sale of the business of which they are a part (called the business in operation), due to their uniqueness arising from their specialised nature and design of the buildings, their configuration, size, location or otherwise. Examples include refineries, power stations, docks, specialised manufacturing facilities, public facilities, churches, museums (RICS, 2003a: Glossary).

9.6.3   The rationale for standards applied to financial statements

The development of standards to govern valuations for financial statements has taken place within the UK over a 30 year period. Whilst the current regulations are mandatory on RICS members, the appraiser should also be aware of both the International Valuation

Standards published by the International Valuation Standards Committee (IVSC) and the European Standards published by The European Group of Valuers Association (TEGoVA). There is much commonality between the standards issued by all three bodies, but only those of the RICS are mandatory for their members. When the standards were first introduced by the respective bodies there was considerable inconsistency between them, but over time convergence has been an ambition that is gradually moving towards achievement, although it has not yet reached this point (Sayce *et al.*, 2003).

The need for consistent standards arose as a result of growing awareness and concern in the early 1970s that there was inconsistent practice between organisations regarding the way in which properties were entered into company accounts. Some were valued on the basis of a market value (a value in exchange), and some on a 'going concern' basis (value to the business); others were simply carried at their historic cost. There was generally no requirement to revalue. The result was that assets could be represented at figures far *below* their market value (as derived from the historic cost accounting convention), rendering the company susceptible to takeover and asset stripping. Alternatively, the figures could be far *above* market value (for example, where additional value to a special purchaser, or a personal planning permission, might exist), in which case the company would appear to have produced a very poor return on capital employed.

Recognition of this concern led to a dialogue between the Accounting Standards Board (ASB) and the RICS, and in 1974 the first guidance to valuers on the valuation of assets for financial statements was published; it was not until the early 1990s that adherence became mandatory (French, 2003).

As a result of the development of the standards, all property that is owned or occupied by a company within the UK will be entered within its financial statements either at cost or at valuations that are periodically reviewed and are prepared in compliance with the RICS standards, which in turn are prepared in consultation with the ASB. Indeed, from 2005 publicly traded companies within the EU member states must publish consolidated financial statements prepared in conformity with IFRS, as adopted by the European Union. Non-listed UK companies will have the option of adopting UK general accounting principles (GAAP) or IFRS, but it has been suggested that the ASB convergence project will eliminate virtually all differences between IFRS and UK GAAP by 2008 (Cairns, 2004).

Until 2005 the ASB rules allowed for property to be 'carried' in the accounts on the concept of 'value to the business' which has been interpreted by RICS within their standards as relating to a replacement cost (that is, what it would cost a company to replace the service capacity of the building in the event of deprival). In the case of property that is owned for investment purposes, this deprival value will equate at all times to the market value of the asset, as defined (RICS, 2003a: PS3.2). However, under the concept of value to the business, owner-occupied property (including property held by way of lease) has been valued on the basis of its 'existing use value' (RICS, 2003b).

Existing use value is deemed to be market value with the addition of two further assumptions (RICS, 2003a: UK PS 1.3). It states that there shall be disregarded:

- any potential alternative uses; and
- any other characteristic of the property that would cause its market value to differ from that needed to replace the remaining service potential at least cost.

9.6.4   Appraising for occupational assets: the existing use debate

The rationale for the existing use concept is the notion that the company should hold assets at their effective worth to the organisation. This, it is argued, may or may not be the same as their value on the open market. The circumstances in which the value to the organisation may not be the same as that on the market depend on the type of building under considera-tion and the type of business being carried on.

To summarise, under the IVS there is only one basis of valuation that is acceptable for financial statements; this is market value (MV). However, under RICS rules an additional basis is recognised in respect of UK properties; this is existing use value (EUV). At the time of writing the position, especially in relation to UK properties, could be regarded as in a state of transition, as outlined below.

9.6.5   Appraising non-specialised properties

Under the current guidance from IVSC, properties that are non-specialised are appraised using market value established by whatever method is deemed to be appropriate by the valuer, in consultation with the client. In establishing the method to be used IVS 1 makes it clear that DCF is an acceptable approach (IVSC, 2003: IVS1 1.3). Within the RICS standards, however, the explicit DCF approach is not specifically mentioned as an accepted methodology except in the context of social housing. This is due in part to the differences in the structure of the two sets of standards. The IVS contain very few principles and details regarding process but have a wealth of information on methodo-logy, as is appropriate to a publication that is advisory only. The RICS standards contain very little instruction on method as they are confined primarily to principles and process; guidance on method is issued separately through a series of information papers. None-theless, the difference does point to the seeming reluctance within the UK to accept DCF as a method of market appraisal in addition to its use in calculating worth.

The market value, as advocated within the IVS, is calculated 'without regard to costs of sale or purchase and without offset for any associated taxes' (IVSC, 2003: IVS1 3.3). The RICS takes a similar approach to the treatment of costs by specifically requiring exclusion of costs with the exception that where these are requested by the client they can be stated separately (RICS, 2003a: UK PS1.7). The rationale for this is to ensure that consistency prevails between valuers and as far as possible between the valuations of assets in different countries.

Although the treatment of costs is consistent between the standards, the basis of valuation differs. Within the RICS standards, the valuation of non-specialised owner-occupied properties in the UK is prepared on the basis of existing use value (EUV), as stated above. In most cases the EUV will be the same as market value (MV), in which case no issue arises.

However, there are times where the two figures may be significantly different. The RICS information paper (2003b) cites several examples. These are set out in the paper at paragraph 2.2 and include, *inter alia*:

● where an occupier is operating with a personal planning consent that could restrict the market in the event of the owner vacating;

- where a property is known to be contaminated, but the continued occupation for the existing use is not inhibited or adversely affected, provided there is no current duty to remedy such contamination during the continued occupation; and
- where the existing buildings are old, and so have a limited market value, but would have a higher replacement cost to the business.

The MV and EUV will also be different if the subject property has a much *higher* value for development purposes or for a different alternative use. Where there is a significant difference between MV and EUV, the valuer is under a duty to report both figures to the client.

The rationale for the use of EUV is based on the need for a company to issue a balance sheet that provides a realistic 'snapshot' of the value of the assets. Advocates of EUV would argue that this basis does this, as it excludes from the valuation those elements of value that are realisable only if the business use of the building is terminated (that is, in the event of development value) and includes those elements that are specific to the business. They would also argue that, as a market value is also reported where EUV and MV differ, there is adequate information available for a fair assessment to be made of the real worth of the company's fixed assets.

However, this view has come under challenge as being inconsistent with the notion of 'fair value' as included in the International Accounting Standards with which the ASB is due to comply during 2005, following an EU Directive. Under the International Financial Reporting Standards (IFRSs) published by the International Accounting Standards Board, owner-occupied assets will either be valued at cost or at 'fair value'.

The definition of 'fair value' is 'the amount for which an asset could be exchanged or a liability settled between knowledgeable willing parties in an arm's length transaction' (IAS 16, para. 6; as quoted in IVSC, 2003). It had been generally accepted that fair value equates to market value as defined (RICS, 2003b), not existing use value. It would follow that the requirements for owner-occupied property should shift from EUV to MV. The expectation has therefore been that RICS would drop the use of EUV. However, this is far from certain and an exposure draft of IVSC (IVSC, 2004a) has indicated that 'fair value is not necessarily synonymous with Market Value' (IVSC, 2004a: 5.3.3) although it acknowledges that 'there remains a lack of clarity as to the underlying assumptions that should be made when making fair value assessments of fixed assets for different purposes' (IVSC, 2004b).

Whatever interpretation is taken as to what constitutes fair value, there is general agreement that it is 'usually determined from market-based evidence by appraisal that is normally undertaken by professionally qualified valuers' (IVSC, 2004a: 5.4).

In conclusion, the situation with regard to non-specialised owner-occupied assets is far from clear. Many properties are held on the books at cost, but where they are carried at valuation the situation in the UK is that they will currently be valued to existing use value. Whether, given the adoption of IFRS by ASB, this will continue is still under debate.

9.6.6   Appraising property for specialised uses

Many companies will own and occupy property for which there is no ready market other than as a sale of part of the business. Almost by definition such properties will only fall within the owner-occupational estate as the restricted number of potential occupiers renders them unattractive to property investors. However, despite the lack of evidence of value, these properties are still required to be entered into the financial accounts. The lack of comparable evidence means that the market-based appraisals methods of valuation used for non-specialised properties are not available. Therefore a depreciated replacement cost (DRC) approach is used. The DRC approach is described by IVSC as a surrogate for market value, in that it is used where there is insufficient market data to arrive at market value by means of market-based evidence (IVSC, 2005: 4).

Under the RICS standards, DRC was previously regarded as a basis of valuation used exclusively for the determination of existing use value of specialised property. However, from 2005 it has been redefined as a method of estimating market value, where 'more reliable methods, such as market comparison or an income (profits test), cannot be applied' (RICS, 2003a: Appendix 3:1).

DRC works on the hypothesis that the value of the property to the business relates to its cost of construction together with the value of the land; this is because if it were deprived of the asset the company would, in order to continue functioning, have to replace the property by rebuilding rather than by buying a replacement. It also acknowledges that the actual asset being valued may not be new and will accordingly have suffered from some obsolescence and depreciation.

To carry out a DRC involves several steps but at all times the IVSC requires that the methodology must incorporate market observations by the valuer with regard to land value, current cost and depreciation rates. The valuer is required to:

- Provide a valuation for the land.
- Calculate the 'gross replacement cost' of the building.
- Assess the future economic life of the building.
- Depreciate the gross cost by an appropriate amount having due regard to any:
  o physical deterioration;
  o functional or technical obsolescence;
  o economic or external obsolescence.

The use of the DRC approach is fraught with difficulties and for this reason some explicit guidance is provided within the standards. Of the four elements of the valuation, that of establishing land value is perhaps the most difficult. To the IVSC, DRC is a surrogate for market value and as such the land value is assessed with reference to the market value of the land. The RICS accepts that the valuation of the land may 'present difficulties, since by definition, the property as a whole is being put to a use for which there is no market' (RICS, 2003a: Appendix 3, amended 2005). The advice to the valuer is that in such cases it may be necessary to take a 'prevailing use' approach.

The valuation of the gross replacement cost is also difficult. Should the valuer assume a straight replacement or a modern substitute? The advice provided is fairly ambivalent and requires the valuer to use personal discretion, bearing in mind that a simple modern substitute may be achieved at a lower cost but may in some circumstances not be a practical alternative as in the case, for example, of a listed building.

The issues of establishing future economic life and depreciation are similarly difficult and should be considered in consultation with the client. Some techniques for quantifying

depreciation have been proposed and adopted: for example, depreciation may be calculated on a 'straight line' basis, or a sagging curve may be applied (Britton *et al.*, 1991); or it
may be calculated on an 'S curve' basis (Johnson *et al.*, 2000).

Whatever approach is taken to the calculation of DRC, the end result tends to be heavily
dependent on the assumptions made; additionally, it is no guide to the figure that could be
realised in the event of a decision to sell. For this reason any valuation so based has to be
treated with extreme caution and in particular cannot be used for raising finance (that is,
for loan security purposes). Where a building is fairly new and has a high replacement cost
due to specialised fittings, it is possible that the figure produced is considerably more than
the premises could realise if offered on the open market. Accordingly, to enter the property
in the accounts at such an amount could distort the company's apparent return on capital
employed. For this reason, if for no other, any valuation carried out by DRC is normally
reported as being subject to the test of the adequate potential profitability of the enterprise
to carry the amount. Where the property lies within a public sector portfolio, the caveat is
that the valuation is subject to the prospect of continuance of the service potential. The
final decision as to the figure to be entered will rest with the client, not the valuer.

In summary, the DRC approach is still regarded as a last resort approach, due to
its inherent subjectivity. Nonetheless, in the absence of market evidence it is the only
appropriate methodology to be used; but the result should always be treated with caution.
The approach should be discussed in detail with the client and the limitations to its use
made clear.

9.7   Corporate property: fund managers' and equity analysts' attitudes

For companies with a stock market listing, the views and attitudes of fund managers, and
the equity analysts in the investment houses who write buy/hold/sell notes on companies,
can be an important factor in the eyes of the board of directors.

The survey by Rodney *et al.* (2001) identified the following attitudes amongst fund
managers and equity analysts:

- Property holdings of UK listed companies are not very significant in the determination
  of the company's share price.
- Operating lease structure is not an important issue, but companies should seek to match
  the length of their leases with the nature of their operations:
  o profitable activities could sustain long leases;
  o low margin activities should opt for short/flexible leases or services accommodation.
- The switch from owning to leasing was considered to have a beneficial impact on
  the company's return on capital employed (ROCE) and return on equity (ROE).
- Views were mixed on the impact of the switch from owning to leasing on earnings
  per share (EPS) and earnings before interest, tax, depreciation and amortisation
  (EBITDA).
- Companies were viewed as being able to add value by:
  o undertaking sale and leasebacks;
  o using debt securitisation.

- There was no clear consensus on the ASB's proposals to bring operating leases on balance sheet, but it was thought that telecoms, brewers, hotels and retailers would be affected most, and that this might put pressure on them to rationalise their property holdings.

Post the Enron debacle, fund managers and equity analysts place value on corporate transparency and risk management processes. This theme from the perspective of the corporate accountancy advisers has been developed by Cooper and colleagues at the Cranfield School of Management (Cooper *et al.*, 2004). Complex sale and leaseback or real estate structuring deals may thus be counterproductive.

9.8   Appraisals for corporate decision-making: the hold/sell/finance decision

How property appraisals for corporate decision-making purposes are viewed will depend, to a large extent, upon the circumstances of the company. A useful indicator of the financial state of a company is its credit rating as assessed and reported by the likes of Standard & Poors or Moody's, and the margin that its fixed rate debt is trading over the benchmark bond. A company with say an AA Standard & Poors rating and a debt margin of say 100 basis points can be viewed as being in sound financial health.

Property ownership decisions for such a company can be made in the context of their long-term benefits to the business. These benefits may be measured in financial terms with reference to the company's weighted average cost of capital plan (WACC) and the impact that the property transactions would have on the WACC, and whether they offer economic value added (EVA). EVA is a residual income-based performance measure developed by Stern Stewart Management Services in New York. EVA is the difference between a company's net operating income after taxes and its weighted average cost of capital.

Companies with poor credit ratings (for example, B grade) that show high margins over benchmarch bonds often face short-term cash flow difficulties. In such circumstances the sale of property assets may be the only feasible way in which the company can find cash flow to sustain its business activities. In this case, the company may be close to being, or may even actually be, a forced seller.

Commercial property investment market appraisals are in the form of a DCF analysis. Whilst DCF analysis has a role in the corporate occupier sector, the in-house corporate decision-making process focuses more on the profit and loss implications after the property transaction and into the future. Thus the company's analysis considers the position of the company's current and prospective net operating income after taxes with the property assets as existing, and these figures are compared with the position after the proposed property transaction. If the EVA is positive then the move from property ownership to leasing is financially beneficial; if the EVA is negative, the move from property ownership to leasing destroys shareholder wealth.

DCF appraisals may be undertaken by the property adviser to the corporate on the basis of estimating the net present cost of leasing, applying the WACC as the discount rate to the after-tax cash flows. This is then compared to the cash released by the property sale.

If a release of capital is proposed, the finance director has a range of options to consider:

- Sale and lease back.
- Outright sale (perhaps coupled with a new planning consent for a more valuable use), and finding accommodation elsewhere.
- Finance lease.
- Using the property assets as collateral for a bond securitisation issue (see Chapter 10).
- Using the property as security for a mortgage.

In such instances, it should be remembered that the property values set out in the balance sheet are in many cases prepared on a historic cost or market value basis, and thus may not give a sufficiently full picture or enough information as to the property's open market value.

9.9   Summary

This chapter has explored some of the issues that affect the decision-making process of corporate occupiers, and in particular the buy/lease decision and the criteria they will employ in terms of evaluating their property selection. What is clear from the analysis is that the accounting and financial structures are critical to corporate views. The current changes to the accounting provisions and their related valuation regulations are seen as potent catalysts for change. It is also apparent that the rise of corporate social responsibility will have a key role in the ensuing years as the need to take a wider perspective than the single bottom lines starts to affect property decisions.

In the past the need of investors to be responsive to the corporate agenda was limited, as demand for property tended to outstrip supply. Additionally, the prevailing lease structures produced a relationship between landlord and tenant that was both antagonistic and distant. Although there is significant evidence that leases are becoming shorter and more in line with those of other European countries and the US, the flexibility within lease structures that has been promoted by both government and the property industry, has so far had little impact on the operation of the markets. It is the effect of financial, market and CSR factors that may, in the end, result in changing structures and a wider range of options for the corporate occupier.

References

Accounting Standards Board (2000) *Inside Track*. London: ASB.

Apgar, M. (1995) The strategic role of real estate. *Corporate Real Estate Executive*, 05/95: 20–3.

Arthur Andersen (1995) *Wasted Assets? A Survey of Corporate Real Estate in Europe*. London: Arthur Andersen.

Avis, M., Gibson, V. and Watts, J. (1989) *Managing Operational Property Assets*. Reading: University of Reading.

Ball, M., Lizieri, C. and McGregor, B. (1998) *The Economics of Commercial Property Markets*. London: Routledge.

Baum, A. (1991) *Property Investment Depreciation and Obsolescence*. London: Routledge.

Baum, A., Callendar, M., Crosby, N., Devaney, S., Law, V. and Westlake, C. (2004) *Depreciation in UK commercial property markets*. Paper to the IPD/IPF Conference, Brighton, 18–19 November.

Bootle, R. and Kalyan, S. (2002) *Property in Business: A Waste of Space?* London: RICS.

Brand, S. (1997) *How Buildings Learn: What Happens After They're Built.* London: Weidenfeld & Nicolson.

Brealey, R. and Myers, S. (2002) *Principles of Corporate Finance.* Irwin: McGraw Hill.

British Property Federation/Investment Property Databank (2004) *The BPF IPD Annual Lease Review.* London: BPF/IPD.

Britton, W., Connellan, O. and Croft, M. (1991) *The Cost Approach to Valuation.* London: Kingston Polytechnic/RICS.

Cairns, D. (2004) *Accounting under IFRS.* Paper to the RICS Valuation Conferences, London, 25 November.

Commercial Leases Working Group (2002) *A Code of Practice for Commercial Leases in England and Wales.* London: RICS.

Commission of the European Communities (2002) *COM 0192 Directive on the Energy Performance of Buildings.* Brussels.

Cooper, D., Taffler, R., James, K. and Kwiatkowski, R. (2004) *The shadow of the balance sheet: the spectre of Enron and how accountants use the past as a psychological defence against the future.* ISPSO Annual Symposium, Germany.

Currie, D. and Scott, A. (1991) *The Place of Commercial Property in the UK Economy.* London: London Business School.

Debenham Tewson Research (1992) *The Role of Property – Managing Cost and Releasing Value.* London: Debenham Tewson & Chinnocks.

Eccles, T.S. and Holt, A. (2002) International Accounting Standards: a paradigm shift for corporate real estate? *Journal of Corporate Real Estate,* 4 (1): 66–82.

Edwards, B. (2003) *Green Buildings Pay,* 2nd edn. London: Spon Press.

Edwards, V. and Ellison, L. (2003) *Strategic Property Management.* Oxford: Blackwell.

Estates Gazette (2005) Occupiers need convincing to adopt lease code. *Estates Gazette,* 08/01/05.

French, N. (2003) The RICS Appraisal and Valuation Standards. *Journal of Property Investment & Finance,* 21 (6): 495–501.

Gibson, V. (1994) *Is property on the strategic agenda?* Paper to the Cutting Edge RICS Research Conference, City University, London, September 1994.

Gibson, V. (1995) *Organisational change and the property resource.* Paper to the Cutting Edge RICS Research Conference, Aberdeen University/RICS, London, September 1995.

Holt, A. and Eccles, T. (2003) Accounting practice in the post Enron era: the implications for financial statements in the property industry. *Briefings in Real Estate Finance,* 2 (4): 326–40.

Imhoff, E.A., Lipe, R. and Wright, D. (1991) Operating leases: impact of constructive capitalization. *Accounting Horizons,* March: 51–63.

International Valuations Standards Committee (2003) *International Valuation Standards 2003.* London: IVSC.

International Valuations Standards Committee (2004a) *Draft International Valuation Application 1: Valuation for Financial Reporting* (Revised 2005). London: IVSC.

International Valuations Standards Committee (2004b) *News Alert.* Press release, 15 November. London: IVSC.

International Valuation Standards Committee (2005) *International Valuation Standards 2005.* London: IVSC.

Johnson, T., Davies, K. and Shapiro, E. (2000) *Modern Methods of Valuation.* London: Estates Gazette.

Johnson Controls (2001) *CREMRU-JCI Annual Survey of Corporate Real Estate Practices 2001.* University of Reading Corporate Real Estate Management Research Unit.

Kincaid, D. (2002) *Adapting Buildings for Changing Uses.* London: E&FN Spon.

Krumm, P.J.M.M. (2001) History of real estate management from a corporate perspective. *Facilities*, 19 (7/8): 276–86.

Krumm, P.J.M.M., Dewulf, G. and Jonge, H. de (1998) Managing key resources and capabilities: pinpointing the added value of corporate real estate management. *Facilities* (16)12.

Leishman, C. and Watkins, C. (2004) The decision-making behaviour of office occupiers. *Journal of Property Investment & Finance*, 22 (4): 307–19.

Lizieri, C., Crosby, N., Gibson, V., Murdoch, S. and Ward, C. (1997) *Right Space, Right Place? A Study of the Impact of Changing Business Practices on the Property Market*. London: RICS.

Macgregor, A. and Then, D.S.-S. (1999) *Facilities Management and the Business of Space*. Oxford: Butterworth Heinnemann.

Nelson Bakewell and OPD (2003) *Occupational Flexibility and Corporate Strategy 2003*. London: Nelson Bakewell/Occupiers Property Databank.

Nourse, H.O. (1994) Measuring business: real property performance. *Journal of Real Estate Research*, 9: 431–44.

Occupiers Property Databank (2004) *International Total Occupancy Cost Code*. London: OPD.

Pett, J., Guertler, P., Hugh, M., Kaplan, Z. and Smith, W. (2004) *Asset Value Implications of Low Energy Offices Phase 2 Report*. London: Association for the Conservation of Energy.

Rodney, W. *et al.* (2001) *The Impact of Property Holdings on Shareholder Value*. Land Securities Trillium research report, City University Business School, London.

Ross Goobey, A. (1992) *Of Bricks and Mortals: The Dream of the 80s and Nightmare of the 90s: The Inside Story of the Property World*. London: Random House Books.

Royal Institution of Chartered Surveyors (2003a) *RICS Appraisal and Valuation Standards*. London: RICS.

Royal Institution of Chartered Surveyors (2003b) *Valuation of Owner-Occupied Property for Financial Statements: Valuation Information Paper 1*. London: RICS.

Sayce, S. and Ellison, L. (2003) Towards sustainability indicators for commercial property occupiers and investors. *Proceedings of the International Sustainable Development Research Conference*, Shipley, 24–25 March.

Sayce, S. and Ellison, L. (2004) *Sustainability and commercial property investment – understanding the impact of direct effects and policy development on asset values*. Paper to the IPD/IPF Conference, Brighton, 18–19 November.

Sayce, S., Iball, H. and Parnell, P. (2001) *The business case for sustainable property*. Final Report to the Construction Confederation (unpublished).

Sayce, S., Walker, A. and McIntosh, A. (2004) *Building Sustainability in the Balance: Promoting Stakeholder Dialogue*. London: Estates Gazette.

Scott, P. (1996) *The Property Masters*. London: E&FN Spon.

Sustainable Construction Task Group (2000) *Reputation, Risk and Reward*. Garston: BRE.

Taffler, R. (1997) Enhancing equity returns with Z-scores. *Professional Investor*, July/August.

University of Reading (2004) *Monitoring the Code of Practice for Commercial Leases: Interim Report*. London: ODPM.

Veale, P.R. (1989) Managing corporate real estate assets: current executive attitudes and prospects for an emergent discipline. *Journal of Real Estate Research*, 4 (3): 1–21.

Warren, C. (2003) New working practices and office space density: a comparison of Australia and the UK. *Facilities* 21 (13/14): 306–14.

Weatherhead, M. (1997) *Real Estate in Corporate Strategy*. Basingstoke: Macmillan.

World Commission on Environment and Development (1987) *Our Common Future*. Oxford: Oxford University Press.

Zeckhauser, S. and Silverman, R. (1983) Rediscover your company's real estate. *Harvard Business Review*, Jan/Feb: 111–17.

Further reading

Baum, A., Crosby, N. and MacGregor, B.D. (1996) Price formation, mispricing and investment analysis in the property market: A response to 'A note on "The initial yield revealed: explicit valuations and the future of the property market"'. *Journal of Valuation & Investment*, 14 (1): 36–49.

Evans, M. and Weatherhead, M. (1999) *Think Profit Act Property*. London: RICS Corporate Property Users Group.

Imhoff, E.A., Lipe, R. and Wright, D. (1997) Operating leases: impact of constructive capitalization. *Accounting Horizons*, June: 12–31.

Investment Property Databank (1999) *The First OPD Conference: Information and Performance in Corporate Property*. London: IPD.

Investment Property Databank (2004) *Investment Property Databank, Property Indices* at www.ipdindex.co.uk

Manning, C. and Roulac, S. (1999) Corporate real estate research within the academy. *Journal of Real Estate Research*, 17 (3):265–79.

O'Mara, M. (1999) *Strategy and Place: Managing Corporate Real Estate and Facilities for Competitive Advantage*. New York: The Free Press.

Oxford Brookes University and University of Reading (1993) *Property Management Performance Measurement*. Oxford Brookes University and GTI Wallingford.

Peto, R., French, N. and Bowman, G. (1996) Price and worth: developments in valuation methodology. *Journal of Property Valuation & Investment*, 14 (4): 79–100.

Sayce, S., Connellan, O. and Plimmer, F. (2002) Global standards for a global profession: developing understanding for 'value in use'. *Proceedings of the FIG International Congress*, Washington DC, April.

Then, D. (2000) The role of real estate assets in supporting the fulfilment of corporate business plans. *Facilities*, 18 (7/8): 273–80.

10 Funding and financial structures

Aims of the chapter

- To provide a rationale for the use of debt in financing property investments.
- To describe and explain the terminology used in property finance.
- To set out the differences between debt and equity finance, and their respective returns.
- To describe the impact of gearing (leverage).
- To consider how debt finance can be used in practice, and the types of finance available.
- To consider how interest rate risks can be managed.
- To describe the structure and types of vehicles available to investors.

10.1   Introduction

In this chapter we look at methods of funding real estate purchases and consider how a combination of debt and equity can be used to finance real estate investment purchases.

Most real estate valuation and investment text books adopt the approach that investors will undertake real estate investments using 100% equity (100% their own money). Whilst for the institutional market this has often been the case, for the majority of other investors a combination of debt and equity is a common occurrence.

Why do investors bring debt on board? The reasons include:

- To increase the returns on their equity.
- To limit their exposure to single investments and to expand the amount of money available, thereby enabling a larger property portfolio to be purchased, and the risks to be spread.
- Because it is often part of the structure of a special purpose vehicle (SPV) or a limited partnership (section 10.11).

Using debt financing to supplement the use of equity money is known as 'gearing up' the finance and, as explained below, this can increase the return on equity. However, the use of gearing comes at a cost in terms of interest and capital payments, and accordingly it affects the risk/return trade-off of the equity investor.

In this chapter we will explore different types of debt finance and consider how these types of finance will impact:

- The net cash flows coming from the property investment. In the US these are called the net operating income (NOI).
- The risk/return profile of the investor's equity as assessed by IRRs and NPVs (Chapter 5). The IRR can be apportioned into an income and an exit ratio, thereby splitting the

impact that the net income returns and the capital gains (or losses) have on the investment returns.

- The investor's tax position. The different figures that investors use will also be identified.

Firstly let us consider some definitions for debt and equity.

10.2   Debt

Debt finance is the principal amount borrowed. It remains constant throughout the borrowing period, unless capital repayments are made during the term of the loan. Where repayments are made during the loan period the loan is described as a repayment or amortising loan. Alternatively, all the capital may be repaid at the end of the loan: this is known as an interest only loan or, where interest on the loan is also deferred, a balloon payment loan.

Interest is paid at an agreed rate per cent. This rate may be a fixed rate for the term of the loan, in which case for short- to medium-term loans the interest rate will be linked to the prevailing SWAP rate at the beginning of the loan, plus a margin. For long-term fixed rate loans with a life of ten years plus, the interest rate is linked to the gross redemption yield on long-dated gilts with a comparable life, plus a margin. Alternatively, the loan may be a variable rate loan linked to bank base rate or, more normally, linked to the three or six month London Inter Bank Offer Rate (LIBOR). Interest is paid on pre-determined dates; this may be monthly, quarterly or half-yearly in arrears, depending upon the type of borrowings. Interest, capital repayments and the lender's fees are contractual obligations that have to be paid to the lender before a return can accrue to the owners of the equity.

Thus to the lender, the return on debt capital is the interest received. However, the lender is also mindful that the capital needs to be repaid. If there is a default on either the interest payments or the capital repayment, the lender's returns will be reduced or wiped out or may become negative. In an attempt to be seen to be lending on very competitive returns, a growing number of lenders are using their fees for lending the money as a further way of earning a return on the loan.

Commercial property lenders undertake detailed credit assessments of borrowers. Where large sums are involved the lender frequently looks to one of the major credit rating agencies, such as Standard & Poors, Moody's or Fitch, for a credit rating of the company. The company is given a credit rating that reflects its ability to meet its financial obligations in different economic environments.

At the end of the chapter we consider the impact that Basle II will have on the ability of banks to lend money. Basle II sets up the risk assessment criteria that banks will be required to undertake. This will impact on their capital adequacy ratios and their scope to lend money.

The risk of non-payment of the interest and capital outstanding is known as the default risk. Credit ratings for the three main credit rating agencies are summarised in Table 10.1.

Please see Spreadsheet 21 for a more detailed comparison of the credit rating criteria of the main credit rating agencies, plus links to their web sites.

Table 10.1   Comparative credit rating systems explained.

Credit risk	Moody's	Standard & Poor's	Fitch/IBCA
Investment grade			
Highest quality	Aaa	AAA	AAA
High quality (very strong)	Aa	AA	AA
Upper medium grade (strong)	A	A	A
Medium grade	Baa	BBB	BBB
Not investment grade			
Somewhat speculative	Ba	BB	BB
Speculative	B	B	B
Highly speculative	Caa	CCC	CCC
Most speculative	Ca	CC	CC
Imminent default	C	D	C
Default	C	C	D

Table 10.2   Investment terminology by profession.

Type of professional	Description	Example of when used
Chartered surveyor	Equity	Property finance
Banker	Equity	Lending agreements
Equity analyst	Net asset value	Stockbroker's reports on listed property companies
Fund manager	Net asset value	Analysis of shares in a property company
Accountant	Shareholders' funds	Preparation of a company's accounts

   In addition to the loan documentation, which sets up a number of financial ratios to which the borrower must adhere, lenders seek security (legal, fixed and floating charges) over the company, the property and the rents in question. Debt returns are relatively stable and secure but are dependent upon lenders meeting their obligations.

10.3   Equity

Equity is the investor's own money invested in the property. This equity input is described differently according to whom one is talking to. Table 10.2 summarises who uses which terminology in relation to the investor's moneys invested in the property. In addition to there being different terminologies for equity among the various professionals, there is also a different understanding of gearing or leverage in US parlance. Gearing is the ratio that describes the amount of debt and equity invested in a deal. However, the gearing ratio has two different methods of calculation:

$$\text{Debt to equity} = \frac{\text{Debt}}{\text{Equity}} \qquad \text{(D to E)}$$

$$\text{Loan to value} = \frac{\text{Loan}}{\text{Property value}} \qquad \text{(LTV)}$$

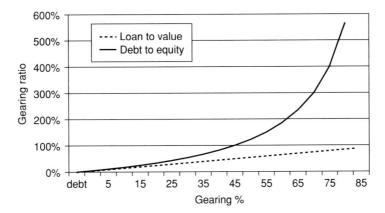

Fig. 10.1   Loan to value v. debt to equity.

The lender will wish to confirm that the property has an appropriate value. The property's value is assessed at the lower of the property's purchase price and its independent market valuation (or external valuation, if the lender is not worried about conflicts of interest). This valuation should be prepared in accordance with the RICS Appraisal Standards (RICS, 2003).

The figures produced for debt to equity (D to E) and loan to value (LTV) are significantly different, such that if when speaking to a property investor you say that you have achieved '120% gearing' they are likely to be mightily impressed, in that they perceive that you have borrowed 20% more than the purchase price. However, from the perspective of a corporate banker 120% gearing may be viewed as relatively modest, in that on a loan to value basis this is just under 55%.

Fig. 10.1 shows the difference in the gearing ratios for different levels of debt. The example relates to a property investment costing £100 million. The x axis shows the amount of debt used and the y axis shows the two different ratios.

10.3.1   Return on equity

For equity investors, the measure of their returns is the return on equity. It is important to establish return on equity (RoE) as well as the overall project return figures, as measured by IRRs. These figures are often very different. The RoE is the return over either an accounting period or a holding period. The IRR is an annualised return as discussed in earlier chapters of the book.

Gearing enhances the returns on equity, when the internal rate of return (IRR) of the investment or project exceeds the cost of debt. In contrast, gearing destroys equity or shareholders' funds or net asset value when the costs of debt exceed the IRR of the property. In Chapter 11 we look at the measuring of returns and describe the calculation and use of IRRs.

For those using net present values (NPV), gearing enhances their NPV when the cost of debt is less than the discount rate (cost of capital) used in the NPV calculation. Currently, only a small minority of property investors use NPV. In part one might suggest that the property investment industry is uncomfortable with the use of weighted average cost of capital (WACC) as the discount rate for assessing the NPV of property investments and projects, when a combination of debt and equity are used. However, we will discuss in Chapter 12 the implications of the advent of new finance, which places doubt on the appropriateness of WACC derived from the capital asset pricing model. This doubt is particularly raised where a market is not efficient that is, where price anomalies exist.

In practice, the major property investment players will use gearing to enhance returns and achieve high IRRs. Frequently these IRRs are in the range 15–25%. Their required rates of return are set in the context of those sought by their shareholders. A number of investors use WACC as their net of tax hurdle rate, and for many listed property investment companies this figure is set out in the back of their published report and accounts.

10.4   The impact of gearing

As the level of gearing to finance an investment increases, so too does the volatility of the achieved returns; namely the return on equity becomes more sensitive to the underlying returns of the property investment itself. The extra variability of the residual cash flow is proportional to the 'income gearing ratio'. At the same time the level of gearing impacts on the risk profile of the debt capital from the lender's standpoint.

If high levels of gearing are used, the lender is vulnerable to falls in property values. Where property values fall below the amount of borrowings, the lender is exposed to a potential loss as there are insufficient assets to meet the repayment of the borrowings.

A key skill for long-term property investors is being able to recognise that the performance of the property market is cyclical and to identify the expected returns from their investments. Helical Bar plc in particular have been very successful in identifying the cycle. They have used gearing in rising markets where the property IRR exceeded their cost of debt and then, prior to the downturns in the market, have reduced the scale of their property holdings and used the sale proceeds to reduce their gearing.

In contrast, property lenders do not consider the upside potential of the properties they are financing. They are focused on the downside risk. In their analysis of the net cash flows they will ignore potential increases in rents (unless contractually binding) and capital values. The cash flows are considered in a risk averse manner. Later in this chapter we will consider the four key lending ratios used by banks.

The returns to the equity investor are the net income flows and the capital retained by the investor after interest charges, bank fees, and capital repayments and other outgoings have been accounted for. These are measured using IRR and NPV performance measures, or in terms of accounting measures as shown below.

Example 10.1: the effect of gearing

To see how gearing can 'turbo charge' the returns of an investor, let us consider a £100 million property investment portfolio. We will assume it is financed by £60 million of debt and £40 million of equity. This will show that gearing increases return to the investor.

To simplify the figures in this example we will at first make the assumptions that:

- the borrowings are interest only;
- the net rental incomes equal the interest costs of the debt plus the running costs of the company;
- there are no retained earnings; and
- the debt level remains constant.

The ladder diagrams in Figs 10.2 to 10.6 show the property company's balance sheet according to the scale of its assets (property investments) relative to how they are funded by debt and equity. The ladder diagram is to scale and, as accounts must balance, the two sides of the ladder match each other. Accordingly, as the property portfolio (assets) in the company change in value, these changes are reflected by changes in the liabilities.

When constructing ladder diagrams, figures from the accounts are used with the split between liabilities and assets. The *liabilities* are the moneys used to fund the assets. These are shown with the shortest term liabilities at the bottom and the longest term liabilities at the top. In this way the debt can be layered to differentiate between short- and long-term debt finance. The *assets* are stacked with the most liquid assets at the bottom and the least liquid at the top. So if the company has cash in its balance sheet, this would go at the bottom on the assets side of the ladder.

At the start of our analysis the property investor's position is as shown in Fig. 10.2. At the end of the year in 2005 the property portfolio has increased in value by 10%, representing a £10 million revaluation surplus. The ladder diagram, following accounting conventions, needs to balance so £10 million needs to be added to the assets side of the ladder. Debt remains constant so the extra £10 million is added to the revaluation surplus as an increase in the equity (Fig. 10.3).

The result of this is that, as shown in Fig. 10.4, the equity has increased from £40 million to £50 million, representing a 25% increase. As a consequence of the use of gearing, a 10% increase in property values has been transformed into a 25% increase in the investor's equity (or the net asset value of the company or their shareholders' funds).

In contrast, had the property portfolio fallen in value by 10% to £90 million, there would be a revaluation deficit of £10 million (see Fig. 10.5). This deficit would be deducted from the equity which would reduce from the original £40 million to £30 million, representing a 25% diminution (see Fig. 10.6).

Year end 31/9/2005

Liabilities	Assets
Equity shareholders' funds net asset value £40m	Property investments
Debt finance	
£60m	£100m

Fig. 10.2 Liability and asset split as at September 2005.

Year end 31/9/2005

Liabilities	Assets
Increase in equity + £10m	Increase in values £10m
Equity shareholders' funds net asset value £40m	Property investments
Debt finance	
£60m	£100m

Fig. 10.3 Liability and asset split in 2005 showing value and equity growth.

Year end 31/9/2005

Liabilities	Assets
Equity shareholders' funds net asset value £50m	Property investments
Debt finance	
£60m	£110m

Fig. 10.4 Liability and asset split in 2005 showing increase of equity relative to debt.

Year end 31/9/2005

Liabilities	Assets
Decrease in equity −£10m	Decrease in equity −£10m
Equity shareholders' funds net asset value £40m	Property investments
Debt finance	
£60m	£100m

Fig. 10.5 Liability and asset split in 2005 showing equity decrease.

Year end 31/9/2005

Liabilities	Assets
Equity shareholders' funds net asset value £30m	Property investments
Debt finance	
£60m	£90m

Fig. 10.6 Liability and asset split in 2005 showing increase of equity relative to debt following value decline.

Gearing may thus be seen as a 'two-edged sword', turbo-charging returns in a rising market whilst destroying equity in a falling market.

Taking the basic example above, let us now remove the simplifications. We will assume there was a profit and this figure (net of tax and any dividends paid out) is added to the equity figure, and part of the debt is amortised (by capital repayments). From the same starting point of £100 million of property assets, financed by £40 million of equity and £60 million of debt, let us now assume that the company:

- makes an after tax profit of £4 million;
- pays a dividend of £1 million; and
- uses the surplus cash flow to repay debt of £3 million.

As before, we make the assumption that the property portfolio has increased in value by 10%. The starting point is as before (see Fig. 10.2).

At the year end the balance sheet will look like Fig. 10.7. Due to the retained after tax profits of £3 million (also known as retained earnings), plus the £10 million revaluation surplus, the equity has increased from £40 million to £53 million. In contrast to the underlying 10% increase in property values, this is an impressive increase of 32.5%.

If the surplus cash flow of £3 million were kept by the company, the debt would have stayed at £60 million and cash of £3 million would go into the assets side of the ladder diagram, below the properties, as shown in Fig. 10.8. As before, the equity has increased to

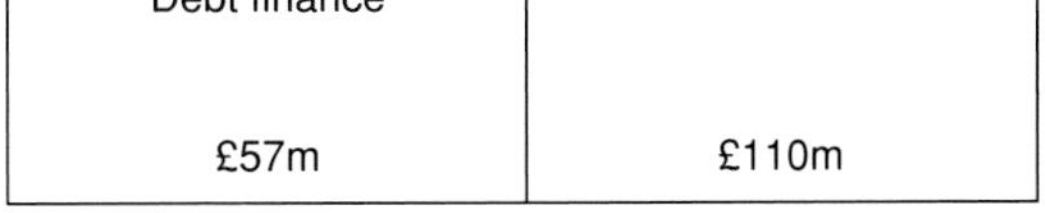

Year end 31/9/2005

Liabilities	Assets
Equity shareholders' funds net asset value £53m	Property investments
Debt finance £57m	£110m

Fig. 10.7   The impact of retained profits on the asset/equity split (1).

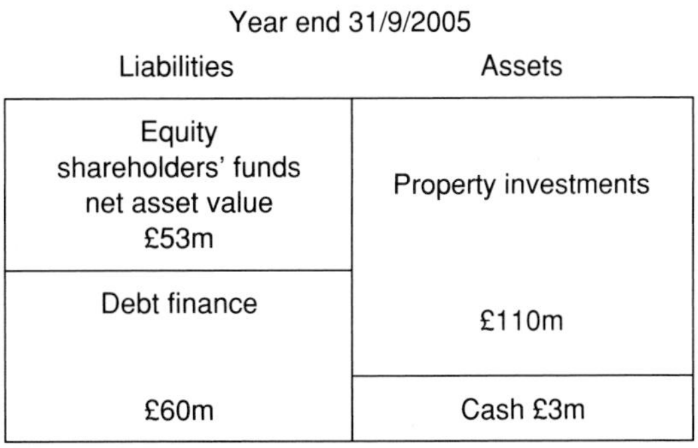

Year end 31/9/2005

Liabilities	Assets
Equity shareholders' funds net asset value £53m	Property investments £110m
Debt finance £60m	Cash £3m

Fig. 10.8   The impact of retained profits on the asset/equity split (2).

£53 million – an increase of 32.5%. This similar result is because it is the impact on the shareholders' funds/equity/net asset value section of the liabilities side of the ladder that is being measured. This provides a pictorial view of how gearing impacts on the debt and equity position of a property investment or the company in which it is held.

Gearing has not always been of advantage to investors. For the 20 years up to 1993, property was subject to a reverse yield gap (see Chapter 3), meaning that property yields were less than long bond yields. Also property income returns were less than short interest costs on debt. This resulted in deficit financing. Where interest costs are greater than rental returns, the deficit needs to be paid by surpluses generated by trading profits from property sales. If the wrong properties were chosen, investors found themselves in financial difficulty.

More recently, since the UK left the exchange rate mechanism in 1993, the country's interest rate structure has changed. With the advent of low interest rates across the yield curve, the property market has benefited because rental yields have exceeded bond yields and the average cost of borrowing. This position, which has prevailed since the mid 1990s is a return to the fundamental situation that prevailed in the decade from the early 1960s. During that period property out-performed both equities and bonds in a similar way to that which was seen in the years 2000–2005.

Please see Spreadsheet number 22 for a working example of the impact of gearing on a set of property company accounts, alongside which are the IRR calculations.

As we will see in the next section of this chapter, the timing of interest payments can vary according to the type of financing. For example, bank interest may be charged monthly or quarterly in arrears, whereas interest on mortgage debentures is half-yearly in arrears and rental incomes are normally quarterly in advance. This timing advantage of property's rental incomes is beneficial to the investor and has the effect of enhancing the geared IRR figures.

10.5   Financing property transactions

Frequently, when financing a property transaction, the numbers are viewed only from the perspective of the investor (that is, the borrower). However, it is important to look at and understand the risk and return profiles of *both* lender *and* borrower.

When considering the merits of a property transaction with finance, it is the *net* cash flows that are important. These cash flows are used by both the investor and the lender to produce IRRs and NPVs. IRRs are useful in that they combine both income and capital figures.

However, in a property investment the rental incomes are a contractual obligation between landlord and tenant for the duration of the lease. In contrast, capital values are subject to the ability to sell in the marketplace, and thus can be seen as subject to the vagaries and cyclical nature of the market. In order to reflect this in the IRR performance figures, the tendency in the US is to apportion IRRs into two components: the part that comes from the net rental incomes and the part that comes from the return of capital from property sales.

The IRR is apportioned into an income and an exit ratio, where:

- *Income ratio* is the percentage contribution of the expected net income cash flows of an investment relative to the total net cash flows.
- *Exit ratio* is the percentage contribution of the expected exit value (or salvage value) of the investment that relates to the total net cash flows. This is used to identify the importance, or otherwise, of the exit value to the worth of an investment.

To calculate these ratios, both the net income and net property proceeds elements of the cash flows have to be discounted at the internal rate of return. (In this context the DCF Analyst Excel Add-In software provides the analyst with the ability to calculate the income and exit ratios simply.)

Please see Spreadsheet 23 for a worked example of the apportioning of IRRs into income and exit ratios for property investments with and without gearing.

Before we consider the impact of different types of finance on the return profiles of the parties involved in property finance, we need first to consider how the lender looks at the lending proposition and the factors that are important to the lender. The lender's primary concern is to ensure that the interest payments, their fees and the capital repayments will be paid on the due dates. In the loan agreement the lender sets out a number of default covenants. These are of vital importance, such that if a default covenant is breached during the term of the loan then either the loan becomes repayable – and usually a higher interest rate becomes payable – or additional 'comfort money' (capital injection) is required.

Whether the bank is lending short, medium or long term, on fixed or variable rate interest, with or without amortisation, gearing and operating ratios are set to which the borrower must adhere. The four main ratios are:

- initial loan to value;
- exit loan to value;
- interest cover;
- debt service ratio.

10.5.1   Loan to value ratio (LTV)

The LTV is assessed in one of two ways, as described below.

Initial loan to value (ILTV)

This is calculated by dividing the loan by the value. A similar ratio is the capital cover ratio which is the reciprocal of LTV.

The value is taken to be the lower of the initial value or cost. These are usually net of purchaser's costs. Historically the valuations were carried out by valuers on behalf of the investor, but now the practice is for the valuer to be instructed by the bank, and it is usual for the valuer to be independent of both the bank and the investor. Such valuations are usually undertaken on a market basis, in accordance with RICS practice statements.

A typical LTV in the industry is 70–80%. However, where there are strong cash flows to support amortisation of the loan, a higher figure of 85–90% may be seen.

The LTV measures real estate financial risk. Default risk rises proportionally with the size of the LTV ratio. Where the LTV is greater than around 80%, the risks are seen to rise proportionately higher. It is at this point that senior debt lending stops and mezzanine finance cuts in (see section 10.6 for more detail).

Exit loan to value

This is calculated by dividing the loan by the exit value. The exit value is determined by taking a percentage of today's investment value, or a percentage of today's vacant possession value. The value is not normally anything to do with the value at the exit (end) of the loan. The percentage of the value will be dependent upon the property and:

- The impact that obsolescence and depreciation will have on the property value.
  - o For new properties let on long leases, the percentage may be set against the investment value.
  - o For older properties, the percentage will often be set such that it represents the underlying land value.
- The relationship between the underlying site value and the property value.
  - o Where land values are relatively high, these underpin the property value and provide the lender with comfort against the property becoming vacant and being subject to redevelopment.
  - o The percentage will also be dependent upon the bank's stance towards commercial property lending. Aggressive lenders may take 80% of the investment value, whilst conservative lenders may drop down to 20% or less of the current vacant possession value.

Lenders often seek an exit loan to value ratio in the range of 60%. When this percentage is contrasted with the ILTV of some 80%, and the discount to the current value is also taken on board, the required maximum outstanding amount at the end of the loan will frequently be significantly less than the loan granted at day 1. This gives rise to the need for amortisation, whereby part of the loan principal is repaid during the loan. This repayment of loan principal (capital) enables the borrower to have a lower LTV at the expiry of the loan.

10.5.2   Interest cover ratio

This is calculated by dividing the annual net rental income by the annual interest payments. The ratio is also known as income cover.

The interest cover ratio figure is dependent upon the quality of the rental income, in terms of the credit rating of the tenants and the unexpired lease terms. For a property let on long leases to blue-chip tenants, a ratio of 115+% might be expected. Where the tenants are of relatively poor covenant strength, a ratio of around 150% would be more appropriate.

10.5.3   Debt cover service ratio

The debt cover service ratio is calculated by dividing the annual net rental income by the total of the annual interest payments plus the annual capital repayments. As with the interest cover ratio, the debt service ratio figure is linked to tenant quality. A ratio of over 110% may be expected, with 125+% for multi-let properties where the covenant strength is not good.

The debt service cover ratio includes capital repayments, which are the element that constitutes amortisation of the loan such that a proportion of the loan is repaid during the loan term. These capital repayments eat into the surplus cash flows, and where large amounts of amortisation are required the debt service ratio is usually the limiting factor that determines the amount of borrowings that can be made.

Where the net rental income is expected to rise within the following couple of years, the lender may grant an amortisation 'holiday' such that the loan is interest only for say the period up to a rent review or for the first couple of years whilst any element of vacant accommodation is let. Often, an amortisation holiday is granted for the first year, enabling the purchaser of an investment to gain sufficient cash flow to reimburse their acquisition costs.

When dealing with amortised debt, the interest payments will be tax deductible, whereas the capital repayments need to be met out of net of tax incomes. The debt service cover ratio does not include tax, but tax payments should be included in the DCF analysis.

Please see Spreadsheet 24 for a worked example of how the initial and exit loan to value ratios, the income cover ratio and the debt service cover ratio are calculated for a property investment financed with bank borrowings.

From the above it can been seen that there are normally four key bank lending ratios that need to be met during the term of the loan. The object for most borrowers is to maximise their initial loan to value ratio whilst staying within their other lending ratios. One approach is to undertake a series of 'what-if' calculations using Excel's Goal Seek facility. However, a useful alternative is to use Excel's solver function. Using the solver function it is possible to set up a routine whereby the initial loan to value is maximised whilst keeping within the exit loan to value, income cover ratio and debt service cover ratio constraints.

Please see Spreadsheet 25 for a worked example of how to use Excel's solver function so that the initial LTV ratio can be maximised subject to constraints set for the exit LTV, the interest cover and debt service cover ratios.

Three other ratios can be used in the lending assessment: break even point, expense ratio and cash on cash return. These are usually used to assist those involved in the lending process but not written into the loan document itself. They are described below.

10.5.4   Break even point

Break even point calculates the percentage of occupancy that a building must achieve in order to service all of its financing obligations, on the basis of an LTV set normally in the

65–80% range. This ratio is useful when dealing with properties that are not fully let and it is commonly used for speculative developments.

The break even point includes operating expenses and the debt service payments. It looks at these expenses relative to the net rental incomes receivable. Most borrowing takes place in a special purpose vehicle (SPV). The SPV, which owns the property and into which the borrowings go, is usually a company (though it can be a limited partnership). The SPV will have costs associated with it, and these plus taxes to be paid are included in the operating costs.

10.5.5   Expense ratio

The expense ratio is used as a comparator with other property although by itself it tells very little. It provides information on non-recoverable outgoings and expenditures made by the landlord which keep the property competitive. The ratio is likely to be significantly higher for second-hand than for new buildings.

10.5.6   Cash on cash return

This is a single period or 'static' profitability measure. It measures, in an accountancy context, the profits that accrue to the equity investor annually. Thus from the net rental incomes (net operating income in US parlance) are deducted the interest and other operating costs not already deducted from the rents. This figure is divided by the equity invested in the property by the investor.

Generally cash on cash returns are seen as accountancy-based figures and so amortisation costs are ignored; however, a number of players include capital repayments when calculating cash on cash returns.

Typically the first year's cash on cash return is expected to be in the range 8–14%. This is achievable when interest rates are less than net rental income returns. However, when interest rates rise and property yields fall, this ratio is squeezed.

- Please see Spreadsheet 26 for a working example of the calculation of the break even point, the cash on cash return, and the expense ratio for a geared property investment.

When dealing with the analysis of debt financed schemes, a number of different performance figures and IRRs may be calculated. These include the project or ungeared IRR, the equity IRR and the after tax IRR (see Chapter 7 for more information).

10.5.7   On-going financial analysis required

During the term of the loan the lender usually requires on-going financial analyses. These analyses include keeping within the LTV and income cover and debt service cover ratios. If these are breached or are about to be breached, the lender is likely to require an equity injection (comfort money) that rectifies the position and brings the ratios back in line. The lender will usually make provision in the loan documentation such that they can call upon revaluations of the property. This is not popular with the investor as it incurs costs, but in volatile or weak markets the lender may seek a revaluation to be aware of their exposure.

10.6   Lending terminology

The main tranches of money used in the bank financing of a property are: senior debt, mezzanine finance and equity (Fig. 10.9). Sub-categories of these include junior debt, senior mezzanine and junior mezzanine.

The senior debt lenders comprise US, German, Continental European and UK retail banks, the investment banks, building societies and life insurance companies.

- The US players (retail and investment banks) are generally short-term lenders of say five to seven years. They are not always the most flexible of lenders but they aim to offer a pricing advantage through the capital markets exit strategies of debt securitisation and conduit facilities. They offer floating or fixed interest rates and tend to prefer property investment portfolios with low risks and strong covenants and a good portfolio spread. Transaction sizes tend to be large (£50 million ++). Their lending margins can be very competitive, but their fees can be relatively high and their loan agreements can seriously disadvantage the financial health of the borrower if breached. The active players include: Morgan Stanley, Lehmans, GMAC and Goldman Sachs.
- In the UK, the Scottish banks (Royal Bank of Scotland and Halifax Bank of Scotland) are currently very active in both property investment and development finance lending activities. They offer both floating and fixed interest rates, but usually require interest rates hedging. They are very competitive on low risk, low margin lending and can offer high (85%) LTVs. The UK banks often have more appetite for risk than German banks and are active in the corporate market.
- The German banks currently dominate the medium to large end of the prime property lending markets. Their loan margins typically are in the range of 0.75–1.5%. Significant players currently include Aareal, HVB International, EuroHypo, West LB and Bayerische Landesbanken.
- Many of the UK building societies have reincorporated as banks, leaving only a few building societies of any significant size. Of these the Nationwide and Bristol & West have become active commercial property lenders. Generally they focus on low risk

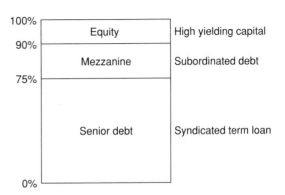

Fig. 10.9   Layered debt.

investments, and offer low interest rate margins. Where the unexpired leases are long and the tenant quality is good, they can do high LTVs. They are often competitive where there are long-term cash flows and offer amortised lending co-terminus with the unexpired lease term. They place less importance on the requirements for sophisticated interest rate risk hedging.

- UK life insurance companies have become an active force in the long-term lending markets, where they use long-term property loans as a method of hedging their annuity liabilities. Thus they will offer long-term fixed rate borrowings secured on properties let to good covenants on long unexpired leases. These loans are priced relative to long dated gilts and the margins are in the order of 125–250 basis points (bp). They can offer high LTVs when the cash flows are sufficient to amortise the loan over the life of the occupational leases. In particular, Norwich Union, Axa and Prudential are big players in this market.
- Other European lenders have made their mark by focusing on niche markets. For example:
  o syndications;
  o smaller lot sized properties and portfolios; and
  o leisure properties.
  Active players in this market currently include French, Dutch, Austrian and Irish banks; for example, Erste Bank, Fortis, KBC and Société Générale.

10.6.1   Current finance availability

Currently, finance is readily available for office, retail and industrial sectors. However, in the specialist sectors of leisure and hotels there are not many active lenders. Generally loans are available from under £1 million to £200 million and above. The most active market is between £10 million and £30 million. Portfolio and multi-let properties have become increasingly popular because of their risk diversification benefits.

Development finance is a specialist sector of this market. Generally substantial pre-lets, and in some instances forward commitment for a sale, are required by lenders before they will consider this form of lending.

10.6.2   Senior debt

Typically, senior debt has loan to values ratios of up to 70–80%. This is lower where the security relates to properties let on internal repairing and short-term leases. Some lenders will offer up to 85+%, where the unexpired term of the occupational leases are long and the tenant quality is good. However, the interest rate is higher for such loans as this includes in effect a blended tranche of mezzanine finance. This is sometimes called 'stretched debt'.

Interest margins for senior debt vary, but the majority of prime deals are in the 90–125 basis points range. Secondary deals are around 125–200 basis points. Tertiary deals are approximately 250++ basis points and may include additional exit fees. Many banks offer competitive lending margins but claw back additional returns by requiring either or both up-front and exit fees. These fees can include:

- arrangement costs (30–50 bp);
- commitment fees (15–25 bp);
- exit fee (10–25 bp).

In addition there may be break fees – particularly for fixed rate lending, where they can be expensive – and monitoring fees.

For most senior debt lending the bank will require amortisation, such that the exit LTV comes down to a modest figure. This is linked to a percentage of the current vacant possession value. Where there are strong covenants and on portfolios, interest only periods or amortisation holidays can be offered.

The loan terms for senior debt are between one and 20 years, with five to seven years being the most common; most lenders require the borrower to enter into hedging agreements.

As at 2003, the Bank of England put senior debt lending secured against commercial property at £92 billion, of which 70% was by UK registered banks. If the life insurance companies, building societies, conduit lending and securitisation are included, the figure rises to around £130 billion. This compares with total outstanding residential mortgages of £697 billion, and total UK bank lending of £4150 billion (data sources: DTZ Money into Property and Jones Lang LaSalle, 2003).

The active lenders in the market change from year to year. For example, in 2004 there were 550+ lending institutions in the UK, of which approximately 100 were active lenders on property, either at a corporate level or on an asset specific basis. A valuable annual review of those active in the property market and the prevailing terms and conditions of property loans is undertaken by De Montfort University in conjunction with Kingfisher Property Finance (www.kingfisherpropertyfinance.co.uk).

10.7   Mezzanine finance and participating loans

As we saw in Fig. 10.9, mezzanine finance sits between senior debt and equity. The lenders of mezzanine finance do not have a first charge on the property and the rents, and are therefore taking on board additional risk. Accordingly, they look for enhanced interest returns and a percentage of the performance of the investment.

Mezzanine finance usually provides the lender with three elements from which to earn returns:

- *Interest rate*: this is set at a higher margin to reflect the higher risks involved.
- *Fees*: these are charged up front, but may be added on to the loan amount. In terms of the cost of the funds, fees can be significant. In some instances an exit fee may be charged, but this is normally subject to negotiation.
- *Performance link*: a performance related element is usually included, which gives the lender a percentage of the surpluses. The documentation of mezzanine finance requires careful wording so that these moneys can be classified as interest payments to the borrower (and thus tax deductible) as opposed to capital costs.

The risk to the mezzanine provider is that the property value against which the loan is partially secured falls to a point where part or all of the mezzanine loan is uncovered by security. If the mezzanine provider has a portfolio of mezzanine loans then part of the downside risk may be diversified away. Where there are two funders providing mezzanine finance, one will be 'senior' and the other 'junior' and, as the words suggest, the senior mezzanine funder will take the less risky 'slice' of the income and the junior funder will be in the more vulnerable position.

> Please see Spreadsheet 27 for a worked example of the inclusion of mezzanine and senior debt to finance a property investment. This includes the calculation of the equity investor's, and the mezzanine provider's IRRs.

10.8   Interest rates

Interest rates or cost of funds are set as follows:

- *Variable rate lending*: normally fixed in relation to either the three or the six month London Interbank Offer Rate (LIBOR).
- *Fixed rate lending*: fixed in relation to either SWAPs, where the duration of fixed funding is between about five and seven years, or in relation to long-dated gilts of similar duration where there is a requirement for longer-term fixed rate finance.

> Please see Spreadsheet 28 for information on SWAP rate curves and gilt yield curves and web sites that provide additional information on variable and fixed rate debt for commercial property lending.

Commercial property lending frequently takes place via a special purpose vehicle (SPV). Accordingly, one of the key questions to be determined will be 'does the bank have access to any security other than that held within the vehicle?'

Non-recourse debt is where, on default, the lender is given access to only the property asset and, via a floating charge, to the SPV. There is no access to the borrower or the borrower's other assets. This is very useful to the borrower when economic times are difficult. This term essentially makes the debt a 'put option' from borrower to lender. It is not clear what the borrower is paying for this option in the price of the loan, but it is not very much and will depend on the strength of the borrower's covenant.

10.9   Management of interest rate risks

When an investor purchases a property using debt secured on the property and the property is placed into a 'ring fenced' vehicle or company (such as an SPV), this is often known as 'project debt'. The intention is that the rents from the property will service the interest payments and the capital repayments if the debt is an amortising loan. This leaves the property investor exposed to interest rate volatility and thus interest rate risk. If interest rates rise significantly, it is likely that the rental incomes will be insufficient to meet the interest and capital repayment liabilities. This puts the borrower, and in some instances the lender, at risk. In consequence, most property lenders ask or even insist that the borrower takes on board one or more interest rate risk hedging instruments. The need to hedge is usually dictated by prudence.

The financial markets are very sophisticated and a range of interest rate hedging instruments are available. The key main instruments used by property investors are caps/floors/collars and SWAP instruments. In addition, floating rate agreements, interest rate futures and droplocks may be used.

The alternative is for the lender to use fixed interest debt as opposed to variable rate debt. Fixed rate interest removes the risk of interest rate movements. However, fixed rate interest is often significantly more expensive, and if repayment is made before the due date substantial penalties may be levied. Also, there is an opportunity loss when fixed rate finance is used during periods of declining interest rates.

These interest rate risk management techniques are described below.

10.9.1   Caps/floors/collars

- A *cap* is a traded interest rate option. Caps are, in effect, tradable insurance policies whereby the lender or the borrower is reimbursed if the interest rates move above or below pre-determined limits. Thus a cap limits the borrowing costs on short-term money rates in return for the payment of an up-front premium. The purchaser of a cap continues to pay short-term rates with the guarantee of the interest rate payable not exceeding a 'strike' level. The strike level is the interest rate at which the third party makes payments to reimburse the interest costs above the strike rate, therefore a cap provides the borrower with a ceiling on the interest rates payable. If interest rates exceed the level of the cap, the borrower is reimbursed.
- A *floor* provides the lender with a minimum interest rate. If interest rates fall below the level of the floor, the lender is reimbursed. Floors are used to reduce the up-front cost of a cap.
- A *collar* combines a cap and a floor. It is thus cheaper for borrowers, but ties them into a specified minimum interest rate. It is possible to construct a zero-premium collar. This is where the premium from the sale of the floor totally compensates for the cost of the cap.

With a cap, if interest rates fall, a lower cost of finance is foregone. This represents an opportunity loss, but is the price to be paid for financial security. The price of a cap is influenced by the shape of the yield curve. If interest rates are expected to rise (upward sloping bond yield curve), then caps will be more expensive than in stable or falling interest rate environments.

10.9.2   SWAP instruments

SWAP instruments form a significant part of the financial markets. Investment and commercial banks make markets in the interest rate SWAPs. The banks 'warehouse' the risk in SWAP portfolios and manage the residual interest risk.

A SWAP contract allows one party to exchange variable interest rate obligations with fixed rate obligations, or vice versa. In the property market significant use is made of the

SWAPs market, usually to SWAP variable rate borrowings into fixed rate debt. SWAPs contracts are separate from the lending agreement and are tradable instruments.

Interest rate risk management is complex, with SWAPs maturing on a daily basis and a variety of similar but not identically matched products. In practice, a major bank acts as a counterparty (guarantor) to these transactions.

As SWAPs are tradable contracts, standard contracts are used for dealing purposes, with fixed rates priced on the SWAP yield curve and floating rates based on six month LIBOR.

The holder of the fixed rate borrowings usually has a good credit rating and has secured the fixed rate debt out of the bond markets. The holder of variable rate debt often may have a lower credit rating. The parties' credit ratings will be reflected in the margin charged over the SWAP rate. Lastly, the bank may charge a 'facility fee' for arranging the SWAP transaction.

10.9.3   Other options

The financial markets in both the UK and the US are sophisticated, and a range of other financial instruments and solutions are on offer including, for example, floating rate notes (FRN), droplocks and interest rate futures.

- *Floating rate notes* are short- to medium-term debt instruments which pay interest in line with short-term money rates. The interest rates tend to be linked to LIBOR rates plus a margin, and the coupon shown is the minimum. FRNs can offer a number of features that make them of particular interest to larger property investors; FRNs that convert for example, into fixed rate interest at the option of the investor (debt convertible).
- *Droplocks* are FRNs that become long-term fixed rate debt when a benchmark bond yield falls to a specified level.
- An *uplock* is where the switch into fixed rate debt is triggered by an upward move in long interest rates.
- *Interest rate futures* are financial futures contracts that enable borrowers and investors to obtain protection against future movements in interest rates. Interest rate futures contracts are tradeable and vary from three month LIBOR to long bond contracts.

In conclusion, there are a range of risk management products. Which one should be used will depend on the timing: what is likely to happen to interest rates in the future, the needs of the investor and their credit rating. The qualities that they can offer include:

- protection from risk;
- flexibility of funding arrangements;
- reduced costs of borrowing over time;
- an ability to avoid 'spikes' in interest costs.

Simple (so-called 'vanilla') products are preferred as they are easier to understand and tend to be efficiently priced. These vanilla products are normally in a standard contract form, and thus are usually cheaper and more liquid than over-the-counter (OTC) customised products.

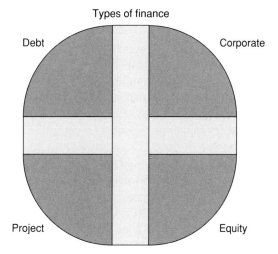

Fig. 10.10 Types of finance.

10.10   Corporate finance

In the first section of this chapter consideration was given to bank finance. In this section we consider finance raised via the stock market.

Before going on to detail the various types of stock market finance, it is helpful to recap on the main types of finance available. These fall into four categories as shown diagrammatically in Fig. 10.10.

At the top left is shown debt. This may be obtained either on a project-specific basis (such as an asset-based mortgage) or by way of corporate debt secured against the company (such as a debenture). At the bottom right is shown equity. This too may be gained on a project-specific basis (for example, by setting up a special purpose vehicle) or on the basis of an equity-sharing arrangement in the company (for example, a partnership arrangement).

In reality the range of structures that can be used is almost endless. The following are the most important types of corporate finance and they will be considered further below.

- mortgage debentures;
- loan stocks;
- convertible unsecured loan stocks;
- convertible preference shares;
- deep discount and zero coupon bonds;
- warrants;
- initial public offerings and rights issues;
- vendor placings.

10.10.1   Mortgage debentures

Mortgage debentures are a sub-category of debentures. They can be issued by property companies with public limited liability status and are secured on property assets and rental incomes. They are used when long-term finance is required and generally have a life of between 15 and 40 years.

There are two particular financial ratios that need to be considered in detailing mortgage debentures. These are income cover, which is usually in the range 105–115%, and capital cover, which is usually around 150%. In establishing the capital valuations, the processes and basis required in the RICS Red Book will be used. The legal charges on the properties and rents are often administered by an insurance company's trust department acting as trustees for the mortgage debenture holders. In this role they carry a significant duty of care to the mortgage debenture investors. In consequence, potential contaminated land issues require proper attention and surveys, adding to the complexity of this form of finance.

Mortgage debentures have interest only payments, and the capital is repaid at the redemption date. The interest is at a fixed coupon, paid half-yearly in arrears, and linked to long gilt yields. The margin over gilt gross redemption yields is usually in the range 75–250 basis points. They are a tradable form of debt funding. They will be listed on the stock exchange and are dealt in by gilts market makers. As they are tradable, liquidity is important and the larger the issue size the better; ideally this will be in excess of £50 million.

It has already been said that mortgage debentures are long term. From the corporate perspective they are inflexible as they can only be redeemed by going back into the market and repurchasing: if companies want to restructure their debt they have to buy out the owner of the debenture rights. Historically, debentures have been both important and useful to the property industry. To the property company they have provided good long-term finance; for institutional investors they have been a 'way in' to the property sector, as by providing this fixed rate finance they have been able to gain a working relationship with the property company that is seeking finance. In a number of instances this has resulted in joint venture projects being undertaken, particularly on the development front.

As fixed rate debt, they are stated in a property company's accounts at cost. However, under FRS 13 the company is required to show in its accounts the market value of this debt. This is known as marking debt to market. If fixed interest rates fall then the negative value of the mortgage debenture rises. This reduces the equity/shareholders' funds/net asset value of the company.

Please see Spreadsheet 29 for a worked example of marking fixed rate debt to market.

The advantage of mortgage debentures for long-term investors is that they do not have any amortisation, and the interest payments are linked to long-dated gilts, which tend to be competitively priced.

Please see Spreadsheet 30 for a worked example of a property portfolio funded by mortgage debenture finance, and the impact on the before and post gearing, plus before and post tax IRRs.

An alternative to the issue of mortgage debenture stock as a means of raising finance is to take a long-term mortgage as provided by life insurance companies. The differences are:

- the insurance company mortgages are simpler to obtain;
- there is no listing process;
- the issue costs are lower; and
- there is a less rigid stance towards land contamination issues.

However, insurance company mortgages will require high levels of amortisation and the margin over the benchmark gilt will frequently be higher than for mortgage debentures, so the overall costs may well be higher.

10.10.2   Other bond-style debt

Fixed interest debt can be issued at 'par' or at a face value less than par. In the case of the latter the running cost of interest is less than the total cost of interest, as part of the interest payment is 'rolled up' and repaid at redemption. This type of finance is called a discounted bond. The advantage to the property company is that the interest payable during the term of the loan is reduced, thereby increasing the net cash flows available to the company. This may be crucial during a time when a company is still seeking to obtain full occupancy of a multi-let scheme or where it is anticipated that strong future rental growth will occur.

Please see Spreadsheet 31 for a working example of using discounted bond finance for a property investment.

A zero coupon bond is where there is no interest payable and the entirety of the interest is rolled up and paid at the redemption of the bond. This method of finance offers the property company excellent positive cash flows during the life of the bond, plus tax credits on the accrued interest. Where the investor is a tax exempt fund, such as a pension fund, no tax is paid on the rolled up interest at the redemption of the bond. From the pension fund investor's perspective, as all the interest is reinvested any problems relating to reinvestment risk are removed.

In a low inflationary environment the inherent uplift in the repayment which is due on a predetermined date in the future needs to be carefully considered, given that commercial property performance is cyclical in nature.

Please see Spreadsheet 32 for a worked example of the financing of property investments using a zero coupon bond, to include pre- and post-tax IRRs and the apportionment of the IRRs.

10.10.3   Unsecured loan stocks

Unsecured loan stocks are used where short- to medium-term debt finance is required and the debt normally has a maturity of less than ten years. The finance is raised either via the stock market or via the commercial banking sector. Interest is payable half-yearly in arrears. As the loan is not secured, it does not 'use up' any property assets on the balance sheet. However, the ability to raise such debt depends upon the company's credit rating and it is usually more expensive than mortgage debentures. In practice it is often the forerunner to a 'large deal', in that the debt is relatively simple to bring on board, does not use up any property assets, and thereby leaves the property company able to purchase a large property or portfolio using the loan stock cash as the equity element. The company will subsequently refinance the deal to achieve a lower cost.

10.10.4   Convertible unsecured loan stocks (CULS)

Convertible unsecured loan stocks are similar to loan stocks in that, up to the redemption date, the investor receives interest half-yearly in arrears, and at the redemption date the investor can receive the return of capital invested. However, during predetermined periods as set out in the loan stock agreement, the investor can elect to swap the loan stock for new shares in the company at the predetermined conversion rate. Because of this the interest payments are usually at a lower coupon due to the equity element. From a property company's perspective the use of CULS usually results in less dilution of the underlying net asset value than a rights issue. The issue of a CULS defers the dilution of directors' shareholdings until such time as the conversion takes place.

CULS are used as a way of keeping ownership of a special purpose vehicle (company) off balance sheet, as until such time as the conversion takes place they are seen as an investment in a debt instrument.

Until the accountancy rules changed in the late 1980s, convertible preference shares were often used instead of CULS. The advantage of convertible preference shares was that they paid dividends and not interest, and thus their cost came out of the after tax earnings, which enhanced the pre-tax figures. Changes to the accounting treatment removed this opportunity to enhance the profit and loss account. However, it should be remembered that preference shares and convertible preference shares pay a dividend that can be paid only if the company has retained earnings.

10.11   Property investment vehicles and structures

The diversity of the type of investors who are active in the property market has broadened over the past decade, especially with the growth of specialist vehicles. This growth has in part been driven by the interest rate differential between income returns on commercial real estate investments and the cost of debt. The exit of sterling from the exchange rate mechanism in 1993 was followed by a sustained drop in the cost of interest rates across the spectrum of the SWAP rate curve. For the property investor this provided the opportunity of being able to borrow money at a cost lower than the income returns on property.

The question for investors was what structure to use to bring the debt on board to finance the property investment (Adams and Venmore-Rowland, 1991). In practice, three main property investment vehicle structures have been used (Venmore-Rowland, 1995):

- companies;
- limited partnerships;
- open-ended funds.

In terms of gross property assets, the gross assets of the main vehicles can be summarised as set out in Table 10.3.

Table 10.3 Property investment vehicles.

Vehicle type	Gross portfolio size	Source
UK private investment companies	Ceiling £150 bn	Merrill Lynch/DTZ
German closed end funds	€147 bn	Jones Lang LaSalle
UK listed property companies	£60 bn	Merrill Lynch
German closed end funds	€147 bn	Jones Lang LaSalle
German open end funds	€70 bn	Jones Lang LaSalle
Other European vehicles including opportunity funds	€41 bn	IPD
UK limited partnerships	€26 bn	ABN AMRO/IPD
UK property unit trusts	€15 bn	Merrill Lynch
Continental European listed property companies	£15 bn	Morgan Stanley
German open end special funds	€14 bn	Morgan Stanley

It has been estimated that within the UK the property assets of local and central government and the corporate occupier sector are worth up to £564 billion, whilst the direct property assets of institutional investors are around £90 billion. A proportion of these assets will be non-commercial property. In this context, the property assets held in public and private property companies are estimated at £210 billion, limited partnerships at £20 billion and property unit trusts £10 billion.

These figures demonstrate that property company vehicles represent a very significant proportion of the property sector. The individual vehicles are described below. First we consider general aspects of the vehicles and to do this it is necessary to refer back to the distinction made between debt and equity earlier in this chapter. It will be recalled that the debt/equity relationship influences the returns to the investor and the risk profile. However, the structure of the vehicle affects how it is taxed and regulated, where it is registered and how it is controlled.

- Taxation is seen as an important factor. The ideal solution is to have a tax-transparent structure, where in the eyes of the tax inspector the vehicle does not suffer tax and all the tax liabilities are passed through proportionately to the investors. Tax transparency is achieved where the same tax consequences result for the ultimate investors whether they invest directly in the asset or through the legal structure by which the asset is held. An example is a limited partnership.
- Vehicles that are set up to collect investment moneys from third party investors – for example, the public – are regulated, and come under the Financial Services and Markets Act 2000. Listed vehicles also come under the rules and regulation of the stock exchange on which they are traded. Private vehicles, in contrast, are broadly unregulated.
- The location where the vehicle is set up is important, as this sets the jurisdiction for the vehicle's tax regime and legal responsibilities. An offshore investment relates to investment vehicles established outside the UK, historically in lower tax areas such as the Isle of Man or the Channel Islands. In recent years the European Union's encouragement of cross-border financial marketing has resulted in new tax havens such as Luxembourg

and Ireland becoming established. Such offshore investment funds are subject to different legislation, lighter regulation and lower tax than funds invested in the UK.

Many of the more complex funds are not recognised by the Financial Services Authority (FSA) which means that they are not subject to the scrutiny of UK regulatory bodies put in place in the interests of consumer protection. Hence their attractiveness in fiscal terms may be offset in part by the additional risk of lack of regulatory protection.

- How a vehicle is controlled is an important factor for the investor. Some investors seek the returns available from property but wish to delegate the management to professional managers or directors. Other investors seek to maintain control over their investments and operate a 'hands-on' investment and management policy. In the case of companies, control of a vehicle is usually dependent upon who holds the majority of the votes.

The directors of a company may be removed by the holder(s) of a majority share-holding. For partnerships the control is vested in the general partner who manages the business and the property investment activities. It is more difficult for the limited partners to remove the general partner. The importance of who controls a vehicle should never be underestimated,

10.11.1 Property companies

Public listed property investment companies have specific listing requirements. They are taxed at vehicle level, and in consequence investors are taxed twice: once within the vehicle and then again at investor level. Thus they suffer double taxation and they are not tax transparent. Private property companies do not have their shares traded on an exchange and cannot seek external equity investment. However, they are frequently used by investors, and may be registered in the UK or established offshore with non-resident tax status, which confers capital gains tax advantages.

A frequent use of the property company structure (Fig. 10.11) is in the form of a special purpose vehicle (SPV). This is a vehicle set up for a particular project or to hold an asset or assets. The company is formed with a limited purpose or life to serve as a conduit or cash flow 'pass through' mechanism. An SPV is often used to contain insolvency risk or to make it easier to give a lender a floating charge. They are created for various mortgage-backed, real estate or loan transactions.

A special purpose vehicle is often set up as a joint venture (JV) company. A joint venture company is one where there is a formal arrangement under which two or more organisations undertake a project, using a vehicle specially incorporated for the purpose; the participants will normally have proportional interests in the JV. Lending to a JV is usually but not always supported by other security from the joint venturers. If it is not supported with guarantees or third party collateral it is said to be 'ring fenced' and the funds are 'non-recourse' to the originating companies. However, the use of JVs has been superseded in recent years by limited partnerships which have become more popular because of tax transparency advantages.

The issued share capital of a property company is the value of the share capital as issued to the shareholders. This may equal the authorised share capital, but cannot exceed it. Those who hold the issued shares have the voting rights, and they can therefore determine

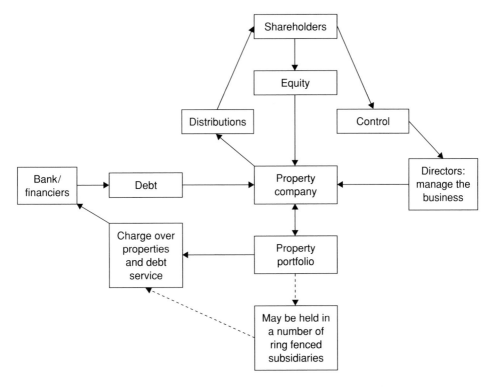

Fig. 10.11   Property company structure.

the composition of the board of directors and the articles of association at general or extraordinary meetings of the company's shareholders.

The net asset value of a share or unit of investment is the difference between the total market value of all investments and the liabilities divided by the number of shares or units outstanding. Net asset value is synonymous with the accountancy term shareholders' funds or, in property or banking terms, equity. For more information on the structuring and workings of company accounts, see Holmes *et al.* (2005).

Listed property companies are usually valued on the basis of a discount or premium to the current estimate of their fully diluted net asset value or NAV (Adams and Venmore-Rowland, 1990). A problem with property companies as an investment sector is that they tend to trade at a discount to their NAV. This acts as a constraint on new issues, as who would wish to sell something for say £80 as shares in a company when the underlying net property assets are worth £100 in the direct property market? Initial property offerings for property investment companies act like other new stock market issues, whilst for property development companies a period of substantial underperformance follows (Gerbich *et al.*, 1995, 1999).

The European Public Real Estate Association (EPRA) provides coverage of the listed EU property vehicles and a forum for debate. Research papers held on the EPRA web site cover a number of topics, including the reasons for property companies to trade at discounts to their underlying net asset value (EPRA, 2004). The research findings concluded that the key issues were:

- Company risk is the most significant determinant of the discount.
- A measure of economic concentration (focused investment strategy) of the company was also found to be important.
- Vehicles with tax transparent structures had much lower discounts.
- Company financial factors, such as gearing, had only a modest influence on the discount.

> Please see Spreadsheet 33 for a working example of the calculation of a property company's net asset value, and triple net, net asset value, both current and prospective.

10.11.2   Real estate investment trusts (REIT)

A real estate investment trust (REIT) is a closed-end investment company that buys real estate properties or mortgages and passes virtually all the profits on to its shareholders. A minimum of 90% of funds from operations is required to be distributed. These properties can be apartments, shopping malls, office buildings or other acceptable real assets. The trust is subject to a number of constraints to which it must adhere in order to keep its tax-transparent status. These constraints may include, for example, no trading of properties, no pure development activities, gearing limits, limits on non-property income and anti-takeover provisions.

REIT-type structures, which are broadly similar to those of a company, are available in all the major economy counties (the G8 group) with the exception of the UK. The main difference lies in the regulations imposed on the directors, which need to be adhered to if the REIT is to maintain its tax-transparent status.

In 2004 the UK Government launched a consultation on the proposed introduction of a new form of property investment vehicle, which is effectively a REIT but is referred to as a 'property investment fund' (PIF). The consultation document was issued partly in response to concerns that the tax system might be contributing to distortions in the market for property investment, resulting in poor liquidity, barriers to entering the market and high debt financing levels. The Government hopes that the introduction of PIFs will lead to a more efficient and flexible property market that is accessible by the private sector and fair to all taxpayers, but at the same time will not reduce the overall tax revenue from the property investment market. The broad objective is to create a new property investment vehicle that offers after-tax returns more closely aligned to those achieved from holding property directly. When the introduction of a UK REIT was first mooted it was promoted as a possible solution to the lack of investment in new housing stock, but in reality it is the commercial property sector that is likely to pick up on REITS in the first instance.

To the investor, the advantage of a REIT is that there is no double taxation, so the tax charge relates to the tax position of the investor. REITs, unlike property companies, are normally not allowed to trade properties on or be developers and this, it is argued, will help their performance to track that of direct property more accurately.

10.11.3   Limited partnerships

Limited partnerships are tax-transparent vehicles which can be set up to invest in property. The partners are each taxable on their own share of the partnerships profits. The limited

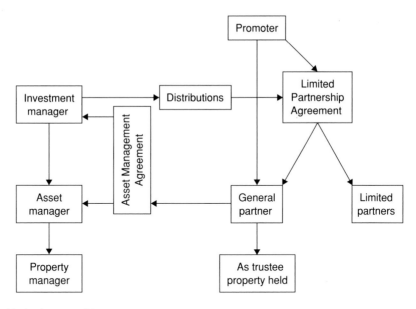

Fig. 10.12   Limited partnership structure.

partners each have a limited liability, capped at their investment in the partnership. In contrast, the general partner who manages the partnerships assets and the distributions has unlimited liability. Limited partnerships tend to have fixed investment lives, with seven years being a popular period. This fixed life helps counteract the inherent illiquidity of these vehicles. The tax position on a change of general partner or sale of limited partnership shares in the partnership may crystallise the contingent capital gains tax liabilities for all the partners. The structure of a limited partnership is shown in Fig. 10.12.

10.11.4   Open end funds

The two main forms of UK open end funds are property unit trusts and open ended investment funds or companies. They may in due course be stock market listed as an open ended investment company (OEIC) as in general terms their popularity is increasing.

The structure of a property unit trust is shown in Fig. 10.13. The structures can become more complicated, as is the case with a German open ended fund as shown in Fig. 10.14.

Property unit trusts are unauthorised efficient investment vehicles for tax-exempt investors, such as pension funds. Their structure is also utilised as a feeder fund for other tax-exempt investors, such as SIPPs for private individuals, to invest in vehicles like limited partnerships (for further details, see www.aput.co.uk). As they are unauthorised for inclusion on the stock markets, they can not be marketed directly to the public and are thus designed for professional investors and fund management groups. They are often structured such that they meet the needs of exempt investors (for example, pension funds) or smaller institutions seeking to gain diversified exposure to the property market.

Offshore property unit trusts have become increasingly popular. This structure allows exempt and non-exempt investors' investment funds to be pooled. The structure enjoys the

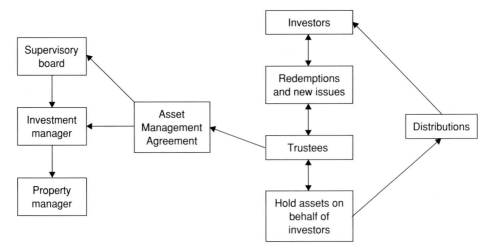

Fig. 10.13   Property unit trust structure.

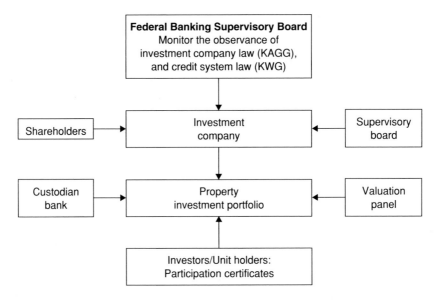

Fig. 10.14   German open ended fund structure.

benefits of non-resident status, such that tax liabilities are only triggered on the remittance of the profits back into the UK.

10.11.5   Private equity funds and other pooled vehicles

In addition to the vehicles detailed above, there exist a number of other financial mechanisms employing a variety of structures and geared to property investment. Of key importance will be their tax position; accordingly, many are set up as offshore funds.

Private equity funds are actively managed collective investment vehicles that can specialise in property. They invest almost exclusively in assets that are not publicly listed or traded or that will cease to be publicly traded after acquisition by way of a 'public to private' transaction. Many private equity funds are specific as to sector, size and/or location.

Another form of investment is via an opportunity fund which will be formed by a group of high net worth investors seeking high returns coming together to create the fund, usually via an investment bank or specialist property/fund management team acting on the fund's behalf. These opportunity funds have been noted for taking an aggressive stance towards the property market in recent years. They have sought returns of over 20% equity IRRs, through moving in at the bottom of a cycle, undertaking development opportunities and employing high gearing ratios.

10.11.6   Direct versus indirect property investment

Of key importance when investing in property vehicles is a consideration of the likely future performance. Many investors use indirect property investment (investing through vehicles) as a substitute for direct property investment. For many investors, it is important that the performance characteristics of indirect property investment vehicles at least track those of the direct property market.

Myer and Webb (1992) considered the performance of US real estate investment trusts and found that their performance was more akin to that of common stocks. But Myer and Webb also found that, by incorporating time lags into the REITs data series, the REITs index related, by 'Granger causation', to the direct property returns also measured by an index. Newell *et al.* (1997) found that, for the UK market, the FTSE property share index 'Granger caused' the IPD monthly property index but with a seven to nine month time lag.

10.11.7   Debt securitisation

The terms structured finance and securitisation are usually used interchangeably. The former is broader by definition and includes traditional asset backed securitisations, as well as the more creative and innovative financial and risk transfer techniques (Merrill Lynch, 2000). For property it is usually referred to as securitisation, but it must be borne in mind that property securitisation is only a small part of the large securitisation market.

In recent years securitisation has become increasingly important to the property sector. Its growth in popularity has been caused by the drop in interest rates such that medium and long bond yields became significantly less than the net initial income returns seen on commercial property. Investment banks spotted an arbitrage opportunity (see Chapter 12). Property cash flows were packaged up into bond-style cash flows and then sold into the bond markets, and in the process a substantial profit was made.

The debt securitisation market comprises both asset backed securities and mortgage-backed securities (see Fig. 10.15). Almost any asset type can be securitised if it meets a number of basic conditions. Merrill Lynch (2000) identified five key characteristics relating to debt securitisations:

- There will be a legal segregation between the assets and the securities.
- There needs to be an ability to have a bankruptcy issuing vehicle remote from management.

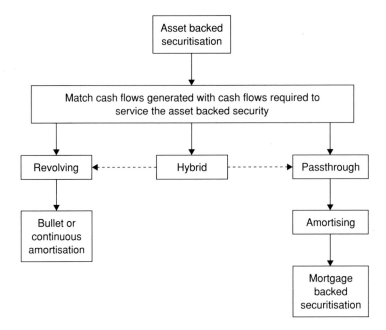

Fig. 10.15   Basic asset and mortgage backed structures.

- There must be no investor recourse to the asset originator in case of losses in the asset pool.
- The credit rating on senior notes must exceed the rating of asset originator.
- There will be higher yield and more protections for investors.

The main types of asset backed securitisation are set out in Fig. 10.16. This illustrates where mortgage backed securitisations (MBS) can fit in. MBS can also be secured on a pool of property mortgages, thus enabling banks to earn higher returns on the capital employed by in effect refinancing their loan books.

Thus the advantage with asset and mortgage backed securitisations is that a higher loan to value ratio can be achieved, to the significant benefit of the returns on equity. Two indicative structures of debt securitisations are set out in Figs 10.17 and 10.18.

For the originator, the main benefit of the securitisation is that it is a cost efficient method of off balance sheet financing. For the investor it gives wider portfolio exposure and diversification benefits, plus a 'yield pick-up'.

In the UK market British Land plc at Broadgate, London, and Canary Wharf plc at Canary Wharf in London Docklands have both launched large and successful debt securitisation issues. But the use of securitisation has not been restricted to major landmark developments. One sub-sector of the property market that has been particularly susceptible to securitisation has been the public house market which has found difficulty in attracting conventional finance due to the strong relationship between property values and the management quality of the operator.

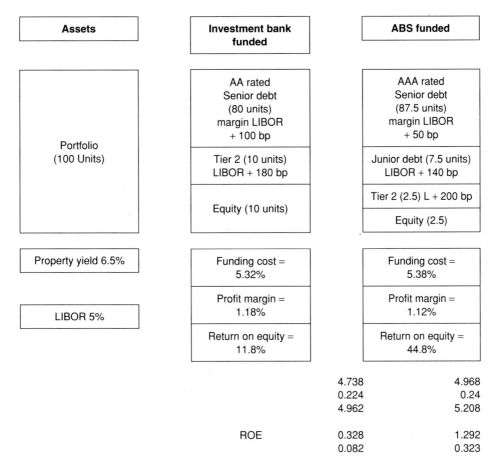

Assets	Investment bank funded	ABS funded
Portfolio (100 Units)	AA rated Senior debt (80 units) margin LIBOR + 100 bp	AAA rated Senior debt (87.5 units) margin LIBOR + 50 bp
	Tier 2 (10 units) LIBOR + 180 bp	Junior debt (7.5 units) LIBOR + 140 bp
	Equity (10 units)	Tier 2 (2.5) L + 200 bp
		Equity (2.5)
Property yield 6.5%	Funding cost = 5.32%	Funding cost = 5.38%
	Profit margin = 1.18%	Profit margin = 1.12%
LIBOR 5%	Return on equity = 11.8%	Return on equity = 44.8%

	4.738	4.968
	0.224	0.24
	4.962	5.208
ROE	0.328	1.292
	0.082	0.323

Fig. 10.16   Bank debt v. asset backed securitisation.

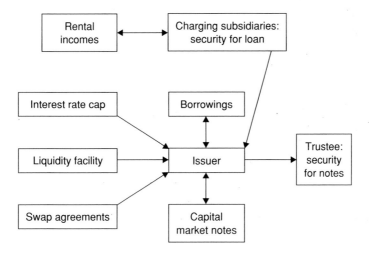

Fig. 10.17   A typical debt securitisation structure.

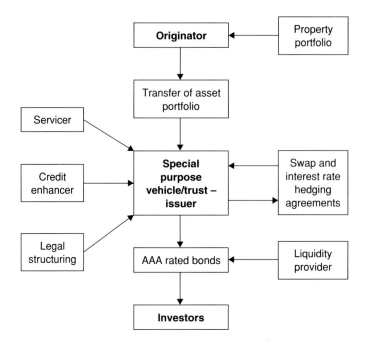

Fig. 10.18 Generic securitisation structure.

10.12 Summary

In this chapter we have explored a range of methods by which commercial property investments can be financed. An integral part of the process from the property analyst's point of
view is to undertake the DCF calculations and to put the resultant IRRs into a risk/return
context. For this activity the use of spreadsheets, and in particular Excel, is very important.

> Please see Spreadsheet 34 for a worked example of a number of useful Excel finance func-
> tions (PMT, IPMT, PPMT, Group Function, SUBTOTAL) that can be used in the analysis of
> geared investments.

However, the DCF calculations undertaken by property analysts should be considered
in the context of the investment vehicle being used by the investor: for example, the
management charges, transfer costs, exit strategy of the vehicle's fund manager, and the
tax position.

References

Adams, A. and Venmore-Rowland, P. (1990) Valuation of property company shares. *Journal of
   Property*, 8 (2): 127–42.
Adams, A. and Venmore-Rowland, P. (1991) Property investment vehicles. Journal *of Property
   Valuation*, 9 (4): 287–94.

DTZ Money Into Property and Jones Lang LaSalle (2003) *Corporate Finance*. London: JLL.

European Public Real Estate Association (2004) *Discounts to net asset value for European property companies*. Research Paper. www.epra.com

Gerbich, M., Levis, M. and Venmore-Rowland, P. (1995) Property investment public offerings. *Journal of Property Finance*, 6 (1): 38–54.

Gerbich, M., Levis, M. and Venmore-Rowland, P. (1999) Property investment and property development firm performance around IPO and rights offerings: UK evidence. *Journal of Real Estate Finance & Economics*, 2 (2): 207–38.

Holmes, G., Sugden, A. and Gee, P. (2005) *Interpreting Company Reports and Accounts*. Harlow: Financial Times/Prentice Hall.

Merrill Lynch (2000) *Introduction to Securitisation*. London: Merrill Lynch.

Myer, N. and Webb, J. (1992) Return properties of equity REITs, common stocks, and commercial real estate: a comparison. *Journal of Real Estate Research*, 8: 87–106.

Newell, G., Matysiak, G. and Venmore-Rowland, P. (1997) *Do Property Company Shares Perform in the Same Way as the Property Market?* London: RICS Foundation Publications.

Royal Institute of Chartered Surveyors (2003) *Appraisal and Valuation Standards*. London: RICS Foundation Publications.

Venmore-Rowland, P. (ed) (1995) *Property Securitisation*. Investment Property Forum Report.

Further reading

Stevenson, S. (2001) A re-examination of the inflation-hedging ability of real estate securities: empirical tests using international orthogonalized and hedged data. *International Real Estate Review*, 4 (1).

Venmore-Rowland, P. (1991) Direct versus indirect property investments. *Journal of Property Valuation*, 8 (3): 272–89.

11 Measuring return

Aims of the chapter

- To explain the requirement to measure investment performance.
- To introduce the concept of performance measurement.
- To discuss the nature and construction of property indices.
- To describe the role of investment benchmarks.
- To assess performance to benchmarks.
- To explain and detail common methods of return measurement.

11.1 Introduction

Performance measurement has become increasingly important in the property market as investors have become more sophisticated and demanding. Fund managers are expected to meet or exceed a specified benchmark on a regular basis. In order to facilitate calculations and comparisons of individual property and portfolio performance, common standards have evolved.

This chapter examines a number of methods used to calculate returns grouped under two main methodologies: money-weighted returns and time-weighted returns. Returns can be defined simply as the income and capital appreciation from an investment, expressed as a percentage of capital invested. Accordingly, total returns can be segmented into income returns and capital growth. Returns provide a consistent measure to assess the investment performance across the assets of an investor.

A distinction should be made between yields and returns. Generally yields are a ratio of current annual income from an investment expressed as a percentage of current value. Yields tend to be a 'snapshot' at a given moment in time. For instance, an initial yield on a property investment is the ratio of net annual income to gross capital value. Returns relate to income and capital gains over a specific period, such as a month or year. However, the distinction is blurred by yields such as redemption yields on bonds, which are the internal rate of return on a bond held to redemption at the current price.

11.2 Simple return

Simple return is a straightforward method used to calculate a return over a period. The formula below includes start and end period and market values plus cash flow over the period.

$$TR = \frac{EMV - BMV - CE + NI}{BMV}$$

Where: TR = total return expressed as a percentage
    BMV = beginning market value
    EMV = end market value
    CE = net capital expenditure
    NI = net revenue income

Despite the formula requiring inputs under different headings, the calculation is simply the amount 'made' or returned to the investor divided by the initial investment.

The cash flow could simply be the net cash flow over the period. However, for property investment, where cash outflows can be revenue expenditure against rental income or capital expenditure to enhance the capital value, it is helpful to distinguish between the cash flows. This allows the returns to be broken down into the income and capital gain components, as examined later.

Typically in the UK, revenue expenditure is considered to be those expenses incurred to keep the property income-producing such as management costs, ground rent payments, service charge shortfalls, rent review fees, letting fees, repairs and maintenance. Expenditure such as refurbishment, capital inducements and retentions is recorded as capital expenditure. There are differences between the categorisation of costs in different countries – for example, US practice is to define agents' letting fees (or leasing commissions) as a capital cost.

Accordingly, the cash flow is broken down into net revenue income and net capital expenditure, which could include the impact of sales and purchases as capital receipts or expenditure if calculating the return on a portfolio.

Example 11.1 uses the simple return formula to calculate an annual return for an example property.

Example 11.1

Consider a property with a start year market value of £100 000, an end year market value of £110 000, capital expenditure of £5000 and net revenue of £10 000 over the year.

$$\frac{110\ 000 - 100\ 000 - 5000 + 10\ 000}{100\ 000} = 15\%$$

Accordingly, the return is simply the net capital gain and net revenue expressed as a percentage of capital invested: £15 000 divided by £100 000.

The 15% total return is evidently composed of two components – the net revenue generated by the capital invested, and the net growth in capital. The contribution of these components can be simply calculated using the formulae below:

$$IR = \frac{NI}{BMV}$$

$$CR = \frac{EMV - BMV - CE}{BMV}$$

Where: IR = income return expressed as a percentage
    CR = capital return expressed as a percentage.

For the example property, the income return is 10% and the capital return is 5%, which sum to give a total return of 15%. The formulae above indicate why it is useful to differentiate between revenue costs that are incurred in maintaining the property's income flow and capital expenditure that is made to enhance capital value. If an all-inclusive net cash flow figure were used for the whole property, the income and capital components of total return would be rolled into one figure. Many investors adopt strategies that target properties that they expect to produce returns tilted towards either capital growth or high income (or a blend), so being able to break down the return into components indicates the style of return generated.

Returns are usually expressed as annual percentages. If a simple return is calculated for periods other than a year, the return can be annualised as follows:

$$TR_{Annualised} = (1 + TR_{Period})^{1/T} - 1$$

Where: $T =$ is period of return expressed as a multiple of a year

For example, a simple return calculated over a six month period will need to be compounded by two in the above formula, and a return over two years will need to be compounded by a half (or square-rooted). In all cases you have to add one to the return you are annualising before taking it to the required power and deduct one from the result to give the annualised return. Calculating returns from multiple periods is dealt with in section 11.4.

11.3 Money-weighted returns

This is the term given to calculations where the return is calculated as the income and gains expressed as a percentage of money employed in the investment over the period of analysis. The returns are said to be 'money-weighted' because periods in which more capital is employed in the investment contribute more to overall returns. Each unit invested is assumed to grow at a constant rate of return over the analysis period. This rate of return is referred to as an internal rate of return (IRR).

Although the calculation of money-weighted returns can be tedious if carried out by hand, the principle of the calculation is simple: the internal rate of return is the rate of interest that discounts all future income/expenditure and capital appreciation from an investment to equal the initial value over the period of analysis. Most spreadsheet packages have built in IRR functions that calculate money-weighted returns and this speeds up calculations greatly.

To calculate an IRR you need to produce a cash flow that poses the question of how frequent the 'stops' are (the points in time where the cash inflow/outflows are positioned): for example, inflows will be the points at which rent is collected. Using spreadsheets makes the actual calculation simple so the limitation on the period between the stops will be decided by the frequency of the input data for the investment. However, if you were calculating the IRR using a calculator or present value tables and interpolation then a quarterly cash flow is likely to be sufficient for a property investment.

The cash flow in Fig. 11.1 has been calculated in Microsoft Excel using the details of the property in Example 11.1. This is very simplistic in that it has two stops – the start and end

Years	Capital Value	Capital Exp	Net Income	Cash Flow
0	100,000			−100,000
1	110,000	5,000	10,000	115,000
			Total IRR	15.0%

Fig. 11.1   Calculating the IRR of a simple cash flow, discounting on an annual basis.

Years	Capital Value	Capital Exp	Net Income	Cash Flow
0.00	100,000		2,500	−97,500
0.25			2,500	2,500
0.50			2,500	2,500
0.75			2,500	2,500
1.00	110,000	5,000		105,000
			Total IRR	16.0%

Fig. 11.2   Calculating the IRR of a simple cash flow, discounting on a quarterly basis.

of a year. Excel's built in IRR function can be used to calculate the IRR. As can be seen, the start value is shown as a negative under the cash flow heading as this is the capital employed at the start of the year (the purchase price that would have to be paid to acquire the investment). The total return for this cash flow is 15% – the same as the result from the simple return we calculated over a period of a year.

From a property perspective, rents are usually collected in advance of the period for which they are due. Most UK commercial leases specify quarterly in advance and the flexibility of an IRR calculation allows the cash flow to be set up to better reflect the actual timings of the cash flow. Fig. 11.2 uses the same details but assumes that the rent is received quarterly in advance while the capital expenditure is still made in one payment at the end of the year.

Note that Excel's IRR function assumes that cash flows are at the end of each year so the result needs to be compounded by four periods using the annualised return formula. The solution (that is, the internal rate of return) is calculated as shown in the following equation.

$$= (1 + IRR\ (E2{:}E6))\wedge 4 - 1$$

where range E2:E6 is the cash flow assuming Figure 11.2 was entered into a spreadsheet with Years in cell 1, etc.

The resulting total return indicates that receiving the income quarterly in advance increases the total return by 1%. This increase reflects the fact that the rent collected will offset the capital employed thereby increasing the return on capital, or that it can be reinvested elsewhere. (This issue is examined in more detail later.)

The cash flow can be modified to calculate income return and capital growth. However, such calculations can produce anomalies and these are examined below.

To calculate income return, the effect of capital gains or losses needs to be removed from the cash flow. In Fig. 11.3 the end capital value is the sum of the initial value plus capital expenditure, instead of the final capital value as in the total return example.

Calculation of capital growth return can simply be calculated by subtracting the income return from the total return, which for this example equals 5.3%. This result can be

Years	Capital Value	Capital Exp	Net Income	Cash Flow
0.00	100,000		2,500	–97,500
0.25			2,500	2,500
0.50			2,500	2,500
0.75			2,500	2,500
1.00	105,000	5,000		100,000
			Income IRR	10.7%

Fig. 11.3   Calculating the income return of a simple cash flow.

Years	Capital Value	Capital Exp	Net Income	Cash Flow
0.00	100,000		2,500	–97,500
0.25			2,500	2,500
0.50			2,500	2,500
0.75			2,500	2,500
1.00	110,000	5,000	–10,000	95,000
			Capital IRR	5.3%

Fig. 11.4   Calculating the capital growth return of a simple cash flow.

calculated as shown in Fig. 11.4. Here, the reduction in capital employed due to the receipt of rent is reflected by including net income through the cash flow. Total rent collected through the year is then deducted from the final capital value so the net rent received through the year is zero.

It should be noted that the capital growth is the growth in capital expressed as a *percentage* of the capital employed through the year. This is in contrast to the simple return result which was just the net increase in capital value divided through by the start of period capital value. It recognises that the capital employed over the total measurement period may change.

However, this approach does not give consistent results. As the length of the cash flow grows, so does the discrepancy between the capital growth calculated and the difference between the total return and income return. This results from the interaction between income and capital compounding in the cash flow.

A different approach could just use the capital elements of the cash flow and ignore the income offsetting capital. This would show a result of 5% – the same as the simple return. This still will not reconcile the capital growth and income return components consistently over different cash flows. Accordingly, a simple solution could be to use the difference between the income return and total return as the capital growth.

IRR calculations have further shortcomings:

- On a theoretical level, the calculation assumes that income is reinvested at the IRR. In practice, the income will be invested or employed elsewhere at a different rate of return. Modified internal rate of return approaches that include reinvestment and financing rates can be used to address this issue, although in most cases these will be considered too complex and the standard methodology will be acceptable.
- On a practical level, cash flows that include inflows and outflows can occasionally produce more than one IRR solution: there is more than one rate that can equate the

Years	Capital Value	Capital Exp	Net Income	Cash Flow
1.00	100,000		0	−100,000
2.00			50,000	50,000
3.00			120,000	120,000
4.00			140,000	140,000
5.00	100,000	350,000	30,000	−220,000
			Total IRR 1	11.4%
			Total IRR 2	19.6%

Fig. 11.5   A cash flow that produces multiple IRR solutions.

discounted cash flow with the initial value. Software such as Excel has the option to specify a 'guess' rate and will provide the answer closest to the guess. Fig. 11.5 shows a cash flow with multiple answers.

11.4   Time-weighted returns

Prior to the 1970s, most money managers used money-weighted IRR calculations to present their performance (see, for example, Spaulding 1997:19). However, there are shortcomings to this approach: fund managers will not usually have control of contributions and withdrawals by their clients. Accordingly, time-weighted returns address this by neutralising the weight of capital invested and instead take into account the period for which the capital is invested.

In 1968 the Banking Administration Institute (BAI) introduced a calculation standard that advocated the use of linked IRRs over sub-periods to reduce the money weighting issue (BAI, 1968). However, before the widespread use of computers the calculation of IRRs was a long-winded procedure, so simpler methods were adopted that calculated the return by formula instead of by an iterative process. These formula methods of calculation are now used extensively by performance measurement providers such as the Investment Property Databank (IPD) and the WM Company.

The ideal time-weighted return is produced by calculating a simple return for each period between cash flows. Each period's return is then compounded (often referred to as 'chain linking') to give the total return for the period analysed, say a year. This is shown in the formula below.

$$TR_A = (1 + TR_1) \times (1 + TR_2) \times \ldots \times (1 + TR_T)$$

Where: TR_A = annual total return expressed as a percentage
     1 to T = periods representing the interval between cash flows summing to one year

It should be noted that returns can also be summed instead of compounded if it is assumed that capital appreciation and income are not reinvested at each measurement point.

This makes for an increasingly complicated calculation as the investment has to be re-valued every time there is a cash inflow or outflow. This is not feasible for a property where valuations are only provided on a periodic basis. Accordingly, approaches have been developed that make an approximation as to the timing of cash flows between valuations.

To place expenditure and receipts at either the start or end of a period is straightforward and involves changing the denominator of the calculation. The denominator is the capital employed over the period for which the return is being calculated. If money is received at the start of the period, it is simply subtracted from the beginning market value; if it is paid, it is added. Conversely, if it received or paid at the end, no adjustment is made to the denominator.

The formula below is the simple return formula modified to reflect capital expenditure being incurred at the start of each period.

$$TR = \frac{EMV - BMV - CE + NI}{BMV + CE}$$

Where: TR = total return expressed as a percentage over the period
       BMV = market value at the start of the period
       EMV = market value at the end of the period
       CE = capital expenditure
       NI = net revenue income

In this formula, as capital expenditure is made at the start of the period, it is added to the capital employed for the whole period.

The most widely used approximation for timing is referred to as the Dietz method (Kirschmann and Dietz, 1983). The Dietz method formula makes the assumption that all cash flows through the period of analysis occur at the mid-point of the period. An alternative interpretation is that income and expenditure are continuously accrued through the period of the calculation. This is achieved by adjusting the denominator by half of the cash flow in the period, thereby adjusting the capital employed by cash inflows or out-flows. If the investment has generated income through the period then the denominator will be reduced by half of the net income, thereby giving a higher return due to the reduction of capital employed as it is offset by income collected.

The Dietz method formula below has the capital expenditure and net income elements stated separately for application to property. Returns for part periods of a year can be chain linked to calculate annual returns.

$$TR = \frac{EMV - BMV - CE + NI}{BMV + \frac{1}{2}CE - \frac{1}{2}NI}$$

This formula can be changed to deal with income return by removing the market values and capital components from the numerator. For capital return, the net revenue income term should be removed from the numerator. If the income return and capital return/ growth are chain linked for multiple periods, their sum may not come to exactly the same figure as the total return. This is due to the cross product of income and capital compounding in the total return calculation.

To allow for a more accurate reflection of the timing of cash flows, the modified Dietz method can be used (Kirschmann and Dietz, 1983). This method weights the return on each cash flow by the time it is employed in the investment and assumes a constant rate of return over the period analysed. It is given by the formula below.

$$TR = \frac{EMV - BMV - \Sigma CE + \Sigma NI}{BMV + \Sigma(CE \times w) - \Sigma(NI \times w)}$$

Where: $w = \dfrac{T - t}{T}$

$\qquad$ T = total number of days in the period

$\qquad$ t = number of days since the beginning of the period T in which cash flow t occurred

To illustrate the calculation of w, a cash flow made on 3 October will give a w of 0.9 (that is, $(31 - 3)/31$) when included in the calculation for the month of October. In the denominator, the Σ symbol denotes that each individual day dated item of capital expenditure and revenue income once multiplied by w should be summed and the total used in the formula.

The practical application of the modified Dietz method is best shown in an example, as follows.

Example 11.2

Use the assumptions from Fig. 11.2. These are a start value of £100 000, an end value of £110 000, capital expenditure incurred at the year end of £5000 and net income of £10 000 per annum received quarterly in advance. For simplification, a quarterly valuation frequency will be used with each period's return chain linked as shown.

The property value is assumed to rise on a linear or straight line basis through the year.

$$TR_{Q1} = \frac{102\,500 - 100\,000 + 2500}{100\,000 - (2500 \times 1)} = 5.1\%$$

$$TR_{Q2} = \frac{105\,000 - 102\,500 + 2500}{102\,500 - (2500 \times 1)} = 5.0\%$$

$$TR_{Q3} = \frac{107\,500 - 105\,000 + 2500}{105\,000 - (2500 \times 1)} = 4.9\%$$

$$TR_{Q4} = \frac{110\,000 - 107\,500 - 5000 + 2500}{107\,500 + (5000 \times 0) - (2500 \times 1)} = 0.0\%$$

$$TR_{YEAR} = (1 + 0.051) \times (1 + 0.050) \times (1 + 0.049) \times (1 + 0.000) = 15.8\%$$

Note that each quarter's return would need to be annualised to compare on a like for like basis to the annual return. For example, Quarter 2's return of 5.0% would produce an annualised return of 21.55%.

The total return in Example 11.2 is slightly lower than that calculated by the money-weighted calculation over the period of a year (Fig. 11.2). This is mainly due to the return reducing as the capital employed increases quarter by quarter with the growth in capital value, while the net income remains constant. As the period of analysis increases, the

Years	Property 1 Capital Value	Capital Exp	Net Income	Property 2 Capital Value	Capital Exp	Net Income	Cash Flow
0.00	100,000		2,500				−97,500
0.25			2,500				2,500
0.50			2,500				2,500
0.75			2,500				2,500
1.00		5,000	2,500	110,000		2,500	−110,000
1.25			2,500			2,500	5,000
1.50			2,500			2,500	5,000
1.75			2,500			2,500	5,000
2.00	140,000			140,000			280,000

	Total IRR	30.1%
	Total Modified Dietz	26.6%

Fig. 11.6   Calculations of returns showing variations produced by using both money-weighted and time-weighted return bases.

results from time-weighted and money-weighted returns may increasingly diverge, especially if cash inflows and outflows occur. This divergence provides a measure of the impact of investment timing.

To illustrate, consider that, after holding our example property for a year, a second identical property was bought and that in the second year capital values grew strongly so that each property was worth £140 000 by the year end (Fig. 11.6). We assume that capital values again rise through each year on a straight line basis and no transaction costs were incurred.

The answers indicate that on a money-weighted basis the total return of 30.1% was 3.5% better than on a time-weighted basis. Neither answer is wrong, but they have a different interpretation. For an investor who has discretion over when to invest and is actively seeking to identify times when the market offers the best value, the money-weighted return is a more representative reflection of performance. However, for fund managers who have to invest the funds that they have been allocated into the market, the time-weighted return is more representative as it reflects the performance of the stock selected.

11.5   Aggregation of individual assets' returns

When returns are aggregated over a portfolio of investments, a decision needs to be taken as to how the individual components should be weighted together. There are two basic choices:

- *Equal-weighted return*: the composite return is calculated as the mean average return across individual assets. This is simple to calculate but of limited use. An example of its use would be analysing performance associated with characteristics of individual properties, for instance multi- or single-let properties. Here you would not want the total return for each group weighted by each component's value as this would distort the comparison: one extreme return to a large property in each group could have a large impact on results.
- *Value-weighted return*: this is the most common method where the composite return is calculated as the capital weighted sum of individual returns. The easiest way to calculate

Property	A	B	C	Total
Start value	1000	800	1900	3700
End value	1050	750	2000	3800
Day				
6	50		200	250
20		−100		−100
29	−20		−80	−100
Total	30	−100	120	50
Total days = 30				
Day weight				0
0.80	40	0	160	200
0.33	0	−33	0	−33
0.03	−1	0	−3	−3
Total	39	−33	157	163
Mod Dietz R1n	8.3%	−18.0%	12.6%	4.2%
Equal weights	0.33	0.33	0.33	1.0%
Start value	1000	800	1900	4.8%
Adj start value	961	833	1743	4.2%

Fig. 11.7   Calculating value-weighted returns.

this is to total each investment's values and cash flow as shown in Fig. 11.7 in the column headed 'Total'. The composite total return for the portfolio over the period is 4.2%.

The shaded rows in Fig. 11.7 show three ways of aggregating returns from individual assets into the portfolio return. The first way is by equal weighting which we have outlined above. The second is by start value. Using the start value will give the wrong answer if there have been any cash flows through the period. Using the end value will also give the wrong answer as this will skew the returns result towards assets that had the strongest capital growth. The best answer is to adjust the start value by the time-weighted cash flows (that is, weight each individual return by the denominator of its modified Dietz method calculation).

Aggregation of the original Dietz method formula is simpler than Fig. 11.7 as the cash flows are all weighted by half their value so the calculation does not need to factor in the true timing.

For IRR calculations, a value-weighted method can be used if the IRRs from each individual asset are for the same time period. However, this method will only ever give an approximation. A better and more flexible approach is to combine the cash flows to produce an overall multi-asset or portfolio IRR.

11.6   Further return calculation issues

11.6.1   Inputs – accruals and costs

There are two basic ways of accounting for cash inflows and outflows to an investment: the cash method and the accruals method.

The cash method is the simplest and records the inflow or outflow on the date that it occurred. This is commonly used in IRR calculations as they reflect the timing of payments and receipts within the calculation. Also, they have the benefit of being able to use functions built into spreadsheet packages, such as the XIRR function in Microsoft Excel, that produce results based on the day cash inflows or outflows are made. Alternatively, periodic stops can be used and income for the preceding period combined into one figure at the stop.

A further consideration is whether to time the cash flows to the dates when they occur or the dates when they are due. It is usual practice to record rents when they are 'receivable' as opposed to when they are 'received', although if a tenant defaults where rents are recorded on a receivable basis the rents the tenant has failed to pay will need to be written off at some point.

Time-weighted returns are calculated using accrual accounting where income during a period is matched against expenses. This method gives a more accurate picture than the cash method if the analysis periods are short, say monthly. A practical example is rent which, although likely to be paid quarterly in advance, is accrued to the months to which it relates. Quarterly rent paid on the 29 September would be split by day into two days in September, 31 days in October, 30 days in November and 24 days in December up to the quarter day on 25 December. This smoothes out the rental income through the year, which would otherwise spike in quarter months. One-off costs are recorded against the period they relate to, but costs such as utilities will be accrued across periods. Accordingly, you record income when it is truly earned, and you record expenses when they are incurred and not necessarily when paid.

11.6.2 Portfolio returns

As shown earlier, returns from individual assets can be aggregated into a portfolio. However, just combining the returns from the assets may overstate the true return to the portfolio as by so doing costs incurred that are not apportioned to individual assets are excluded. Examples of such costs are legal fees incurred on abortive purchases, portfolio valuation fees and fund management fees.

In determining which fees to deduct it is important to consider the purpose of the portfolio return calculation that is being undertaken. For instance, if the calculation is for comparison to a market index or benchmark, the assumptions used to calculate the index or benchmark will need to be known to allow a fair 'apples with apples' comparison.

It is often the case that published returns indices do not include transactions (see below) and do not reflect portfolio level costs apart from an allowance for basic property manage-ment. In the case where fund management fees include property management services, the return measurer may deduct default fees from rents to provide a comparison between the performance of the underlying assets in each portfolio, excluding the impact of varying levels of fund manager fees.

11.6.3 Real returns

This chapter has examined calculating nominal rates of return that do not allow for the impact of price inflation over the period of the return. Investors whose liabilities are denominated in real terms, such as defined benefit pension funds whose liabilities grow with wage inflation, will be interested in what returns they achieve after the deduction of inflation.

Calculating real returns is simple for time-weighted rates of return as the return figure calculated can have inflation for the corresponding period deducted using the formula below:

$$RTR = \frac{(1 + NTR)}{(1 + I)} - 1$$

Where: NTR = nominal total return expressed as a percentage over the period
     I = inflation rate expressed as a percentage over the period
     RTR = real total return expressed as a percentage over the period

The periodic real returns calculated can be chain linked together for calculating the real return over longer periods.

For money-weighted rates of return calculated over periods longer than a year, it is more accurate to either deflate each item or stop in the cash flow by the rate of inflation from the cash flow start. The exception to this is where a constant rate of inflation over the whole cash flow is used and the formula above can be used to calculate the real return.

11.6.4   Geared returns

Borrowed funds are often used by property investors to purchase assets. This is referred to as gearing in the UK and leverage in the US.

At the start of this chapter, returns were defined as the revenue income and capital appreciation from an investment expressed as a percentage of capital invested. If borrowed funds are used to purchase a property then the capital invested by the investor (equity) will be less than the market value and associated purchase costs of the asset at purchase. Of course, they will also have to service the interest costs and any amortisation of the debt from the income.

Accordingly, the return to an investor will be increased or decreased due to the gearing, depending on the movements in the value and income from the property.

Example 11.3

Using the details of the property in Example 11.1, with a start year capital value of £100 000, an end year capital value of £110 000, capital expenditure of £5000 and net income of £10 000 over the year we can calculate a geared return (see Fig. 11.8). It is assumed that a 50% loan to value ratio with interest only paid on the debt and an interest rate of 7% is agreed with the lender. The simple return formula is used to calculate the return, with interest charged deducted from income (numerator) and debt outstanding deducted from the capital employed (denominator). Acquisition fees and any debt arrangement fees have been ignored.

	Ungeared return	Geared return
Value at start	£100 000	£100 000
Borrowing	£0	£50 000
Equity invested	**£100 000**	**£50 000**
Gross income	£10 000	£10 000
Interest charges	£0	£3500
Net income	**£10 000**	**£6500**
Value at end	£110 000	£110 000
Borrowing	£0	£50 000
Equity invested	**£110 000**	**£60 000**
Total return	**20.0%**	**33.0%**

Fig. 11.8 Calculating a geared return.

	Ungeared return	Geared return
Value at start	£100 000	£100 000
Borrowing	£0	£50 000
Equity invested	**£100 000**	**£50 000**
Gross income	£10 000	£10 000
Interest charges	£0	£3500
Net income	**£10 000**	**£6500**
Value at end	£90 000	£90 000
Borrowing	£0	£50 000
Equity invested	**£90 000**	**£40 000**
Total return	**0.0%**	**-7.0%**

Fig. 11.9 Calculating a geared return demonstrating the risks involved of borrowing.

Gearing in this example has added 13% to the annual return, as the income return and the capital growth are both based on an initial equity investment of £50 000 instead of £100 000.

While gearing improves returns when capital growth and income exceed the cost of servicing the debt, it can significantly reduce returns when values fall, rents fall or interest rates rise as shown in the example with an assumed £10 000 fall in values over the year (see Fig. 11.9). Accordingly, taking on debt can be seen to increase the risk of an investment.

For a money-weighted return calculation, the calculation is simple. If the debt financing straddles the period of analysis then the debt outstanding can be deducted from the start and end valuation, with interest deducted from the intervening income. Alternatively, the points at which debt is drawn down and repaid can be treated as income and expenditure. Interest is simply a periodic deduction, with interest on commercial loans generally paid quarterly in arrears in the UK.

Using the inputs from Example 11.3, Fig. 11.10 shows the IRR on an ungeared and geared basis assuming rents are received in advance and interest paid in arrears. Note that the quarterly interest rate is the annual rate divided by four as opposed to the compounded fourth root of the interest rate – this is normal market practice. By allowing for rent payments in advance each quarter plus interest payments in arrears, the IRR calculation produces an additional 3.5% return over and above the simple return calculation. Also note that market indices such as the IPD Annual Index do not include the effect of gearing and it is assumed that the return on each asset is based on a 100% equity interest.

					Cash Flows	
Years	Capital Value	Net Income	Debt	Interest	Ungeared	Geared
0.00	100,000	2,500	50,000		−97,500	−47,500
0.25		2,500		875	2,500	1,625
0.50		2,500		875	2,500	1,625
0.75		2,500		875	2,500	1,625
1.00	110,000		−50,000	875	110,000	59,125
				IRR	21.3%	36.5%

Fig. 11.10   Calculations of an IRR on a quarterly basis showing both geared and ungeared calculations.

11.6.5   Industry standards

In the UK and Continental Europe, the Investment Property Databank (IPD) is the leading supplier of property investment performance indices and property performance analysis services to investors. IPD's methods are generally recognised as the industry standard.

Since December 2001, IPD have adopted a time-weighted return methodology using a monthly frequency to calculate all their returns for UK property investments. Although this had always been used for their monthly index, their annual returns had previously been based on a single calculation for the whole year using the Dietz method formula. For periods longer than one year, the results were compounded to give a time-weighted rate of return. IPD implemented the monthly time-weighted methodology across all the national markets that they cover for the year to December 2004 and have recalculated historic returns on the same basis.

Of course, IPD's method requires monthly valuations. The most common frequencies of valuations for investment property are annual and quarterly, so IPD extrapolate the intervening valuations using the most appropriate monthly index of capital value movement for the type of property being measured. In practice, unless values have risen dramatically and then fallen back to their original level or vice versa, assuming values changed on a straight line basis between valuations will not give a materially different answer.

Across all asset classes, the Global Investment Performance Standards (GIPS) published by the Chartered Financial Analyst Institute (formerly known as the Association for Investment Management and Research) are voluntary standards by which firms calculate and present investment performance to clients and prospective clients (CFAI, 1999).

The GIPS standards are based on the underlying principles of fair representation and full disclosure. By providing a consistent basis for calculation, they allow a fair comparison of returns generated between investment advisory firms. The GIPS standards requires a time-weighted rate of return using a valuation frequency at least monthly. They accept the use of daily approximation methods such as the modified Dietz method, although a proposed higher 'gold' GIPS standard in draft form may require a true time-weighted return. Accrual accounting must be used for income and expenditure and cash held by funds must be included in the calculation as this can dilute the return. Non-reclaimable withholding taxes are also included.

For real estate it is not practical for all investors to have monthly revaluations so annual valuations are acceptable, but if these are produced in-house there must be an external valuation every 36 months. From 2008, this standard will be quarterly valuations with an external valuation annually (CFAI, 2003). The source of the valuation, the manager's discretion over funds to invest and the calculation methodology need to be disclosed with the results.

Real estate returns should also be split into capital and income return. It is recommended to include a since inception IRR (money-weighted return). Where the manager has discretion over the timing of investor capital call tranches, it is recommended that an MWR and TWR since inception is reported based on the terminal value as the current market value and the book cost (excluding unrealised gains/loses), and on a net and gross of fees basis. Where an IRR is used, it should have at least quarterly cash flow aggregations.

11.7   Indices and return

11.7.1   Background

Indices provide a way of recording performance data through time. Using a base of 100 at a given point in time, an index records the compound growth or return of a variable such as consumer prices or the stock market. Indices provide a method of comparison irrespective of the units in which the underlying variable is measured.

Using the quarterly returns calculated in Example 11.2, Fig. 11.11 shows an index of total return for this property on a quarterly basis. Time zero is taken as the base point and given the value of 100. The index is then calculated by compounding the index value at the start of each period by the return during the period.

The return over any period can be calculated by dividing the end of period index number by the start of period index number and subtracting one to find the percentage change. This figure can be annualised if required, as explained earlier in this chapter. Given that the information in the index is the ratio between index numbers, the absolute values are not important and the base year could be any value. The value 100 is selected as it is easy to interpret results relative to this figure; for instance, in Fig. 11.11 it is easy to see that the growth over the year to 115.8 equates to a 15.8% return.

Indices are often rebased with a new point allocated as 100 to make the updated index easier to interpret. This has happened a number of times with the UK Retail Price Index and, while the index numbers change, the ratio between points remains the same. Indices such as the FTSE 100 are not rebased as their index numbers are quoted and their absolute level is used as a yardstick of the state of the market. However, it should be noted that a 100 point jump in the index translates to a different percentage change depending on the level of index.

Time	Index Start of Period	Total Return over Period	Index End of Period	Index
0.00	100.0	5.1%	105.1	100.0
0.25	105.1	5.0%	110.4	105.1
0.50	110.4	4.9%	115.8	110.4
0.75	115.8	0.0%	115.8	115.8
1.00				115.8

Fig. 11.11   An index of total return calculated on a quarterly basis.

Published market indices for total returns usually ignore transactions. For the FTSE 100, this is purely the capital growth or total return, should you hold a portfolio of all the 100 stocks in the same proportion to their market capitalisations. It ignores any trading costs. Similarly, property indices such as the IPD Annual Index ignore trading and instead record the return of what are defined as 'standing investments' (those properties held and not bought or sold between points in the index). For this reason, published indices do not make suitable performance benchmarks as most property investors trade to some degree. Organisations like IPD do produce indices that include the impact of trading on the returns of the portfolios that contribute to their 'universe' or index portfolio, but these are not usually available to the public and are only provided to clients. This issue is examined in more detail later in the chapter.

11.7.2   Property indices

While indices of capital growth and total return have existed for the equity and bond markets for many years, property indices are a relatively recent development. It was during the 1970s that early attempts were made by some of the larger firms of property consultants to compile their own indices. However, it was the creation of the IPD Index and its rise to prominence in the 1980s that has provided investors for the first time with anything approaching a reliable index. Although the setting up of IPD marked an enormous step forward, the question of the reliability of indices and whether they properly reflect the underlying movements of the property market has been aired on a theoretical basis and the mathematical problems highlighted (Brown and Matysiak, 1995, 1997; Brown, 2001) as discussed below.

The rise of interest in indices mirrors the rise of institutional involvement with property, and all the major indices track property that is held in institutional portfolios. The IPD Index is the biggest sample in the UK and includes a large number of property companies and unitised funds together with institutional funds.

One of the main drivers behind both the development of, and continued debate surrounding, property indices lies in the fact that property is competing against other investment media as a home for financial funds. Therefore it is driven by the need to understand, compare and monitor performance. Property indices must be viewed in comparison with other financial indices, if for no other reason than that they are produced primarily to enable comparison to be made with other media. For indices to have value to the user they must be based on reliable data – and this normally implies a large sample. With shares this is quite possible, but even here the index of top 100 shares can become quite quickly at variance with the results obtained from the all-share index. Therefore whenever the results of an index are examined it must be in the context of its data source.

Property investment indices are used:

- for performance evaluation;
- as an indication for market movements;
- for comparison, both nationally and internationally and across sectors;
- to inform and thus influence both the purchase/sell decisions and the setting of investment objectives; and

- for the execution of many valuations and investment worth calculations, particularly if the valuation is undertaken by equated yield models where the level of return indicated by the indices may provide guidance in the establishment of investor hurdle rates.

It follows that valuers, investors and property advisers use indices either explicitly or implicitly. Morrell (1995:8) argues that due to their technical nature they seem 'far removed from the work of the investment surveyor. Property indices are therefore often poorly understood.'

Within the general financial markets, the movement of indices is critical in its effect on market sentiment – and can be a major contributor to volatility in performance – as markets react to movements of the index.

11.7.3   Types of property indices

Within the equity markets it is the share price indices that are the most important, and they are constantly updated. Within the property market there is simply not the same level of transparency.

Within the property markets the indices are usually either:

- rental growth; or
- capital growth; or
- total return.

Most indices are aggregated using a notional or actual portfolio that is supposed to be representative of the market. However, they may also be dis-aggregated by:

- sector (shop, office, industrial); and/or
- sub-sector (shopping centres, standard shops, retail warehousing); and/or
- location (south-east, central London, Greater London).

It is interesting to note that early attempts to build up indices on an international level met with very little success, due primarily to a paucity of data and lack of institutional interest to drive and populate the index. However, the situation has now changed and many European-based indices have commenced within recent years.

Early indices tended to be concentrated on rental values – for which most evidence has been available – but overall returns now tend to feature. Few indices outside the major commercial sectors exist apart from house prices, which are tracked by different organisations. Within the UK, indices are generally of commercial property.

11.7.4   Major property indices

IPD produce separate monthly and annual indices and together these form probably the most comprehensive property database in the world. The technical calculation of the index is a time-series of chain linked time-weighted returns for their constituent portfolios. It is valuation driven as opposed to price driven, which is possible for quoted markets such as equities and bonds.

The composition of the IPD index has been a matter of debate over the years, as has the base date, and some years ago there was a lively discussion as to whether its composition should be frozen so that as new funds joined the service their historic returns did not change the index results back through time. The IPD sample portfolio contains data on a very large number of portfolios and in this way it can claim to be a representative index. However, the sample portfolio is heavily skewed in terms of value to London and the south-east of England, reflecting the regional spread of institutional portfolios. It is therefore not representative of the UK commercial property market as a whole but rather of the regions where large investors are active and hold stock. For small property investors in provincial locations, there is little incentive to pay IPD to measure the performance of their holdings.

The composition therefore reflects the investment sentiment of investors, so it is dominated by the conventional industrial, retail and offices sectors. Attempts by IPD to set up a public houses index were made in the mid-1990s but abandoned. Although some leisure sits in the index, it cannot be separately disaggregated as the value and number of the units held in these categories are still small. However, IPD have been running an index of historic (listed) properties and this has yielded some interesting results. In particular, such properties tend to be more volatile in terms of their return characteristics.

The number of firms providing valuations that are incorporated in the index at any one time is small. Therefore there is a danger that any one firm can have a significant impact on movements in the sample portfolio.

It is misleading to refer to *the* IPD index. As stated above, over recent years this has developed into a family of indices, so there now exists the annual and the monthly index. There are important differences between the indices in terms of their composition. The funds that contribute to the monthly index are only those where valuers undertake monthly valuations, such as unitised funds. The annual index is the bigger index, and may be regarded as more representative. However, the time lag and valuation inefficiencies mean that the annual index is not sufficiently sensitive for many investors' use.

Another issue for the index is that of bias: the index is driven by valuations, not prices. Therefore when a property is to be sold it has to be removed from the index as it is based on standing investments. These technical issues can create internal issues of accuracy.

Other well-known indices are published by the following firms:

- Jones Lang LaSalle
- CB Richard Ellis.

Each is based on a different composition and the base dates, method of computation and presentation also vary. This makes comparison very difficult (see, for example, Morrell, 1995; Turner and Thomas, 2001a,b). Some smaller specialist indices also exist, with firms such as Christie and Co. and Fleurets maintaining indices in relation to hotels and public houses, but these are not widely disseminated.

11.7.5   Index composition

In constructing an index various bases can be used, as described below.

Sample based

With sample-based direct property indices, actual valuations are used. They rely therefore on adequate numbers of valuations and accuracy in the valuation process. It is also important that a coherent balance between types of property is maintained.

The critical issue is the overall size of the index and particularly its size at the sub-sector level. This must be sufficient to ensure that non-systematic risk items can be excluded for the reason that the index needs to take account of issues such as:

- properties undergoing active management;
- voids;
- recent and proposed transactions.

With sample-based indices the time-lag problem is very real, and hence there has been a call to develop a 'real time' index to emulate the stock market index (Fisher, 2002).

Notional or hypothetical based

With these indices it is general market movement that is monitored instead of individual asset value movement. Accuracy may therefore be hard either to prove or disprove.

The concept behind such indices is to take valuations at current rental levels and the yields of a hypothetical property. Hence the problems of ageing stock are overcome and effectively the index reflects the movements of prime rents and prime yields or new fully let top grade stock. Turner and Thomas (2001a,b) argue that the effect of this is to constantly 'overegg' possible investor returns, as no-one can invest in such a moving portfolio. The reality is that properties become reversionary and age!

Transaction based

By definition such indices contain a constantly changing base. They are generally used for house prices where the number of transactions is (normally) large and where no firm rental information is available. Christie and Co. also use transactions as the basis of their public houses index.

It is of course also the basis on which the equity indices work. However, in the case of the equities markets the transaction volume is significant and large, and there is a homogeneous product that is traded over time. This is certainly not the case for property. Only if hedonic pricing models can be perfected is there any realistic prospect of a representative transaction-based index for property emerging – and even then the level of transactions is likely to be simply too small.

11.7.6   Problems associated with property indices

Size of portfolio

If the index is to be meaningful then a sufficient sample size is essential – particularly if it is to be disaggregated. In essence it must be large enough to diversify away specific risk. With property the added problems of the effects of voids, refurbishment, reversions and over rents all impact on the figures contributing to the index. It is on this basis that IPD scores over competitor indices. However, even IPD indices are not immune from these issues and they have various mechanisms to minimise the effects. These technical issues lead to differences between the results obtained from monthly and annual indices.

The size of IPD's sample portfolio does allow them to disaggregate and extract, for example, listed buildings as well as types. However, they only hold properties in a limited number of towns and this distorts the index.

Lack of data

The general lack of public domain information on property is a serious defect when establishing the parameters for an index. This is still very much the case for Europe where the lack of fully developed institutional investment markets over time results in insufficient data. Even in the UK it is recognised as a concern.

Valuation driven

Most (though not all) property indices are valuation driven and as such they are not entirely reliable, although Carsberg (2001) argued that valuations are much more accurate than has sometimes been suggested. Despite this they lag market activity and there is no room for complacency. Indeed, Carsberg specifically called for the RICS to discuss ways forward with IPD.

IPD now track the sale prices achieved subsequent to valuation for the index to monitor the performance of the valuers. The fact remains that when a valuation base is used and the transactions market is thin, the prediction of price is fraught – and it is often argued that where markets are rising or falling fast there may be an inbuilt bias to the figures. This gives rise to what is known as the smoothing effect, which has been much explored by some academics. However, whilst it could be perceived as a problem, the contra-argument is that it does help property markets to maintain a lower level of volatility as compared to stock markets.

Lack of central market place

The lack of a central market means that a transaction base is not currently achievable. It is interesting that in many countries that have a very low level of sophistication within the property market central records are maintained of all transactions – so potentially transaction-based indices could be established there.

Heterogeneity

The very nature of property – its heterogeneity – means that any index based on a sample of properties is inevitably not necessarily representative of the entire market. Whilst a large sample should alleviate the problem, it will not eradicate it completely. Also, as with any index based on an actual or hypothetical portfolio, the property stock will constantly vary – and as it changes, so the true chain link nature is distorted.

Distribution of rent review patterns and lease structures

Not only will the distribution of rent review patterns produce distortions: so, for example, will the presence of voids. This again has a dampening effect on volatility (Turner and Thomas, 2001a).

Distortions of thin or abnormal markets

If the market is thin then evidence to back up valuations is also thin and this can produce distortion. With transaction-based indices the situation is very much worse. This problem is found not only in property indices but in share price indices as well.

Distortion of active management

Active management will inevitably affect the return of an individual stock – for example, with voids and capital expenditure. In the short term, if an undue number of properties within the index base are subject to active management at any one moment, distortion can take place.

Construction base

Perhaps the biggest problem for the designer of a property index is the base on which to construct and the nature of the index. The issues include balance, size, level and type of disaggregation, method of computation, time series v. cross-sectional approach, discrepancy between the statistical characteristics of the index sample portfolio and the portfolio being analysed.

11.7.7   The major differences

Morrell (1995) identifies the major differences in the main published indices under the following heads:

- *Composition*, with IPD being significantly the largest and thus statistically the most reliable, although it is predominately of institutional portfolios and is thus not a representative sample of commercial property as it excludes owner-occupied and smaller property company owned estates.
- *Construction*, with some indices constructed on a monthly basis, some quarterly and others annually. Additionally, differences occur in the treatment of improvements and developments and many exclude the cost of managing units.
- *Disaggregation*, which is often not possible – indeed only IPD can really disaggregate successfully – due to sampling size deficiencies.
- *Results*, which as noted earlier can vary by amounts that are large enough to sway the decision-making process.

Recommendations for improvements in the provision of indices were made by the SPR (Society of Property Researchers) and the RICS (Brown *et al.*, 1994). This led to a re-weighting of the IPD index and the recommendation to set up a tracker index, and

Beginning market rent	£100
End market rent	£105
Beginning yield	7.0%
End yield	7.5%
Calculation	$= ((105/7.5\%)/(100/7.0\%) + 7.0\%) - 1$
Total return	5.0%

Fig. 11.12   Calculating returns using indices of return.

consultation taking place with other bodies (such as the Institute of Actuaries) to move towards the convergence of methodologies to facilitate more comparability. This has since moved on with the recommendations of Carsberg (2001) and the RICS response thereto (RICS, 2002).

11.7.8   Approximating market returns from market indices

While providers such as IPD give performance data based on the actual cash flows from properties in their sample portfolios, it is possible to construct 'synthetic' returns series from notional or hypothetical property-based indices published by many property agents. This data usually takes the form of a prime rent and yield series. A simple method of estimating the return achieved on these markets is to assume that all rental growth over the period is reflected in the capital value.

The formula below is used in Fig. 11.12 and illustrates a simple one-period calculation.

$$TR = \left(\left(\frac{EMR/EY}{BMR/BY} \right) + BY \right) - 1$$

Where: TR = total return expressed as a percentage over the period

BMR = rental value at the start of the period

EMR = rental value at the end of the period

BY = yield at the start of the period

EY = yield at the end of the period

There are some fundamental problems with the approach set out above that should be considered when comparing it to returns based on sample portfolios. First, it assumes that all rental growth is reflected in the valuation at the end of the period. In reality, as the benefit of rental growth is usually deferred – for instance, for up to five years in the UK market – only a proportion of this growth will be reflected in the valuation. Second, the yield is assumed to be the income yield, with rents received at the end of the return period with no deductions.

Of course, in practice, with more information about the basis of the data used, adjustments to the calculation can be made to better reflect the return generated if the hypothetical asset that this type of data is usually based upon were actually held. This would include costs, depreciation, timing of income, income growth and deferment of the reversion in the capital value to produce a reliable synthetic returns series.

11.8   Establishing benchmarks

The primary objective of property investment is to purchase assets that will produce a financial return either as revenue or as capital gain. The financial return investors will require will depend on factors such as their risk tolerance and the style of returns needed to meet their investment objectives.

A simple requirement may be an absolute target, such as to produce real returns of 6% per annum. However, for some investors this may conflict with their requirements for controlling risk. If the property market were producing a real return of below 6% in a given year, then an investor might have to take on unacceptable levels of risk in comparison to the average property investor to meet this objective.

To illustrate this point further, consider the example of a pension fund with a multi-asset portfolio diversified into equities, gilts and property. The fund's primary objective will be to provide its pensioners with an income in their retirement. The lure of investments with a high return may be tempting, but this will need to be offset against the risk of loss if those investments turn bad. Accordingly, the fund diversifies.

Having chosen to invest in the property market, it has made a calculated decision that property provides some degree of diversification against downside risk in its other investments. This decision will be based on historic observations of the relationship between the property market and the equity and bond markets, plus a view of how this relationship will continue in the future. In this case the style of returns produced by the property market in given economic circumstances will be required by the investor.

The pension fund may therefore feel it is more appropriate to specify a financial return target that is not absolute but is relative to the performance of the property market in general or to other investors with similar investment objectives. For a pension fund, comparison against all the assets recorded by IPD may not be appropriate as it includes assets held by investors with shorter-term investment objectives.

The pension fund may decide the most suitable benchmark is the performance of other pension funds' property portfolios, and this could be further focused into a size bracket. This service is provided in the UK by companies such as IPD, Russell/Mellon CAPS and the WM Company. IPD records the performance of the largest segment of the property market and can offer benchmarks that reflect the type and size of investors. Size can be important as small funds are restricted by the lot size of properties they can invest in. To some extent style, such as where an investor only invests in a certain market segment, can also be reflected.

Many fund management contracts specify benchmarks, which if consistently exceeded by the fund manager result in bonus fees.

11.9 Summary

Return (both actual and anticipated) is perhaps the most important consideration in making buy/sell/hold decisions. Accordingly, it is very important that this can be measured accurately and in a way that enables the investor to compare performance between one asset and another. At the aggregated level, it will be required to measure the performance of one portfolio against another.

However, in reality there is no one simple way of measuring return. At best it is an approximation and contains assumptions that may not hold good in reality, such as the reinvestment decision that underpins the IRR calculation. Whilst it is acknowledged that return measurement is possible using a number of different equations, it is consistency of approach that is perhaps the most important thing to achieve as only if returns are so measured can performance be compared. In this the role of property indices has gained importance, with IPD having now become the industry standard. However, even this index is not comprehensive as it only records the returns that valuers estimate to have been achieved for institutional property holdings. In time more progress will undoubtedly be made towards greater consistency; for now, it is important that property professionals have both a good understanding of the mechanics of return calculations and a recognition of their limitations.

References

Banking Administration Institute (1968) *Measuring the Investment Performance of Pension Funds.* London: BAI.

Brown, G. (2001) A note on the effects of serial cross-correlation. *Journal of Property Research,* 18 (3): 249–57.

Brown, G. and Matysiak, G. (1995) Using commercial property indices for measuring portfolio performance. *Journal of Property Finance,* 6 (3): 27–38.

Brown, G. and Matysiak, G. (1997) Sticky valuations, aggregation effects and property indices. *Journal of Real Estate Finance and Economics,* 20 (1): 49–66.

Brown, S., Morrell, G.D., Unsworth, R. and Ward, C.W.R. (1994) *Property Indices Research Report: The Commission's Findings and Recommendations.* Society of Property Researchers, Technical Paper No. 1. London: SPR.

Carsberg, B. (2001) *Report of the Carsberg Committee to RICS on Commercial Property Valuation.* London: RICS.

Chartered Financial Analyst Institute (1999) *Global Investment Performance Standards.* London: CFAI.

Chartered Financial Analyst Institute (2003) *Real Estate Provisions for the GIPS Standards.* London: CFAI.

Fisher, J. (2002) Real time valuations. *Journal of Property Investment & Finance,* 20 (3): 213–21.

Kirschmann, J. and Dietz, P.O. (1983) Evaluating portfolio performance. In: *Managing Investment Portfolios* (eds J.L. Maginn and D.L. Tuttle). Boston: Institute of Chartered Financial Analysts.

Morrell, G. (1995) Property indices: a coming of age? *Journal of Property Valuation & Investment,* 13 (3): 8–21.

Royal Institution of Chartered Surveyors (2002) *Response to the Carsberg Report* www.rics.org.uk

Spaulding, D. (1997) *Measuring Investment Performance.* Boston: McGraw Hill.

Turner, N. and Thomas, M. (2001a) Property market indices and lease structures – the impact on investment return delivery in the UK and Germany. Part I. *Journal of Property Investment & Finance,* 19 (2): 175–94.

Turner, N. and Thomas, M. (2001b) Property market indices and lease structures – the impact on investment return delivery in the UK and Germany. Part II. *Journal of Property Investment & Finance,* 19 (3): 296–322.

Further reading

Brennan, L. (1992) Techniques and challenges in developing property indices. *Journal of Property Valuation & Investment,* 10 (1).

Frost, A.J. and Hager, D.P. (1986) *A General Guide to Institutional Investment.* London: Heinemann.

Hargitay, S. and Yu, S.-H. (1993) *Property Investment Decisions.* London: E&FN Spon.

Hoesli, M. and Macgregor, B. (2000) *Property Investment: Principles and Practice of Portfolio Management*. Harlow: Longman.

Investment Property Databank/Drivers Jonas (1988) *The Variance in Valuation*. Annual report. London: Drivers Jonas.

Investment Property Databank/Drivers Jonas (1993) *The Variance in Valuation*. Annual report. London: Drivers Jonas.

Lundstrom, S. (2000) *Valuation for Performance performance Measurement measurement – the implications for research and practice*. IPD/IPF Property Investment Conference 2000.

Maginn, J.L. and Tuttle, D.L. (eds) (1983) *Managing Investment Portfolios*. Boston: Institute of Chartered Financial Analysts.

Morrell, G.D. (1991) Property performance analysis and performance indices: a review. *Journal of Property Research*, 8: 29–57.

Moore, R. *et al.* (1982) Property indices: do they make sense? *Journal of Valuation*, 1 (2): 197–201.

12 Handling risk within the portfolio

Aims of the chapter

- To place property investment into a portfolio and multi-asset risk context.
- To consider the nature of risk in financial assets and its relationship with property investments.
- To consider risk in the context of constructing efficient portfolios.

- To trace the evolution of finance theory and the assumptions underpinning modern portfolio theory.
- To set out alternative approaches to portfolio construction.
- To consider the use of expected factor models and their application to property.

12.1 Introduction

This chapter considers the application of portfolio theory to real estate investment portfolios. The approach taken is to examine the risk/return profile of the portfolio rather than that of the individual assets. Traditionally, as described in Chapter 8, the real estate industry has focused on risk at a single asset level. However, for reasons that are explored in this chapter, to most investors risk related to the whole portfolio is equally important; hence there have been concentrated efforts over recent years to apply investment theory developed in financial markets to real estate.

Real estate has its analytic foundations embedded in traditional finance. The analysis of the property – its legal position, design and specification – has formed part of valuation methodology and property investment appraisal. However, as explored in previous chapters, this was historically considered in isolation from other investment media. The real estate industry was slow to adopt modern financial techniques, and it is only since the 1980s that it has been seeking to apply them to 'optimise' property portfolio construction.

As will be argued in this chapter, the move from single asset risk analysis to portfolio analysis and portfolio optimisation is not unduly complicated. However, it does require additional data sets, and for many this may be a limiting factor.

The literature and methodologies relating to portfolio construction and portfolio optimisation have in the main come from finance literature, often from the United States and as applied to the equities markets. This finance literature can broadly be categorised as modern portfolio theory (MPT). Whilst real estate academics and practitioners (see, for example, Brown, 1991; Dubben and Sayce, 1991; Baum and Crosby, 1995; Brown and Matysiak, 2000; Hoesli and MacGregor, 2000) have examined this literature and have sought to apply MPT to the construction of property portfolios, two key issues are raised:

- Do real estate investments and equities share similar fundamental characteristics, and, if not, will this alter in the future as new methods of holding property are developed? If so, how should we perceive the application of the finance literature and MPT?
- Is MPT in itself the right tool to assist analysts and appraisers in constructing optimal real estate investment portfolios? Or are there alternative theories that, separately or in conjunction, can provide real estate fund managers with more appropriate tools for the construction of optimum portfolios?

In this chapter, first the conventional wisdom relating to real estate portfolio construction is explored. Following that, the issues that are raised and that question the validity of MPT are assessed in the light of the implications for property portfolios. In particular, the application of expected return factor models is considered.

12.2   The nature of risk in financial assets

Before explaining the concepts of MPT and portfolio optimisation, a definition of risk is provided.

Risk can be defined as the degree of likelihood that an expected outcome will not happen. It is therefore a measure that can be linked to probability. The higher the risk, the less able we are to predict the outcome. With an individual asset the classic measure of risk, as was explained in Chapter 8, is in relationship to standard deviation. The more closely clustered outcomes are around the average outcome, the lower the standard deviation and hence the lower the risk. Intuitively, investors seeking a lower than average level of risk will accept a lower than average return; conversely, to achieve a higher than average return, intuitively an investor will have to accept a higher level of risk.

However, where groups of assets are considered the very act of combining the assets may affect the level of risk. It will depend on both the type of risk and the risk profile of each asset. The aim of the theorists has been to devise models that can enable investors to build portfolios of risk-prone investments that, when combined, decrease the overall exposure to risk without an equivalent reduction in expected returns. The attempts collectively are known as portfolio theory.

Fundamental to these theories is an appreciation of the types of risk that affect assets. These can be divided into two main types:

- systematic (market-related) risk; and
- non-systematic (specific) risk.

12.2.1   Systematic risk

Systematic risk is typically perceived as market risk, and is driven by general sentiment; it is therefore a risk that an individual investor cannot independently control. It is seen as an important source of price volatility in an investment.

Systematic risk may be broken down into a number of key characteristics. These include, for example:

- Market risk:
  - o interest rate risk;
  - o GDP growth rate risk.
- Inflation risk:
  - o purchasing power risk;
  - o interest rate risk;
  - o unexpected inflation risk.
- Political risk:
  - o tax imposition risk;
  - o regulation risk;
  - o legislation risk.
- Exchange rate risk:
  - o currency risk.

For property investments, market risk also includes:

- local economy;
- local GDP;
- employment.

Systematic risk is seen as non-diversifiable risk and investors' choice relates to their level of exposure to systematic (market-related) risk. From the analysis above it is clear that systematic risk will often be very much higher with non-domestic investments.

12.2.2   Non-systematic risk

Non-systematic risk relates to the specific risks to which an investment is exposed. For equities, there exist a wide range of risks that impact on the expected performance. These include:

- industry risk
- sector risk
- management risk
- operating risk
- financial risk
- default risk
- credit risk
- information risk
- liquidity risk
- poor regulation risk
- poor transparency risk.

From a real estate perspective, the diversifiable non-systematic (specific) risks overlap (for example, default and financial risk) but also include:

- covenant strength
- location

- lease terms
  - break clauses
  - repairing obligations
- obsolescence/depreciation
- tenant
- planning.

To these can be added a new class of specific risk: that relating to sustainability. This concept was introduced in Chapter 8. Work by Sayce and Ellison (2004) reveals that it is increasingly possible to model a property's vulnerability to the growing needs for compliance with the principles of sustainability.

12.2.3   Introducing risk analysis as a mechanism for portfolio construction

For any asset or portfolio, the risk as measured by the variability or variance of return can be split into two elements:

Variance of expected return = Systematic risk + Non-systematic risk

This may be rephrased as:

Variance of expected return = Market related risk + Diversifiable risk

Portfolio theory states that at portfolio level investors strive to eliminate specific risks through diversification. This leaves them with varying degrees of exposure to market risk. Their expected return will be a function of their exposure to market risk.

Diversifying away non-systematic or specific risks at a portfolio level will benefit the portfolio by reducing the level of overall variability and risk. It is this risk reduction that is the key to portfolio optimisation and it is on this concept that the principles of modern finance, as detailed below, are based. If markets work efficiently – and this notion is debated below – investors should not be 'rewarded' for specific risk, as by judicious choice of assets they will be able to diversify this away. Whether or not this hypothesis is sound is discussed in the remainder of the chapter.

12.3   Portfolio management under modern portfolio theory (MPT)

Under MPT, investors may be seen as seeking to maximise their risk/return trade-off. Their expectations are seen not necessarily in terms of a single point return, but rather in the context of a range or distribution of possible rates of return. The risk/return trade-off thus relates to the expected return and the range of expected returns, measured in terms of variance or standard deviations. Combining investments tends to reduce the standard deviation (risk profile) of the portfolio. Under MPT, the benefits of diversification relate to the reduction of non-systematic risk, leaving systematic risk as the residual.

The impact on risk of combining different investments relates directly to the correlations between the assets contained in the portfolio. Correlation is a measure of how two investments perform relative to one another. If the performance of the two investments

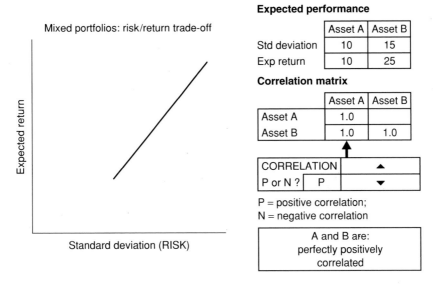

Fig. 12.1 Two-asset portfolio showing perfect positive correlation.

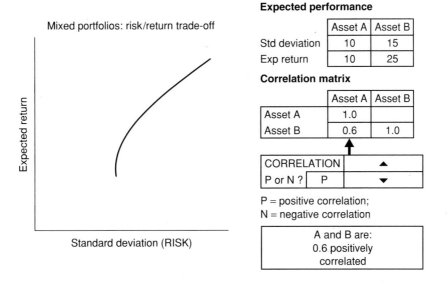

Fig. 12.2 Two-asset portfolio showing positive (not perfect) correlation.

moves in step then they are said to be correlated. If, however, they do not move in step and the movements are unrelated, they are said to be uncorrelated. When the movements are in opposite directions they are said to be negatively correlated.

As Figs 12.1 to 12.4 show, when negative (or low) correlations are found significant diversification and risk reduction benefits will accrue; in contrast, if there is perfect positive correlation then no diversification benefits accrue.

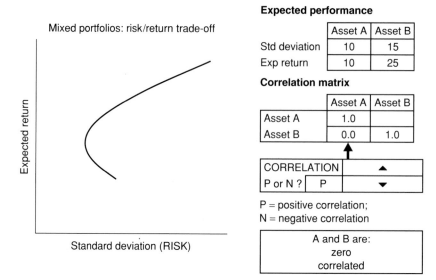

Fig. 12.3 Two-asset portfolio showing zero correlation.

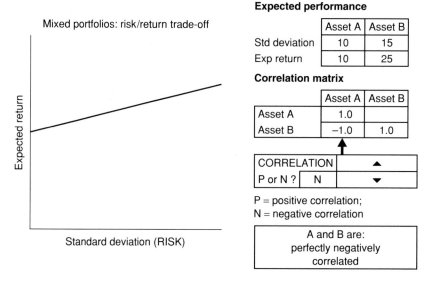

Fig. 12.4 Two-asset portfolio showing perfect negative correlation.

Please see Spreadsheet 35 for a worked example of the impact of different correlations between two investments when they are combined together in different proportions. The returns are shown to be a weighted average, and are not affected by the correlation figure.

As the graph in Spreadsheet 35 shows, for assets that exhibit negative correlations it becomes possible to reduce risk significantly. However, it is seldom possible to achieve the desired negative correlation as most investments, in practice, tend to show some degree of positive correlation over and above the market risk. In consequence, there tends to be some non-systematic risk that can not be diversified away.

The equation for calculating the risk of a portfolio is set out below:

$$Var(x) = p_a^2\sigma_a^2 + (1 - p_a)^2\sigma_b^2 + 2p_a(1 - p_a)Cov(x_a, x_b)$$

Where: $Var(x)$ = variance of returns

p_a = proportion (or % weighting) of asset a
$p_b = (1 - p_a)$ = proportion (or % weighting) of asset b
σ_a^2 = variance of returns of asset a
σ_b^2 = variance of returns of asset b

Alternatively, this can be rewritten as:

$$Var(x) = p_a^2\sigma_a^2 + (1 - p_a)^2\sigma_b^2 + 2p_a(1 - p_a)R\sigma_a\sigma_b$$

Where: $R\sigma_a\sigma_b$ = coefficient of correlation between returns of two investments a and b where:

$$R\sigma_a\sigma_b = \frac{Cov(a, b)}{\sigma(a)\sigma(b)}$$

In which Cov (a,b) = covariance between two random variables, a and b

σ_a = standard deviation of the returns of investment a
σ_b = standard deviation of the returns of investment b

Thus the risk as measured by, or considered in terms of, standard deviations (the square root of the variance) can be split into two components:

- The first component of this equation relates to the risk inherent in each investment. This figure is the square of each investment's portfolio weighting times the square of the investment's standard deviation of returns.
  - Thus for a property representing 10% of a portfolio which has a standard deviation of 10% about the expected return, this figure would be $(0.1)^2 \times 10^2 = 1.0$. The standard deviation of expected returns is the square root of the variance.
  - As the portfolio size increases and the weighting of the investment decreases, this figure drops significantly. If the investment represented 2% of the portfolio, and with a standard deviation of 10%, the figures become $(0.02)^2 \times 10^2 = 0.04$. This is 25 times smaller.
- The second component of the equation relates to the 'correlation effect' between the assets. For each pair of assets (in the correlation matrix), their investment weightings are multiplied together. The product is multiplied by the standard deviation of return for each asset in the pair, and then by the correlation of the returns for the pair of assets. The figures for each of the pairs are then summed.

The correlation figures, individually, are relatively small, but when added together they become significant. Where negative correlations exist this will reduce the total figure, showing the benefit of diversification. However, if correlations are highly positive the gains are minimal.

Whilst calculating the equation for a portfolio comprising very few assets is a simple exercise and can be done without computing power, for large portfolios the mathematical computations become complex.

Please see Spreadsheet 36 for a worked example of the impact on the variance (and standard deviation) of returns of a portfolio where the portfolio has different numbers of assets, of different lot sizes and with different correlations.

When seeking to apply this theory to a portfolio, there are some key factors that must be considered. There are three components to the variance (and standard deviation) of a portfolio's expected returns around the mean expected return. A portfolio manager adopting a MPT approach to portfolio construction should be mindful of:

- The number of properties in the portfolio.
- The standard deviation of return of each investment from the mean expected return.
- The correlations between the properties.

From a practical viewpoint, a number of issues arise from this approach and should be given close consideration:

- The benefits of diversification increase with portfolio size; however, so will the costs of portfolio management. Portfolio management costs may therefore be a limiting factor in determining portfolio size as measured by the number of individual properties.

  Property is a management-intensive asset class, and if left on 'autopilot' it usually does not deliver optimum returns. Even when the day-to-day management is outsourced, the asset manager/fund manager still needs a sound understanding of each property in the portfolio, and the factors driving its returns and its risk profile.
- Equities are homogeneous so, for example, one share in BP is like any other share in BP. This is not the case with direct property investment. Is a new, well-located City of London office investment valued at £150 million let to one tenant the same as a similar £150 million investment that is multi-let? Intuitively the answer is no, but to what extent are they different in their contribution to portfolio risk? Instead of the number of properties, should it be the number of tenancies in the portfolio that is used, as tenant risk is a major element in establishing specific risk?
- Alternatively, is a mixed-use property, with say basement car parking, ground-floor retail, three storeys of offices over and two floors of residential above the offices, a single property or four properties for portfolio purposes?
- In both the examples above, the market practice is to value the property as one. But in performance terms it is likely to be both the individual leases and the user type that influence expected returns and the risk profile of the investment.
- Generally it is perceived that gearing increases risk but does not alter the underlying risk profile of the portfolio. Is this a realistic proposition?
- What is the investment rationale behind the portfolio? Is it to match liabilities (life insurance companies and pension funds) or is it to enhance shareholder wealth (property companies)? In the former case, diversification benefits of property are sought; in the latter, the aim is to maximise returns and shareholder wealth.

As is considered later in the chapter, this last point is of key importance. For institutions (life insurance companies and pension funds), the role of the property investment portfolio is usually to act as an income-producing asset that also acts as a diversifier. If this is the case then the fund manager will be seeking to hold a real estate investment portfolio that tracks the performance of the real estate market. The benchmark for the UK commercial property investment market is usually taken to be the IPD Annual Index (see Chapter 11). Portfolio construction and diversification for institutional investors are therefore aimed at creating stable real estate returns that are closely linked to the property market, for which the IPD index acts as a proxy.

For property companies, the analysis methods need to be different. Their primary objective is to maximise their shareholders' wealth and therefore they will be seeking to maximise returns whilst containing risk. However, they are not able to apply MPT in the same way as financial institutions because, by definition, their assets are in property and they do not have – nor can they – equity portfolios to aid diversification of their asset base.

Accordingly, their aim is to pursue enhanced returns whilst seeking property assets whose performance displays low volatility. Diversification in terms of the number of properties and their type can assist in providing the stability, but the applicability of MPT may be limited, as we will consider in the last part of this chapter. Instead, property companies need to pursue other ways of identifying opportunities for out-performance.

In summary, there are a number of reasons why MPT may not be the most appropriate solution for determining the shape of a portolio for a property investor. Accordingly, in the next section we consider how MPT has evolved and seek to establish whether there may be alternatives to MPT that are better suited to the characteristics of property and the needs of investors.

12.4   The evolution of finance theory

In the first part of this chapter the argued benefits that can accrue to a portfolio through diversification have been outlined. We now take a step back and consider how finance theory has evolved, and how it may be applied to real estate investment.

The real estate investment market has characteristics different from those of the equities market, for which much of the finance theory and methodology was constructed. There are three main phases to its evolution:

- *Traditional finance.* This relied on fundamental security analysis, in which the reports and accounts of each company are analysed. This includes the analysis of the financial policy, the legal rights of financial claims and the time value of money and discount rates. Traditional finance adopts a single asset approach, and involves close scrutiny of each asset.

- *Modern finance.* This utilises financial economics and its application to portfolio construction, and is based on an assumption of informed rational economic behaviour. It seeks to provide a framework for 'portfolio optimisation'; it promotes the 'irrelevance' of the financial structure of the firm; it develops a system of portfolio choice built on structured diversification (MPT), which has been applied to both single asset pricing models (the capital asset pricing model (CAPM)) and multi-factor models (the arbitrage pricing theory (APT)); and lastly, it is underpinned by a reliance upon the 'efficient market hypothesis'.

- *New finance*. The new financial paradigm casts doubt on the underlying tenets that bind modern finance together. In particular, it questions market efficiency and whether single-factor models (CAPM) or multi-factor models (APT) actually do achieve the optimum returns required by investors. Instead, it focuses on inductive 'ad hoc' factor models, which apply statistics, econometrics and behavioural psychology, and it relaxes the simple assumptions underlying MPT.

The move from the beliefs underlying modern finance to those of the new finance theories is gaining ground in a growing number of quarters. New finance will rewrite the finance text books and suggest alternatives to the strict application of MPT. It is therefore ironic that at a time when the property industry has recently started to apply MPT, others in the financial field are moving on to newer methodologies!

This is not to dismiss the value of the modern finance theories. For those seeking stable real estate returns and diversification benefits, CAPM and single-index models provide a valuable framework for portfolio construction and for linking returns to those of the real estate market. However, new finance provides alternative approaches which aim to identify assets that are inefficiently priced and that when combined together have the capability to produce superior returns.

Property investment analysts are well versed in the application of traditional finance, through their use of the discounted cash flow analysis of property investments. Traditional finance approaches form the 'rock bed' of the portfolio manager's analytical approach to ranking property investments. These approaches will provide useful data, which can be utilised when considering modern finance and MPT applications.

12.4.1   From traditional to modern finance: the underlying paradigms

To place modern finance and MPT into context, it is necessary first to consider its application to equity investment portfolios. Modern finance has underlying it four interlocking paradigms.

The first paradigm was a catalyst for this style of thinking. It was the brainchild of Harry Markowitz in the 1950s (Markowitz, 1959). He presented a new analytical technique for the building of investment portfolios which exhibited an optimum risk/return profile. Through his work the concept of portfolio optimisation was born. However, lack of computing capacity and the complexities of the figures for other than simple portfolios rendered the theory difficult to apply at the time when it was first presented.

The second paradigm came a little later when two economists, Modigliani and Miller, developed their 'M & M irrelevance theorem' (Modigliani and Miller, 1958). This contended that it was the assets rather than the liability structure of the balance sheet that was important. They argued that the gearing of an investment, whether internal (within the company) or external (by the investor secured on their shares), did not matter.

The third paradigm, typified by the work of James Tobin on liquidity preference (Tobin, 1958), William Sharpe on capital asset prices (Sharpe, 1964) and John Lintner on the selection of risky assets (Lintner, 1965), developed Harry Markowitz's portfolio

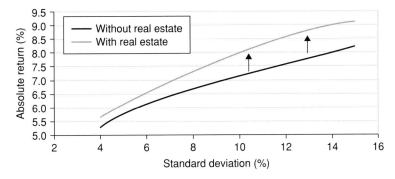

Fig. 12.5   The efficient frontier showing the effect of adding property as a diversifier to a mixed asset portfolio.

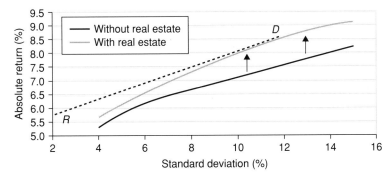

Fig. 12.6   The securities market line formed by adding a risk-free asset to the portfolio.

optimisation tool and developed the capital asset pricing model (CAPM). CAPM uses a market portfolio which includes all assets and from which an efficient frontier can be calculated (see Fig. 12.5) and from this a securities market line is created (Fig. 12.6), by combining the market index with varying amounts of a risk-free asset (usually taken as short-term Treasury bills). This is one step on from a single-index model which uses a benchmark index to calculate the beta of a portfolio relative to the benchmark index.

The analysis of the different risk/return characteristics of different portfolios can be made such that a series of efficient portfolios can be identified. The graph in Fig. 12.6 depicts an efficient frontier showing the risk/return relationship as measured by standard deviation of returns, and expected returns, respectively. The addition of a risk-less asset into the available pool of assets for inclusion into the portfolio enables the so-called security market line to be produced, as depicted by the dotted line RD in Fig. 12.6, where R is the risk-free rate of return, and D is the tangent of the efficient frontier.

The single index model and CAPM (see the equation below) imply that if investors all used portfolio optimisation techniques it is possible to simplify Markowitz's covariance matrices model to a model with a single factor that drives expected returns. This single factor is the exposure to market risk, since investors would hold fully diversified portfolios, which would have removed all non-systematic risk through diversification.

The relationship between risk/return is determined by the investment's or portfolio's beta (β), which represents its variability in returns to the benchmark index. This variability is measured by the portfolio or investment beta. A beta is calculated by regressing the performance of an investment or a portfolio against that of the market.

$$E(R_p) = R_f + \beta(R_m - R_f) \pm \varepsilon$$

Where: $E(R_p)$ = expected rate of return for portfolio p
R_f = risk-free rate of return
β = measure of market risk
R_m = market rate of return
$\pm\varepsilon$ = + or − an error term

Please see Spreadsheet 37 for a worked example of the calculation of a beta for a property portfolio relative to the IPD Annual Index. This example also considers the goodness of fit of the regression line (R^2) and its relevance to the beta figure.

Please see Spreadsheet 38 for a worked example of the calculation of a beta for a listed property company relative to the FTSE All Share Index. This example also includes an example of how the beta figure can be used in the calculation of the company's weighted average cost of capital (WACC).

The fourth paradigm was published in the 1960s by Eugene Fama who put forward the 'efficient markets hypothesis' (EMH) (Fama, 1968). In an efficient market investments are priced such that their value equals their worth; that is, the value in the market fairly reflects the net present value of their future expected returns. In an efficient market the prices of investments move randomly, in that price movements cannot be used to predict future price movements. This is a point that a number of leading real estate academics have considered, in particular Brown and Matysiak (1999).

12.4.2   An examination of the assumptions underlying MPT

An underlying assumption to the first three paradigms (optimum portfolios using MPT, M & M irrelevance theorem and CAPM) is that efficient markets prevail and that all information is both known and acted on, resulting in a lack of price distortion. Under this, price must equal worth.

Please see Spreadsheet 39 for a worked example of the calculation of the efficient frontier for a simple property portfolio. This example uses Excel's Solver wizard to move from naïve diversification to weightings that maximise returns for given levels of risk.

If the efficient markets hypothesis does not hold (so that values do not equal worth) then the application of modern finance becomes flawed and open to question. However, the real estate investment market has become increasingly sophisticated and the ability to pick winners and discard losers is far from simple, and moreover is difficult to achieve particularly over the medium to long term.

A number of assumptions underpin the efficient markets hypothesis. These are:

- *Information efficiency*: the market and its assets exhibit strong form information efficiency, in that all information is in the price of the assets in the market. Lower levels of information efficiency exist where:
  - o in a semi-strong market, all publicly available information is in the share prices;
  - o in a weak form market, previous price movements cannot be used to predict future price movements.
- *Analysis*: all investors are skilled and informed analysts.
- *Tradability*: with the advent of new information, investors trade on price anomalies and prices quickly reflect this new information.
- *Taxes*: taxes are ignored.

In addition to the efficient markets hypothesis being satisfied, a number of other assumptions are also made to support and validate modern portfolio theory.

- A single time period is used for analysis and returns are maximised for a given level of risk over this period.
- All assets are perfectly divisible and marketable and have nil transaction costs.
- There are no taxes.
- A higher return is always preferred to a lower return.

The first assumption is perhaps a reason why, in the UK, five year analysis periods are common, due largely to the lead taken by Prudential Property Investment Managers who were at the vanguard of measuring property portfolio performance relative to other asset classes.

In contrast, US investors tend to adopt a ten year analysis period, perhaps due to the significant impact of debt finance in the market, plus debt running with the land (that is, not necessarily repayable on the sale of a property), and the large involvement of investment vehicles and private individuals in the market using debt finance.

The assumption that all investors seek to optimise their portfolio returns requires the following further assumptions:

- The market itself gives the optimum expected return for its level of risk.
- The different expected returns of investors will be determined by the betas of their portfolios.
- All investors use CAPM methodology to optimise their portfolio's risk/return profile.
- From the market index (of all investments) comes the securities markets line.
- The efficient frontier represents the highest level of return for a given level of risk and cannot be exceeded as the market is efficient.
- The market index is an efficient portfolio.
- Investors structure efficient portfolios and in consequence do not suffer tracking errors.
- It is the reduction of the variability of returns rather than tracking errors that is seen as being important.

12.4.3   Newer developments in MPT: the arbitrage pricing theory

The concept of CAPM was further extended by Ross (1976) who published the arbitrage pricing theory (APT). APT is a multi-factor model with an underlying assumption that investors will seek to eliminate the difference between the risk/return of two portfolios through a process of arbitrage.

In APT the view is that investments have a number of factors (not one, as is the case with CAPM) that drive performance. Each of these factors has a beta (β). These factors, when combined collectively, account for all the relationship between the investment performance and that of the market. Correlations between investment returns and the specific factors (such as inflation and GDP) give a result such that each investment responds in a similar manner to each factor. APT also makes the assumption that the relationship between the various factor betas and the expected return is linear, and not curved (which it tends to be in practice).

The concept of APT seems very plausible, but the model itself is difficult to build and its prediction powers have been found not to be as strong as might be expected (Haugen, 1999). The predicted return in the APT model comes from the unbiased estimates of the factor betas for the following period. This can be a problem in that betas often vary over time. In consequence, it is not easy to estimate the next time period's beta for each factor. More importantly, it is not an accurate process. This produces a significant shortcoming of the APT model even over a single time horizon; it becomes increasingly difficult, if not meaningless, over a series of periods. Nevertheless, APT provides a useful insight into the factors that drive the performance of an investment and a portfolio, and the understanding that diversification benefits come from the diversification of the components of market (economic) drivers.

The risk/return profile of investments needs, however, to be put into the context of the factors and items of analysis that influence prices. In the CAPM and APT models, items relating specifically to the investment itself are ignored in that it is assumed that they can be diversified away; as such they form no part in the pricing process, and thus items relating to specific risk do not form part of these risk/return models.

In summary, the progression has been from a single factor model, to CAPM, to a multi-factor model (APT). Now we will consider what factors drive expected future performance in markets in which some assets may not be efficiently priced.

12.4.4   Difficulties in application

It has been argued above that modern finance has been built on an assumption of efficient markets. However, it is very questionable whether efficiency does occur. Intuitively, it can be recognised that inefficiencies come from a number of features of the markets and the assets that lie within them. These include:

- Different exposures to taxes.
- The imposition of round trip dealing costs (buy $\leftrightarrow$ selling costs).
- In tight markets there is illiquidity, and small changes in volume (buying or selling) influence prices to a larger extent than in actively traded – liquid – markets.
- Some assets may be difficult to trade and thus become more expensive.

- Other market inefficiencies render markets less than perfect. These include:
  - o information, in terms of both quality and quantity;
  - o analytical techniques applied by investors;
  - o ability to trade on price anomalies.

12.5   The move towards new finance: expected return factor models

The shortcomings of MPT have led to financial analysts seeking other approaches to the portfolio construction issue, including expected return factor models. These seek to predict share price returns in the future from a more fundamental standpoint.

Unlike MPT-style models which focus on factors that drive the correlations between shares, expected return factor models focus on the factors that help explain and predict which shares have tended to – and should continue to – move up or down relative to other shares. These factors tend to be specific share characteristics that differ in scale from share to share. Using multiple regression techniques, those factors that are present in shares exhibiting abnormal expected returns are identified.

Expected returns are calculated as the sum of the products of the expected factor returns (using 12 months' previous data) and the factor exposure for the period of analysis. The shares are ranked by their expected returns and placed into deciles. The shares in each decile are reallocated at the end of each analysis period.

Haugen and Baker (1996) considered the grouping of the drivers of expected returns of investments into 'families' of factors. These families of factors, which may influence returns and indicate where inefficient pricing may exist, can be summarised as follows:

- risk
- liquidity
- cheapness (relative pricing)
- profitability
- technical
- sector.

12.5.1   The families of factors

Using historic performance data from the US equities market, Haugen and Baker (1996) considered how the individual risks in these families of factors influenced asset and portfolio returns, and developed multi-factor analytical models to identify which of the factors influenced abnormal returns.

Part of their premise was that the equities market could be split into a series of ten deciles whereby the shares were categorised according to special characteristics. The performance of these deciles was then monitored using historic data, and where decile 10 showed relative out-performance the factors causing it were noted.

In more detail, they broke down the categories (families of factors) as set out below. This approach is interesting in the context of the characteristics of the property investment market.

Risk factors

These were given priority of place under the analysis, thanks to their perceived importance in influencing returns. Risk measures included were as follows:

- Market beta (single index model and CAPM).
- Factor betas for APT.
- Standard deviation of return.
- Residual variance risk resulting from non-systematic risk not being diversified away.
- Various accounting ratios:
  - o earnings – standard error;
  - o net operating income to interest payable;
  - o variability in the running yield on the investment.

Liquidity factors

Liquidity is perceived as being important as, when coupled with a market's supply and demand characteristics, it influences how prices perform.

These liquidity factors were split into the following:

- market capitalisation;
- trading volumes;
- trading volume trend.

Cheapness (relative pricing)

This element of the pricing model considered the measures of cheapness in a competitive market place. The underlying premise was that companies with high profit margins held onto these, until such time as new entrants and competition depressed profit margins. Where low or non-existent profit margins exist, this will reduce competition due to competitors leaving the market, thus providing the surviving players with the ability to build up their profit margins. The markets in which the companies operate are in an ever-changing state of flux. The view is that profit margins for each company are cyclical and move up and down over time.

Corporate prosperity leads to growth expectations, which lead to higher multiples and share prices. Firms with low margins and poor growth prospects have relatively low market prices and low multiples. Haugen and Baker (1996) viewed the former as being potentially expensive and the latter as potentially cheap.

In this approach a key issue is the perceived barrier to entry for each market in which each company operates, and thence the time it takes for those with high margins to suffer the effects of competition. This time period is open to estimation by the equity analysts and they may be expected to be over- or under-optimistic a proportion of the time, thereby creating pricing inefficiencies. Such measures of cheapness or relative pricing risk include:

- price earnings ratio;
- price earnings ratio trend;
- enterprise (book) value to price;

- trend in enterprise (book) value to price;
- dividend yield;
- dividend yield trend;
- cash flow to price;
- cash flow to price trend;
- sales to price ratio;
- sales to price ratio trend.

Measures of profitability

Measurers of profitability relate to the analytical framework and calculations that determine the profitability of companies, and the accuracy of these figures. The greater the level of imprecision, the larger is the potential return. The accounting/analytical ratios that are considered include:

- profit margin and its trend;
- sales to assets and its trend;
- return on assets employed and its trend;
- return on equity and its trend;
- earnings growth record;
- a measure of earnings surprise.

Technical factors

A study of technical issues is known as chartism. The technical analyst seeks to interpret the past cycles of behaviour on the market and interpret these to arrive at predictions for future pricing.

In a world where market efficiency is seen as the norm, chartists in many quarters struggle to gain acceptance of their professional skills in interpreting price trends. However, as market efficiency is not a 'given' and price anomalies are observable in the market place, there is merit in including excess return measures, over a number of time periods.

Sector factors

An analysis of sector factors involves a consideration of the influence over returns exercised by the exposure to a specified market sector. The main sectors are examined in terms of their relationship with the company's share price returns. They are broken down as follows:

- durable goods;
- non-durable goods;
- utilities;
- energy;
- construction;
- business equipment;
- manufacturing;

- transportation;
- finance; and
- business services.

12.5.2   The impact of families of factors on return

Having established the families of factors, Haugen and Baker analysed the specific factors that were driving the returns of traded equities (Haugen and Baker, 1996). In the US it has been found that the factors were:

- excess returns for specified periods;
- the trend in the trading volume of the share;
- the price/earnings ratio;
- cash flow yield;
- return on equity;
- cash flow to price variability;
- six month excess return;
- return on assets;
- payout ratio; and
- trading volume to market capitalisation.

In the UK equities market, Haugen and Baker determined that the components in the multi factor model were:

- excess returns for specified periods;
- book value to price;
- cash flow to price;
- price earnings ratio;
- gearing ratio;
- variance of total returns;
- residual variances of returns; and
- return on equity.

12.5.3   Applying expected return factor models to equities

From the above it is possible to put together a stock selection process for picking winners and discarding losers. The key is to identify the drivers of performance of desirable shares. Such shares would fit the profile of large market capitalisation: liquid, high turnover, financially sound, low risk companies with upward momentum in the market, profitable with rising profits. Companies with these characteristics would undoubtedly not be cheaply priced, but shares without all the components might be. The benefit of a portfolio would be to combine the relevant attributes and diversify away the poor characteristics.

Undesirable shares – for example, those with a relatively small market capitalisation, illiquid, risky, financially weak, prices falling relative to the market, poor profitability and getting less profitable with relatively high prices – would be avoided.

Shares in the market would be split up into deciles in which the lowest expected return is decile 1, and decile 10 the highest.

12.5.4   Pricing net cash flows

Cash flows can be split into normal returns on the capital outlay, and abnormal returns, in terms of their net present values. The anomaly is that whether the abnormal profits are full priced or not, they can be sustained in the short term but not in the longer run.

So, given the above, how should we consider the construction of optimal property investment portfolios? At the moment this is very uncertain, and additional property-specific research requires to be undertaken. Nevertheless, a number of approaches can be put forward that will assist fund managers in their quest for optimising their portfolios and gaining relative out-performance.

12.6   Expected return factor models – application to property portfolios

The application of expected return factor models to the equity portfolios has been shown to produce enhanced returns when using historic data series. A significant amount of intellectual capital has been invested in MPT, and it can be predicted that it will still be some while before expected return factor models are used to a wider extent.

In the context of constructing real estate investment portfolios, the methodology of expected return factor models intuitively has much to commend it. The focus on factors specific to property investments fits in well with many current investment analysis practices and would form a logical extension.

12.6.1   Qualitative analysis

Whilst in the UK quantitative analysis predominates, in Continental Europe a greater use of qualitative ranking methods are used. In particular PEST and SWOT analysis are used.

As has been argued in Chapter 7, PEST analysis takes a 'helicopter' view and incorporates political, economic, social and technological issues. It ranks the factors identified, and point scores may be applied to them.

SWOT analysis looks at the strengths, weaknesses, opportunities and threats. It considers them for investment properties and their location from the perspective of both the occupier and the landlord. It also ranks the factors identified, and point scores may be applied to them so that a ranking can be achieved.

12.7   Other approaches to portfolio construction

In this section of the chapter a number of other approaches to portfolio construction are considered, particularly in the context of property portfolios for which there is a scarcity of historic performance and associated data.

12.7.1   Scenario approach

A scenario approach to portfolio construction can be used, where the properties in a portfolio and prospective purchases and sales are analysed. The expected returns of each property are calculated for five to ten years into the future. These returns are estimated on the basis of a range of different (but realistic) economic scenarios. The resultant annual or periodic performance figures are used to determine the correlations and variances between the investments under the different scenarios. Probabilities are applied to each scenario and from this, using Excel's Solver wizard, optimum portfolios can be determined.

> Please see Spreadsheet 40 for a worked example of the calculation of optimum portfolios using a scenario approach to property performance forecasts. This example uses Excel's Solver wizard to calculate the figures.

The approach of using economic scenarios to determine the future performance characteristics of a property portfolio can also be used to help identify the liability matching characteristics of a property portfolio using stress testing techniques.

The combination of qualitative methods with quantitative analysis methods has a role to play, in that the qualitative analyses provide an underlying framework for the quantitative analysis. In addition, these will both potentially give a better perspective of additional factors that expected return factor models should consider incorporating in their multiple regression analysis models.

12.7.2   Attribution analysis

In the UK property investment performance has been shown to be driven to a significant extent by stock selection skills (Brown & Matysiak, 2000). To determine specific factors resulting in under- and out-performance, a number of techniques are being used in the property industry. One such method is the application of attribution analysis to the properties in a portfolio and to those that make up the IPD annual and monthly indices.

12.7.3   Cluster analysis

An alternative method of grouping properties and their performance characteristics is the application of cluster analysis. This analysis identifies the underlying factors that are driving the performance of specific groups of property investments.

The application of cluster analysis is relevant since investors tend to look at property investment by categories such as use, location or quality. Cluster analysis enables a more detailed view of the drivers of performance and how a portfolio can be grouped into clusters with similar risk return profiles.

12.8   Summary

In this chapter, and with the use of six working examples set out in the Spreadsheets, we have seen how traditional financial analysis techniques relied upon fundamental analysis. We have explored the world of finance theory as applied to property portfolios using modern portfolio theory and discovered the benefits of diversification. The importance to MPT of the efficient market hypothesis has been identified, and we have considered the factors that make the property investment market potentially less than efficient.

Whilst MPT has started to gain acceptance in real estate fund management circles, we considered the advent of expected return factor models and how these multiple regression models focus on both asset specific and economic drivers. MPT models assume market efficiency. In contrast, the expected return factor models focus on potential market inefficiencies and aim to use these pricing anomalies to construct optimum portfolios with the potential to produce abnormal returns.

References

Baum, A. and Crosby, N. (1995) *Property Investment Appraisal*, 2nd edn. London: Routledge.

Brown, G.R. (1991) *Property Markets and the Capital Markets*. London: E&FN Spon.

Brown, G.R. and Matysiak, G.A. (2000) *Real Estate Investment: A Capital Market Approach*. London: Pearson Education Limited.

Dubben, N. and Sayce, S. (1991) *Property Portfolio Management: An Introduction*. London: Routledge.

Fama, E. (1968) Risk, return and equilibrium: some clarifying comments. *Journal of Finance*, 23 (1): 29–40.

Haugen, R. (1999) *The New Finance: The Case Against Efficient Markets*. Englewood Cliffs, NJ: Prentice Hall.

Haugen, R. and Baker, N. (1996) Commonality in the determinants of expected stock returns. *Journal of Financial Economics*, July.

Hoesli, M. and MacGregor, B. (2000) *Property Investment: Principles and Practice of Portfolio Management*. Harlow: Longman.

Lintner, J. (1965) The valuation of risk assets and the selection of risky investments in stock portfolios and capital budgets. *Review of Economics and Statistics*, 47: 13–37.

Markowitz, H. (1959) *Portfolio Selection: Efficient Diversification of Investments*. New York: John Wiley and Sons.

Modigliani, F. and Miller, M. (1958) The cost of capital, corporation finance and the theory of investment. *American Economic Review*, 48: 261–97.

Ross, S. (1976) The arbitrage theory of capital asset pricing. *Journal of Economic Theory*, 13: 341–60.

Sayce, S. and Ellison, L. (2004) *Sustainability and commercial property investment – understanding the impact of direct effects and policy development on asset values*. Paper to the IPD/IPF Conference, Brighton, 18–19 November.

Sharpe, W. (1964) Capital asset prices: a theory of market equilibrium under conditions of risk. *Journal of Finance*, 19 (3): 425–42.

Tobin, J. (1958) Liquidity preference as behaviour towards risk. *Review of Economic Studies*, 25: 65–86.

Further reading

Cavaglia, S.F. and Moroz, V. (2003) Risk and return properties of global equities. *AIMR ConferenceProceedings*, Association of Investment Management and Research.

MacLeary, A. and Nanthakumaran, N. (eds) (1988) *Property Investment Theory*. London: E&FN Spon.

13 Forecasting

Aims of the chapter

- To detail the nature and aims of forecasting and place these within the context of property investment and management.
- To distinguish between a forecast and an appraisal.
- To provide an overview of current practices and techniques used within the real estate industry for undertaking forecasts.
- To describe methods of establishing trends, including the examination of sources of data and their reliability.
- To explain regression analysis in its various forms (simple, multi-variate, linear and non-linear).
- To discuss the relevance of property cycles in forecasting techniques, and the use of barometers and lead indicators.

13.1 Introduction

Whenever investment or operational property purchase decisions are made, some sort of forecast will be used either explicitly or implicitly. In many cases this will be an intuitive forecast based on purchasers' experiences of past trends which they project into the future. In the case of the operational owner the forecast will inevitably concentrate on the ability of the property to meet business requirements, but it should nevertheless also include reference to future property markets. For the investor, however, the need to forecast likely future changes in property market conditions and, in particular, the ability of the individual property to perform in the future will be of great significance in the decision-making process.

Over the past 20 years the availability of data to investors on property markets has improved enormously. This has notably been through the medium of IPD (Investment Property Databank) who produce short- and long-run data on 90% of institutionally owned assets. The increased flow of reliably sourced data, combined with an increasing availability of computer-based statistical software, has enabled investors to access and apply statistical techniques. It is now possible to undertake relatively sophisticated modelling techniques in respect of market movements, rental levels and yields, to produce better cross-media comparison in ways that were previously unavailable. The question remains as to whether these techniques do and will enable investors to improve their risk/return profiles. In this chapter the various techniques now available and increasingly in use are explored. First, however, it is necessary both to define a forecast and to distinguish it from an appraisal.

13.2   Forecasting and appraisals

Investing in property usually implies a long-time commitment. The average holding period for property held within the IPD annual property index is estimated at around seven years. Therefore both owners and investors need to satisfy themselves that their purchase appraisals are founded in well-based forecasts of the future. However, a forecast is not the same as an appraisal; the latter projects cash flows into the future but uses market assumptions, whereas a forecast encompasses the use of many different techniques.

In a discounted cash flow framework the future expected values for these variables can be determined at one end of the spectrum by practitioner/professional judgement and at the other by forecasts derived from sophisticated models. In practice a combination of the two is often used. Put simply, an appraisal is an investor's view of the worth of an investment property. In this appraisal there are a number of assumptions relating to the future. These assumptions or variables drive the projected performance of the investment and that in turn provides the estimate of worth of the asset to the investor or corporate occupier.

The nature of an appraisal has been defined in earlier chapters and it is important here to distinguish between an appraisal and a forecast. In essence an appraisal will provide the investor or owner-occupier with an estimated net present value (NPV) of the property at a given date based on primarily market-derived evidence and using a discount rate that is considered appropriate to the class of property, including any specific and market risk factors. The market data used will relate to current and projected rental values and yields, including estimates of rates of likely depreciation. As with all discounted cash flow analyses, the analysis period will be set; this will frequently be between 5 and 15 years. At the end of the cash flow period an 'exit' value will be taken and this will relate to projections of the most likely market conditions.

In preparing an appraisal, estimates must be made. In establishing these inputs to the calculations some quantitative forecasts may have been undertaken or commissioned. However, the appraisal itself is not a forecast of future value: it is the interpretation of a range of data that will enable the investor or owner to form a view as to whether the market is currently under- or over-pricing the asset. In the event that those operating and advising in the market are fully aware of the same forecast materials as the appraiser, convergence between market value and appraisal may result. So, in summary, a forecast can *inform* the appraisal but an appraisal is not a forecast, nor is it necessarily dependent on one.

13.3   Aims of forecasting

The aim of any forecast is to provide a 'best estimate' of the future in relation to specific elements of likely change. Essentially, therefore, its purpose is threefold:

- To highlight where there are opportunities for future successful activity.
- To pinpoint areas of risk.
- By quantification, to inform decision-making both at the point of purchase and subsequently.

Within a property context, forecasting can be used to:

- Detect market level trends that may effect either whole portfolios or sectors within the portfolio, either positively or negatively.
- Predict future rental growth or yield patterns by analysing likely movements in their underlying 'drivers'.
- Establish projected financial performance.

It is in the nature of all forecasting that it is an essentially inaccurate activity. Therefore care must be taken in assessing the confidence that can be placed in any forecast. For this reason, as detailed below, forecasts are frequently considered in probability terms.

Whilst every property appraisal and valuation has a perception of the future built within it, this has in the past normally been predicated on experience and intuition. Increasingly, investors are now seeking quantitative approaches to assist them with their decision-making. This will be of importance especially at times when either economic uncertainty prevails or the property market is weak and data hard to establish. The RICS recognises this within its appraisal standards (RICS, 2003: GN5) but only deals with the issue in very general terms.

Within a management context, forecasting details such as levels of future rent may be critical in the hold/sell decision.

13.4 Methods of forecasting

13.4.1 Time series

Many forecasts involve the use of time series analysis. A time series is an ordered sequence of values for a variable taken at equally spaced points through time. Forecasting time series movements can be approached from two different basic angles:

- Identifying historic patterns in the time series and self-projecting the series into the future (trend analysis).
- Identifying relationships between variables and the market, and using those variables to project the movement of the market into the future (regression analysis).

This chapter identifies and introduces the self-projecting methods of forecasting, but focuses on regression analysis. Regression analysis is the basis of most commercially available forecasts of the property market so knowledge of how to construct a model is beneficial when interpreting and using the results. Detailed time series analysis and econometrics as a discipline are considered to be outside the scope of this book; coverage is restricted only to topics that are likely to be useful for the property professional.

13.4.2 Decomposition analysis

Decomposition analysis is based on the premise that time series are composed of a number of elements or components, normally defined as seasonal, trend/cycle plus a random or irregular variation.

If these components are assumed to be independent of each other, then the time series is the sum of the components. If they are assumed to be interrelated, then a multiplicative approach is used.

Once the values of each component have been determined, they can be recomposed by addition or multiplication to project them forward and create a forecast. Software packages such as SPSS (Statistical Package for Social Scientists) have built-in procedures that can isolate these components and provide forecasts using, for example, de-trended or de-seasonalised data.

13.4.3   Forecasting using smoothing analysis

Time series data is expected to exhibit some form of random variation through time. Additionally, it may exhibit an underlying cyclical, trend or seasonal component. To identify these components, smoothing analysis can be used to remove unwanted variation and project the time series forward.

- *Moving average models* self-project the time series into the future by averaging past periods and projecting that view forward. The optimal number of periods to average will need to be found by trial and error, although some statistical packages may do this automatically. Basically, the assumption used is that the average of values at the end of the series is the best estimate of the current mean value around which the data is fluctuating.
- *Exponential smoothing* works in a similar way to the moving average model, except that the model assigns exponentially decreasing weights to past observations, so more recent observations have more impact on the forecast.

Whichever approach to time series is taken, the underlying principle is the same: the view of the future is found by an analysis of past transactions and context. Whilst the various types of time series analysis develop different ways of dealing with abnormalities and variation, there is an underlying assumption that the past is a good guide to likely future performance. If that underlying assumption is ill-founded, so too is the forecast.

13.5   Forecasting using linear regression models

Linear regression analysis is used to examine the relationship between one dependent variable and one or more independent variables. The results from the analysis can then be used to forecast the dependent variable using known values of the independent variable or variables.

The following sections examine the steps involved in building forecasting models using regression. However, each step needs to be considered within the constraints of the following five assumptions which will become clearer further into the chapter:

- The dependent variable is a linear function of the independent variables plus an error term.
- The error terms sum to zero.
- The errors at each point are random from the previous error and show no trend.

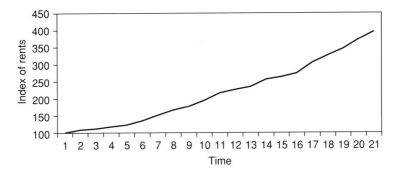

Fig. 13.1   A rental growth index.

- Independent variables are fixed.
- Independent variables are not perfectly correlated with each other (multi-collinearity) and there are more observations or points in the time series than independent variables.

On the last point, it is generally considered that the longer the series, the better, as this will reduce the possibility of error.

13.5.1   Stationary time series

Linear regression requires the meaningful calculation of a number of statistical tests such as means and variances. These rely on the times series exhibiting what is known as 'stationarity'.

A stationary time series is one that does not exhibit trends and cycles over time, with the result that the mean and variance of the series remain constant over time and each subsequent observation is a 'random step' from previous observations. A characteristic often seen in non-stationary series is a constant increasing in the variable over time. Fig. 13.1 shows an example of a variable increasing over time – in this case a rental growth index, which would not be a suitable time series to use as a variable in regression analysis.

In order to conduct time series analysis, it is necessary to transform non-stationary series using any one of a variety of mathematical techniques to produce stationary series. A technique commonly used to achieve this is 'differencing'. This transforms the series by taking the change in level of the series from one point in time to the next. Fig. 13.2 shows the results of differencing the rent index series used in Fig. 13.1.

For Fig. 13.2, the differencing was simply the difference between each successive index figure. This is referred to as the first difference and it will have the effect of reducing the number of observations in the series by one. The resulting series can be tested for stationarity statistically or be judged visually from a sequence plot – in this case the first differenced series can be seen to still trend upwards through time.

If stationarity cannot be achieved from first differencing as shown in Fig. 13.2, then the second difference can be calculated. The second difference in the present example would be the difference in the index change each period, and the results are shown in Fig. 13.3.

If stationarity *can* be achieved but not a completely random series, then the series exhibits what is known as autocorrelation or lagged correlation. In these circumstances

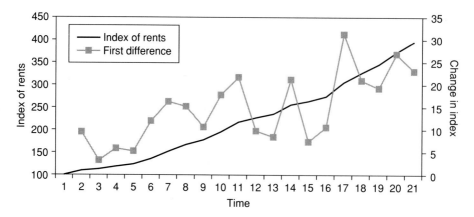

Fig. 13.2   Transforming time series by differencing: first stage.

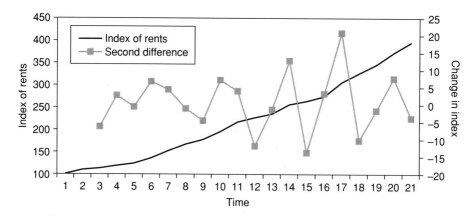

Fig. 13.3   Transforming time series by differencing: second stage.

a moving average, autoregressive model or combination of both models may be more appropriate. One example of such a model is the autoregressive integrated moving average (ARIMA) model.

Given that the time series used in Figs 13.1–13.3 is an index of rental growth, it would be more appropriate to take the first difference as the percentage change between points in the index instead of subtracting one index figure from another. When compared to Fig. 13.2, the percentage change shown in Fig. 13.4 eliminates the trend or drift; the series fluctuates around a mean point with no distinct cycle. Simply subtracting index numbers as in Fig. 13.2 does not allow for the effect of compounding in the series, hence it has a definite trend.

Other examples of transformations are achieved by the used of logarithms and square rooting. If required, the forecasts eventually produced can be untransformed back to the original time series basis.

Instead of taking the percentage change as the difference in indices, and provided the index series contains only positive values, it is common practice to take either the natural or base 10 logarithm of the index series and then to subtract the previous value from the

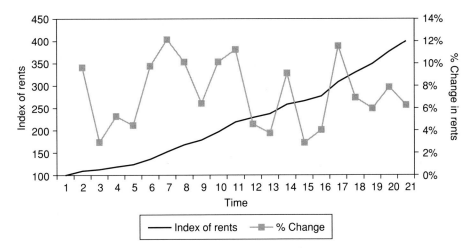

Fig. 13.4   Transforming time series: producing an index of rental growth.

current value. This provides a series of differences that is approximately equal to the percentage change.

Quite often, first differencing applied to economic and property data still does not provide a time series that exactly fits the strict requirements for statistical modelling. It may still exhibit what is known as weak stationarity. In practice, some flexibility and judgement is needed in interpreting statistical requirements, and weak stationarity can often be assumed to be close enough.

13.5.2   Selecting independent variables using scatter plots and correlation analysis

To build a regression model you will need to select a variable or variables that will influence the dependent variable you are looking to forecast. The selection of these independent variables will require economic and analytical thought.

The use of simple scatter plots can help identify whether an independent variable has potential to be used in a model. Fig. 13.5 shows three scatter plots of potential independent

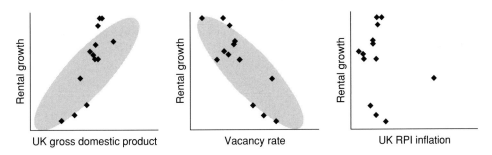

Fig. 13.5   Scatter graphs showing the relationship between independent variables and office rental growth.

variables against a dependent variable, which is prime office rental growth. Looking across the charts in Fig. 13.5, the first compares annual rental growth against UK gross domestic product (GDP). As would be expected on an intuitive basis, rental growth appears to be stronger in years when the economy is growing at the greatest rate. Here there is a discernable positive relationship as growth in one variable reflects growth in the other and the relationship is demonstrated by the pattern of plots shown rising from left to right. Additionally, the emerging trend appears to be linear and so suitable to be modelled using regression to develop a 'line of best fit'. If the trend appeared to be curved, then using a logarithmic transformation of the variables might provide a linear solution suitable for modelling using regression.

The middle chart compares annual rental growth against the office vacancy rate. Logically, it would be expected that stronger rental growth would occur in years when the vacancy rate is low. Accordingly, the correlation relationship in this case is negative – a fall in one variable reflects growth in the other.

The third chart compares rental growth to inflation. Here there is no noticeable relationship, and it is likely that inflation, on its own at least, would have little value in a forecasting model, as the two variables appear to display little or no correlation; they are driven by different factors. However, it may be that inflation could demonstrate a positive or negative relationship when taken in combination with other variables. If it is considered that this could be the case, then it should be included in a model tested. Also, the inflation series could be used to deflate the rental growth series to provide a more accurate model.

Rental growth is primarily a product of supply and demand. Accordingly, forecasting models that incorporate these factors as independent variables are likely to provide the most logical and robust forecasts. However, there are no direct demand measures for property, so proxies such as economic or employment growth for offices, consumer spending for retails and manufacturing output for industrials need to be found. Supply measures are also difficult to find for all markets.

Whilst scatter plots provide a visual means to identify potential independent variables, correlation, which is considered below, provides a statistical technique to quantify the strength of the relationship between two variables. Just as the regression scatter diagram could only suggest a relationship, so correlation does not indicate, per se, a causal relationship.

In real estate decision-making practice, the interpretation of the revealed relationship is normally undertaken intuitively and with the use of other market intelligence. The same applies to the choice of which variables to regress. Accordingly, there is always the potential for error. Even if the time series for each variable does prove to be validated by future movements, the *relationship* between them may not hold good. Misinterpretation as to the real nature of the relationship can lead to inappropriate decision-making.

13.5.3 Granger causality

There are statistical tests that can help determine whether observed relationships are, in fact, causal. One of the best known of these techniques for identifying specific causality is the Granger causality test (Darnell 1994:41–3). The bivariate Granger causality test is a statistical technique that can be used in a time series analysis when the question is whether or not one economic variable or data series can help forecast another economic variable or data series.

A frequently quoted example that is well documented relates to the observed relationship between economic recession and oil prices. It has been observed that, for nearly all of the post Second World War period, economic recessions have been preceded by large increases in oil prices. How can one find out statistically whether there is a relationship between oil price shocks and subsequent recessions? Granger, by his causality test, proposed a methodology for testing such observational hypotheses and this was then taken up by Sims (1972, 1980)[1].

In a property context such methodology may be applied to, for example, the relationship between the stock exchange FTSE property share index (or listed companies within that index) and a direct property index such as the IPD monthly property index. Myer and Webb (1993) looked at the relationship between listed real estate investment trusts (REITs) and the direct US property market and found Granger causal relationships for some REITs. Newell *et al.* (1997) determined that, with a time lag of between seven and nine months, the indirect property index could be shown to Granger-cause direct property indices, and found a small number of listed property companies that also had similar characteristics.

13.6   Correlation

A correlation coefficient measures the degree to which two variables move in step with each other. However, finding a correlation between two variables does not necessarily imply that changes in one cause changes in the other.

There are two main methods for calculating the correlation between two series of numbers. Spearman's technique is used primarily for ordinal data, such as rankings, and Pearson's product moment technique for interval- or ratio-type data as set out above. For more on the statistics and mathematics behind this and other frequently used statistical measures in property, please refer to Adams *et al.* (2003).

Both methods produce a correlation coefficient that can vary from −1 to +1. A positive correlation indicates that an increase in one variable is reflected by an increase in the other up until the point where they move in lockstep, when the correlation would be one. If the variables work against each other the correlation will be negative. A correlation of zero

---

[1] Testing the relationship between the data series as to whether there is causality, in the Granger sense, involves using F-tests to determine whether lagged data for an independent variable provides any statistically significant information about a dependent variable X in the presence of lagged X. If there is no relationship, then it is said that 'data series Y does not Granger-cause data series X.' The concept of causality is straightforward; however, the statistical techniques behind Granger causality tests are rather more complicated and convoluted. In practice there is more than one way in which to implement a test of Granger causality. One method, for example, uses the autoregressive specification of a bivariate vector autoregression, and assumes a specified autoregressive lag period and using ordinary least squares estimates the unrestricted regression equation. An F-test of the null hypothesis is also carried out. In Granger causality regressions using lagged dependent variables, the test is only valid asymptotically. Another caution is that the choice of lag length period in Granger causality tests is important as the answer is very sensitive to this variable. Also, consideration needs to be given to the methods employed in dealing with any non-stationarity of the time series.

Table 13.1   Correlation matrix.

	Rental growth	Vacancy rate	GDP	Inflation
Rental growth	1.00			
Vacancy rate	−0.84	1.00		
GDP	0.84	−0.78	1.00	
Inflation	−0.18	0.51	−0.34	1.00

indicates no relationship. To demonstrate this, the Pearson's correlation coefficients for the variables in Fig. 13.5 are shown in the correlation matrix in Table 13.1.

Earlier in the chapter it was noted that non-stationary time series can cause spurious results; for this reason, differencing and other techniques are used to produce stationary series. Using the example above in illustration, it can be found that correlating the non-stationary index values for rental growth against inflation would result in a correlation of 0.23.

The correlation matrix also shows the correlation coefficients between the independent variables, which can be useful when selecting variables as two or more variables may have a strong relationship with both the dependent variable and each other; this is known as multicollinearity. This is undesirable in a model as both variables will have the same effect on the independent variable: accordingly, one variable should be dropped. If a model was constructed using *both* GDP *and* the vacancy rate, it is possible that a high negative correlation would result and in turn this could lead to multicollinearity in the model.

Statistical confidence intervals and significance can be calculated for Pearson's correlation coefficients, although the diagnostic tests from the regression analysis can be relied upon to assess independent variables' suitability. The use of the correlation coefficient is to provide information on the confidence that can be placed in the resulting correlation statistic: for example, it is possible to get the result of a 0.1 coefficient (which suggests that there is virtually no relationship) and be 95% confident of this result. Alternatively, it is possible to obtain a 0.95 coefficient and not be confident of the result.

The important point is that if the regression statistics flag up a variable as being significant, then it is not necessary to calculate the significance of the correlation coefficient as well.

13.6.1   Lagged dependent variables

In practice, historic values for the dependent variable are sometimes used in forecasting. As highlighted earlier, successive observations in time series are not always random. Property value and return indices are often autocorrelated due to 'valuation smoothing', and including previous values can help to forecast subsequent values. These are known as 'lagged dependent' variables, with the technical term for their use known as 'autoregression'.

The presence of autoregression in a data series violates one of the assumptions of the classical linear regression model, as one of the *independent* variables is now based on the *dependent* variable. In consequence, this is not fixed if the model is used to forecast further ahead than the lag period.

However, if it is logical to include a lagged dependent variable and this significantly improves the model, then it is usually acceptable in practice. This is one area in which real estate analysis is particularly complex as the amount of actual transaction price data will inevitably be below that obtainable for other investment media. Accordingly valuation, as opposed to transaction, data is used to populate many forecasts and time series. The result of this is that the data does contain elements of lagging and possible inaccuracy or/and bias. This makes property particularly susceptible to concerns as to the reliability of forecasts.

Once variables are selected for potential use in a model, a forward or backward elimination process can be used to assess their contribution. Some statistical software also provides automated processes to select the optimum model from independent variables.

13.7   Ordinary least squares and multiple regression

Regression takes a statistical step *beyond* correlation (which merely measures co-movement) by allowing one or more variables to forecast the movement in another variable. Using more than one independent variable is known as multiple regression and is the most common statistical forecasting model used in property markets.

Regression uses a technique that simply finds a constant equation combining values of the independent variables to plot a line with the least difference to the dependent variable. Regression will produce differences or errors at each point in the time series, known as residuals. These must and will add up to zero; that is, positive errors will be cancelled out by negative values. This is shown in Fig. 13.6, in which the regression line has been created from the GDP and vacancy rate series in order to produce a line of prediction for rental growth.

The line of best fit is achieved by minimising the squared differences between the regression line and the dependent variable; this technique is often referred to as 'ordinary

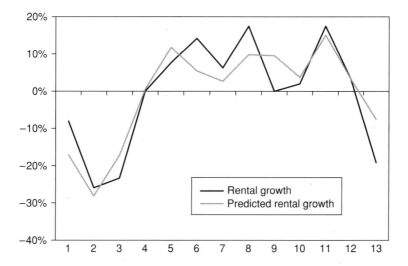

Fig. 13.6   Predicted office rental growth found by regressing GDP and vacancy rates.

least squares' (OLS). There are other regression methods, such as weighted least squares, that have uses in specific situations where OLS regression is not the most appropriate method.

The equation of the regression line comprises a constant (or intercept) and a coefficient (or slope) for each independent variable. As the equation does not fit the dependent variable exactly, there is also an error term. The dependent variable is usually referred to as the y variable and the independent variables as the x variables. The equation takes the form shown below with a further coefficient for each independent variable:

$$Y = \text{constant} + (\text{coefficient} \times X) + \text{error}$$

13.7.1   Regression statistics

Spreadsheet packages such as Microsoft Excel contain functions to calculate regression lines that produce results on the accuracy of the model. Table 13.2 shows the output for the regression equation used to produce the predicted rental growth line in Fig. 13.6. The multiple 'R' statistic is simply the correlation coefficient between the dependent variable and the predicted series with values ranging from −1 to +1. The R squared statistic takes the correlation coefficient one stage further by identifying the proportion of variance in the dependent variable that can be explained by the regression equation. The remaining element is that which is unexplained between the two variables.

Adding more variables to the regression analysis will never reduce the R squared; it will either stay the same or increase. The adjusted R squared measure takes account of the number of independent variables – in simple terms, more independent variables reduce the

Table 13.2   Output for regression equation.

(a) Summary output						
Multiple R			0.8917			
R squared			0.7952			
Adjusted R squared			0.7542			
Standard error			0.0731			
Observations			13			

(b) ANOVA						
	df	SS	MS	F		Significance F
Regression	2	0.2073	0.1036	19.4119		0.0004
Residual	10	0.0534	0.0053			
Total	12	0.2607				

	Coefficients	Standard error	t Stat	P-value	Lower 95%	Upper 95%
Intercept	0.0477	0.1152	0.4145	0.6873	−0.2089	0.3044
Vacancy rate	−1.3279	0.6497	−2.0439	0.0682	−2.7754	0.1197
GDP	4.5050	2.1757	2.0706	0.0652	−0.3428	9.3528

confidence you can have in the results. The R squared and adjusted R squared will be the same for models with one independent variable, but for multiple regression equations the adjusted figure is the best measure of overall model accuracy.

The standard error is the standard deviation of the points in the regression line from the dependent variable. Like the standard deviation, it can be used to form confidence intervals around the forecasts produced by the regression equation.

The significance and reliability of each coefficient, and therefore each independent variable, is determined by the so-called 't' statistic. It is outside the scope of this book to give a detailed analysis of this and other statistics but, as a rule of thumb, a 't' statistic should be more than +2 or less than −2 to be significant, although the actual figure will depend on the number of observations in the time series minus the number of parameters estimated. This figure is known as the *degrees of freedom*. In this case it is 13 minus the two independent variables and constant, summing to 10. The actual figure for the 't' statistic at different levels of confidence can be found in statistical tables. In some packages, an 'F' statistic may also be shown; this is the square of the 't' statistic.

Another important measure is the P, or probability value. This measures the probability that the coefficient is actually zero and therefore not significant in the model. A 95% confidence interval would mean that the P value needs to be less than 0.05. Whilst a greater or lesser level of probability may be acceptable, depending on the circumstances, 95% is commonly adopted as the acceptable level of probability.

The confidence intervals show the range within which you would be 95% confident that the coefficients fell. A smaller confidence interval is better. MS Excel allows you to specify different levels of confidence for this measure.

13.7.2 Interpretation of regression results

The first point to draw out from examination of the example is that the overall model accuracy is good, with 75% of the variance in rental growth explained by the model. However, there are some problems with the 't' statistics and P values.

It is often the case that the 't' statistic on the intercept/constant is not significant. However, unless there is a structural or theoretical reason to remove it the constant is left in, although MS Excel does give you the option to have the constant at zero. Removing the constant can lead to violating the assumption that error terms sum to zero by biasing the intercept. In a perfect world the intercept would be zero as all relevant independent variables would be included, alleviating any bias in the regression line.

Using statistical tables both 't' statistics are significant at 90% confidence level with 10 degrees of freedom (1.81), but not significant at 95% (2.23). This may be due to multicollinearity between the variables as a result of their high correlation. In practice, you would try other variables that might work better in combination with the GDP and vacancy rate data and therefore produce significant 't' statistics at 95% confidence.

The equation for the regression line at each point in the time series will be:

$$\text{Predicted rental growth} = 0.0477 + (\text{Vacancy rate} \times -1.3279) + (\text{GDP} \times 4.5050)$$

Forecasts of the rental growth time series can then be projected by substituting future estimates of vacancy rate and GDP into the above equation.

It should be noted that the error term is calculated as the difference between the predicted rental growth and actual rental growth so that:

Rental growth = Predicted rental growth + Error

13.8   Diagnostic tests

To check whether the model estimated conforms to the five assumptions outlined earlier in the chapter, diagnostic tests should be run to identify problems such as:

- *Heteroskedasticity*: the error terms' variance is not constant through time, indicating that the model's accuracy is varying through time.
- *Autocorrelation*: the error terms have a trend indicating that the model is more accurate at some points in time than at others.
- *Outliers*: reduce the goodness of fit of the regression line.
- *Multicollinearity*: two or more independent variables are highly correlated.

While these tests can be carried out in MS Excel, the use of specialised econometrics packages such as E-Views, which have many tests as built in functions, will be preferred if this level of sophistication is required on a regular basis.

13.9   The use of forecasts

The forecasting techniques examined in this chapter are only valuable tools if they are used to provide insight and help forecasters to make more informed judgements. While the techniques are sophisticated, they are susceptible to the GIGO (garbage in, garbage out) syndrome. Forecasting is therefore part science, part art.

The first thing that anyone using forecasts based on statistical techniques should consider is that they are not point estimates: they are probability distributions. The figure calculated from regression analysis is in the centre of the probability distribution. Unless you know the confidence and potential for error in forecasts, you cannot make informed decisions from them. Furthermore, if forecasts of independent variables are used to forecast the dependent variable, as will often be the case, it is inevitable that the potential for error in the forecast is increased.

13.10   Forecast equations and their calibration

A variety of quantitative forecasting models are used in the commercial property market. These range from simple to complex techniques and include:

- Single equation models, which include variables such as GDP, employment levels and financial variables in order to forecast rental growth, returns or yields.
- 'Inter-active' simultaneous equation models, which can be described as behavioural or structural models.

The aim of the forecasting model builder is to identify those models that produce useful and superior results. This task needs experience and expertise. The modeller should be aware of the characteristics and quality of the data used. A feature of many property models is that they incorporate data and information relating to the general economy and business conditions. These tend to be openly available, but at a cost, and can provide useful early signals: for example, consumer spending, output, employment (Matysiak, 1997).

Many forecasters seek to identify key variables that pick up changes in rental values. In practice, it has been found that the set of explanatory variables varies by sector. In the office sector, for example, it has been found that the gross domestic product, output and employment in financial and business services, unemployment, interest rates and operating expenses produce the highest statistical relationships. Consequently, it is these variables that are built into the models.

The vacancy rate is thought by many to play an important role. The logic is that if the variables that affect vacancy rate can be identified, then as the vacancy rate affects rental growth, a model can be constructed. In particular, it is the gap between actual vacancy rate and structural vacancy rate that matters (Hendershott *et al.*, 1999).

In the retail sector expenditure, lagged retail profits and the GDP seem to be the most successful demand side indicators. In the industrial market, the GDP and manufacturing output seem to be the most significant variables in the UK literature (RICS, 1994; Thompson and Tsolacos, 1999, 2001). Attempts to incorporate supply side variables in the models have generally not worked, and this quest has been hindered by the discontinuation of the official HMSO (now TSO) floor space data.

Regression analysis (as described earlier in the chapter) is one approach that can be useful in helping to identify the relationships in the underlying data. The aim with regression equations is to find the regression figures that produce the highest coefficient of determination, R^2, for an appropriate lead-lag period. In regression models, the set of variables may be split into soft/financial and hard indicators. For each of these categories, individual series are ranked according to their explanatory power as measured by the R^2 statistic from a bivariate regression between the variable of interest y_t, such as rental growth or take-up, and the individual indicator (denoted $x_{i,t}$) in which the retained lag of the indicator is selected automatically according to statistical criteria. This is summarised as:

$$\Delta \ln(y)_t = \beta(L)_i x_{i,t} + \varepsilon_{i,t}$$

In this equation, we seek to explain and/or anticipate changes in variables, such as rental growth or take-up, by using variables that lead rental growth or take-up.

Based on work undertaken by Matysiak, examples of some economic/financial variables that have been found to be useful in forecasting various property variables such as rental growth or investment yields at the sector level are shown in Table 13.3 (Matysiak and Tsolacos, 2003). In forecasting models, these variables are often useful at highly aggregated levels: for example, at the retail, office or industrial sector level. However, in order to forecast local market movements for rental growth, yield changes or take-up, local data is required.

13.11   Property market barometers and lead indicators

Property forecasters tend to use sophisticated modelling techniques; however, property market barometers are relatively straightforward in their construction. Barometers provide

Table 13.3   Economic financial variables.

Gilts yields	Car registrations	Net lending to consumers
Export orders	Volume of expected output	Financial surplus/deficit
Consumer confidence	Stock of finished goods	Real money supply M4
Changes in inventories	Consumer credit	Personal disposable income
Industrial production	Unit labour costs	Gross trading profits
House building starts	Yield curve	Manufacturing investment
Real money supply M0	Press recruitment ads	Private to total credit
New orders in manufacturing	FT All Share Price Index	Manufacturing output
Manufacturing employment	Retail sales	Gross domestic product

real estate decision-makers with an indicator of market trends and sentiment, and can help forecasters to identify turning points in the market. Barometers gather the current views of key players as to say yield or rental value movements. They give a market view as at a point in time.

In contrast, lead indicators seek to identify data series that are statistically linked to the way in which the market will move. The benefit of identifying lead indicators has been reiterated by Matysiak and Tsolacos (2003). Lead indicators are viewed as being particularly useful to analysts involved in DCF appraisals in helping to clarify their cash flow projections. Examples of lead indicators are changes in:

- lease length;
- roll-over percentages (percentage of tenants that renew their leases);
- break options;
- time vacant space is on the market;
- volume of investment transactions.

Individual lead indicators may be combined in order to produce a composite measure that is likely to provide a more reliable indicator of future market conditions.

When regression-based forecast models are used, their accuracy may be enhanced by the inclusion of a composite lead indicator. This composite indicator would consist of timely local property data, appropriately weighted (Matysiak and Tsolacos, 2003).

13.12   The role of forecasts in financial and property lending markets – value at risk

In this section consideration is given to two areas where forecasting expertise and risk analysis skills are becoming increasingly important. These are 'value at risk' and stress testing. Both are tools to assist in the risk management of assets.

Every investor would like to reduce or eliminate risk; however, to do so is not possible nor would it be consistent with the need to achieve a satisfactory level of return. If this is accepted then it is risk measurement and risk management that become the key concerns, within which forecasting has a distinct role. Additionally, the development of risk management techniques that rely on estimates of the future may be expected to have a growing impact on both the scope and depth of the skills base required in the property market. In particular, it is likely that the skills offered by accomplished forecasters, who tend to be few and far between, will became increasingly sought after.

A role of forecasts is to identify future performance patterns for properties and portfolios. Where the property assets are highly geared, the equity investor can be exposed to downturns in the markets. The worry for equity investors and the banks financing them will be their exposure to downside risk or losses.

Value at risk is a measure developed by J.P. Morgan with a view to establishing a market standard. They released their value at risk model under the badging 'RiskMetrics' as long ago as 1994. The RiskMetrics software program contains simplified risk assessment calculations and provided an important impetus to the growth in the use of value at risk amongst smaller financial institutions, non-financial corporations and institutional investors. In particular, its appeal was amongst the major derivatives dealers for measuring and managing market risk.

Value at risk is a single, summary, statistical measure of possible portfolio losses. It is a measure of losses that might be expected as a result of 'normal' market movements. The model identifies the size of the (normally) small probability where losses greater than the value at risk might be suffered. The underlying concept of value at risk can be summarised as a way to describe the magnitude of the likely losses to the portfolio.

Value at risk is not a cure-all. It is a single, summary, statistical measure of normal market risk to which the company is exposed. The value at risk numbers will frequently be supplemented by the results of other risk measures: for example, scenario analyses and stress testing.

Stress testing is also important in forecasting risk. It often begins with a set of hypothetical extreme market scenarios. These scenarios might be created from predetermined extreme scenarios (such as the market moving by five or ten standard deviations from its central tendency) for each of the sectors in which the business operates. The linkage (correlation) between potential losses is considered and an overall picture is gained of how the investment or banking activities might fare under extreme conditions. The property market has endured a number of cycles, the two worst of which in recent times were observed to bottom in 1973 and 1990. If property losses are correlated to other financial losses at such points in time, the bank may find its capital adequacy ratios under pressure. Value at risk seeks to identify these cross-relationships and the point at which market movements could place a financial institution in jeopardy.

There are alternatives to value at risk, as value at risk may not be appropriate for all entities. The two alternative methodologies are sensitivity analysis and cash flow at risk. Sensitivity analysis (discussed in Chapter 8) is less sophisticated than value at risk. In contrast, cash flow at risk can be considered more sophisticated than value at risk. Cash flow at risk focuses on the robustness of cash flows rather than changes in market-to-market values. Cash flow at risk measures are typically estimated using simulation techniques and focus on a longer time horizon than value at risk measures.

Such techniques are currently rarely seen in the real estate market. However, they are established within the financial and business communities, and professionals operating in the real estate investment market should be aware of how competing markets deal with estimating the exposure to market risks in a future context.

Additionally, for those involved in property lending, the Basle Capital Accord is bringing risk measurement and forecasting techniques onto the 'radar screen'. The implications of this are now explained.

13.13   Basle Capital Accord

Under the Basle Capital Accord agreement and related banking supervisory regulations, banks are required to have minimum capital adequacy ratios. These ratios measure the relationship between the bank's equity base (regulatory capital) and the size of its loan book. Principle I of the Accord requires banks to have a capital requirement of 8% for credits (loans) granted. Thus equity of 8 is required to support loans granted of 100. The figure for pure real estate loans is reduced to 50%, giving a capital requirement of 4% of the amount loaned. Where a bank fails to meet the necessary capital adequacy ratio it is not normally able to operate in the inter-bank money markets, and this seriously impedes it ability to undertake business.

In due course, a further tightening of capital adequacy regulations is envisaged with a second accord, known as Basle II. The objective is to get banks to undertake several different approaches for calculating how sensitive their regulatory capital base is to the degree of risk in individual financing transactions. The Basle Committee on Banking Supervision, a division of the Bank for International Settlements (BIS), is currently working on a completely new capital accord for credit institutions. After an initial consultation phase, there are plans to bring into force the new Basle II Capital Accord with effect worldwide from a likely date in 2008/9 for all international banks.

Basle II will place a greater onus on banks to calculate and manage their risk positions, in the context of the size of their capital base. The risk rating would serve as the basis for calculating the bank's capital requirements, along with the associated probability of default. As a result, the risk structures of individual financing transactions will have a much stronger influence on margin amounts in the future.

In summary, Basle II proposals comprise three regulatory areas, to which banks will be required to adhere if they wish to operate freely in the inter-bank money markets. First, there is the prospect of the introduction of differentiated credit risk assessment, requiring that operational and other banking risks must be re-analysed, measured, and backed with regulatory capital; second, banks would be required to comply with supervisory requirements relating to their reporting requirements; and third, to adhere to stringent legal disclosure obligations.

The fundamental view put across by the Committee on Banking Supervision is that worldwide minimum capital requirements should remain unchanged, at an average of 8% for all banks. The extent to which Basle II will call for this average to be raised or lowered in the context of a bank's specific loan portfolio and other derivative or investment exposures is likely to be based on:

- the loan portfolio structure of each individual institution;
- the structure and risk degree of the individual financings; and
- how the individual bank overcomes operational and other risks.

In calculating capital requirements, Basle II thus calls for the consideration of bank-specific factors, in addition to those of the individual transactions. Basle II provides for the use of external credit ratings for banks and, as many banks are unrated, it also provides for the use of internal ratings determined by the bank itself. The internal ratings will determine default probabilities and use them as the basis for the rating grades.

13.13.1   Real estate implications flowing from Basle II

The advent of Basle II will place additional requirements on banks when undertaking lending. That much is certain. Real estate underpins a significant proportion of bank loan transactions. The prospective thrust for real estate will be the requirement for more than just valuations for loan purposes. A requirement for prospective cash flow ratios – for example, long-term debt service cover ratios – will require forecasting expertise in a property-specific context. Also, property and property debt will need to be placed into a portfolio context.

The risk assessment techniques that are proposed under Basle II, and the requirement to provide cash flow forecasts in the context of prospective debt service cover ratios, will bring the risk and cash flow forecasting methodologies of the financial markets into the wings of the property marketplace. This in turn will require an increase in appropriate skills amongst the property adviser community.

13.14   Summary and conclusions

In this chapter the forecasting methods used within the property market have been explored and placed into the context of the wider capital markets.

Forecasting methodologies employed in the financial markets by econometricians tend to be complex in nature and beyond the knowledge and skills base of many in the real estate marketplace. In the past there was a good reason for this. Those who operate within the financial markets have long had access to substantial data series (daily, weekly or monthly). In stark contrast, forecasters operating in the real estate markets have two issues that make accurate or meaningful forecasting significantly more difficult. Primarily, these relate to the paucity of data that exists. Data series within the direct property market tend to be at best monthly, and frequently quarterly or even annually. Matters are further complicated in that whilst in the equities market the main indices are transaction based, in the property market the indices are appraisal- (or valuations-) based (Matysiak and Wang, 1995). Furthermore, the fact that a number of the commonly used data series exhibit non-stationarity provides another complication.

When considering property forecasts, care should be taken to understand the drivers of the model employed and the sensitivities of the outputs of the model to the input variables. In practice, forecasting models require calibration and need to be set against that which agents are seeing happen or are expecting to see happen in the short term.

In conclusion, property forecasting currently suffers from an inadequacy of both appropriate skills and data. Great strides have been made in terms of the latter in recent years; it is incumbent on practitioners and analysts to address the former.

References

Adams, A., Booth, P., Bowie, D. and Freeth, D. (2003) *Investment Mathematics.* London: Wiley Finance/John Wiley & Sons Ltd.

Darnell, A.C. (1994) *A Dictionary of Economics.* Aldershot: Edward Elgar.

Hendershott, P., Lizieri, C. and Matysiak, G. (1999) Workings of the London office market. *Real Estate Economics,* 27 (2): 365–87.

Matysiak, G. (1997) Modelling and forecasting in commercial property. Editorial. *Journal of Property Finance,* 8 (4).

Matysiak, G. and Tsolacos, S. (2003) Identifying short-term leading indicators for real estate rental performance. *Journal of Property Investment & Finance,* 21 (3): 212–32.

Matysiak, G. and Wang, P. (1995) Commercial property market prices and valuations: analysing the correspondence. *Journal of Property Research,* 12 (3): 181–202.

Myer, N. and Webb, J. (1993) Return properties of equity REITs, common stocks and commercial real estate: a comparison. *Journal of Real Estate Research,* 8 (1): 87–106.

Newell, G., Matysiak, G. and Venmore-Rowland, P. (1997) *Do property company shares perform in the same way as the property market?* London: RICS Foundation Publication.

Royal Institution of Chartered Surveyors (1994) *Understanding the Property Cycle: Economic Cycles and Property Cycles.* London: RICS.

Royal Institution of Chartered Surveyors (2003) *Appraisal and Valuation Standards.* London: RICS.

Sims, C. (1972) Money, income and causality. *American Economic Review,* 62 (4): 540–52.

Sims, C. (1980) Macroeconomics and reality. *Econometrica,* 48 (1).

Thompson, R. and Tsolacos, S. (1999) Rent adjustments and forecasts in the industrial markets. *Journal of Real Estate Research,* 17 (1/2): 151–67.

Thompson, R. and Tsolacos, S. (2001) Industrial land values – a guide to future markets? *Journal of Real Estate Research,* 21 (1/2): 55–67.

Appendix A: Valuation and finance formulae

Aims

- To provide readers with the main formulae used in the book and in the real estate market.
- To give a context to the construction and use of each table.
- To provide a link between these formulae and Excel Spreadsheet-based paste functions.

- To consider the impact of the timing of income receipts in terms of nominal, effective and true interest rates.
- To contrast in arrears formulae with in advance formulae.
- To consider formulae for annual cash flows and periodic (more than one per annum) cash flows.

Introduction

Property valuations and discounted cash flow analysis share the same fundamental financial theories, namely the concepts of:

- The 'time value of money' or, in layman's terms, £1 receivable today is worth more than the right to receive £1 in say four years' time.
- Compound interest.

In valuations, as discussed in Chapters 1 and 2, the valuer determines the passing rent, the estimated open market rental value and the valuation yield from comparable evidence. The valuer then uses one (or more) valuation formula(e) to determine the appropriate multiplier(s) to be applied to the rental value(s) to produce the value. In this methodology, each rental stream that is valued is deemed to remain constant for a certain period, and implied into the valuation yield are such items as risk and growth. In contrast, discounted cash flow sets out the anticipated cash flows and these are discounted to present day values to produce a net present value and/or an internal rate of return.

Valuations are thus described as being implicit and DCF as an explicit appraisal methods. Both use the same financial tenets. In consequence, the underlying mathematical principles are similar but the input figures are from different perspectives.

This appendix follows in the steps of Bowcock (1978) who, through his *Property Valuation Tables*, sought to fill the gaps relating to traditional valuation tables (Davidson, 2002) used by practitioners, which assume annually in arrears rental incomes whereas in practice rents are normally receivable quarterly in advance. The importance of this timing difference has been highlighted by the Investment Property Forum, who publish quarterly in advance figures on their web site (IPF 2005) and recommend their members to switch from annually in arrears, nominal equivalent yields to quarterly in advance 'true equivalent yields'.

This appendix sets out to provide a comprehensive list of the valuation and financial formulae that underpin the calculations undertaken by the valuer and investment analyst. Thus it considers a range of deterministic formulae in order to provide the valuer or investment analyst with an insight into how the formulae are constructed and what is implied into their figures.

With few exceptions, valuers and property investment analysts rely on bespoke software packages or spreadsheets to carry out their calculations. The increase in the use of spreadsheets by property professionals (Bowcock & Bayfield, 2000, 2003) provides an opportunity to save time and to work more efficiently. However, at times there may be a lack of consistency or errors and the formulae have set out with this in mind.

The aim here is to place the formulae into a practical context. The advent of bespoke software packages has transformed the ease with which valuations can be undertaken. The complexity of the valuation formulae used has for many become of secondary importance as the numbers are calculated effortlessly.

Also, Excel and Spreadsheets offer a wide range of functions that simplify the use of formulae, with drop-down boxes into which the variables are put; the number is then calculated and returned to a specified cell. Excel has been further empowered by a number of Excel Add-Ins that provide the user with extended functionality. In a property and financial analysis context, the DCF Analyst Add-In (DCF Analyst, 2005) uniquely incorporates a comprehensive range of property and finance functions, risk wizards and auditing functions. This provides the user with, for example, access to all the years purchase tables and many other functions and wizards in Excel.

Those interested in finding out more about the mathematics that underpins the financial formulae are referred to Adams et al. (2003), whilst Levy (2002) and Melicher and Norton (2003) place the non-property formulae into a financial context.

The formulae

The variables for the formulae have been standardised as follows:

Variable	Represented by
Nominal interest rate, % per annum (or valuation yield for years purchase single rate and in YP in perpetuity formulae)	i
Years	n
Periods per annum	p
Remunerative rate % per annum (in YP dual rate formulae)	m
Accumulative rate % per annum (in YP dual rate formulae)	a
Tax rate	t
Years deferred	d
Inflation rate	h
Real rate of interest (inflation adjusted tate)	r
Growth rate	g
Sinking fund formula	SF

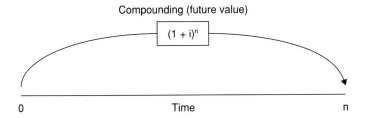

Fig. A.1   Compounding (future value).

Table A.1   Differences between simple interest and compound interest.

Years	5%		15%		25%	
	Compound	Simple	Compound	Simple	Compound	Simple
5	1276	1250	2011	1750	3052	2250
10	1629	1500	4046	2500	9313	3500
15	2079	1750	8137	3250	28 422	4750
20	2653	2000	16 367	4000	86 736	6000
25	3386	2250	32 919	4750	264 698	7250

Amount of £1

The amount of £1 formula, or compounding formula, lies at the heart of many financial formulae. The formula returns the amount an investment will grow to after a number of years at a stated interest rate. This is the compound interest formula. It assumes that the interest earned at each period is re-invested and therefore accumulates interest in subsequent periods along with the original amount. It is how banks calculate interest on savings and how rents are deemed to grow over a period of years. The formula is:

$$(1 + i)^n$$

It can be represented graphically, as in Fig. A.1. The impact of compounding is frequently substantial. As the rate of interest earned and/or the length of time that the money is invested for increases, the investment grows significantly.

Set out in Table A.1 is an example of the difference between simple interest, where there is no compounding of the interest earned, and compound interest. With high rates of interest and long investment periods, the differences can be huge.

Present Value of £1

This is the reciprocal of the amount of £1 formula. It can be used to determine the current or present value of a future cash flow, where the date, amount of money and discount rate are known: in other words, how much a future cash flow is worth in current money terms. As such, it is a fundamental element in discounted cash flow analysis calculations. It can also be used to calculate the investment that must be made now in order to accrue to the

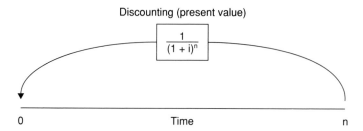

Fig. A.2 Discounting (present value).

Table A.2 The impact of rising discount rates.

Years	Discount rate p.a.						
	2%	5%	10%	15%	20%	25%	30%
5	906	784	621	497	402	328	269
10	820	614	386	247	162	107	73
15	743	481	239	123	65	35	20
20	673	377	149	61	26	12	5
25	610	295	92	30	10	4	1

amount required at a given annual interest rate. Thus if you need £150 in the future, you can put aside less now because it can earn interest in the meantime.

In the formula, i is known as the discount rate, and the formula is:

$$\frac{1}{(1+i)^n}$$

This is represented graphically in Fig. A.2.

It is important to appreciate that the relation between increasing and decreasing discount rates is not linear: as Table A.2 illustates, when discount rates rise their impact becomes increasingly severe. The example in the table shows what £1000 receivable at a future date is worth over time at different rates.

Thus for an opportunity fund with a target rate of return (discount rate) of say 30%, for example, £1000 receivable in 10 years' and 20 years' time is now worth to them £73 and £5 respectively. In contrast, for an overseas life insurance company with a target rate of return (discount rate) of say 5%, £1000 receivable in 10 years' and 20 years' time is now worth to them £614 and £377 respectively. The differences are substantial. As a consequence, the opportunity fund will place great importance on the short-term cash flows, whilst the life insurance company will be interested in both the short- and long-term cash flows.

Amount of £1 per annum

Returns are the future sum that a series of equal cash flows will amount to if invested at a given interest rate. For example, an investment of £1000 per year for five years with an interest rate of 5% accumulates to £5526. In contrast, if the interest rate were 15% p.a. then the sum would grow to £6742. Moreover, if the investment period were extended to 15 years, the money with 5% interest would become £21 579 and that with 15% would become £47 580. This reinforces the impact that regular savings can have on one's wealth!

The amount of £1 per annum formulae are:

In arrears cash flows   *In advance cash flows*

$$\frac{(1+i)^n - 1}{i} \qquad\qquad \frac{(1+i)^n - 1}{1-(1+i)^{-1}}$$

Inflation: real and nominal interest rates

A real rate of interest or growth is an inflation-adjusted rate, whilst a nominal interest rate or growth rate is an actual rate that does not take the effects of inflation into account. Adjusting for the impact of the rate of inflation requires the application of the following formulae (it is not just a simple matter of adding or deducting the numbers):

Real interest rate to a nominal interest rate

$$i = (1+r)(1+h) - 1$$

Nominal interest rate to a real interest rate

$$r = \frac{(1+i)}{(1+h)} - 1$$

Annual sinking fund

The annual sinking fund is the amount that is required to be invested at the end of each year in order to accumulate to £1 by the end of the final period. It is a useful formula when dealing with prospective capital expenditures where the costs are to be spread over a number of years.

$$Formula = \frac{i}{(1+i)^n - 1}$$

Periodic sinking fund

This is similar to the annual sinking fund, but here the payments may be in arrears or in advance, and more than one payment may be made per annum. The formulae are as follows:

In arrears payments   *In advance payments*

$$\frac{p[(1+i)^{1/p} - 1]}{(1+i)^n - 1} \qquad\qquad \frac{p[1-(1+i)^{-1/p}]}{(1+i)^n - 1}$$

Annuity

The annuity formula calculates the income stream generated annually in arrears over a specified number of years by an original investment of £1, for a given interest rate. The income stream includes within it the repayment of capital. The figure returned is the annual in arrears figure.

The annuity formula is the reciprocal of the years purchase single rate formula, and the formula for more than one payment per annum is:

$$\text{Formula} = \frac{p[1 - (1+i)^{-1/p}]}{1 - (1+i)^{-n}}$$

The years purchase 'family' of formulae

These formulae have been grouped together as they are similar in concept. Each formula assumes that the rental income is constant and does not grow. As an aside, in discounted cash flow terms the formulae could be viewed as being the sum of the annual (or periodic) present value figures.

Years purchase (YP) dual rate, in arrears

For one payment per annum the formula $= \dfrac{1}{(i + SF)}$

which becomes, for rents receivable for more than one period per annum:

$$\frac{1}{p[(1+r)^{1/p} - 1] + \dfrac{p[(1+a)^{1/p} - 1]}{(1+a)^n - 1}}$$

YP dual rate, in advance, for more than one period per annum

$$\frac{1}{p[1 - (1+r)^{-1/p}] + \dfrac{p[1 - ((1+s)^{-1/p})]}{(1+s)^n - 1}}$$

YP dual rate with tax, in arrears, with one or more periods per annum

For one payment per annum the formula $= \dfrac{1}{\left(i + SF\left(\dfrac{1}{(1 - t)}\right)\right)}$

which becomes for rents receivable for more than one period per annum:

$$\frac{1}{p[(1+r)^{1/p} - 1] + \dfrac{p[(1+a)^{1/p} - 1]}{[(1+a)^n - 1][1 - t]}}$$

YP dual rate with tax, in advance, with one or more periods per annum

$$\frac{1}{p[1-(1+r)^{-1/p}] + \dfrac{p[1-(1+a)^{-1/p}]}{[(1+a)^n - 1][1-t]}}$$

YP in perpetuity, in arrears

This is a simple and easy to remember formula: $\dfrac{1}{i}$

Which becomes, for more that one rental receivable per annum:

$$\frac{1}{[(1+i)^{1/p} - 1]}$$

Or for the multiplier for the periodic rental income:

$$\frac{1}{p[(1+i)^{1/p} - 1]}$$

YP in perpetuity, in advance, with one or more periods per annum

$$\frac{1}{p[1-(1+i)^{-1/p}]} \qquad \text{Times the periodic rent}$$

YP single rate, in arrears

$$\text{With one or more periods per annum} = \frac{1-(1+i)^{-n}}{p[(1+i)^{1/p} - 1]}$$

YP single rate, in advance

$$\text{With one or more periods per annum} = \frac{1-(1+i)^{-n}}{p[1-(1+i)^{-1/p}]}$$

Years purchase deferred

This formula is used where there is a period before the rental income commences and can be valued. The deferred element of the formula is simply a present value of £1 formula (see above) times the relevant years purchase multiplier. The rate of interest used in the present value calculation is, by convention, the valuation yield.

Gordon's growth model, or the dividend discount model

This formula is used in the equities markets as a valuation tool, where p is the market price, d is the next prospective income (dividend) receivable, k is the cost of equity and g is the rate of income (dividend) growth. Levy (2002) covers this topic in detail. The market price is determined as follows:

$$p = \frac{d}{(k - g)}$$

Rearranging the cost of equity can be determined as follows:

$$k = \frac{d}{p} + g$$

Calculating the implied rental growth rate

Valuation yields have an implied growth rate built in to them. The growth rate (g) over the rent review period will be a function of the investor's target rate of return, (e) (equated yield) and the rent review pattern (p) in years. An element of the formula can be simplified to the annual sinking fund formula (annually in arrears incomes), giving for an equivalent yield (k) the following formula:

$$k = e - (SF \times p)$$

Internal rate of return

The internal rate of return (IRR) is the discount rate that equates the future cash flows of an investment with the purchase price such that the net present value equals zero. The answer is calculated via an iteration process. The formula is:

$$\sum_{t=1}^{n} \frac{ncf}{(1 + d)^t} = I_0$$

Where: ncf = net cash flow from periods 1 to n

d = internal rate of return (for quarterly cash flow periods, a quarterly IRR is returned)

I_0 = initial capital outlay.

Non-conventional cash flow

A conventional cash flow is one where there is more than one change of sign in the cash flows (for example, purchase of a property = negative cash flow; rent receivable = positive; property refurbishment = negative; property sale = positive: so two changes of sign).

Mathematically, if there is more than one change of sign then more than one IRR could be in existence (Levy and Sarnatt, 1996). To resolve this, a modified IRR can be calculated where the second and subsequent negative cash flows are cancelled out by implied borrowings, which are then amortised against the subsequent cash flows. (Beware that Excel's MIRR function for this calculation produces counter-intuitive results and can produce erroneous answers.)

Net present value

The net present value is arrived at by summing all the discounted net cash flows (ncf) using a specified discount rate (r). The formula is:

$$NPV = \frac{ncf_n}{(1+r)^n}$$

Income and exit ratios

An internal rate of return (IRR) may be apportioned into an income ratio and an exit ratio. The two ratios added together equal one.

The income ratio is the percentage contribution of the expected net income cash flows of an investment relative to the total net cash flows. The income ratio is the percentage of the cost (gross purchase price) of the investment that the net income cash flows represent when they are discounted at the internal rate of return. It is an analysis ratio which is used to identify the importance, or otherwise, in returns terms, that the net income streams represent as compared to the exit value.

The exit ratio is the percentage contribution of the expected exit value (or salvage value) of an investment relative to the total net cash flows. It is an analysis ratio which is used to identify the importance, or otherwise, in returns terms that the exit value represents as compared to the net income streams.

Compounding up

This formula can be used to compound up, for example, growth rates or interest rates. The formula is:

$$(1+i)^p - 1$$

Where: i is the periodic rate
p is the number of periods per annum.

Compounding down

This formula can be used to compound down, for example, growth rates or interest rates. The formula is:

$$(1+i)^{1/p} - 1$$

Where: i is the annual effective rate
p is the number of periods per annum.

Effective $\leftrightarrow$ nominal interest rates

Nominal interest rates assume the receipt of interest annually in arrears. In practice, interest is charged either monthly, quarterly or half-yearly. This earlier payment of the interest results in a higher effective interest rate being paid by the borrower. The formula is:

$$\left(1 + \frac{i}{p}\right)^p - 1$$

Where: p is the number of periods per annum that interest is added (compounding periods)
i is the nominal annual interest rate.

True equivalent yields ↔ nominal equivalent yields

True yields are used to adjust nominal (annually in arrears) yields to reflect the receipt of the incomes periodically in advance. In the case of commercial property rental, incomes are frequently receivable quarterly in advance. Thus the nominal yield under-states the position. The formula that calculates the true equivalent yield (T) for a rack-rented property with a nominal equivalent yield of N, and with rents receivable in advance p times per annum is:

$$T = \frac{1}{\left(1 - \dfrac{N}{p}\right)^p} - 1$$

Gross and net of costs yields

The gross and net refer to whether or not the purchaser's costs are reflected in the valuation yield. In the UK the commercial property market normally uses net yields, whereas in Germany, for example, gross yields are often used as it is argued that the purchaser's costs can vary significantly. The simple property valuation in Fig. A.3 shows how these yields are calculated.

Initial, equivalent and reversionary yields

Where a property is let at less than the prevailing open market rental value (OMRV) it is said to be under-rented. In the valuation, the assumption is that at the next rent review or at the reversion the rent will rise to the OMRV. The initial yield is an income return represented by the initial passing rent divided by the value (see above for gross or net). The equivalent yield is a 'blended' yield, and sits between the initial and reversionary yields. The equivalent yield is the valuation yield used in the years purchase formulae to calculate the value, as shown in Fig. A.4.

Initial yields, net or gross of repairs

In Continental Europe, the initial yield method (capitalisation method in the US) of valuation is frequently used. Yields net or gross of costs have been discussed in the above section. Consideration also needs to be given to the treatment of repairs in yield

Rack rent receivable		500 000	
x YP in perpetuity @	6.00%	16.666667	
			8 333 333
Less purchaser's costs @	5.7625%		454 044
Property value			7 879 289

The net equivalent yield $= \dfrac{500\ 000}{8\ 333\ 333} = 6.00\%$

The gross equivalent yield $= \dfrac{500\ 000}{7\ 879\ 289} = 6.35\%$

Fig. A.3   A valuation of a rack-rented property investment showing the calculation of yields.

Rack rent receivable		400 000	
x YP in perpetuity @	6.00%	16.6667	
			6 666 667
Increase on rent review			
Current ERV		500 000	
Less rent passing		400 000	
Extra on review		100 000	
x YP in perpetuity deferred			
3 years @	6.00%	13.9937	
			1 399 365
			8 066 032
Less purchaser's costs @	5.7625%		439 480
Property value			7 626 552

$$\text{Net initial yield} = \frac{400\ 000}{8\ 066\ 032} = 4.96\%$$

Fig. A.4   A valuation of a reversionary property investment showing the calculation of yields.

$$\text{Net reversionary yield} = \frac{500\ 000}{8\ 066\ 032} = 6.20\%$$

$$\text{Net equivalent yield} = 6.00\%$$

calculations. The normal practice in the UK is to quote yields on the basis of net rents; however, in a number of Continental European countries yields are quoted on the basis of rents before the deduction of non-recoverable outgoings and landlords' repairing obligations. The latter gives an inflated figure for the yield.

Gross redemption yields

Whilst property yields normally relate to an income return measure, in the bond market the term gross redemption yield is a performance measure as it combines both income and capital returns. The gross redemption yield is thus the internal rate of return of a bond's cash flows.

Running yield

This is the rent passing per annum divided by the purchase price for a gross running yield, or the price plus purchaser's costs for a net running yield. The running yield may be stated for a number of different years.

In traditional valuations prospective rents are on the basis of todays rental levels, whereas discounted cash flow analysis grows the rents. Thus valuations and DCF analysis can produce different running yields.

Exit valuation yield

The exit valuation yield (or kick-out yield in the US) is the valuation yield used to value the net rental incomes at the end of the cash flow. In the UK the convention is to take the rent passing and estimated rental value as at the exit date. In contrast, in the US the following year's net operating income (or the stabilised net operating income) is capitalised.

Cash on cash return

This is a measure of the net income receivable expressed as a percentage of the investor's capital outlay. For net cash flow after debt service there are two approaches: the first adds back in capital repayments made during the period; the second looks at the net cash flow receivable. In an accountancy context, cash on cash returns relate to profit and loss items and adopt the first method.

Discount rate/target rate of return/required rate of return/equated yield

These terms are synonymous. Discount rate/target rate of return/required rate of return is terminology used in discounted cash flow appraisals and represents the return that the investor is seeking. Equated yield is the term used in valuations. When value or price equals worth, the internal rate of return is the same as the discount rate/target rate of return/required rate of return/equated yield.

Reverse yield gap

This is a measure of the growth potential of property. It is the difference between a property's equivalent yield and the gross redemption yield on gilts (government bonds). However, it makes no allowance for the relative riskiness of the two assets. In recent years there has been a positive yield gap, with property yields greater than gilt yields.

Summary

In this appendix a wide range of valuation and financial formulae have been considered. The aim has been to provide the reader with a point of reference, rather than a full explanation. Thus the appendix should be considered in conjunction with the main text of the book.

References

Adams, A., Booth, P., Bowie, D. and Freeth, D. (2003) *Investment Mathematics*. Wiley: Finance Series.

Bowcock, P. (1978) *Property Valuation Tables*. Basingstoke: MacMillan Press.

Bowcock, P. and Bayfield, N.J. (2000) *Excel for Surveyors*. London: Estates Gazette.

Bowcock, P. and Bayfield, N.J. (2003) *Advanced Excel for Surveyors*. London: Estates Gazette.

Davidson, A.W. (2002) *Parry's Valuation Tables*. London: Estates Gazette.

DCF Analyst – Excel Add-In Software (2005) i-Analysis Ltd free demonstration version available from http://www.i-analysis.com

Investment Property Forum (2005) *Quarterly in Advance Adjustment Figures*. www.ipf.org.uk

Levy, H. (2002) *Essentials of Investment*. London: Prentice Hall.

Levy, H. and Sarnatt, M. (1996) *Capital Investments and Financial Decisions*. London: Prentice Hall.

Melicher, R.W. and Norton, E.A. (2003) *Finance: An Introduction to Institutions, Investments, and Management*. London: John Wiley & Sons Inc.

Further reading

Baum, A. and Crosby, N. (1995) *Property Investment Analysis*. London: International Thompson Business Press.

Gordon, M.J. (1958) Reported in: Bringham, E. (1982) *Financial Management: Theory and Practice*. London: Dryden Press.

Gordon, M.J. and Halpern, P.J. (1974) Cost of capital for a division of a firm. *Journal of Finance*, 29: 1153–63.

Appendix B: Worked examples in the chapters: how to download spreadsheets from the web site

In this book we have provided a practical view of property appraisals and analytical techniques. A familiar feature for those undertaking real estate appraisals and analytical techniques is the use of spreadsheets and Excel. Instead of providing a series of Excel screen shots of spreadsheets, the authors have produced a number of downloadable spreadsheets, which show how a number of the appraisals and analytical techniques discussed in the chapters can be undertaken in a practical spreadsheet environment.

The Excel spreadsheets can be accessed by going to

www.blackwellpublishing.com/sayce

To facilitate navigation and to assist in downloading the relevant spreadsheets, there is on the web site an index of the various spreadsheets cross-referencing them to the chapters in the book.

The authors hope that the spreadsheets will provide the reader with a valuable insight into a number of the practicalities involved.

Index